Hot Topics, Public Culture, Museums

Hot Topics, Public Culture, Museums

Edited by

Fiona Cameron and Lynda Kelly

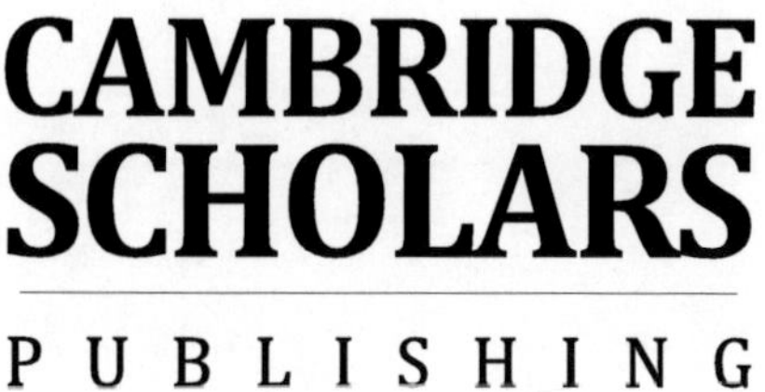

CAMBRIDGE SCHOLARS PUBLISHING

Hot Topics, Public Culture, Museums,
Edited by Fiona Cameron and Lynda Kelly

This book first published 2010

Cambridge Scholars Publishing

12 Back Chapman Street, Newcastle upon Tyne, NE6 2XX, UK

British Library Cataloguing in Publication Data
A catalogue record for this book is available from the British Library

ISBN (10): 1-4438-1974-3, ISBN (13): 978-1-4438-1974-9

TABLE OF CONTENTS

List of Illustrations

FOREWORD

CELEBRATING THOSE WHO CREATE CHANGE[1]

ELAINE HEUMANN GURIAN

In a profession generally resistant to change and where alterations in practice can be measured in what seems like geologic time, it is books like the one the reader is now holding that helps move the process along.

Books are substantial and seen as trustworthy. The reader can hold them (or now read them on a screen). The authors create footnotes, which help confer a respectable authenticity. The writing is put into a framework that allows one idea to sit next to another as if both had always been related to each other like siblings. The very processes of book production, which take time and have many steps, might possibly help move the subject of controversy from its fringe position into established acceptance. This important book, about museums incorporating difficult and contested subjects into their work, the consequences of doing so and reviews of the theory and practice that surround such decisions, helps merge isolated examples into a more coherent and acceptable practice.

Each illustration coheres to the next and an almost viral, seemingly intentional, plan seems to evolve. The creators of the activities written about are made more highly regarded and they, by association, are able to join the company of others, some of whom they may never have known before. In real life the same museum directors cited probably met resistance by staff and their public when inaugurating these very activities.

We must likewise be grateful to the editors, Cameron and Kelly, for persisting in researching and writing about controversy and its value, for gathering authors who now know each other, and most of all for helping to move formerly marginal parts of the museum world onto centre stage for emulation by others.

Why is it that many museums are resistant to change? And when museum directors insist on change, why are museum personnel so expert at thwarting and avoiding it? Does this resistance have to do with the specificity of museum work, or is it ubiquitous wherever organisational change is proposed?

In museum work we find people who have chosen their careers based on their individual philosophy, life style and interest. Their choice of profession is often very specific and may have been committed to from a very early age. Choosing to work in museums is certainly not based on remuneration, since salary levels are low when compared to the pay similarly educated people tend to get elsewhere. I conclude that most museum staff are self-selected based on a mix of personal reasons, which include the role museums have played in their lives, a commitment to the nobility of the work itself, and pleasure with the position they hold in society because of it. This is especially true of those who choose employment in the specialised museum functions (curation, museum education, exhibition development and collections care, for example). Museum workers can appear messianic in defence of their notion of what museums are all about. Their definition of appropriate museum activity is often tied, I believe, to their view of themselves as vigilant guardians of patrimony (physical objects) for future generations and benign enlighteners of present day visitors. These staff members envision themselves standing at the barricades fighting against those who, like the authors of these chapters, wish to propose change because they believe in a different definition of museums. These museum workers, as self-appointed custodians, fear that these individuals might be misguided, advocating the transformation of the institutions they love into something they will no longer recognise.

I now sometimes thank such resisters—a funny position for one who has advocated inclusionary change for nearly 40 years. Let me confess that I find the object-based temple of the contemplative—the places I have so long sought to change, such as the Metropolitan Museum of Art and the Louvre—divine.

Equally surprising to me is that my young grandchildren are similarly entranced, no matter their age or their prior subject-matter knowledge. For all of us, going to the Met is indeed like entering the rarefied magical world of the imagination. The journey is closer than I care to admit to the mystical literature favoured by these same grandchildren. Entering satisfies aspirations of being powerful, rich and endowed with super-human powers because, in some sense, we know those places diverge exotically from our daily environment and reflect more of the values of the people who formerly owned these objects than those who made them.

Allow me to name these museums as the "classicists". These are the object-drenched gorgeous spaces whose installations have intentionally omitted explanatory labels that might help most mere mortals. These are the places that are indeed overwhelming and memorable—at the same time as they exasperate by reducing the uninitiated to feelings of insignificance. The indelibleness of the Metropolitan may be based in part on its indecipherability. And there are some smug few who fear that the exclusive ambience would be compromised if more people understood it.

Let me be clear: there are few such classic places so perfect as to be worthy of my total forgiveness. I would still contend that most classic museums do not reach the Met's level of delightful astonishment. Instead they often evoke mystification, and ultimately boredom and frustration in their visitors.

In contra-distinction, there are "inclusionists' museums" with whom I proudly associate myself, that are committed to wide accessibility, that associate with daily experience and the important issues of the world around them. I would contend that the examples cited in this volume belong predominantly to this category. These institutions have intentionally modified and even wilfully destroyed the impenetrable atmosphere so treasured by the classicists. But they often intentionally give away their other worldly magic by doing so. These institutions take as their stance a more egalitarian political position asserting that the material evidence we call collections belongs to everyone and that any systemic change that welcomes the less initiated is for the good.

The tension between the "classicists" and the "includers" has existed from almost the beginning of museums themselves and there have been side-by-side contemporaneous developments of excellence by each "team" in every age. The inclusionist museums tend to be numerically fewer and are often considered generally less powerful than their more traditional siblings. They are often children's museums, science centres, community and culturally specific museums—institutions that the classicists might not always consider "real" museums. The influence of these inclusionary institutions is huge because they experiment with multiple strategies of interactivity, interesting administrative techniques and controversial subject matters that push the boundaries of the field as a whole. The subject matter, points of view, and techniques employed by these museums are the ones that slowly make their way into the mainstream, first by imitation at other inclusionary museums and then via acceptance by the more flexible classicists, where any change is often heralded as revolutionary.

Thereafter there is an acceptance of this self-same technique by even the most reticent, using a process that could be called "wanting to be the third on your block". The approval comes after many others have tried it, most especially after the supplest of the classic museums have incorporated it into their own programs. Peter Linett writes: "It is unrealistic to expect any major museum to venture out on the limb alone" (Linett 2009).

I now understand that so many museums resist change because they aspire to remain in the "classic" camp, most especially aligned with the social elite and reinforced by the stereotype of museums found in movies and literature. The lack of basic change among the majority of the world's museums has, I now believe, been intentional and the resistance to change has been successful overall. It also is the case that neither the majority nor the powerful have demanded it. Quite the contrary, the controlling stakeholders, whether the social elite, political officials, or the newly rich, have more often funded "classic" institutions over others in their locale. And these stakeholders have sometimes required those who stray to return to the fold, instructing others of the dangers of experimentation.

The advocacy of museum inclusion has remained the province of the political left, the mostly disenfranchised cultural minorities, academics and free-choice educational philosophers. These advocates usually have insufficient political clout to effect major transformation. But publications like this one can encourage and legitimate further experimentation.

When classicists' museums begin direct work with under-served audiences, institute a social web blog, or publish an exhibition calendar that includes seemingly controversial subjects, such activities might be seen as gestures in response to external pressures so that the museum core can remain inviolate. Such actions often remain episodic or ancillary, without permanent adoption within the museum's programming, and sometimes exude a patronising feeling that I am sure the staff did not intend. By contrast, inclusionist museums tend to experiment with systems that enhance their dialogue with visitors and in doing so care less about old definitions of patrimony than do their classic siblings.

I now believe that museums transform only when their directors *will* it. It is more personality based than I would like. Such directors are the indefatigable visionaries who know how to advance from idea to operation. And eventually those who join him or her share the vision and form a band of believers—a passionate coterie.

Visionary directors appear in both museum categories—inclusive and classic. Those who foster experimentation in classic museums tend to expand on examples already seen elsewhere (but do not violate the boundaries of their sector) while visionary directors of inclusionary museums often defy traditional boundaries. These far-sighted inclusionary directors are the "first on their block", often vulnerable to firing, or oversee museums small (or deemed insignificant) enough to fly below the radar. It is such directors who are most often cited in this book.

Classicist directors attempting change move their institutions and their field in small successive steps that can be emulated by others. They recognise that their museums are incrementalists. They borrow ideas from the more experimental branches of the museum community and choose those most ripe for acceptance.

These directors are brave, but not foolhardy. They pay with their personal social capital to make change happen. It is because of their clout that such departures from established practice can be embraced by other classic museums and come to be seen as acceptable, traditional and even timeless. The classic sector, when cautiously emulating the more avant garde change-agent museums, forgets (or intentionally does not acknowledge) the source material they've adopted. As a political move, expanding the acceptable methodology of one's own cohort is smart. It makes the director into an acknowledged pioneer. I admire such directors. Those who succeed in changing the procedures of their class are, of necessity, persistent and valiant. But their aim is to be the second, not the first, on their block. That makes those who emulate these expanders the "third" on their block.

I do not know who will tackle new museum issues in the immediate future but I remain impressed by and grateful to those who dare to be the first on their block, as well as those are brave enough to be the second. I admire this book, which allows the ideas of the "firsts" to be highlighted, and encourages the "seconds" to follow their lead. Both of them will give heart to all of us "thirds" as we eventually try new things.

References

Linett, P. 2009. Reinstallation Rorschach: What do you see in the renovated Detroit Institute of Arts? *Curator,* 52 (1): 5–12.

Notes

[1] Parts of this foreword incorporates elements of a key note address "Being the Third on Your Block" written for the Michigan Museum Association, and delivered in October 2009.

ACKNOWLEDGEMENTS

Hot Topics, Public Culture, Museums has been a long and rewarding endeavour, made possible by the generosity of the 16 authors whose work forms this collection. The authors' willingness to contribute their thoughts, research and time to producing such a publication made it possible for the editors to produce a work of significance to the sector. We thank you all. Most importantly we would like to thank Cambridge Scholars, UK and in particular commissioning editor, Carol Koulikourdi for accepting the proposal for publication and steadfastly steering the collection from its inception to a successful conclusion.

This collection was conceived out of an Australian Research Council SPIRT grant *Exhibitions as Contested Sites: The Roles of Museums in Contemporary Societies* and a Canadian Museums Association grant for *Contested Sites Canada,* led by Fiona Cameron, with Lynda Kelly, Linda Ferguson and Jenny Ellison as investigators (also first-investigator on the Canadian project). The project's findings form many of the discussions. The successful completion of this book would not have been possible without the support of these funders and partnering institutions: the University of Sydney, the Australian Museum and the Australian War Memorial along with the 28 institutions and staff in the US, UK, Canada, Australia and New Zealand who contributed to the study.

We would also like to extend our gratitude to Elaine Heumann Gurian, an esteemed thinker and practitioner, for producing her thought-provoking foreword. A special acknowledgment also goes to Stephen Garton, Professor of History and Provost and Deputy Vice-Chancellor University of Sydney for his contributions in the development of the initial research grant. Thanks also to Merilee Robb, Director, Research Development at the University of Sydney and Professors Ien Ang and David Rowe at the Centre for Cultural Research, University of Western Sydney for their support and advice. We would also like to acknowledge Dawn Roach and John McAvity of the Canadian Museums Association who supported the *Contested Sites* research in Australia through the Canadian Government, Department of Foreign Affairs and Trade *Youth Professional International Program* grant by the provision of research assistants consecutively over a four year period. This collection is not the only outcome from this

Canadian-Australian partnership, but more recently the marriage between Adrienne and Steven.

It would not have been possible to produce a collection of such scholastic integrity without the support of the reviewers, many of whom are authors. For this we would like to thank Russell Staiff, Elaine Heumann Gurian, Caleb Williams, Richard Sandell, Des Griffin, Andrea Witcomb, Margaret Lindauer, Juan Salazar, Elaine Lally, Robert Swieca and Linda Ferguson. We also extend our gratitude to Fiona Crawford for her much appreciated and professional editorial contributions in the final stages of the collection's production and to Matthew Tomczak for the stunning book cover design.

INTRODUCTION

FIONA CAMERON

This collection engages the highly problematic and increasingly important issue of museums, their engagement with "hot" topics (taboo subjects, revisionist histories and political issues), and their roles as part of wider conversations in a networked contemporary public culture.

Hot topics such as homosexuality, sexual, racial and political violence, mental illness, massacres, lynching, drugs, terrorism and climate change are now all part of museological culture. A long-established practice of exhibiting "the facts", "truth", "national history" or unproblematic conceptions of "other" places and peoples is no longer sustainable in an environment where the self-evidence of all these things is under question. Unproblematic conceptions of national history and the "other" are now giving way to complex narratives and the portrayal of their unsavoury aspects. Previously considered off-limits, the induction of these subjects and their representation in museums has been problematic. While some museums have successfully and meaningfully engaged hot topics[1], in reality few are willing to do so because they are seen as high risk due to a fear of political and social repercussions, such as funding withdrawal or the alienation of audiences.

Over the last 20 years, Western democracies have witnessed a rise in museum controversies and political debates around disputed interpretations of history, current affairs and topics considered morally and politically transgressive.[2] Clearly controversies suggest that many institutions in the second decade of the 21st century are theatres of struggle over moral values, beliefs and political agendas. Institutions are seen as powerful places for shaping cultural memory and important gatekeepers for directing, opening up or closing down cultural conversations on topics of societal significance.

The new museology has often expressed the need for museums to deal with complex political and social issues, arguing that museums must develop a function of critique and see themselves as a forum for debate. Engaging such topics is an extension of the museum's role in representing diversity and pluralism, however, a reluctance to converse deeply with these subjects is based on a limited understanding of the roles and civic purposes of museums in contemporary society; the social and political contexts in which institutions operate; and how these topics might be purposefully interpreted and engaged in a changing and increasingly politicised world.

Contentious topics such as difficult histories, taboo topics and hot contemporary issues of local and global relevance and significance are difficult to represent because they are unpredictable, involve conflict, are mobile and are inseparable from a range of broader social and political contexts and flows, many of whom cannot be calculated and anticipated (Cameron 2003). Most importantly they embody a divisive dimension, raising alternative answers while challenging an individual's or group's values, beliefs, ideologies or moral position (Cameron 2003). It is for these reasons that the entry of such topics into museums in recent years has been problematic, deemed to challenge the institutional foundations and the philosophical integrity of the museum. Museum metaphors as they currently stand are predominantly orientated towards the production of stable, certain meanings, ordered categories, unified heritage values and socially symbolic meanings such as local or national identity (Cameron 2008).

As Ferguson, Cameron and Koster argue in Chapters 2, 3 and 4 respectively, these blockages are partly due to a schism between the modern museum, based on the notion of certainty; consensual values; the use of expert knowledge systems as factual objects; a lack of focus on impact and relevance; as places to discipline populations by setting moral standards and reforming behavior; and as places to control conversations. Essentially museums have strived to create a world of factual "objects" almost completely separate from human concerns, desires and conflicts (Cameron 2003).

Political theorist John Rawls argues that societies and the culture of public institutions are inherently political, characterised by irreconcilable opinions and values.

> The political culture of a democratic society is marked by a diversity of opposing and irreconcilable religious, philosophical and moral doctrines … within a background of enduring free institutions … What are the grounds of toleration so understood …? how is to possible for there to exist over time a just and stable society … who remain profoundly divided … we must find a way of organizing ideas and principles … in a different way than before. (Rawls 1999, 123)

Re-reading Rawl's argument in the context of museums, controversy is a naturally occurring state in wider public culture, and therefore the ability to express and embrace ideological diversity in terms of the subject and those of audiences is a requirement of many 21st century museums. On the other hand representing contentious topics also engages the political culture of museums—the diverse and opposing doctrines of a range of stakeholders, many of whom have political clout and control public funding.

From these vantage points we might ask the following questions. Although doctrines remain irreconcilable, how can museums effectively engage contentious topics in new ways considering that in a contemporary complex society, pluralism and discursive conflict is an emergent contemporary condition?

Moreover, morality in a postmodern world, according to cultural theorist Zygmunt Bauman (2007), has become re-personalised and individual rather than based on a consensual, collective morality, all traits characteristic of modernist institutions. Therefore it can be argued that engaging divisiveness challenges the epistemological foundations of museums as "objective" knowledge sources and as authorities. For museums, contentious subjects raise more questions than they answer rather than offering consensual positions or knowable "facts". As a result a difficult dilemma arises between the perceived objective basis of knowledge in museums and the subjective interpretations that contentious topics necessarily entail. Museums must navigate the sensitive terrain between facts / opinion, authority / expertise, advocacy / neutrality, censorship / exposure.

New forms of content production and sociality enabled by digital technologies and Web 2.0 through social networking sites such as Facebook, ning, YouTube and Flickr dramatically alter relationships between cultural institutions and public culture in terms of knowledge production and power relations. Accordingly, the borders between the museum as a discrete entity operating above society are eroding as the boundaries between the museum and public culture become increasingly blurred. Museum information now operates within networks that transcend their immediate location, placing institutions in wider flows of interconnected cultural, political, economic and technological ideas, agendas and resources (Cameron 2008). Through these public spaces, museum information and collections, for example, are able to garner greater interest and cultivate meanings within wider cultural and social contexts. Social actors in various locations and contexts are acting on and modifying information according to their interests. For example, museum information and objects are taking an active role in social networks and political agendas. Via Google, collections of Persian objects, used as signifiers of Iranian cultural identity were mobilised to counter negative representations of ancient Persia following the *300* movie controversy about the battle of Thermapylae between the Persians and Spartans in 480BC (Jones 2007). Searches for the film *300* were diverted away from the film to a website Project 300 that displayed contemporary Iranian art, documentaries and links to the British Museum's *Forgotten Empire* exhibition of Persian artefacts (Jones 2007, 6)[3]. Art works were used as a tool to project positive representations of Persian civilisation and bolster contemporary national narratives.

Collections information from the Powerhouse Museum collection on Australian swimmer, Annette Kellerman, the "Diving Venus", who was arrested in 1907 for indecent exposure by appearing in her bathing suit, appeared on the porn blog, Silent-Porn-Star.[4]

Interactions with museum information and heritage collections, some planned, others serendipitous are now being conducted through these multiple and extended connections of people, ideas and objects, across long distances and national boundaries. Museum information is fluid, boundaries no longer exist, enabling all these things to be used and reconfigured within flows (Cameron 2008).

Although museums tend to be locality-bound and represent specific communities, they now simultaneously operate in global networks as nodes in information flows, and within broader heritage regimes. The global offers a different set of competing dynamics, no longer territorially defined and community based. In considering museums as at once local, national and global, this aspect works with the potential to integrate a multiplicity of political, economic, social and cultural economies, linked to various communities, histories and geographical regions of the globe. All these actions and connections have the potential to create and (re) create meanings around museum information in complex ways.

Because the space of information flows is now so flexible and interactive, protocols of communication according to theorist Manuel Castells (2004) between cultures in networks are not necessarily based on shared values but sharing the value of communication. Therefore museum information now operates in an open-ended network of meanings and within many-to-many communication regimes that co-exist but also interact and modify each other on the basis of exchanges. Here museum information and objects are simultaneously connected to locality and institution, but also increasingly play a role in mapping out a public space beyond the museum. Clearly, the more technology facilitates a networked social structure and individual self expression as seen most recently with Web 2.0, the more difficult it becomes for institutions to produce universal or consensual meanings around identity and history. On the other hand, these developments offer new opportunities for museums to become more embedded into and relevant for contemporary societies, operating as part of assemblages and assembling entities around socially relevant issues. What particular contributions museums might make and how institutions might capitalise on these opportunities and confront the challenges posed by these new configurations between hot topics, public culture and museums is the theme of this collection.

These movements and interactions, as detailed between public culture and museum culture, are more closely aligned to what Bruno Latour (2005) calls "object-orientated democracies" (Cameron 2008). According to Latour (2005, 15), and in referring to contemporary issues such as the Islamic veil in France or the latest beheading of fanatics in Falluja, each of these "objects" generates a different pattern of emotions, passions, opinions, disagreements and agreements while drawing together an assembly of people each with their own agendas and ways to achieve a resolution.

In a networked environment, Latour (2005, 19) posits that there is a shift from matters of fact, to matters of concern or matters of interest as the various agendas and opinions are brought together through networks. The museum accordingly is an actor within an object-orientated democracy as competing assemblies of people and ideas coalesce generating changes in conceptions of what is objectivity and what are the "facts" (Cameron 2008). Persian objects from the British Museum exhibition, *Forgotten Empire,* for example, were drawn into the object-orientated democracy around Persian nationhood and identity that emerged around the *300* movie. Here collections and information were used as "objects" in international relations specifically to foreground and assert the matters of concern and interests of contemporary Iranian artists, activists and media about representations of the Persian past and how the Persian empire was portrayed (Cameron 2008).

By the gathering together of different assemblies of relevant and interested people around an object, Latour (2005) argues that the public space and the readings of the object that emerges is profoundly different from that usually recognised under the label of the political. Here the analogy for museum information lies in how this information is operating, read and used in networked public space by different individuals and groups, often in entirely different ways from those imagined under the guise of curatorial authority or heritage significance, value and certainty.

Increasingly, institutions seek to re-evaluate their roles and institutional forms in a diverse, mobile, networked and deeply politicised world to remain relevant, inclusive, viable and vital. But for many, the particular roles institutions might perform under these emerging conditions remains unclear. How might institutions position themselves meaningfully around topics that are divisive, that challenge established or conservative orthodoxies and the values, beliefs, moral positions and political agendas of their stakeholders? How are networked relationships between constituencies enabled by digital technologies reshaping museum-audience relations and wider conversations around socially significant topics, and as part of object-orientated democracies?

Museum scholar Eilean Hooper-Greenhill (2000) suggests that it is timely to reconstruct the museum idea itself to think more deeply about the character and possibilities of museums in a more complex society. Hooper-Greenhill suggests this process involves reviewing, reinvigorating and adapting museum values, practices, authority and knowledge as shaped according to 19th century ideas, and embracing new ones reflecting 21st century conditions. Hooper-Greenhill (2000) concludes that reworking the idea of the museum has much to do with understanding the relationship between museums and their audiences, as well as the recognition and exploitation of the generative power of the cultural sphere.

At this intersection, the initiation of hot topics into museums offers an ideal starting point to interrogate what Hooper-Greenhill proposes. Clearly there is a variable gap between knowledge about and the practices of museums around hot topics in an increasingly complex and networked political world in a context where the idea of shared values, common meanings, disciplinary and institutional authority is now under question. The social, cultural impact and networking capabilities of media technologies and their uses in emergent cultural conversations between museums, audiences and across a variety of social spaces also requires investigation.

This collection fills these gaps by drawing on the findings from the Australian Research Council international research project *Exhibitions as Contested Sites, the Roles of Museums in Contemporary Societies* and *Contested Sites Canada* (Canadian Museums Association).[5] Sustained research in the Canadian, US, UK, Australian and New Zealand contexts is used to theorise and interrogate the contemporary social, civic and political agency of history museums and science museums in public culture. The work of international scholars in other cultural contexts (South America and Continental Europe), contribute to this volume by expanding the discussion on museums, hot topics, and the nexus between institutions, public culture and audiences.

This collection advances the knowledge base of cultural / museum theory and practice by offering new ways of conceptualising and theorising contemporary museums as institutional forms and their place in public culture based on emergent social conditions; alternative notions of how culture is conceived; how the engagement with hot topics is enacted through new forms of sociality, and what this says about building social and cultural competencies (institutions and audiences as both agents / actors). It also contributes to making museums more responsive, integral, valuable and relevant to communities by the consideration of all these things. The various authors in this collection contribute to the formulation of new knowledge about the practice of contentious curatorship within institutional settings including institutional interpretative capacity, curatorial strategies for engaging hot topics from those based on didactic models to ones that also engage the emotions and affect, and the possibilities offered by digital media. And finally authors in Part 2 explore the potential for digital technologies to enable conversations around hot topics examining key themes of museum authority and expertise, the ways museums might be reframed as information sources and what this says about audience, institutional forms and relations in building vibrant participatory cultures.

In **Part 1: Hot Topics, Agency and Institutional Forms,** authors present multifarious musings on museums as institutions and forms in contemporary societies and the changing role of the curator within these assemblages through various philosophical theoretical lens and practice models.

Chapter 1, *The Transformation of the Museum Into a Zone of Hot Topicality and Taboo Representation: The Endorsement / Interrogation Response Syndrome* by Caleb Williams (Justice and Police Museum, Sydney, Australia) presents a new theoretical and conceptual account for the emergence of hot topics in museums (examples include: sexuality, prison riots, ecological protest, forensic work and the history of tattooing). Williams goes on to argue that the current condition of post-modernity at once changes the museum from a space dedicated to truth and fact to interpretation. Here the institution is situated in a new realm of possibilities in engaging two-way conversations around topics of societal relevance and concern. Williams goes on to discuss the practice of contentious curatorship and the limits of the interpretative capacity of the museum in a contemporary world.

In **Chapter 2**, *Strategy and Tactic: A Post-Modern Response to the Modernist Museum* Linda Ferguson (Australian War Memorial, Canberra, Australia) drawing on the *Contested Sites* findings examines a range of topics considered too contentious by stakeholders for museums to display. Ferguson considers what these topics say about the widely accepted roles of museums, and as places for representing identity, certainty and morality early in the 21st century. Here Ferguson situates and theorises museum controversies as evidence of the struggle between the conditions of modernity and post-modernity and notions of what the museum is. She considers museum controversies as an event beyond a simple opposition politics between institutions, audiences and citizens, rather as a legitimate, active and influential actor within an existing field of power relations. From this position Ferguson offers a new reading of how and why exhibitions become contentious within this wider field of relations beyond the museum.

Fiona Cameron (Centre for Cultural Research, University of Western Sydney, Australia) in **Chapter 3**, *Risk Society, Controversial Topics and Museum Interventions: (Re)Reading Controversy and the Museum Through a Risk Optic* offers a new reading of the museum and controversy using Ulrich Beck's (1999) notion of global risk society, the rise of global risks and hazards such as climate change and terrorism and the emergence of new social forms drawing on the findings of the *Contested Sites* research. Although it is clear that museums have a very important role to play in conversations, debates and decisions around topics of societal importance, Cameron argues that previous institutional forms are based on the notion of earlier risk management regimes based on discipline and risk control that inhibit such conversations and debates. In reading the museum in the context of what Beck calls second modernity, ways of engaging controversy emerge pointing to new strategies in which institutions must engage controversy as interfaces between museums and public culture become more intimately interconnected in a networked, globalising world.

In **Chapter 4** *Evolution of Purpose in Science Museums and Science Centres*, Emlyn Koster (Liberty Science Center, Jersey City, US) examines the evolution of science museums and science centres through the optic of purpose as opposed to simplistic binaries based on experience, static versus participatory. Koster argues that in engaging purpose, institutions must strive to attain optimum relevance to pressing science-driven opportunities and challenges in society. Koster tracks the movement of purpose from the establishment of science museums in the nineteenth century and their emphasis on research, education and collecting to the science centres of the 1960s as spaces for increasing science literacy around physical phenomena to world expositions presenting a positive view of the world based on scientific and technological progress. All these rationales, in which Koster regards as examples of first and second generation institutions are mainly pedagogically driven, and accordingly this preoccupation has been at the expense of an equally important criterion of considering impact and relevance, and the place of institutions in science and society. Here Koster argues that both the internal barriers and the external opportunities for science centres and science museums must be tackled in a wholehearted, relevancy-driven state of mind, a defining characteristic of his third generation institution. He concludes by stating that institutions are not only to be safe places but also ideal places for conversations, places that consciously proceed boldly but carefully forward.

Chapter 5, *Curator: From Soloist to Impresario* by Elaine Heumann Gurian (Consultant and member of the Museum Group, US) explores museums as institutions in networked society, sites intentionally or unintentionally now operating in extreme sharing networks of information. More specifically she interrogates the structural change a museum will have to make in order to intentionally share information not created exclusively or edited by staff and how the integration of such information on the exhibition floor must allow the visitor to find answers to their own self generated queries in the presence of objects. Topic choice and the breadth, angle and depth of its exploration tends to remain in control of the institution. This chapter examines what happens when carefully edited museum information around a topic deemed controversial comes together with user-generated content. Heumann Gurian argues that the coming together through multiple avenues of input where different knowledge systems—opinions and values, lived experience and expertise are enabled to interact offers unique opportunities for deeper conversations to occur in museum spaces. Heumann Gurian also examines some of the blockages preventing such engagement around knowledge sharing, which she articulates as a philosophical problem around the notion of the curator.

In her second chapter, **Chapter 6,** *Liquid Governmentalities, Liquid Museums and the Climate Crisis*, Fiona Cameron (Centre for Cultural Research, University of Western Sydney, Australia) extends her thinking about museums as institutional forms in the context of the highly relevant, controversial and compelling topic of climate change. Foucauldian and post-Foucauldian governmentality theory and Beck's notion of world risk society are the predominant means by which the analysis of climate change governmentality structures is conducted. Moreover, the former is the principal paradigm in which museums are theorised, at once as places for discipline (Bennett 1995) and accordingly in risk management. Cameron reads climate change and museums in governmentality flows through these two predominant optics. Cameron then goes onto critique these modes of thinking, proposing a new theoretical idea, "liquid governmentalities" and "liquid museums" drawing on complexity and assemblage theory as a means of moving away from normative views on climate governmentality and the museum. Here the aim is to look at governmentality and the place of museums in these formations as a process rather than as a reflexive exercise in which to tease out the meaning of a particular form, event program or exhibition, and the circulation of power within this ensemble. Here by looking at museums according to a different optic, rather than one that asks *why* to one that looks at the *how* we can look at institutions and interventions as processes, and consider ways that institutions might be shaped and connected to broader networks and flows.

Morgan Meyer (Department of Sociological Studies, University of Sheffield, UK) in **Chapter 7**, *From Cold Science to "Hot" Research* examines the shifting roles of science museums from places for cold research, where secure, closed and fixed knowledge is communicated, to ones that engage hot controversial research and open debates and where novel questions are asked. He demonstrates how contemporary science museums act increasingly as contact zones, that is, "places of hybrid possibility and political negotiation, and sites of exclusion and struggle". Here Meyer, drawing on his research in the UK and France, contemplates new roles for science museums as environments for negotiation between diverse actors and between multiple epistemologies and ontologies.

In **Chapter 8**, *Queering the Museum,* Richard Sandell (Department of Museum Studies, University of Leicester, UK) and Stuart Frost (British Museum) use case examples from the UK and US to explore issues surrounding museum attempts to represent lesbian, gay, transgendered and bisexual communities. The authors go on to interrogate the challenges and opportunities created by museums to combat homophobia and promote equality. Their discussion offers new insights into the museum's relationships with social norms of acceptability and tolerance and examines the social agency of representational practices, in particular the potential for museums to (re)frame, enable and inform the conversations society has about difference.

In **Part 2: Engagement**, a combination of theoretical positions, case studies and research findings are presented by authors that provide new ways to think about working with museum audiences, whether in the physical surrounds of the museum or, increasingly, in the social spaces of the web. Taken together, these suggest that ideas around participation, "citizen curator" and museum authority are key challenges facing museums when engaging with their multiple audiences around hot topics in a rapidly changing and fluid global environment.

In **Chapter 9**, *Controversies in Context: Communication, Hot Topics and Museums in Canada*, Jenny Ellison (History, York University, Toronto, Canada) reports on Canadian research undertaken with museum staff, journalists and museum audiences that explores risks, causes and perceived consequences of presenting hot topics in museums. Ellison argues that these hot topics are shaped by the social and political context within which museums operate and proposes that museums need to provoke conversations in thoughtful and honest ways, while purposefully connecting audiences. Ellison acknowledges both the complexity of these issues, and at the same time identifies the creative possibilities available for institutions to engage their audiences.

Lynda Kelly (Australian Museum, Sydney, Australia) in **Chapter 10**, *Engaging Museum Visitors in Difficult Topics Through Socio-Cultural Learning and Narrative*, considers socio-cultural theory as a conduit for engaging visitors with difficult topics as well as assessing their physical museum experiences. A socio-cultural approach to identifying visitor learning is applied through analysing summative evaluation of visitors to an Australian Museum exhibition that tackled the difficult topic of death. The role of narrative is also considered through examining visitor responses to the more confronting aspects of the exhibition and considering how they felt about death within the context of their personal experience.

Chapter 11, *Making Choices, Weighing Consequences: Pedagogy and Politics of Transportation in America on the Move*, Margaret Lindauer (VCUarts Department of Art History, Virginia Commonwealth University, US) uses the exhibition, *America on the Move* at the National Museum of American History (Washington DC) as a case study for analysing the pedagogical underpinnings inherent in exhibition development. Lindauer argues that while free-choice learning accounts for the wide range of educational outcomes among visitors, it is an insufficient conceptual model for developing an exhibition that would prompt visitors to consider the relevance of the exhibition to their own lives. In her reflexive analysis of the exhibition Lindauer suggests that "critical pedagogy", an educational philosophy aimed at engaging learners in analysing social issues, would have been compatible with curatorial hopes for visitor reception.

Hailing the Cosmopolitan Conscience: Memorial Museums in a Global Age, **Chapter 12** by Paul Williams (Ralph Appelbaum Associates, US), describes how globalisation and physical memorials can be understood as complementary with a growing post-nationalist public that identifies with "cosmopolitan conscience". Williams identifies that as globalisation has affected the moral impetus of memorial museums, it has been only occasionally discussed and little theorised. Williams' chapter remedies this lack of critical attention by elaborating on two connected facts that have become patent over the past twenty years: the flow of instantaneous mediascapes and tourists crossing borders (Appadurai 1996), and a near-worldwide "memorialising moment" realised in the creation of and popular interest in inert memorial structures.

Andrea Witcomb (Faculty of Arts and Education, Deakin University, Australia) in **Chapter 13**, *The Politics and Poetics of Contemporary Exhibition Making: Towards an Ethical Engagement With the Past*, analyses two examples as a way to explore their potential to generate more complex understandings of the past and, in particular, for crossing the boundaries produced by cultural memories and identities. Witcomb begins by describing a visit to Dennis Severs' House in Spitalfields (UK). While acknowledging that this is an extreme example of the new turn to what might be called sensorial or affective forms of interpretation, Witcomb suggests that the kind of "palpable" history Severs created in his house has parallels in contemporary forms of interpretation practice that seek to avoid linear, rational and didactic means of communication to impart information and meaning to visitors. These ideas are further developed and applied to a number of other experiences, including those that engage hot topics.

In **Chapter 14**, *"Mymuseum": Social Media and the Engagement of the Environmental Citizen*, Juan Salazar (Centre for Cultural Research, University of Western Sydney, Australia), invites us to think about how museums and science centres can engage the technologies and practices of social media toward increased citizenship participation in relation to the current hot topic of climate change. Regarding the question of engaging publics in climate change action, it is argued that there is still uncertainty about how social media can play a more fundamental role beyond offering the illusion of participation, access and creative content production. Salazar identifies that although recent literature examines the emergence and impact of social media in opening spaces for participation and co-creation, very few analyses go beyond the new promises of networked socio-technical communities.

Lynda Kelly (Australian Museum, Sydney, Australia) and Angelina Russo (Faculty of Design, Swinburne University, Australia) in **Chapter 15**, *From Communities of Practice to Value Networks: Engaging Museums in Web 2.0*, explore the ideas surrounding communities of practice and how these could be applied in thinking about how to better engage hot topics and museum staff with Web 2.0 at an institutional level. It considers how to encourage a Web 2.0 mindset through addressing issues surrounding organisational change and learning. Kelly and Russo conclude by discussing next generation "value networks" as an extension of communities of practice, that enable audiences to participate with museums on their own terms through drawing relevant information and engaging in discourse that is of value to them.

Chapter 16, *Architectures of Collaboration, Webs of Contention*, Elaine Lally (Faculty of Arts and Social Sciences, University of Technology, Sydney, Australia) examines emerging social networks as conduits for interfacing audiences, museums and hot topics in public culture. Lally asserts that new online social networks like Facebook and Twitter have been drawing a lot of attention as hot topics in their own right, yet while they are clearly becoming important recreational and social spaces, they are also increasingly being mobilised by interest groups, advocacy networks and organisers of topical events. As museums and galleries are exploring innovative ways of engaging with audiences through these new forms of organising, Lally explores the shifting relationships around hot topics as new forms of collaboration between institutions and their active publics.

This collection is the first of its type to look beyond controversies as events and the museum as a separate entity in the engagement of hot topics. The external pressures facing institutions in terms of the digital, new forms of sociality, and a globalising world characterised by individual self culture and contention more than ever requires that the nexus between hot topics, public culture and museums be (re)examined in light of the complexity of both theory and practice. We hope you enjoy this exploration.

References

Appadurai, A. 1996. *Modernity at large: Cultural dimensions of globalization*. Minneapolis: University of Minnesota Press.

Bauman, Z. 2007. *Liquid times: Living in an age of uncertainty*. London: Polity.

Beck, U. 1999. *World risk society*. Cambridge: Polity Press.

Bennett, T. 1995. *The birth of the museum: History, theory, politics*. New York and London: Routledge.
Cameron, F.R. 2003. Transcending fear—engaging emotions and opinions—a case for museums in the 21st century. *Open Museum Journal*, 6, http://amol.org.au/craft/omjournal/journal_index.asp (accessed 18 December 2009).
—. 2008. Object-orientated democracies: Conceptualising museum collections in networks. *Museum Management and Curatorship* 23 (3): 229–243.
Castells, M. 2004. Ed. *The network society: A cross-cultural perspective*. MA: Edward Elgar.
Hooper-Greenhill, E. 2000. *Museums and the interpretation of visual culture*. London and New York: Routledge.
Jones, S. 2007. Building cultural literacy. Paper presented at *New Collaborations: New Benefits—Transnational Museum Collaboration*, International Council of Museums, UK, July 26–27, Shanghai, China.
Latour, B. 2005. *Reassembling the social: An introduction to actor-network-theory*. Oxford: Oxford University Press.
Rawls, J. 1999. *A theory of justice*. Harvard: Harvard University Press.

Notes

---

[1] Examples of "challenging" exhibitions include the New York Historical Society's exhibition *Without Sanctuary: Lynching Photography in America*; the US Holocaust Memorial Museum in its graphic portrayal of the Holocaust; the Imperial War Museum's exhibition *Crimes against Humanity;* the National Museum of Australia's exhibitions on frontier conflict and stolen generations examining massacres and the displacement of Aborigines; *Mining the Museum* at the Maryland Historical Society; British Empire and Commonwealth Museum in Bristol reinterpretation of the history of the British Empire to include a critical examination of its more unsavoury aspects such as slavery and genocide. The Antenna program at the Science Museum in London interrogates contemporary science issues, such as climate change, male birth control, genetically modified foods and cloning.

[2] Examples of controversies include struggles over interpretations of colonialism and slavery (*The West as America* at the Smithsonian's National Museum of American Art, frontier conflict at the National Museum of Australia, the *Trade and Empire* exhibition at the National Maritime Museum), war and genocide (*The Last Act—Enola Gay* exhibition at the Smithsonian's National Air and Space Museum and *Crimes against Humanity* at the Imperial War Museum, London), race and race relations (*Another Side of the Twentieth Century* at the Allen County-Fort Wayne Historical Society and *Treasures of Palestine* at the Powerhouse Museum, Sydney), representations of the human body (*Robert Mapplethorpe: The Perfect*

Moment at the Institute of Contemporary Art of the University of Philadelphia and *Body Art* at the Australian Museum) and relationships between industry and science (*Darkened Waters: Profile of an Oil Spill* at the Pratt Museum in Homer Alaska; *Science and American Life* at the National Museum of American History).

[3] http://www.thebritishmuseum.ac.uk/forgottenempire/ (accessed 15 November 2009)

[4] http://silent-porn-star.blogspot.com/2007/12/kellerman-nude-mermaid.html (accessed 15 November 2009)

[5] The international research project *Exhibitions as Contested Sites—The Roles of Museums in Contemporary Society* (a three year study conducted between 2001 and 2004), funded by the Australian Research Council with partners the University of Sydney, the Australian Museum and the Australian War Memorial involved 28 museums in the US, Canada, Australia, UK and New Zealand. This project aimed to move beyond the specifics of museum controversies to examine the relevance, plausibility and practical operation of history and science museums as civic centres for the engagement of contentious topics. To do this, we used a framework utilising a range of methods from literature analysis of museological, theoretical debates and museum controversies to extend thinking about the roles of museums in contemporary societies, to a program of quantitative (omnibus and exit surveys) and qualitative research (in-depth interviews and focus groups).

Quantitative research involved omnibus surveys of the broader Australian community in Sydney and Canberra drawing on a statistically representative sample of 500 respondents. We asked participants to respond to a selection of 16 topics that Australians might consider controversial and to a series of role positioning statements using a five-point Likert scale (strongly agree to strongly disagree). Exit surveys were conducted at the Australian Museum, the Australian War Memorial with 197 and 248 visitors respectively, and at three Canadian Museums, the Museum of Anthropology Vancouver, the Canadian War Museum and the Musée d'Art in Montreal with 286 visitors. Here participants were asked to respond to the range of questions as in the omnibus to compare with the responses of the broader community. Quantitative exit surveys and questionnaires were then analysed using SPSS (data analysis software) to enable comparisons between all data sets, enabling cross-cultural comparison thereby extending the research sample.

The qualitative phase of the research involved five focus groups, with museum visitors, a total of 40 participants in Sydney and Canberra. Here we sought to discuss the findings from our quantitative research as well as experiences of museum visiting, museum functions and activities, and explore concepts of authority, expertise, trust and censorship.

By comparison, we investigated the perspectives of museum staff, stakeholders and media using an online survey, in-depth interviews and focus group discussions with over 100 staff and stakeholders in 26 institutions in Australia, New Zealand, Canada, the US and UK. Participants were asked to identify topics that were particularly controversial in that country, or for their institution, at that time to capture emerging controversies and contemporary responses. Other questions related to museums, social responsibilities and civic roles, authority, expertise and censorship, the impact of controversies on institutional functioning, successful programming and funding arrangements. In comparing the different geo-political, social, cultural and institutional contexts we were able to illuminate the multifarious challenges, limitations and opportunities that institutions face in presenting contentious subjects. The project was led by Chief Investigator, Dr Fiona Cameron as part of her postdoctoral fellowship along with partner investigators, Dr Lynda Kelly (Australian Museum) and Linda Ferguson (Australian War Memorial). *Contested Sites* Canada, funded by the Canadian Museums Association involved a quantitative survey of three institutions, Museum of Anthropology, Vancouver; Canadian War Museum, Ottawa and Musée d'Art, Montreal and interviews with journalists. This project, funded by the Canadian Museums Association, was led by Dr Jenny Ellison with Dr Fiona Cameron, Dr Lynda Kelly (Australian Museum) and Linda Ferguson (Australian War Memorial).

PART ONE:

HOT TOPICS, AGENCY AND INSTITUTIONAL FORMS

CHAPTER ONE

THE TRANSFORMATION OF THE MUSEUM INTO A ZONE OF HOT TOPICALITY AND TABOO REPRESENTATION: THE ENDORSEMENT/INTERROGATION RESPONSE SYNDROME

CALEB WILLIAMS

> To look at itself a society must cut out a piece of itself for inspection. To do this it must set up a frame within which images and symbols of what has been sectioned off can be scrutinized, assessed, and, if need be, remodeled and rearranged. (Turner 1979, 468)

We live in interesting times. Post-modernity has been called a situation of "undisciplined 'freedom' saturated with nihilism", a space that offers neither truth nor fact, only interpretation (Cheeks 2009). The contemporary museum may refuse to acknowledge that such a thing as post-modernity exists, but will find it harder to deny that a fraught, confusing, and precarious phase of world history is unfolding just beyond its doorstep, evidenced in "global economic crisis", "global war on terror", "global climate change", breakdowns in civility, protests, crimes, bizarre eruptions in popular culture, environmental destructiveness, consumer excesses and addictive behaviors. This ambiguous phase of cultural and historical development offers many possibilities to the museum. It is argued here that the museum becomes a deeper, braver, more empowering and philosophically useful space to audiences when it both engages with, and profoundly interprets, the often bafflingly complex cultural, socio-political and behavioural reality that surrounds it, privileging both *past* and *present* as legitimate targets of museological investigation.

It seems that as one of many observable shifts in direction within the contemporary museum, the coolness of taxonomical representation of the past has started to give way to a hotter and more frictional interaction with the present. This engagement with what is "hot", "difficult" and "taboo" demands critical assessment and reflexivity from both the practitioner and theorist alike. The ideas and observations that emerge within this chapter stem from many years of curatorial activity in the Justice and Police Museum, in Sydney, an institution that due to its core themes, collections and exhibiting practices has dealt with a range of subjects that might be considered taboo, provocative and hot (in the newsworthy sense).

At the time of writing for example, the local media has been dominated by tales of "exploding warfare" between outlaw motorcycle gangs which erupted publicly when 18 members of the Hells Angels and Commancheros clashed in the arrivals lounge at Sydney airport resulting in violent killing (Daily Telegraph 2009). The groups involved in this episode resurrected memories of one of the Justice and Police Museum's earliest forays into the territory of the hot topic in 1996: the exhibition titled *Gangs: Subcultures of the Street* and at various times gang associates (including members of the currently feuding Commancheros and Hells Angels) attended the exhibition to ponder objects, photographs and text connected to gang history, paraphernalia and iconography. Thankfully, in this instance, gang members came and left peacefully, their appearances mainly notable for the periodic rumble of a Harley-Davidson juddering to a halt, or growling back to life, on the footpath outside the museum steps.

The *Gangs* exhibition was the first in a trilogy of shows at the Justice and Police Museum in the mid-1990s that established a signature style of curatorial work within the museum. *Tattoo: A History of the Decorated Body* (1997) followed, and after this came *Protest: Environmental activism in NSW* (1998). These exhibitions allowed the museum to transform itself into a forum-style space, where anthropologies of the local and histories of the present could be developed and sensitised, dangerous or controversial topics could be subjected to serious analysis and encountered in a non-threatening environment by contemporary audiences.

Other local museums have pursued similar projects. The Australian Museum for example has surveyed *Body Art* (2000) and *Death* (2003), and is currently developing a new exhibition, tentatively titled *All About Evil* (2012). Internationally, there is a similar museological embrace of potentially volatile subject matter. For example, museums in the UK have recently produced a variety of exhibitions around sexuality, sexual identity and same-sex relationships: *Queer is Here* (2006) appeared at the Museum of London, *Hello Sailor! Gay Life on the Ocean Wave* (2007) at the Merseyside Maritime Museum and *Seduced: Art and Sex from Antiquity to Now* (2007) at the Barbican (see also Chapter 8). To some extent, then, it seems that contemporary museum and gallery visitors are not only willing to view sophisticated, adult perspectives and interpretations of formerly taboo subject matters, but also to welcome them and support them via attendance at exhibitions.

The first part of this chapter makes observations about a recent paradigm shift in curatorial practice and agenda, and the epistemological and transformational possibilities inherent in the museum in post-modern times. Eight separate theoretical models are then advanced to account for the ascension of the taboo and hot topic in the museum, drawing on the insights of museologists, such as Stephen Lavine, Julie Marcus and Kevin Walsh, as well as thinkers from a range of other disciplines including Lyotard, Baudrillard, Said, Foucault, Barthes, Nietzsche and Jung.[1] The endorsement/interrogation response syndrome in museums, which displays the tension between "celebrating" and "profoundly scrutinising" any subject the museum chooses to interpret is then examined. Finally, at the conclusion of this chapter, a case study from the author's own museum using the aforementioned *Protest* exhibition will be presented as a potential model for handling difficult subject matter effectively within museums.

The museum in post-modern times

Recent museological writings remain optimistic about the museum's capacity to interact meaningfully with contemporary audiences. Cameron has produced extensive research to suggest audiences both need and want interrogative and thought-provoking exhibitions that "challenge views", and "create and stimulate opinions"; museums that, in other words, are as prepared to ask questions as they are to provide answers (Cameron 2003). Heumann Gurian (1996) has famously argued the contemporary museum enables "safe, congregation" in a dangerous world, in a space where visitors feel protected, encouraged to think, feel and scrutinise. Lavine (1991, 151–158) calls museums "zones of intensified seeing" where the normal laws and codes that govern *what* and *how* we look are suspended. Indeed, by authorising and making us feel safe about looking, it has been said that even the most troubling representations can be illuminated, contained, demythologised and deprived of their capacity to harm, inside the museum (Williams 2002). Finally, it has also been demanded that the contemporary museum should provide its visitor: the "unsettling experience of the truly new" (Crane 2000, 60).

Wolfgang Ernst (2000) has written that the task of the post-modern museum is to teach the visitor "how to cope with information" (17–34). But this assertion requires amplification: one of the most important tasks of the post-modern museum is to teach the visitor not only to "cope" with information, but to look beneath its surface, to discover what motive it serves. The post-modern museum can evade the reproduction of knowing in simple terms and encourage the transformational encounter with doubt and the radical over-turning of previously held suppositions. Within the post-modern museum dubiety, paradox and illumination, can be simultaneously served and provocative accounts of knowledge and deep immersions in unknowing allowed to beneficially co-exist. Indeed the ideal post-modern museum may aspire to be a locus of liminal "pure possibility", as a space "betwixt and between" where "the familiar is stripped of its certitude" and strangers reach "an ineffable affinity, where sacred truths are imparted and/or social alternatives explored" (St John 2001).

Museum prerogatives in a time of accelerating change

It seems fair to acknowledge that we now inhabit a phase of museological development in which the traditional role of the curator, with its custodial imperative and scholarly absorption in auratic objects, has been challenged, redefined and expanded. This role now accommodates a proactive understanding of the importance of museum agency and a new consciousness of personal responsibility, where the accuracy of the narratives the museum constructs or reinforces is concerned (Walsh 1992). This new style of curation is flexible. It often supports the understanding of museum as a forum rather than a temple, as a site of exploratory dialogue rather than of authoritative monologue (Cameron 2003). Such an approach to interpretation and display allows the museum to treat multiple discourses, often simultaneously. The new museology, geared toward social inclusiveness, the investigation of community and collective memory, frequently interfused with post-modern scepticism about inherited certainties, has effectively challenged the 19th century notion of the museum as receptacle for received traditions, taxonomies, typologies, culturally-sanctioned knowledges and hegemonic meta-narratives. With this broad-scale reassessment of what a museum does and for whom it speaks when it does it, there has also come an opening of possibilities in terms of subject matter.

The curator no longer desires the status of remote, knowledgeable autodidact but increasingly wants to be regarded as an imaginative, "cluey" and approachable communicator: someone who can engage in meaningful and insightful ways with both the historical and contemporary scene. There is also a strong need to delve beneath surfaces, to overturn comfortable mythologies, to supply contextual depth to popular phenomena understood superficially, to decode and trace genealogies of signs to their root, to restore marginalised voices to contemporary debates and with this, to create contemplative environments for the taboo, hot topic or contentious subject, to be inspected at close quarters.

But the taboo and difficult subject matter does not arrive in the museum simply because curators want to put it there. Part of the purpose of this chapter is to locate the nebulous network of influences, justifications and precipitating conditions that create a favourable micro-climate for the taboo in the museum. Indeed, it should be understood that treatment of hot, provocative and taboo subjects by the museum is part of a much broader confluence of practices and theoretical positions that are shaping thought about the present. The following exposition treats each of these explanatory models as self-enclosed and contra-distinctive. But in reality each museum position will exist in a state of highly competitive interplay, modifying, cancelling out, jostling against, and enhancing, some of the others.

The branding/marketing model

In the 1990s a major shift took place in the marketing and advertising industry and a new and far more sophisticated awareness of the power and importance of branding came into being. It was in this decade that "the brand reinvented itself as a cultural sponge, soaking up and morphing to its surroundings" (Klein 2001, 170) and marketers began to concern themselves with the fundamentals of consumer identity and psychology. The brand became a "stylistic badge of courage" (*New York Times Magazine* 1994, 124) and those involved in the task of brand creation found themselves, "perpetually probing the zeitgeist to ensure that the 'essence' selected for one's brand … would resonate karmically with its target market" (Klein 2001, 8). Many of the most successful brands concerned themselves less with gross exhortations to consume and more with the celebration of concepts, experiences, lifestyles, attitudes and sets of values deemed most seductive and attractive to the sector of the market they were attempting to win over. Consumers were taught to value a branded commodity not so much for its intrinsic usefulness or even the quality and durability of its construction but rather because the brand conveyed a "feel-good" psychic experience to its buyer, and offered the opportunity to join a certain brand-conscious community.

The lesson of this shift in approach to selling things—products, activities and experiences—has not been lost on museums. Indeed, it can be argued that taboo subject matter is currently being used to re-brand some museums in a highly sophisticated marketing exercise. Here the taboo is deployed strategically to suggest that the museum has transformed itself into a vital, contemporaneous cultural zone and is now a receptacle of "highly charged" ideas and representations that possess strong appeal to visitation demographics that would not normally choose to spend leisure time in the museum. The co-opted mystique of the taboo is thus used to renovate the image and reputation of the museum, converting it into a "hip" destination, a place newly connoted with intellectual flair, outré playfulness and cutting-edge risk taking. By exploiting the taboo and its associations with rebellion, excess and danger, the museum re-defines, re-images and to some extent, reinvents itself as a viable, contemporary social technology, newly visible to new audiences.

The post-modern crisis model

Taking a different position to the above, it can be argued that the taboo is currently privileged within the museum as a result of a post-modern crisis of meaning. This crisis is characterised by the failure of meta-narratives, the collapse of cultural hierarchy and the "end of history".[2] Plurality, transgressiveness and ambiguity have thus replaced authoritarian certitudes and society teeters on "the violent edge between ecstasy and decay" (Kroker and Cook 1998, 8–9)· Observing this situation, the museum experiences profound doubt about its former position as cultural arbitrator. Confusion spreads about what the museum should interpret and to whom and a vacuum is created in exhibiting strategies. Nihilistic narratives are appropriated from the media to fill this vacuum, which celebrate consumption, eroticism, behavioural extremes, violence and death. Curators abandon "the modernist project of explaining the world" (Warby 1992, 48) and turn instead to mimesis, pastiche and cultural interplay: "fetishizing the fragmentariness and eclecticism of present humankind" (Baudrillard 1989). The museum admits chaos, excess and multiplicity: confronting areas of human behaviour that were formerly taboo enter exhibition spaces, which now encapsulate and dissect the cultural moment. The apparatus of post-modern critical theory demands interaction with the transformations, quirks and manias of the contemporary scene (or its absence) and the museum provides this. Trapped in a media-generated web of hyper-reality, of simulation and simulacrum, the museum deepens dialogue with and about this pervasive sign system from which it is impossible to escape (Baudrillard 1989). As a marker of the defeat of its former rational enlightenment agenda and a concession to the current notion that “nothing is forbidden”, taboo subject matters become deeply entrenched in the curatorial project.

The emancipatory museum model

A counter-argument might be made about the post-modern hiatus and its precise impact on the museum in regard to the taboo. In this argument post-modernism brings about a much-needed space for reassessment and self-reflexivity that allows an optimistic reconfiguration of energies, outlooks, and interpretative strategies. This reflexivity about purpose and agency moves some museums in an emancipatory direction (Walsh 1992). The emancipatory museum accepts post-modernism’s hybridity but rejects much of its pessimism. The emancipatory museum favours the poetic use of shock in order to generate a rupture in audience conditioning and expectation, and to provide a deeper, more critically alert awareness of “things-as-they-are” (Lavine 1991, 23).

This kind of museum works deliberately at “subverting power in order to reveal” and at creating “moments of illumination to bring to light an unseen order” (Marcus 1996). The emancipatory museum also offers a home to feminism, ecology, anti-imperialism, localism, gay / lesbian perspectives as well as the perspectives of other liberationist and social justice movements. Taboo subjects are treated by the emancipatory museum as part of a wider strategy of resistance against the continuum of an ordered, repressive and hegemonic present where “counter-stories” and “destabilising narratives” are generally unwelcome. Edward Said (1993) has described the emergence of “a new non-coercive culture” that is part of a “genuinely radical effort to start again” (289). This is the fundamental aim of the emancipatory museum. One method of starting again is to examine old ideas about taboos—which anthropologists, such as Mary Douglas have shown are foundational elements in the binary structure that coheres society—in the light of new knowledge and new theory (Douglas 1984).

The museum as agent of democratic exposure model

The rise of the taboo may again, be related to the democratic right of exposure. In this paradigm, exposure has become a modality of power. Its threat or application disciplines, regulates and checks human behaviour, propelling society forward in an orderly, progressive manner. The interrogation of established institutions—the law, the army, the church, the police, the political establishment and the monarchy—was once forbidden, frowned upon and regarded as a taboo act. Yet this taboo no longer stands. Formerly power was shaped as a pyramid and defended the interest of the powerful. Yet within the "panoptic schema" of society that currently has taken hold in the West, as Foucault (1984) has said, "power is everywhere" (93) and our current situation resembles a "transparent building in which the exercise of power can be supervised by society as a whole" (Foucault 1979, 207). We have the right to examine, see and think about what we want to. The privileging of exposure, and of the inevitable surveillance and voyeurism that go with it, allows the journalistic and legal gaze to penetrate wherever it likes—to the Oval Office, Buckingham Palace, elite private schools. The museum's exposure of the taboo may be regarded as one in many gradations of both "light" and "serious" types of exposure occurring all the time. These range from the serious TV documentary on Asian sex-slavery in Australian cities, to the Royal Commission finding on the depths of political corruption, to the tabloid magazine's scoop on a celebrity's extra-marital affair. A negative consequence of this is that the dignity that was once associated with private life and private acts constantly recedes before the new technologies of intrusiveness. More positively speaking, freedom to expose reinforces revisionist interpretation of our selves, our overarching power structures, and those areas of life of which we were once afraid.

The rational museum model

A fifth perspective on the emergence of the taboo links this to the museum's capacity for rational inquiry and the need to lend the community at large the benefit of "enlightening" museologial expertise. With Kant, the rational museum would argue that "enlightenment is the emergence of man from self-imposed infancy" (Honderich 1996, 236). The rational museum thus sets itself the task of removing infantile ideas in regard to the taboo in order to improve man / woman in the ways of reason. Discounting post-modern dubiety in ultimate truth and values, the rational museum maintains "knowledge beyond culture is possible" (Gellner 1992) and "has occurred" (Gellner 1995, 6–8) and looks upon the taboo—and the cluster of fearful, superstitious and stigmatising attitudes that surround it—as a puzzle that learning and intellect can solve. This type of museum approach to the taboo is detached, scientific and non-exploitative. Here, the focus on the taboo does not arise from a crisis in visitation figures (the marketing museum), a political agenda (the emancipatory museum), imitation of nihilistic narratives in popular culture (the post-modern crisis museum), or a random application of the museum's right to scrutinise whatever it wants to (the exposing museum), but from a desire to educate and dispel ignorance using the methodological, interpretative, ratiocinative competence of its highly trained staff. The rational museum's agenda is the disposal of fear, the disposal of what threatens, the disposal of irrationality. Like the combustion engine, or the circulation of blood, or the Gallipoli campaign, the taboo within the rational museum is regarded as infinitely susceptible to technical explanation and scholarly probing.

The auto-anthropology museum model

A sixth perspective on the current curatorial fascination with taboos relates the methodology of auto-anthropology to the museum perspective on the taboo. Auto-anthropology operates by subjecting close-by places to the same kind of scrutiny as places that are far-away, believing "exotica" exists all around us, is locatable beneath our feet (Overing and Rapport 2000). Anthropology traditionally has been only active in sites beyond the West. Here it has confidently sought to report and decipher the customs, practices, social relationships, religion and rituals of primitive cultures, taking a particular interest in sexual roles, food, fertility, taboos and beliefs surrounding death. This kind of scrutiny, mapping, decoding and documenting of the "other" for the benefit of Western learning was long thought perfectly acceptable, particularly if it happened in the context of elsewhere. Western attitudes to death, sex, bodies, ritual and to taboos—of which there are many—went largely unremarked, unscrutinised, mapped, decoded and reported by anthropologists as if they somehow represented a universal standard of "'normality", and those of so-called primitive cultures, an extremely aberrant version of "abnormality". The auto-anthropology movement seeks to reverse this trend, as do modern museums that share its philosophical outlook. The retreat of anthropology from an exclusive concern with the "exotic" to more localised considerations of ritual, otherness, violence, communication and taboo has something in common with the work of Roland Barthes, semiotics—the analysis of signs, has shown that critical exploration of areas once considered "light" or "low" in the cultural spectrum—such as wrestling, striptease or holidays—can disclose underpinning profundity. Within the academy, the increasingly popular discipline of Cultural Studies, which has absorbed the work of Barthes, also promotes startling ways of reading problematic, ideologically inscribed, hegemonically-generated social codes, that are broadly accepted as natural, normal and common-sensical, in the cultural order (Hebdige 1987). These disciplines and the underlying forms of knowledge and theory they embody, like the work of auto-anthropology, direct the museum toward the examination of the taboo in terms of local culture.

The curatorial psychology model

According to Nietzsche, all philosophy is disguised biography, and an "involuntary and unconscious memoir" is to be found within the heart "of every great philosophy" (Nietzsche 1990, 155). The curatorial psychology model accepts this premise, and that curators lack neither desire nor advocacy. Thus an exhibition on a taboo subject can contain biographical impulses and perspectives, and be read as an act of "symbolizing, conceptualizing, and meaning seeking" (Macey 2002, 155) on a personal level, that is transformed into consumable cultural production. In line with this, a strongly held world-view may also be leveraged into community discourse, under the guise of rational demystification and enlightenment for others. Empathy and engagement as well as curatorial ambition, emotion, and careerism are all implicated and subsumed within the exhibition-making phenomenon. The hot topic never derives from the unimpeachable cultural authority of the museum building alone, but from the collegiate endeavour of those who construct their professional lives within this building. The taboo exhibition may be heralded as non-polemical and neutral in intention, but in reality it is marked by the personal consciousness and opinion of the human author. Vested interests of personal voice in museums are disguised by methods of information transmission. The didactic content of an exhibition text is authored (by a person or a team), though often anonymously and invisibly. The illusion that the museum *itself* speaks in an exhibition, with calm, detached, magisterial authority, is thus sustained via the existence of unsigned text, and the motive of the human author concealed. The hot, taboo, or sensitive exhibition topic may seem a like well-reasoned intervention into a certain societal problem, but subterranean drives, overt passions, and private biographical impulses also inevitably play their part in shaping outward form, and inward logic.

The shadow museology model

In Jungian psychology "persona" is the term given to the outward, visible, socially constructed form of the personality—the mask that is exhibited publicly—and the "shadow", is used to define the less visible varieties of impulse, aggression and instinct that exist beneath the surface of normal consciousness (Hall et al. 1973, 44). The “shadow” is also claimed to be the final resting place of all that is hidden, repressed, and denied in conscious life (48). Civilizations too, have their persona and shadow. As do museums and museological projects. In recent times it seems, a museology that actively dissects the shadow-side of our civilization has evolved. This museology replaces the optimism of triumphalist narrative, with a more probing, deeper and darker analysis of cultural, social and political issues that were formerly invisible, repressed or tabooed. This shadow museology gives space to the worst in human nature, as well as the best. It contests prior modelling of sexuality, death, the body, ecology, crime, violence and economic, military and colonial activities in order to reveal what has been concealed, displaced and censored from former accounts of these topics in museums, if indeed they existed at all. Shadow museology faces up to the fact life is dark, and that civilization is a “façade” and when the impulses that surge beneath civilization, are “stringently repressed” and not openly admitted, or illuminated and given space in consciousness, “disaster often ensues” (Hall et al. 1973, 50). By engaging with societal tragedy, repression and denial, in its various forms shadow museology tries to make this disaster less imminent. In classical Jungian analysis the process of “individuation” or self-integration is achieved by becoming more aware of what the shadow contains; honest confrontation produces communal psychic health. Shadow museology admits deep imperfection and underlies all human endeavour but is also hopeful, believing “the balance of light and dark is ultimately possible—and bearable” (Johnson 1991, 15) and that “repair of our fractured world must start with individuals who have the insight and courage to own their own shadow” (27).

The endorsement/interrogation response syndrome

Interrogation and endorsement exist in a state of ongoing tension and interplay in the contemporary museum. To understand how these two competing forces work, a simple analogy can be applied in which the museum converts itself into an interrogative “lens” or endorsing “mirror” in order to treat any subject it chooses to examine. The “mirror” museum generates consensus by transforming itself into a narcissistic field into which an audience gazes to have an opinion, a sense of nostalgia, or a consumerist aspiration flattered. The “lens” museum scrutinises both past and present to bring to light repressed truths that loosen hegemonic constraints, and re-frame previously understood realities. The “mirror” museum interprets in a shallow, de-theorised space that suspends all criticality. The "lens" museum pursues phenomenological complexity, in a space filled with richness and depth. The "lens" penetrates; the "mirror" is facile.

Interpretation that is subtle, nuanced and philosophically rich, and that is prepared to admit multi-perspectival complexity should always be privileged over interpretation that caves in, or becomes altogether absent or compliant, before the sheer difficulty of the politicised or socially sensitive "contentious", "hot" or "taboo" subject that falls beneath the museum gaze. The marketing campaign that advertises the presence of a hot topic in a museum can lead audiences to assume they will encounter a brave speaking-out about previously unspoken, or unspeakable truths and realities. Yet despite this alluring packaging, it can be the case that the mere presence of the taboo, populist or contentious subject within the museum is no guarantor of curatorial profundity. There are several reasons for this non-provision of a truly meaningful and illuminating experience for the visitor. The absence of true criticality can stem from overly circumspect, or fearful curatorship, or from censorship by sponsors, or from political pressure from an overarching authority beyond the museum. This latter reason for the retreat into silence, self-censorship or endorsement rather than interrogation where difficulty presents itself, though deeply lamentable, is at least part of the real politik and "rough and tumble" of cultural practice and provides some excuse for the abandonment of intellectual and philosophical rigour by the institution concerned. Much worse however, is a non-politically mediated or enforced, voluntary absence of critique in texts and interpretative apparatuses as a matter of choice or policy by the museum. In this, the features appear of what cultural critic and philosopher Frederic Jameson has called the "new depthlessness" of post-modernity, which amounts to an abdication of a museum's responsibility to interpret altogether (Jameson 1991, 6). Instrumental in this suppression of depth has been the muzzling of complexity, by museums anxious to avoid charges of bias and/or advocacy and with it the need to pacify rather than provoke their audiences. Words in particular have suffered as texts are shortened and deprived of sophistication in argument placing limits on curatorial engagement, exposition and analysis. Ironically, as taboo and hot topics have become more present in the museum, penetratively insightful discourse, and more profound varieties of literary or philosophical expression by the curator, have also become more absent. This stems from the belief that the modern visitor will happily engage with an interactive, or stand in front of an audio-visual presentation, but will not read. "Thick description" is increasingly hard to find in museums. Stripped of ideational nutrition by internal committees—intent to eradicate both the poetics and provocation contained within text—nuanced arguments tend to be collapsed into ever simpler "bites" of information. In their newly incarnated monochrome brevity some museum texts resemble prose pap that is entirely deracinated of meaning. The net effect of this is to curtail illuminative analysis, while promoting facile interaction with ideas. Taken in combination, these limits on interpretation threaten to turn the museum into a co-opted site of fetishisation and superficial celebration of commercial / cultural products / social phenomena that may indeed ironically possess risqué connotations (hot, contentious, taboo) but deep interpretation is withheld so that the museum becomes a passively endorsing showroom rather than a deeply investigative laboratory. The transformation of the museum into a compliantly reflecting, rather than actively interrogating social agent, needs to be averted. The temptation to ignore the problems and complexities that lie hidden beneath the layers of contemporary culture's surface obviousness is great, as are the monetary and audience rewards for doing so. But in adopting the path of least resistance interpretatively the newly "visible" and "edgily relevant" museum will paradoxically become absolutely redundant as a generator of useful insights and meaningful experiences for audiences.

An exhibition of ecological activism considered

In 1998 the Justice and Police Museum presented an exhibition titled *Protest: Environment Activism in NSW 1968–1998.* The exhibition viewed protest as a powerful but ambiguous democratic mechanism capable of transforming corporate and governmental practice, policy and consciousness and also of delivering broadly positive community outcomes, including legislative change that protected urban and wilderness environments under threat for the community-at-large.

Part of the curatorial strategy became to tease out the paradoxes that surround protest: at best the protester is considered a brave, profoundly conscientious, ecologically aware citizen, at worst an anarchic, anti-capitalist and pseudo-criminal. The exhibition became a signal opportunity for the museum to experiment with its own forum-like potential when dealing with a politically and socially sensitised issue.

In terms of the "frames", "models" and "optics" already mentioned in this chapter, four theoretical models were in fact influential, and were incorporated in some sense, within the exhibition. The emancipatory museum model, with its emphasis on privileging stories from groups that are "silenced" in the overarching official culture, informed interpretation within the exhibition. The auto-anthropology model, that emphasises the foregrounding of localised forms of exotica, manifested in the exhibition's concern to not only document the mechanics of protest events, but also protester sub-culture, its rituals and belief system. The branding model also played a role. The museum's two prior exhibitions *Gangs* and *Tattoo* had been successful with younger audiences: *Protest* was felt to be another topic that would do the same while also strengthening the museum's reputation for tackling difficult subject matter in a sensitive and thoughtful fashion. The curatorial psychology model also influenced the shaping of content; but this was understood more retrospectively than at the time. I had experienced bereavement shortly before research on the exhibition commenced, losing my mother to cancer. She had been a passionate nature lover, believing wilderness to possess both a life-sustaining significance, and a higher "numinous" character. So the exhibition also tapped into "biographical drives" and became a way of implicitly acknowledging, and paying homage to that formative influence.

Research began with a fieldwork phase of dialogue with mainstream conservation groups and their more radical offshoots, police, solicitors and others, building trust and clarifying objectives. We spoke both to those who had been arrested and claimed to have suffered violence as a result of protest activity, and those who carried out arrests. Different generations of protesters were interviewed from Jack Mundey and Joe Owens, the unionists who became architects of 1970s Sydney "Green Bans" as well as various anti-hydro-electric, nuclear, logging, and mining campaigners of the 1980s and those behind the "Reclaim the Streets"' protests of the 1990s. The complexity of the story of eco-protest in New South Wales demanded multi-perspectival interpretation. This ranged from the audio-visual grab to a boldly dated timeline that unraveled key events chronologically, to ponderous text-based ideological confessions in essay format, in the space provided by the exhibition's catalogue.

The exhibition interpreted its subject via two commissioned films, a five-metre timeline, five 700 word text panels, a photographic chronology of key protest moments and a 57-page illustrated catalogue containing four 2,500 word essays. There were the usual didactic object labels and a number of enlarged quotations on walls from police, judges, environmental groups and protesters themselves as well as the material culture of protest and its paraphernalia on display.

Photographic documentation was positioned throughout the exhibition. This showed how various protest campaigns had unfolded: sometimes gently and non-violently, and others in a confrontational spirit with surreal tactics: pipe barricades cemented into forest roads, with protestors chained inside, body burials, limbs "locked on" to machinery, tripod erection, and protestors "living in trees". These photographs were displayed adjacent to tool kits, protest manuals and technologies, badges, masks, posters, pamphlets and costumes from particular campaigns. Particularly evocative were serial protester Benny Zable's black gas mask and robes emblazoned with the message: "Consume Be Silent Die I Rely On Your Apathy Its Costing The Earth" placed next to vertical columns of pristinely emerald wilderness photography by photographer Henry Gold depicting areas saved from logging by protest and later declared national parks.

The films that featured increased the forum-like qualities of the exhibition, allowing different speakers to be heard and diverse viewpoints to be comprehended, including those of the media, protestors, and police charged with managing protest. These films, made by activist film-makers News Unlimited brought a necessary level of noise, emotion, drama, music, adrenalin and physicality and an easily grasped sense of various contested localities, as well as the key issues behind each campaign, to the space of the exhibition. In one of the films on freeway protests in Sydney the stereotypical notion of the protester is powerfully and movingly collapsed. This segment followed Pat, a pensioner aged in her 60s, who goes from supporting younger protesters on the sidelines, to putting her own body on the line, in order to stop the destruction of local forest. She talks candidly about a "moral awakening" and a need to share in the burden, camaraderie and danger of the protest and, after breaking into a fenced-off compound to prevent a large tree from being torn down, is arrested by police. Afterward, Pat speaks of her experience in insightful terms. The footage of the growing radicalisation of this humble, "everywoman" sparks thoughts about conscience, social responsibility and citizenship. Pat's journey argues strongly for local desire, dignity, and difference. Pat's transformation in undergoing her protest is both poignant and thought-provoking. Her bravery and commitment demands respect.

Conclusion

The hot topic exhibition inevitably asks as many questions as it answers: it satisfies an audience by transforming the museum into a meaning-enriched site of plural reflexivity, which also refuses to patronise with easy truths. Such exhibitions possess the potential to be catalytic events. Managed responsibly and interrogatively by the museum, they posses the ability to speak both to our heads and hearts; deepening thought around important issues so that visitors are offered the opportunity to leave the space of the exhibition with expanded perspectives, changed minds and opened eyes.

References

Baudrillard, J. 1989. *Selected writings*. Cambridge: Polity.

Barthes, R. 1972. *Mythologies*. London: Paladin.

Cameron, D. 2003. The museum, temple of the forum. *Curator* xiv: 11–24.

Cameron, F.R. 2003. Transcending fear—engaging emotions and opinions—a case for museums in the 21st century. *Open Museum Journal*, 6, http://amol.org.au/craft/omjournal (accessed 18 December 2009).

Crane, S. A, 2000. Curious cabinets and imaginary museums. In *Museums & memory*. Ed. S. A. Crane, 60–80. Stanford: Stanford University Press.

Cheeks, R. 2009. Transcendence and history by Glen Hughes. *Philosophy Now,* http://www.philosophynow.org/issue72/72cheeks.htm (accessed 18 December 2009).

Daily Telegraph. 2009. Bikie war explodes. March 23.

Douglas, M. 1984. *Purity and danger: An analysis of the concepts of pollution and taboo*. London: Ark.

Ernst, W, 2000. Arch(ive)textures of museology. In *Museums and memory*. S. A. Crane, 17–34, Stanford: Stanford University Press.

Foucault, M. 1979. *Discipline and punish.* London: Penguin.

—. 1984. *The history of sexuality (vol. 1).* London: Penguin.

Gellner, E. 1992. *Postmodernism, reason and religion.* London: Routledge.

—. 1995. Anything goes: The carnival of cheap relativism that threatens to swamp the coming *fin de milleniair. Times Literary Supplement.* 6–8.

Hall, C. S., V. J. Nordby and J. Vernon. 1973. *A primer of Jungian psychology.* New York: New American Library.

Hebdige, D. 1987. *Subculture: The meaning of style.* London: Methuen.

Heumann Gurian, Elaine. 1996. A savings bank for the soul. Paper presented at the Museums of Australia Power and Empowerment Conference, November 30, Sydney.

Honderich, T. 1996. *The Oxford companion to philosophy.* Oxford: Oxford University Press.

Jameson, F. 1991. *Postmodernism, or, the cultural logic of late capitalism.* Durham NC: Duke University Press.

Johnson, R. 1991. *Owning your own shadow: Understanding the dark side of the psyche.* New York: Harper Collins.

Klein, N. 2001. *No logo.* London: Harper Collins.

Kroker, A. and D. Cook. 1988. *The postmodern scene: Excremental culture and hyper aesthetics*. London: MacMillan.

Lavine, S. D. 1991. Museum practices. In *Exhibiting cultures: The poetics and politics of museum display*. Ed. S. D. Lavine and I. Karp, 151–158. Washington: Smithsonian Institution Press.

Lyotard, F. 1986. *The postmodern condition: A report on knowledge*. Manchester: Manchester University Press.

Macey, D. 2002. *Dictionary of critical theory*. London: Penguin.

Marcus, J. 1996. The erotics of the museum. Paper presented at the Museums of Australia Power and Empowerment Conference, November 30. Sydney.

New York Times Magazine. 1994. Variations: Cover Story. December 13.

Nietzsche, F. 1990. *Beyond good and evil.* London: Penguin.

Overing, J. and N. Rapport. 2000. *Social and cultural anthropology: The key concepts.* London: Routledge.

Said, E. 1993. *Culture and imperialism.* Vintage: London.

St John, G. 2001. Victor Turner—What is this thing called liminality in alternative cultural heterotopia. Contest as Australia's marginal centre. PhD thesis www.confest.org/thesis/twopartone.html (accessed 18 December 2009).

Turner, V. 1979. Frame, flow and reflection: Ritual and drama as public liminality. *Japanese Journal of Religious Studies* 6/4 (Dec): 465–499.

Walsh, K. 1992. *The representation of the past: Museums and heritage in the post-modern world.* London: Routledge.

Warby, S. 1992. Post-post-modernism? In *Destabilizing theory: Contemporary feminist debates.* Ed. M. Barrett and A. Phillips, 48. Cambridge: Polity.

Williams, C. 2002. Beyond good and evil? The taboo in the contemporary museum: Strategies for negotiation and representation. *Open Museum Journal* 4 http://amol.org.au/craft/omjournal/journal_index.asp (accessed 18 December 2009).

Notes

[1] This theoretical model both expands and revises ideas presented in an earlier piece in the Open Museum Journal (2001) *Beyond good and evil? The taboo in the contemporary museum.*

[2] See for example Baudrillard (1989) and Lyotard (1986).

CHAPTER TWO

STRATEGY AND TACTIC: A POST-MODERN RESPONSE TO THE MODERNIST MUSEUM

LINDA FERGUSON

Introduction

In her essay, "Pushing buttons: Controversial topics in museums", Ferguson (2006) examines a number of topics that different stakeholders consider too controversial for museums to display. These include terrorism, asylum seekers, religion, racism, sex, and drugs. Her analysis of the reasons museum staff, visitors, and the wider community give as to why these topics should or should not be displayed reveal much about people's perceptions of museums, as well as the roles they consider appropriate for museums in society today. For example, Ferguson argues that visitors value the certainty that museums provide: "they present factual information, things that we as a society know". If museums were to examine topics or issues that are emerging or unresolved, she claims that this could undermine people's certainties about themselves and their world, something that is of concern to both visitors and staff. Ferguson also suggests that at this historical point in time, people's sense of identity is under threat. In a complex global environment in which nations are dealing with issues such as terrorism, war, immigration, asylum seekers, racism, and race relations, she suggests that people value museums because, in the words of Karp, they "tell us who we are and, perhaps most significant, who we are not" (Karp 1991, 15). In addition, Ferguson states that people want museums to be non-judgmental, to show both sides of the story, but not if it could mean advocating activities that fall outside the realm of acceptable social behaviour (such as drug use).

These things that people value about museums—their roles in providing certainty, representing identity, producing "good citizens" and spreading the accepted values of "civilised society", as well as giving a sense of one's place in the world—are inextricably linked to ideas of modernity. They are as much a part of the fabric of museums as the architecture that embodies them and the collections they hold.

Public museums emerged during the 19th century alongside developments in science, technology and historical disciplines, industrialisation, urbanisation, new ideas regarding order, progress, time and space (Walsh 1992), and a growing trend towards governmental control (Bennett 1995). As new institutions, they epitomised many of the key tenets of modernity. They provided evidence that it was possible to present objective, immutable facts and truths about the natural world. Through their exhibitionary techniques, they provided a sense of order and demonstrated a narrative of human progress and development. Their displays allowed them control of the past, and imbued the institutions with knowledge, power and authority. Bennett (1995) argues that their existence allowed for the emergence of new sets of knowledge, including geology, biology, anthropology, archaeology, and art history. These provided new ways of seeing and understanding the world. Furthermore, museums provided a space in which working class peoples could be "civilised", educated and edified, and in which visitors' behaviour would be self-monitored, self-regulated and normalised. Witcomb (2003) claims that museums have played a complex role in the development of modernity; she associates their development with the emergence of urban popular culture, and with consumerism.

Museums have a long and complex history, throughout which, at each period of their existence, they have embodied and shaped public perceptions of what is valuable and important. Museums and their collections are part of the history and philosophy of knowledge, in both the humanities and the sciences, and this history and philosophy is in part also created by them (Pearce 1992). As sites of secular knowledge, museums help to bind a community into a civic body, by identifying that community's "highest values, its proudest memories, and its truest truths" (Duncan 1991, 91). Museums have a unique and important role in preserving a community's cultural heritage. By collecting and displaying "real" objects, museums are able to achieve an apparent "authenticity", and to create apparently authentic representations of the world. This ability, underlain by their alleged innate neutrality, has enabled museums to develop as instruments of power, and as sites of power-knowledge (Karp 1991).

In the 1980s, dramatic changes began to occur within museums; museums began to rethink their relationship to visitors (Lumley 1987), and to question the political, ideological and aesthetic dimensions that accompany the act of collecting (Vergo 1989). Exhibitions such as *Into the Heart of Africa* began to explore new ways of contextualising museum collections (Schildkrout 2004). The use of multiple voices in exhibitions—what Riegel calls "the postmodern dialogic museum mode" (Riegel 1996, 93)—began to be adopted as a way of invoking multiple identities and subjectivities, calling into question the notion that there is one objective truth, or only one way of viewing the world. Other textual techniques such as the use of irony (Riegel 1996) were adopted in exhibitions as an attempt to be self-reflexive and to question the authority of the museum. New museum developments, such as the Jorvik Viking Centre in York, UK, focused attention on "culture" as a way of life rather than as a set of values to which museum visitors should aspire (Lumley 1987). For Lumley, the development of new, high-technology museums, of open-air museums, and of participatory and interactive displays called into question

> the certainty about the museum's separation from the marketplace, and of its educational as opposed to entertainment role ... Whereas the Victorians had clear ideas about what museums were designed to do (to improve minds, celebrate national heroes and history, cultivate taste in art and design etc), today it is often difficult to see what they are trying to achieve. (1987, 82)

It is my contention that many people have struggled to understand the role of museums in the context of these changes. This is evidenced by the degree of conflict that has occurred between audiences and museums, and which has found its voice in the ways that people react to "controversial" exhibition topics. The response of audiences to particular exhibitions is a sign that this struggle is taking place. It is a struggle not just between individuals, groups and museums, but between the conditions of modernity and post-modernity, and between certainty and doubt.

I am not so much concerned as to why exhibitions are controversial, but as to how they become so. What are the specific activities undertaken by individuals or groups—and the actions (or lack thereof) by museums—that lead to controversy? How can we understand these actions as part of the complex series of power relations that exist between museums and audiences? My focus is not on the ways in which museums establish and maintain power relations; much has already been written on this subject (for example Bennett 1995, Dubin 1999, Witcomb 2003, Cameron 2006). Nor is my concern the ways in which museums exercise power, but the ways in which audiences and citizens do—the tactics they use to exert their own influence on museums. In focusing on the actions of audiences and citizens, I hope not to paint their role in museum controversies as "simple oppositional politics" (Witcomb 2003, 16), but instead to position them as legitimate, active and influential players within an existing field of power relations.

Over the past 25 years, a variety of museum exhibitions have erupted into controversy. While the controversies themselves have been well-documented, most commentators have failed to situate them within a broader theoretical framework. This chapter will fill this breach by treating the experience of controversial museum exhibitions as evidence of the struggle between the conditions of modernity and post-modernity. It will offer both a description and theoretical explanation of the reactionary responses to exhibitions that have characterised the post-modern, post-colonial era. Drawing on Foucault's (1984) reconceptualisation of power and resistance, and de Certeau's (1984) critique of practices of power and resistance in everyday life, this chapter will re-examine how a number of museum exhibitions became contentious. Using de Certeau's concept of strategy and tactical resistance, it will examine some of the modes of tactical resistance that audiences have used in reacting to exhibitions, thereby constructing them as "controversial".

Power: strategy and tactic

Power is often conceptualised as something that is exercised in a single direction, from the top down. However, Foucault (1984) teaches us that power is neither sovereign nor found in a single source, but rather that power is everywhere, and thus so because it comes from everywhere. Where there is power, there is resistance—in fact, a plurality of resistances, present everywhere in the power network. These points of resistance can be employed in a variety of ways:

> These play the role of adversary, target, support, or handle in power relations … resistances that are possible, necessary, improbable; others that are spontaneous, savage, solitary, concerted, rampant, or violent; still others that are quick to compromise, interested, or sacrificial; by definition, they can only exist in the strategic field of power relations. (Foucault 1984, 95-96)

Foucault warns against viewing these points of resistance as reactionary, on the rebound, always passive, and doomed to perpetual defeat.

Reconceptualising relations of power within the framework offered by Foucault entails recognising that museums and audiences are in a strategic relationship with each other. Power is not simply something exercised by museums over audiences in a unilateral direction. Instead, power is exercised from multiple points in the interplay of relations between museums, visitors and citizens.

Michel de Certeau (1984) provides a theoretical framework for understanding practices of power and resistance in everyday life. His interest lies in discovering and describing the ways in which various populations and subjects manage to resist the encroachment of discipline and/or power: he is "concerned with battles or games between the strong and the weak, and with the 'actions' which remain possible for the latter" (de Certeau 1984, 34).

According to de Certeau, once a subject with both will and power has been able to claim a place as its own, it is then able to manage its relationships with external groups via the use of strategy. In other words, by establishing a base, a subject becomes able to impose its will on exterior threats and targets (customers, competitors, enemies, objects of research and, I daresay, visitors and citizens). The establishment of a base is accompanied by several important effects. Firstly, the subject achieves what de Certeau calls "a triumph of place over time" (de Certeau 1984, 36), giving themselves the opportunity to capitalise on their current situation and plan future expansions. Secondly, the subject is able to observe what is happening outside of its space, giving it the ability to predict what might happen, thus enabling it to manage external threats. De Certeau calls this "a mastery of places through sight" (de Certeau 1984, 36). Thirdly, de Certeau claims that the subsequent knowledge produced by the subject is both made possible and determined by the power that the subject already possesses. He suggests that a business, an army, a city, or a scientific institution are all subjects that could establish a base for themselves and make use of strategy to manipulate external power relationships. I contend that museums can also be understood as subjects within this framework of place, power-knowledge and strategy.

In opposition to strategy is tactic—what de Certeau calls the "art of the weak" (1984, 37). Those who rely on tactic do not have their own power base from which to operate. Instead, they respond to opportunity as it arises, launching surprise attacks within enemy territory and then disappearing. In this way, de Certeau claims that "the space of tactic is the space of the other" (1984, 37). Those acting tactically use time to their advantage, identifying and acting at the precise instant where a favourable outcome is possible. The art of tactic allows the weak to manoeuvre themselves into the other's place if only fleetingly; it is "a logic of momentary occupation without ownership" (Frow 1991, 55). The prizes won tactically are ephemeral, unable to be stockpiled or kept.

The range of museum controversies that have occurred over the past 25 years can be seen as examples of strategy and tactical resistance. Audiences across the world have used different modes of tactical resistance to react to different exhibitions, thereby constructing these exhibitions as "controversial". In the next section, I examine the most common mode of tactical resistance used by audiences: the tactic of protest.

Protest

The tactic of protest is one that has been used with varying degrees of success for decades. The tactic of protest takes more than one form. At its simplest, it involves *direct intercession.* By this I mean that the protester directly contacts the museum, makes his or her point of view known (often on behalf of a wider interest group), and either requests or demands a change to be made: an exhibition to close, a display to be taken off view, the central theme of a planned exhibition to be abandoned, or the text of an exhibition to be altered. This form of protest has a low profile and is unlikely to be successful as the tactic itself is not much of a threat: there is little at stake for the museum. However, protesters may raise the stakes by threatening the *withdrawal of funds or support.* If the value of these potential losses is high enough, this form of protest may have more chance of success. There is also the tactic of *indirect intercession*, in which a protester may try to raise broader attention to the issue at hand and seek to influence the museum via third parties. This would include, for example, the protester writing letters to the editor of a newspaper or lobbying a senator or Member of Parliament. *Publicity* is a fourth tactic and may involve a protester or protest group releasing statements directly to the media or hosting a website about the issue; the aim is to achieve newsworthiness (Ellison 2003) and to raise broader public attention to the issue, ensuring that it will not go away and calling the museum to make a response or take action. *Mobilisation* of other interest groups is a way of gaining strength through numbers. Rather than trying to achieve broad public attention on the issue, this tactic focuses attention on existing networks that can use their membership to up the ante and duplicate the attack.

The modes described above are fairly intangible, however, other forms of protest are more material. *Picketing* is a way of drawing attention both to an issue and to its source: the museum. Here, protesters take their argument and locate it on the borders of the museum's own space, making their "attack" at the very boundaries of the institution. This form of protest is highly visible in its own right, but can also find itself replicated in other media formats (for example, broadcast on the evening news). Another high-profile form of protest is the *public demonstration or rally;* here, protesters move their attack away from the institution and into the broader community, physically taking to the streets as a way of demonstrating their support for changes to be made at the museum. The involvement of large numbers of citizens and taxpayers is meant to be a persuasive sign of the force of numbers and their "rightness" in the protest. *Boycott,* either of the museum or of an alternative high-profile institution or event (such as the Olympic Games) is an interesting tactic of protest. The tactic of boycott (or even the threat of boycott) succeeds by a double absence, through the act of denial. The protester, without its own power locus, makes its absence felt at the place where the other's power is usually greatest. Despite being based on absence, boycott can be a highly conspicuous means of protest if the boycotters are able to make their cause visible through the media.

A final tactic is to *harness other powerful establishments,* which are then able to use their own strategies to enforce change. Such establishments could include political systems, judicial or regulatory systems, educational structures, organised religion, other museums, and even the broader network of museum professionals and peers. This form of resistance may begin with indirect intercession to a Member of Parliament (from government or the opposition), a bureaucrat or a church leader, who may then choose to take the issue on as his or her own. Alternatively, it could occur as the independent action of an education board following widespread publicity about an issue. The museum may find itself subject to political scrutiny through review boards, questions on notice as to how decisions are made or money spent, the appointment of board members who support the points of view of the protesters, threats to withhold public monies, or undue pressure to remove the museum director or senior curatorial staff. Alternatively, museums and staff could find themselves charged with committing a crime.

In waging a successful attack against a museum, an individual or group may use more than one tactical form of protest; a well-organised group may be able to coordinate several forms into an ongoing tactical campaign. I would contend that such a campaign is tactical rather than strategic, as it appears to develop in an ad hoc manner, taking advantage of what has been gained and new opportunities that arise, rather than planned in full from the start.

How have these different forms of protest been used in creating controversy and influencing (coercing?) museums to change? Which tactics have individuals and groups used to react to museums? Which tactics have been "successful", and in what ways? In the next section of the chapter, I revisit some of the exhibition controversies that we have witnessed over the past 25 years. In so doing, I attempt to move beyond questions of *why* these exhibitions were controversial; instead, I focus on *how* these exhibitions became contentious through the exercise of power and tactic by audiences.

Case studies

One of the earliest well-documented and publicised examples of protest against museums occurred in 1985 (Coombes 1992, Simpson 1996). The protest was made against the London Museum of Mankind's *Hidden Peoples of the Amazon* exhibition. The exhibition was apparently about "the life and culture of the Indian peoples of the South American tropical rainforest" (Simpson 1996, 36). Coombes claims that the exhibition represented these various Indian groups as "productive, active, and evidently in possession of an encyclopaedic knowledge of the complex ecology of their environment" (1992, 45). However, critics of the exhibition claimed that it gave an inaccurate picture by failing to represent the plight that threatened the survival of contemporary Amazonian Indians (Simpson, 1996). Furthermore, critics claimed that the exhibition failed to acknowledge the dialectical and dynamic relationship of diverse Amerindian peoples to culture contact. In particular, there was a lack of evidence of the ongoing struggle between Indians and the Brazilian government; no signs of selective resistance on behalf of the Indians; and no sign of self-determination by the Indian peoples represented in the exhibition (Coombes 1992). The exhibition was picketed by representatives from Survival International as well as by two Indian representatives from different Indian rights organisations. The museum responded to the protest by adding three items to the exhibition: a storyboard about western aid campaigns against the destruction of the Amazonian rainforest and two photographs which evidently demonstrated a thriving "hybrid culture" (Coombes 1992, 47).

In January 1988, the Lubicon Lake Cree people of Alberta, Canada, protested against a major exhibition, *The Spirit Sings: Artistic Traditions of Canada's First Peoples,* which was being put on at the Glenbow Museum to coincide with the Winter Olympics in Calgary. The protest was organised to draw attention to the Lubicon Lake Cree's 40-year-old land claim and had originally been planned as a demonstration and boycott of the Olympic Games. However, the Lubicon Lake Cree turned their attention to the exhibition, which had been sponsored by Shell Oil Canada Ltd to the value of 1.1 million Canadian dollars. The Lubicon felt that the sponsorship of an exhibition of native art work gave the impression that the sponsor supported native rights—when instead, Shell was drilling for oil in the area of the Lubicon Lake Cree's land claim (Coombes 1992, Harrison et al. 1988, Simpson 1996). The protest drew considerable media coverage, and resulted in an internal split within the Canadian museum community; those supporting the boycott, and those believing that the exhibition should go ahead as planned. A number of museums refused to loan objects to the Glenbow Museum in support of the boycott or in concern for the objects' safety. As well, several curators resigned from museums throughout Canada. Others accused the Lubicon of bullying, totalitarian tactics, and of hostage taking—using the exhibition unashamedly to attract international attention to their grievances (Simpson 1996). The exhibition opened with only one allusion to the controversy that surrounded it: a notice at the end of the exhibition that affirmed the museum's commitment to a fair and speedy settlement of land claims and associated issues (McManus 1991). More than 20 years have passed since the initial controversy; according to the Friends of the Lubicon website, the Lubicon Lake Cree are still seeking a land rights settlement with the Canadian government.

The examples given above have been relatively peaceful protests. The dispute surrounding the Royal Ontario Museum's 1989 exhibition *Into the Heart of Africa* was not. It began with a small group of community representatives giving a poor review of the exhibition brochure prior to the show's opening (the museum made changes to the brochure in response to their concerns). Schildkrout (2004) claims that after the exhibition opened, public protests gradually escalated. First, there were complaints to the museum and letters to newspapers (direct and indirect intercession). Four months after the opening, black Canadian protesters established the Coalition for the Truth about Africa, an umbrella organisation for over 15 black community groups (MacDonald and Alsford 2007), and began picketing the museum. Next came street demonstrations and violent encounters involving the Toronto police, with a number of arrests being made. The demonstrations were deemed newsworthy, resulting in extensive and detailed press coverage that may have given the impression that they were larger and occurred more frequently than was the case (Simpson 1996). The museum responded by seeking the involvement of the judicial system, obtaining a court injunction to keep protestors from picketing within 15 metres of the museum entrance. At this point, the educational system became involved in the controversy, seemingly of its own accord: the Toronto Board of Education issued a statement that the exhibition was unsuitable for primary and junior students and only permissible for older students with structured preparation and follow-up. Finally, all four of the museums that were supposed to host the exhibition cancelled (Schildkrout 2004). Simpson (1996, 27) reports claims that *Into the Heart of Africa* was "used as a political platform by black activists".

The most publicised museum controversy, generating an unprecedented amount of commentary, is undoubtedly the *Enola Gay* affair (Dubin 1999). The *Enola Gay* is the B-29 bomber that carried the first atom bomb to its target, Hiroshima, near the end of the Second World War. The National Air and Space Museum (NASM), part of the Smithsonian Institution, planned to exhibit the forward fuselage of the *Enola Gay* in an exhibition that was timed to coincide with the 50th anniversary of the end of the Second World War. Among the museum community, the exhibition is best known as *The Last Act: The End of World War II, The Atomic Bomb, and the Origins of the Cold War,* although it was originally conceived as *The Crossroads: The End of World War II, the Atomic Bomb and the Onset of the Cold War.* According to the Air Force Association (AFA) website (which contains a detailed chronology of events), the controversy surrounding this exhibition commenced in August 1993. Within weeks of the original exhibition concept document being produced, B-29 veterans had collected 5,000 signatures to raise concerns about the planned exhibition and to petition the museum "to display the airplane proudly". The Executive Director of the AFA, Monroe Hatch, and the editor of the *Air Force Magazine*, John T. Correll, became key players in the controversy. Over the next 17 months, they used a variety of tactics to try to ensure that the museum did not display the *Enola Gay* in the way it originally intended. For example, Hatch corresponded with the director of NASM, Martin Harwit, strenuously expressing the Association's concerns with the exhibition. The AFA released a report on the Smithsonian's plans to exhibit the *Enola Gay*, in which they discredited the "Politically Correct Curating" that was "part of the cultural reinterpretation that has swept the Smithsonian complex"; the report also discredited another NASM exhibition that they claimed took a hostile view of airpower. Correll published a shortened version of the report in the *Air Force Magazine.* Having achieved widespread publicity with the release of the report and the *Air Force Magazine* articles, the AFA provided a copy of the preliminary draft exhibition script to the *Washington Times;* at the request of Congressional staffers, the AFA undertook content analysis of the script (an action it repeated for four subsequent drafts). On several occasions, Hatch met with Harwit, Air Force officials, military historians, other veterans' groups, and even the Under Secretary of the Smithsonian, in an attempt to "resolve differences" or "resolve problems with the exhibition". Hatch and Correll were assisted in their task by internal sources within the Smithsonian who leaked documents to the AFA and *Air Force Magazine* (Zolberg 1996).

The controversy surrounding the planned *Enola Gay* exhibit was fanned by the media and leapt upon by politicians who saw a new opportunity to gain attention and win votes (Dubin 1999). Articles were published in newspapers such as the *Washington Post* and the *Wall Street Journal,* as well as in a range of specialised publications. Dubin (1999) claims that most journalists accepted the critics' allegations at face view and failed to corroborate their statements.

The wider community took up the argument, writing to the Smithsonian to vent their disapproval; at one point, the Smithsonian was reportedly receiving "over a hundred letters a week" (Dubin 1999, 200). According to the AFA website, in August 1994, 24 members of Congress wrote to the Smithsonian, expressing their "concern and dismay" about the exhibition; a month later, a "Sense of the Senate" report was passed unanimously, in which the exhibition script was called "revisionist and offensive to many World War II veterans". In December 1994, seven members of Congress wrote to the Smithsonian expressing "deep displeasure" with the way in which the exhibition had been handled. In January 1995, 81 members of Congress called for Harwit to resign as Director of NASM. By the end of that month, the exhibition had been cancelled and by early May 1995, Harwit had resigned.

A key tactic employed by the AFA during the *Enola Gay* controversy was that of citation. De Certeau talks about "tactics of 'making people believe'" including "the claim to be speaking in the name of a reality" (1984, 184-185). He notes the importance of citing someone else:

> Citation thus appears to be the ultimate weapon for making people believe. Because it plays on what the other is assumed to believe, it is the means by which the 'real' is instituted. (de Certeau 1984, 188)

Dubin (1999) reports that the AFA used the tactic of citation by quoting snippets of draft exhibition text out of context and after they had been removed from the exhibition script. One passage in particular, was said to have taken on a life of its own:

> For most Americans this war was fundamentally different from the one waged against Germany and Italy—it was a war of vengeance. For most

> Japanese it was a war to defend their unique culture against Western imperialism. (Dubin 1999, 198-199)

Out of context, the text gave the impression that Americans were racist and vengeful; quoting it was a way of making people believe that this was also the museum's perspective.

The Canadian War Museum faced a similar backlash in 2006 over its depiction of Bomber Command and its bombing raids on Germany's industrial towns in the Second World War. As reported by Randy Boswell at *Canada.com* on 28 September 2006, a national Coalition of Veterans threatened to call a public boycott of the museum if it refused to change the display. The veterans were critical of the text in the exhibition, which they claim implied that Allied bomber crews were war criminals. Somewhat ironically, they also disputed the text's assertion that "The value and morality of the strategic bomber offensive against Germany remains bitterly contested". The museum responded to the veterans' initial complaints, making what they called "substantial alterations" to the Bomber Command display by "adding contextual information and even a quote from Arthur 'Bomber' Harris", the controversial commander of the campaign. However, the veterans wanted further changes to the key text panel. They "issued an ultimatum ... demanding another meeting with curators" about their representation of Bomber Command. The article reports the museum's response that "another meeting on the issue would be futile ... when it comes to representing historical events, it is common for people of good conscience to disagree". Paul Gessell, reporting for *The Ottawa Citizen* on 28 August 2007, says that the veterans threatened to boycott the exhibition, which prompted the museum to undertake what it called the "exceptional step" of seeking input from independent, expert historians. Of the six historians who reviewed the exhibition, four agreed that it presented an accurate view of the air war in Europe, with the remaining two raising concerns about the "tone" and "balance" of the text panel. At this point, the museum made what it said was its final decision, that the text panel would not be changed. However, in June 2007, a Senate subcommittee on veterans' affairs recommended changes that could be made to the text panel. Within a few days of the release of the Senate report, the museum's director "mysteriously" left his job. In August, the museum agreed to revise the panel. As reported by James Adams in the *Globe and Mail* on 11 October 2007, the revised wording was three times as long as the original and was drafted in consultation with many people, including groups and individuals who had protested at the original text, such as the Royal Canadian Legion, the Mayday Committee, and retired army generals. This article includes a comment attributed to the acting museum director Mark O'Neill that the museum "would not entertain the idea of any substantial changes to the revision".

The contention and debate surrounding these two anniversary exhibitions remind us of the difficulty in attempting to reconcile commemoration and interpretation within a museum. Such concerns are not solely related to events that occurred 60 or more years ago, but are equally relevant to events of the last ten years. For example, the International Freedom Center (IFC) was a proposed museum to be built at the World Trade Center memorial site to commemorate those who had died in the 11 September 2001 terrorist attacks. The proponents of the IFC hoped that it would complement the memorial by presenting exhibitions and education programs that could examine the terrorist attacks in the context of an ongoing global struggle for freedom. However, many people (including those who had lost loved ones in the 9/11 attacks) opposed the plans for the IFC, claiming that it would present a "politicized and biased history that would taint the sacredness of the memorial" (Van Orden 2006). A rally was held in 2005, protesting the appropriateness of having museum exhibits at the memorial site. In September of that year, the New York Governor George Pataki decided to remove the IFC from the memorial site. Nonetheless, a new National September 11 Memorial and Museum is due to open at the World Trade Center site in 2013, and will include the hijackers' perspectives. Joan Gralla, reporting for *Yahoo!News* on the eighth anniversary of the attacks, stated that "Museum officials are treading carefully".

A new form of protest has emerged in the 21st century: vandalism. In at least two high-profile incidents, individuals have either damaged or attempted to deface exhibits in a museum. The first such incident occurred at the Sakharov Museum in Russia in January 2003. A contemporary art exhibition on faith and religion, *Caution! Religion,* was vandalised by six men from a Russian Orthodox Church within four days of its opening. As reported by Steven Lee Myers on 2 September 2003 for the *International Herald Tribune Online*, and on 29 March 2005 for the *New York Times Online*, the six men defaced many of the 45 artworks with spray paint, destroyed others, and graffitied the walls of the museum. The police arrived and detained the men within the museum, charging them with hooliganism. Priests from the Russian Orthodox Church denounced the museum. Under the direction of Reverend Aleksander Shargunov, a priest from the church of Saint Nikolai in Pyzhi, (whose parishioners had attacked the exhibition), church members began a letter-writing campaign defending the men. The lower house of Parliament passed a resolution condemning the museum and the exhibition's organisers. Charges against four of the six men were dropped early "for lack of evidence", even though the men had been apprehended inside the museum. The trial of the other two men took place on 11 August 2003, with several hundred Orthodox believers holding a vigil outside the court. The court found that the two men had been unlawfully prosecuted, however it stated that the investigation should continue—not against those who had attacked the exhibition, but against those who had put it together. Subsequently, new charges were laid against the museum director, Yuri V. Samodurov, the museum's curator, Lyudmila V. Vasilovskaya, and one of the artists, Anna Mikhalchuk. According to Jeremy Bransten's *Radio Free Europe Radio Liberty* report on 29 March 2005, all three were charged with inciting ethnic and religious hatred under Article 282 of the Russian Criminal Code. Mikhalchuk was acquitted, but Samodurov and Vasilovskaya were both found guilty, and each fined 100,000 rubles (approximately US$3,600).

The second vandalism incident occurred at the Museum of National Antiquities, Stockholm, Sweden, in 2004. Again, it was a contemporary art exhibition, timed to coincide with a three-day international conference on preventing genocide. According to Tommy Grandell's report at *Salon.com* on 27 January 2004, the exhibition included a portrait of a Palestinian bomber whose suicide bombing had resulted in the deaths of 21 bystanders in Haifa, Israel. The exhibit was created by Israeli-born artist Dror Feiler, who said the piece was meant to show "how weak, lonely people can be capable of horrible things". The Israeli ambassador to Sweden, Zvi Mazel, attempted to vandalise the exhibit at a function, and called for it to be removed from display. In the next ten days, US-based Jewish human rights groups sent almost 14,000 emails to Sweden's Prime Minister, Goeran Persson, requesting that the exhibit and promotional posters of the image be removed. In contrast to the government's response in Russia, the Swedish government claimed that it did not have the right to censure art, or to influence the museum in its actions. The museum refused to take the exhibit from display, although it did remove 26 posters of the portrait that had been used to promote the exhibition from subway stations throughout Stockholm.

My final example of the tactic of protest comes from Malaysia in 2007. As reported online in the *Middle East Times* on 13 April 2007, and in the Associated Press on 14 April 2007, the Negeri Sembilan state museum was hosting an exhibition on ghosts, ghouls and supernatural beings. The exhibition attracted about 25,000 visitors in its first five weeks, but it also attracted the criticism of religious scholars who claimed that encouraging belief in ghosts was un-Islamic. The Malaysian Culture Arts and Heritage

Minister, Rais Yatim, called for the exhibition to be closed on the basis that it was not beneficial to the community. However, the museum refused to shut down the exhibition, stating that its objective was to educate the public. At this point, Malaysia's National Fatwa Council ruled that exhibitions on supernatural beings were forbidden as they could undermine the faith of Muslims. The Negeri Sembilan state government abided by the council's ruling, cancelling the show. The Council's decision was to be presented to all of Malaysia's state governments, for gazetting as religious law.

Conclusion

In the Introduction I identified some of the things that are most valued about museums: their roles in providing certainty, representing identity, producing "good citizens" and spreading the accepted values of "civilised society", and giving a sense of one's place in the world. All of these roles are bound to ideas of modernity. Since the 1980s, museum practice has changed markedly. The postmodern museum puts into doubt many of these most valued things. While there were controversies before the 1980s (McConnell and Hess 1998), there has been an exponential increase in the number and intensity of controversies since that time. I contend that this rise in controversy is in part due to the fact that audiences have struggled to understand the role of museums in the context of these changes. The response of audiences to particular exhibitions is a sign that this struggle is taking place.

By drawing on Foucault's (1984) reconceptualisation of power and resistance, and introducing de Certeau's (1984) theories on strategy and tactic, I have attempted to situate museum controversies within a broader discussion of power and power relations. It is not just museums that exercise power; visitors and citizens are themselves active, influential, and legitimate powerbrokers. By focusing on the range of tactical responses that individuals and groups have used in protesting against exhibitions, I hope to highlight the complexity and multilateral nature of power relations between museums and audiences. The fact that a range of other establishments (political, judicial, regulatory, educational and religious) have also become involved in these controversies intensifies the degree of complexity.

In focusing on *how* controversies have erupted, I have deliberately steered away from questions of *why* exhibitions were controversial. At the most basic analysis, each was controversial simply because the exhibition, its location, and its timing provided an opportunity for a successful tactical attack. This is true even in those instances where museums had strategically tried to circumvent controversy by using advisory boards (as did NASM) or sought community vetting of content prior to a show's opening (as the Royal Ontario Museum did to a limited degree). This raises the question as to how museums can defend themselves strategically, not just respond in a reactionary manner, once a protest has begun. Despite the range of museum reactions in these case studies, most of the protester concerns were eventually borne out: museums added new elements to exhibitions, changed what was planned, removed offensive elements, or cancelled or closed the show. It is not easy to find those instances in which museums have ignored, quashed, or out-manoeuvred a tactical attack with no adverse consequences.

This critique of power, power relations and the uses of strategy and tactic reminds us that there will continue to be controversies surrounding museums. Individuals and groups will continue to find "cracks" (de Certeau 1984, 37) and turn them into tactical opportunities, to harness the influence of existing networks, the media, and political and other establishments, and to turn the broader public attention onto the museum and its need to change. We already know which topics are considered potentially controversial (Ferguson 2006); this critique reminds us of the importance of timing in relation to controversy, and identifies some modes of tactical resistance so that museums can understand the "games" that these protesters play, and the directions in which these games may turn.

References

Bennett, T. 1995. *The birth of the museum: History, theory, politics.* New York and London: Routledge.

Cameron, F.R. 2006. Beyond surface representations: Museums, "edgy" topics, civic responsibilities and modes of engagement. *Online MuseumJournal,*8.http://amol.org.au/craft/omjournal/journal_index.asp (accessed 18 December 2009).

Coombes, A. E. 1992. Inventing the "postcolonial". *New Formations,* 18, 29–52.

De Certeau, M. 1984. *The practice of everyday life.* Berkeley: University of California Press.

Dubin, S. C. 1999. *Displays of power: Memory and amnesia in the American museum.* New York and London: New York University Press.

Duncan, C. 1991. Art museums and the ritual of citizenship. In *Exhibiting cultures: The poetics and politics of museum display.* Ed. I. Karp and S. D. Lavine, 88–103. Washington: Smithsonian.

Ellison, J. 2003. Re-visioning the media, museums and controversy: A preliminary case study. *Open Museum Journal,* 6. http://amol.org.au/craft/omjournal/journal_index.asp (accessed 18 December 2009).

Ferguson, L. 2006. Pushing buttons: controversial topics in museums. *Open Museum Journal,* 8, http://amol.org.au/craft/omjournal/journal_index.asp (accessed 18 December 2009).

Foucault, M. 1984. *The history of sexuality, an introduction.* London: Penguin.

Frow, J. 1991. Michel de Certeau and the practice of representation. *Cultural Studies* 5: 52–60.

Harrison, J., B. Trigger and M. Ames. 1988. Point / counterpoint: The Spirit Sings and the Lubicon boycott. *Muse* 6**:** 12–25.

Karp, I. 1991. Culture and representation. *Exhibiting cultures: The poetics and politics of museum display.* Ed. I. Karp and S. D. Lavine, 11-24. Washington D.C.: Smithsonian.

Lumley, R. 1987. Museums in a post modern world. *Museums Journal* 87: 81–83.

Macdonald, G. F. and S. Alsford. 2007. Canadian Museums and the representation of culture in a multicultural nation. In *Museums and communities.* Ed. S. Watson, 276-291. London: Routledge.

McConnell, M. and H. Hess. 1998. A controversy timeline. *Journal of Museum Education,* 23: 4–6.

McManus, G. 1991. The crisis of representation in museums: The exhibition "The Spirit Sings", Glenbow Museum, Calgary, Canada. In *Museum economics and the community.* Ed. S. M. Pearce, 202-205. London: The Athlone Press.

Pearce, S. M. 1992. *Museums objects and collections: A cultural study.* Leicester: Leicester University Press.

Riegel, H. 1996. Into the heart of irony: Ethnographic exhibitions and the politics of difference. In *Theorizing museums: Representing identity and diversity in a changing world.* Ed. S. Macdonald and G. Fyfe, 83–104. Oxford: Blackwell Publishers.

Schildkrout, E. 2004. Ambiguous messages and ironic twists: Into the Heart of Africa and the other museum. In *Museum studies: An anthology of contexts,* Ed. B. M. Carbonell, 181–192. Malden: Blackwell Publishing.

Simpson, M. G. 1996. *Making representations: Museums in the post-colonial era.* London, New York: Routledge.
Van Orden, V. 2006. Exhibiting tragedy: Museums and the representation of September 11. *Journal of Museum Education*: 31, 51–62.
Vergo, P. 1989. *The new museology.* London: Reaktion Books.
Walsh, K. 1992. *The representation of the past: Museums and heritage in the post-modern world.* London, New York: Routledge.
Witcomb, A. 2003. *Re-imagining the museum: Beyond the mausoleum,* London, New York: Routledge.
Zolberg, V. L. 1996. Museums as contested sites of remembrance: The Enola Gay affair. In *Theorizing museums: Representing identity and diversity in a changing world.* Ed. S. Macdonald and G. Fyfe, 69-82. Oxford: Blackwell Publishers.

CHAPTER THREE

RISK SOCIETY, CONTROVERSIAL TOPICS AND MUSEUM INTERVENTIONS: (RE)READING CONTROVERSY AND THE MUSEUM THROUGH A RISK OPTIC

FIONA CAMERON

Introduction

In an increasingly inter-connected global society uncertainty prevails. Our lives are in a constant state of transformation—characterised by fluidity and mobility. New risks, threats and global hazards emerge such as global financial meltdowns; climate change and terrorism, all requiring action. Increasingly individuals are charged with a greater responsibility for themselves, necessarily requiring them to make decisions in many areas of their lives. Taking cultural theorist Ulrich Beck's (1999) theory of world risk society, in this chapter I firstly critique the modern museum project as a first step towards reconsidering and reframing institutional forms according to these contemporary social conditions.

Museums were established on the basis of earlier forms of social life, and risk control regimes. They operated within a national framework; represented collective patterns of life; and acted as places to set moral standards and control cultural conversations. Engaging controversial topics and controversy is now a fundamental role for many museums in an increasingly complex and globalising world. Controversy is no longer something to be feared, but signals the contemporary relevance of the museum form in public political culture. Secondly, in this chapter I argue that museums have a critical role in activating controversy as a productive means for engaging their audiences; in formulating new knowledge; in contributing meaningfully to current debates to more effectively operate within an increasingly pluralistic society and as spaces operating within new transnational risk management and decision-making flows on matters of societal concern. Thirdly, I illustrate how institutions formerly framed according to an earlier institutional rationale might innovate to engage controversial topics and controversy more purposefully in a transnational world increasingly characterised by global risks and hazards.

Controversial topics, controversy, museums and public culture—the context

The idea that museums *should* engage controversy is strongly supported by the findings of the Australian Research Council and Canadian Museums Association funded international research project, *Exhibitions as Contested Sites: The Roles of Museums in Contemporary Societies.*[1] The findings suggest that according to 60 per cent of those surveyed via telephone in Australia and around 80 per cent of museum visitors interviewed in five museums in Australia and Canada respectively, stated that engaging important challenging and controversial topics and points of view in a democratic, free-thinking society was seen as a key role for museums. For many, museums are seen as one of the few places where these debates can happen. Participants' responses articulated potential interventions more succinctly. According to a Sydney pensioner, museums should act as provocateurs inciting critical and reflexive comment, "It's the role of museums to be provocative, to bring certain things into question and under consideration" (Contested Sites Omnibus Survey, Sydney). Others stressed the potential for museums to incite new ways of thinking, "There are few places in our culture where people dare to take on such issues to force us into a new paradigm" (Contested Sites Exit Survey, Museum of Anthropology).

These sentiments were supported by our online staff survey. Around 89 per cent of museum staff agreed that museums *should* present exhibitions about topics that some people may see as taboo or controversial. Likewise, staff expressed the potential for institutions to act as venues instrumental in transforming ways of thinking about topics of societal relevance. One museum professional based in a US museum articulated this by stating "Museums can provide the perfect setting for discussions and debate around topics that directly influence and shape society" (Contested Sites Online Staff Survey).

The main concerns of staff and stakeholders in regards to exhibiting these topics related to the fear of losing funding support; the need to be politically correct in order to receive and maintain public funding; the risk of alienating stakeholders or lobby groups; determining whose voice and history is told; and the risk of having the museum hijacked as a platform for people who have opinions about that topic (Ferguson 2006; Cameron 2006). These tensions were counter-balanced by the perceived need to remain relevant, to take an active and important role in contemporary societies as places for conversations. This disposition was articulated by one US museum professional, "If we are content to be pretty places that tell safe stories we will quickly become irrelevant and then really be at risk of losing our funding" (Contested Sites Online Staff Survey).

For audiences the fear of engaging controversial subjects rested on the threat of politicising institutions and undermining their perceived impartiality and trustworthiness. Usurping institutional legitimacy and trust according to those we interviewed has the potential to occur when museums present unsubstantiated opinions and openly engage in a partisan debate, "…it would turn [museums] into a different institution altogether if they were trying to lead public opinion … that would border on political" (Contested Sites Visitor Focus Group Transcript AUS#a; Cameron 2007).

Although it is clear that both institutions and communities see museums as having a vital role in the engagement of controversy, and many institutions are indeed tackling "hot" topics, there exists an uneasy tension between how to negotiate their institutional political settings and the multifarious values and agendas of stakeholders. A lack of clarity about their roles and responsibilities and the ways institutions might position themselves around controversial topics in order to maintain perceived legacies of impartiality and trustworthiness were also central concerns. Larger concerns emerge, however, around the potential incompatibility of existing institutional forms and the need to (re)invent new ones to remain relevant while still maintaining trust. Accordingly, many institutions remain out-of-step with emerging social conditions. Therefore the analysis of the latter is critical in this reframing process.

The second part of this chapter interrogates these blockages and proposes with greater clarity, drawing on contemporary cultural theory and empirical data, ways that institutions might (re)formulate their roles as actors and arenas to better embrace controversial topics and controversy in light of emergent social conditions.

World risk society—a new optic for (re)conceptualising controversy and museums

Ulrick Beck's world risk society (1999) is a useful theoretical paradigm to interrogate contemporary social conditions and museum transformations. Here I use Beck's thesis as an optic to critique the museum project, consider current programs and (re)frame museums' roles and institutional forms in a world increasingly characterised by global risks and hazards and their incumbent contestations.

Central to Beck's idea of world risk society is the ethos of risk and related social transformations. Risks, in the form of new technological, economic, social and natural hazards arising from the unintended consequences of modernisation and the means used to foresee, communicate, control and govern them is deemed one of the key motivators in the transformation of society from what Beck calls first modernity to second modernity. According to Beck (1999) social forms connected with his first modernity is the idea of national industrial society based on territorially defined collective patterns of life: the family; the welfare state and the union; the exploitation of nature and the idea of technological and scientific progress. The concept and reality of risk operating within first modernity is conceived as an objective entity, one that is subject to control and hence controllable through calculation, assessment and probability. This risk concept promotes the establishment of risk measurement, control and preventative mechanisms such as expert knowledge systems, museums, the police, government and insurance companies. Institutional forms, such as these used to control human action are inseparable from the politics of risk—real and perceived threats to our fundamental political ideals of liberty, justice, rights and democracy.

Museums, for example, were established as institutions of first modernity. They were conceived as places of precaution, as venues to control risk by monitoring cultural conversations, by setting moral standards and reforming behaviour through education, and by producing moral and responsible citizens. They were framed to celebrate science and technological achievement promoting a radical optimism and certainty about the future by producing knowable, and certain expert knowledge. Expert systems of knowledge based on scientific objectivism promote the former, while social recognition of other forms of knowledge cast as lay, have been withheld. This reading of the museum as an instrument of first modernity is not dissimilar to a Foucauldian governmentality reading of the museum popularised by museum theorist Tony Bennett (1995). The notion of museums as a mechanism instrumental in the circulation of risk and as an instrument for controlling and managing populations reflects a similar sentiment of the museum as an apparatus of discipline. With both readings, the individual and indeed a population is conceived as entities to be disciplined and shaped through a pedagogic lens according to the mores of the governing classes (Bennett 1995). It is not surprising therefore that controversy has no place and is indeed incompatible with this institutional formation, given the emphases on risk control, discipline, the collective, audiences as objects of governance, expert knowledge systems and rationality, and the exclusion of the non-expert voice. The legacy of this form was expressed by one staff member at the National Museum of the American Indian, "… we do very well at being intellectual bastions; we don't do very well at giving social experiences … if we become better social experiences we may be more able to deal with controversial topics" (Contested Sites Staff Focus Group Transcript USA#b).

The reworking of the museum idea in the 1970s, in philosophical terms as the new museology (Cameron 1971) and in practice as the forum for debate from the 1980s, offered new hope in the representation of difference and contention. Partially borne out of disputes over the representation of women, gay and indigenous communities in museums and the rise of post-modern and post-structuralist thought, this model is posited on the idea of identity politics and the ontology of difference rather than commonality and interaction. Through modalities of representation, identity acts as the predominant social organising principle as separate class, ethnic and gender groupings in exhibition spaces and programs. This is evident in the popularity of community access spaces in the 1990s. These notions of pluralism and diversity tend to describe and represent the idea of identity as "community", and as celebratory, separate and non-interacting, while at once seeking to recover subaltern, and at times, sensitive histories previously denied in museum spaces. Examples of this approach can be seen at the Smithsonian National Museum of American History in exhibitions *Our Peoples: Giving Voice to Our Histories*. While sensitive topics may be represented, controversy—the inherent disputatiousness of particular subjects is controlled within certain limits through the curatorial editorial process. Many museums are still reluctant to openly encourage interactions between the various parties instead privileging their own or authorising certain narratives. This represents a continuation of a modern risk regime in which many museums continue to control cultural conversations within certain boundaries, a position claimed by staff as a means of maintaining institutional trustworthiness and hence credibility (Reconceptualising Heritage Collections Powerhouse Museum curatorial focus group, 20 March 2008).

The erosion of first modernity and the museum project

The erosion of first modernity, the museological project and the incumbent need for new institutional forms around controversy that take into account emerging social forms is driven by the unintended consequences of the success of industrialised society—the emergence of hazards and others deemed as potentially threatening. These new risks include the degradation of the environment and climate change, terrorism, nuclear accidents, global financial meltdowns, threats to food supplies, genetically modified foods, BSE (mad cow disease), cloning, and infectious diseases such as HIV Aids. As hazards become more prominent and numerous and along with globalisation, individualisation (a process in which neo-liberal policies place a greater emphasis on the individual as responsible for their own self care), and reflexive modernisation (a greater interest in critiquing society, expert systems, institutions and government), new interdependent social forms and risk conflict and management structures emerge as global risk society.

Moreover, as these manufactured risks become prominent and are made objects of expert, public and personal concern, the failure of rational expert systems to manage uncertainty and calculate risk precipitates an erosion of trust in science, corporations and government. This leads to doubt, uncertainty about the future, insecurity, instability and the emergence of new dialectics of conflict and notions of justice from one based primarily on the distribution of wealth through class and unionised struggles to include those based on the distribution of "bads", risks or hazards such as climate change.

A recent online survey we conducted on climate change and museum interventions across Australia and the US clearly indicates the rise of the notion of risk society around this hazard, and the ensuing process of reflexive modernisation.[2] Climate change in recent years has become a global risk of expert and governmental concern, requiring action on a global scale as evident with the establishment of the Intergovernmental Panel on Climate Change, the Kyoto Protocol and most recently COP15, the Copenhagen talks. Other indicators of the emergence of this risk society disposition and an emerging interest in critiquing societies and institutions across the wider population is evident in a distinct breakdown of trust in governments, corporations and industry as information providers on risk threats. For example around 66 per cent (of 1500 respondents) in Australia and 73 per cent in the US sample (comprising 600 participants in New York State, New York City and New Jersey State) lacked confidence in national governments, and a further 81 per cent expressed a distrust of industry and corporations as information sources on climate change (Cameron et al. 2009). While a certain level of trust remains with expert systems such as scientific organisations and museums as information sources, with the sample indicating 70 per cent and 66 per cent respectively in Australia and the US, and 55 per cent and 56 per cent in regards to museums, this is surprisingly low. The qualitative responses in the survey are indicative of an emerging scepticism towards expert systems and institutions. In referring to the government's handling of climate change, one respondent stated, "I feel lied to and embarrassed to be an Australian" (Cameron et al. 2009). Another Australian respondent stated "I feel sceptical due to its intense politicisation" (Cameron et al. 2009).

Both the US and Australian sample positions museums and science centres as key institutions in climate change risk management flows as trusted information sources (Cameron et al. 2009). In terms of content, this includes information on cutting-edge science, dissenting opinion and the politics of climate change, ways to reduce greenhouse gas emissions and lifestyle changes, new renewable technologies, and post carbon futures (Cameron et al. 2009). The findings also express the emergence of risk conflicts over responsibility for and the distribution of climate change risk. In the US sample 69 per cent suggested that corporations and 68 per cent indicated that governments should take a greater responsibility for reducing greenhouse gas emissions rather than placing the onus on individuals and families (Cameron et al. 2009). The Australian sample however was more definitive, with 79 per cent stating that governments and 75 per cent suggesting big business and industry be held liable (Cameron et al. 2009).

Risk operates in an immaterial form as mediated and contested definitions of risk and in a material form as tangible events, often requiring decisions and action, at times controversial. Beck (1999) therefore argues that in the shadow of global dangers and uncertainties, society opens to the sub-political. Individualisation, scepticism and diversity become written into society, the latter two dispositions borne out in the survey findings. According to Beck the rise of the concerned and responsible individual, globally networked sub-political movements outside representative government, transnational institutions, the emergence of discourse coalitions involving alternative knowledge systems are all indicative of these transformative processes (Beck 1999). These structural and social shifts are clearly evident with the proliferation of grassroots sub-political activities around the climate change issue from locally based action groups to larger global organisations such as Climate Action Network involving 287 non-government agencies worldwide.[3] The Australian based GetUp e-democratic movement with more than 300,000 members across Australia is another case in point and has become a powerful lobby group to government on a range of issues.[4] Within the museum / science centre sector, the recent Association of Science and Technology Centres IGLO International Action on Global Warming[5] initiative to raise worldwide public awareness on global warming involving more than 500 science centres in activities across the globe also demonstrates the rise of transnational risk communities within the cultural sector.

The theoretical orientations of cultural theorists Manuel Castells (2004), Zygmund Bauman (2007) and John Urry (2003) more clearly articulate what these social and institutional forms look like and how a global risk society emerges through the lens of emerging digital technologies, one that Beck fails to address. Drawing on these digitally mediated platforms of interconnectivity, Castells (2004) describes contemporary society as an ontology of network cultures, as a new social morphology that substantially modifies the operations and outcomes of processes of production, experience, power and culture.

Bauman (2007, 1) uses the analogy of a transformation from a solid structure to one resembling unpredictable liquid flows. According to Bauman's thesis, solid frames for structuring human actions give way to a networked society, a matrix of random connections and disconnections of an infinite nature on which endemic uncertainty prevails. These fluids, according to Urry (2003), are partially structured by the various scapes of the global order, the networks of machines, technology, organisations, texts and actors that constitute various interconnected nodes along which flows can be relayed. Here he argues societies are lying truly wide open, materially and intellectually, impotent to decide their own course with any degree of certainty.

The erosion of the modern museum and its reframing within transnational flows is clearly evident within these network formations. As the boundaries between the museum and the social space of lived experience become blurred the potential for new institutional forms and types of exchanges emerge. The unmanageability of contemporary threats particularly in the world of Web 2.0 social networking technologies, and the internet—a medium that promotes debate and citizens as producers—questions the validity of institutions as rational and risk-regulating, and their ability to limit and control danger, to regulate cultural conversations, to act as moral and reforming technologies around hot topics, and to act as authorities in promoting social mores. For example, museum collections data is being consumed and appropriated in social networks for political purposes outside the ambit of the museum (Cameron 2008, 233). Iranian protesters angered over the Hollywood movie *300* launched in early 2007 and the representation of Persians in the battle of Thermopylae with the

Spartans in 480BC mobilised museum collections through Google to counter negative representations of their culture and politics and bolster a sense of identity (Jones 2007). Searches for the film *300* were diverted away from the movie to the website Project 300 that aimed to present positive representations of Iranian culture through contemporary Iranian art, documentaries and through links to the British Museum's *Forgotten Empire* exhibition of Persian artefacts (Jones 2007, 6; Cameron 2008, 233). Similarly collections data and photographs from the Powerhouse Museum collection on Australian swimmer, Annette Kellerman, the "Diving Venus" who was arrested in 1907 for indecent exposure by appearing in her bathing suit, appeared on the porn blog, Silent-Porn-Star (Chan 2007; Cameron 2008, 233).

Clearly the risk regime has changed. As industrial projects and their incumbent and perceived risks become political, institutions necessarily can become intentionally co-opted or unintentionally immersed in conflicts, as demonstrated with the *300* movie controversy, and as part of risk management structures around the climate change issue evident with the online survey findings as detailed. Therefore museums as contemporary venues where science and society meet require a consideration of these new social relations. Because they represent science and technology, institutions must address global hazards and their risk conflicts. Topics deemed controversial and those identified as part of the research such as genetically modified foods, biotechnology, war, terrorism and environmental degradation are necessarily part of the flows of risk conflicts articulated around competing definitions of risk and their various material forms. The erosion of institutional authority and a growing scepticism towards expert systems, the regime in which museums operate, necessarily requires institutions to re-think science in society in ways that admit and legitimate other forms of knowledge. Becoming cosmopolitan through globalisation also means that institutions are linked into wider sub-political movements, debates, transnational institutions and risk communities through the internet and Web 2.0 technologies. As individuals become active content producers evident through the popularity of social networking spaces such as MySpace, Twitter and Facebook and blogs, they demand opportunities to express their opinions, influence and make decisions. And as institutions of first modernity and spaces that promote scientific and technological development, they too become the subject of critique.

The museum form of second modernity and its role in transnational risk flows and institutions as actors in the engagement of controversial topics therefore necessarily takes a new turn. Embracing these new risk contexts can be viewed as a bold initiative. Beck (1999) suggests that in this age of uncertainty and ambivalence, with constant threats be it disasters, events or debates, we need to re-invent our political institutions and establish new ways of conducting politics at social sites previously considered apolitical. Accordingly, there are three responses to risk: denial, apathy or social transformation (Ekberg 2007). Clearly to embrace risk in all its uncertainties, and in order to take on a more proactive place in risk flows within wider public political culture, museums must think and to a degree be organised somewhat differently. Furthermore, the transnationalising effect of discourses such as global climate change, for example, requires institutions to re-form themselves according to new ontologies of the social that cross national boundaries, and the notion of multiplicity and complexity beyond the idea of the binary and plural. Put simply, institutions need to deal with a shift from their predominant rationalistic tendencies of controllability, certainty and security to engage risk as a discursive construction and all its inherent conflicts as a natural predisposition. Institutions are also required to reform a series of relations of definition around nature-culture, rationality, debate and conflict, certainty and uncertainty, utopia and dystopia.

Museums, risk regimes, and as institutions of second modernity

So according to my own assessment of Beck, Castells, Bauman and Urry, and drawing on the research findings of the *Contested Sites* project, what might the institution of second modernity look like? How might this analysis inform ways to more meaningfully engage controversial topics and risk issues given shifting social conditions and circumstances? As risk regimes move from the concept of control and governance and become politically reflexive, how can new social forms and interactions operate with the museum? What opportunities do these new formulations of risk science and risk conflict offer in terms of interventions given that institutions are inevitably tethered to global risk structures? Where do the tensions lie between interventions formulated within an older risk ethos and newer ones? Unsurprisingly, the predominant stressors expressed by staff working against a more politically reflexive agenda is the institution's relationship to what Beck (1999) calls agencies of "organised irresponsibility". This refers to the coalition of politicians and policy makers, business, and experts who, while often instrumental in the production of the uncertainties and risks of global risk society, disavow their responsibility, instead placing the burden on the individual to mitigate risks. Scepticism towards these actors and their motivations on one hand and their potential conflict of interest as funders, for example board members and sponsors in the museum setting, was clearly expressed through the survey findings. The uneasy tension between the former, for example government as an agency of organised irresponsibility in this instance promoting environmental degradation, and museums as agencies of government is clearly evident in interviews with staff at a state museum in Ontario, Canada

> The current government is very pro-business, right-wing. It is now possible in Ontario to clear thousands of hectares of forests but there's no way that this museum could talk about that because we get so much money from the province. In the environmental community this is a very serious issue. (Contested Sites Staff Focus Group Transcript CAN#c)

Beck (1999) defines this as the political contradiction of the "self endangerment" of risk society. That is between an emerging public awareness of risks, such as environmental degradation on one hand, the lack of attribution of systemic risk to the system on the other, and the coercion of the museum in the promotion of such irresponsible risk discourses, actively or by omission. Given institutions' key role as trusted information sources within these risk management structures, how can institutions effectively navigate these conflicting agendas?

In considering museums as instruments of second modernity, the following attributes suggest a way forward in planning institutional roles as agents in all these things.

Life politics, global risk biographies and the self-interested visitor. One of the key social forms in second modernity is the notion of individualisation. Here the views of staff and audiences differ on how they conceive the instrumentality of individualisation in the museum context. In considering this relationship in terms of curatorial perspectives many saw their role in reforming behaviour as inciting people to perform morally right actions "It's not simply preserving the past or doing the housekeeping well. It's also what we think of the future, what are the options, are there things we should be doing that might be ameliorating damage, and improving the situations" (Contested Sites Interview Transcript UK#b). Focus group research clearly suggests otherwise showing the loci of responsibility for engaging controversial topics and for reform remains with the visitor through the use of museum information to inform their own biographical solutions. Here and within the museum the individual is reshaped from solely an object of discipline to one that is also reflexive, political and driven by self-interest. The use of museum information in the formation of biographical details is evident in this response by a visitor to the Canadian War Museum, and typical of many others, "Museums give a non-biased view of events and issues and allows people to form their own opinions" (Contested Sites Exit Survey, Canadian War Museum).

For around 25 per cent of focus group participants, museums act as spaces for *historical reflexivity* (Cameron 2005, 220–1). They are venues to gain information on hot topics and events in the historical record. Audiences use this symbolic content to look and learn about the past by engaging their own capacities for inner reflection and to evaluate their own values and beliefs, "Museums are reflective, there is … an opportunity to reflect on the past" (Contested Sites Visitor Focus Group Transcript AUS#a). This is likened to media theorist John Thompson's (1995, 42–3) analysis of media content. He argues that audiences appropriate messages and make them their own in a process of self formation and self understanding.

For the majority, 55 per cent, *contextualisation* acts as a reforming tool (Cameron 2005, 221). Applied to current, as well as historical topics and events, this approach enables audiences to understand their origin, complexities and likely ramifications, "with September 11 and the Bali bombing for example, a museum's role is to build up a historical picture of where these events originated …" (Contested Sites Visitor Focus Group Transcript AUS#e; Cameron 2007, 338).

Symbolic content is deployed for locating, constructing and reforming self; understanding others; in reshaping stocks of knowledge; testing feelings; attitudes; re-evaluating moral positions and expanding horizons of experience, "It is important to get some reference to where you sit in the scheme of things—where is my place in all this" (Contested Sites Visitor Focus Group Transcript AUS#e; Cameron 2007). This position resonates with diagnostic reporting, the deconstruction of problems, the analysis of causes and in portraying the context in which the story is taking place (Alagiah 1998 referenced in Tester 2001, 39).

For around 20 per cent, reform referred to activist agendas, involving the active re-shaping of an individual's behaviour to bring about change (Cameron 2005, 222–3). That is, by opening people's minds to alternative views on a given topic and offering suggestions on how audiences might become active to bring about change, "If museums are to continue to exist as people friendly institutions, they have to have programs to educate people about the history of terrorism, why it happens and the role of civil society to combat terrorism ..." (Contested Sites Visitor Focus Group Transcript AUS#e). Here symbolic content acts with self to interrogate choices, motivations and frame action, "I like the idea of an exhibition being empowering—in presenting good ideas and how do you turn that into action" (Contested Sites Visitor Focus Group Transcript AUS#b; Cameron 2007, 339).

This research suggests that relationships between museums and audiences in the engagement of controversial topics require a new account of self as a symbolic project that is self-acting, more open-ended and reflexive (Cameron 2007, 339). According to 80 per cent of audiences surveyed institutions are seen as having the power to challenge people's ways of thinking and shift an individual's point of view (Cameron 2005, 225). The means of constituting and reforming self, however, refers to a greater ability to self-regulate, evaluate and process a range of information on their own terms, "museums should not express an opinion, they should provide good information and arguments .... We have our own opinions" (Contested Sites Visitor Focus Group Transcript AUS#a; Cameron 2007, 340).

Considering all these things, how can institutions innovate further to allow their audiences to be more politically reflexive around controversial topics and matters of risk? This represents a shift from the moral individual, to rights, to knowledge, and to have a say in risk management. Given that reflexive notions of the future and hazards disrupt and critique science and technological notions of progress and forms of rationality, how can institutions facilitate involvement in decision making and discussions about scientific research and technological development for an unknown and uncertain future? Are museums capable of moving beyond the individual as responsible in terms of choice and burden, to one of collective individualism? And can institutions question systems of organised irresponsibility (governments, business, industry and science), the agencies from whom sources of risk tend to originate, and challenge celebratory notions of science and technology? The allocation of risk, in which science controversy is a central theme, suggests a new political project for museums in terms of risk conflicts, and in building transnational risk communities.

Engaging risk conflicts. Risk is a discursive construction. Far from being characterised as subject to the rational exercise of scientific knowledge and dispassionate decision making, risk operates rather as clusters of subjectivities, emotions and irrationalities. Given that risk conflict and conflictual co-existence are central elements of a transnational risk society, how can institutions re-position these dynamics at the centre of the museum while maintaining institutional legitimacy and trust? On the other hand, our research also shows that the legacy of the modern museum as a place to control risk and monitor cultural conversations continues to be an important one for many audiences. Although many focus group participants expressed the importance of museums as non-judgmental, to show both sides, there are some topics like terrorism and drug use that were deemed unworthy of a balanced consideration (Ferguson 2006). In these cases, presenting the "other side" was seen as legitimising certain "extremist" values and "deviant" behaviours "presenting these topics could give legitimacy to something that has no legitimacy" (Contested Sites Visitor Focus Group Transcript AUS#c; Cameron 2007, 336). The Contested Sites findings suggest a way forward. For 90 per cent of audiences surveyed, enabling risk conflicts to emerge and circulate is tantamount to offering opportunities for audiences to express their opinion, "… everyone should have the opportunity to express their political view whether others agree with it or not…" (Contested Sites Visitor Focus Group Transcript AUS#b; Cameron 2005, 226). For others it also involves engagement with other visitors, the institution and the ability to leave evidence of debates in exhibitions, "with more discussion, people would be better informed and therefore form their own opinions" (Contested Sites Omnibus Survey, 20). Clearly museums have a role in the staging of self, the expression of values, beliefs and opinions. So how can institutions move beyond the individual's own expression of opinion and individual actions, to facilitate opportunities for other forms of collective political reflexivity through engagement with sub-political movements, in building shared communities of risk in transnational contexts?

Certainty/uncertainty. Because the notion of risk shifts our attention to the far future and because that future is unknown and uncertain, we have a trajectory here that at once challenges particularly the accepted museum position within time, and moreover highlights tensions in which institutions are seen as places that at once offer certainty in uncertainty. In a recent series of focus group interviews undertaken for the Australian Research Council grant, *Hot Science, Global Citizens: The Agency of the Museum Sector in Climate Change Interventions* the tensions between offering certainty in an uncertain world around the topic of climate change ranged from those who saw institutions as rational entities offering certainty to a more multiplicious interpretation as one that engages multiple views of the future, acting as sites for information rather than certainty. The former was expressed by one Sydney older male participant, "It certainly can play a role of being a place to offer certain concrete facts about what actually is going on" (Hot Science, Global Citizens Focus Group Transcript, Sydney adults, older families). The notion of multiple views of the future was expressed by a younger Sydney male "[museums and science centres] ... gives us an awareness ... of different ideals and different thoughts and different options" (Hot Science, Global Citizens Focus Group Transcript, Sydney, adults, younger families). This research offered a way forward, the first contingency being for institutions to highlight uncertainty as a contemporary condition "Say something is uncertain—museums and science centres [should] highlight the uncertainty—prepare people for an uncertain future" (Hot Science, Global Citizens Focus Group Transcript, Sydney adults, older families). And second to see institutions as sites for information rather than rational certainty, "I'm thinking that museums and science centres are places to offer you information but not certainty" (Hot Science, Global Citizens Focus Group Transcript, Melbourne adults, older families).

Interestingly many expressed the fact that there are few places they can go to get a consideration of the options and alternatives. In summary, museums and science centres are seen as strategic sources of information offering views on alternatives and options and where people are encouraged to be reflexive " [museums and science centres] can and are providing information about real alternatives as a form of education that we can understand" (Hot Science, Global Citizens Focus Group Transcript, Sydney, adults, younger families).

Discourse coalitions and reflexivity. In these new risk contexts museum expertise and the future are reformulated. The findings from the *Contested Sites* project show that museum information is still respected and influential, "... museums have a reputation like university professors, and you expect to see things which have the backing of scientific method. It is not just some ratbag sprouting propaganda, it's a well thought out established viewpoint". Despite Beck's assertion that the authority of expert knowledge systems has been largely lost, museums are still seen as trusted and respected in a world of uncertainty within the context of a burgeoning information society (Reconceptualising Heritage Collections Designers Focus Group 2008). An institution's struggle for primacy however has been to an extent displaced. Instead museum expertise becomes just one of the many narratives that operates with others as part of discourse coalitions in public debates, albeit a very important one in framing self, "Museums could present lots of different views that call into question people's views" (Contested Sites Visitor Focus Group Transcript AUS#a; Contested Sites Visitor Focus Group Transcript AUS#b). To this end reflexive strategies become paramount both in terms of the institution as self-critique and in the interpretative framing that operates to inform self. For 70 per cent, this involves techniques that facilitate critical thinking. Here the institution acts as a facilitator through carefully selected and authoritative scholarly information; multiple perspectives and opinions on given subjects; source transparency; interpretative guidance and the framing of content to show how judgements are formed and decisions made. Clearly this represents a reformulation of the notion of institutional trust to one of active trust firmly based in the concept of self. It is premised on the notion of dissent, rather than consensus, and rests firmly on the recognition to the rights to "one's own life".

Nodes in global networks—transnational institutions and risk human rights. In second modernity the public fora are (re)written on the basis of a new ontology of institutions as nodes in fluid networks, where the value of communication and interaction rather than the ontology of difference as explained in the earlier discussion operates. The ability to link, embed and connect museum information to public culture debates and harvest information from a range of sources is enhanced via Web 2.0 and with the emergence of social spaces such as MySpace, YouTube, Flickr, Facebook and Second Life. Museum information now operates in fluid, global networks connected to other social, political, cultural resources and agendas. These contexts in which people more easily become content producers, interact with, share information, engage in social action and participate in social networks pose a series of new risks and opportunities for museums—the latter to reconnect with public culture debates and build communities around risk human rights. Clearly when considering museum-public culture interfaces there is a move from museum hierarchical organisational forms as separate and standing above society, to ones that are more flexible, open, dynamic, relational and interactive that operate as nodes in networks able to connect with other resources (Cameron 2008). New roles emerge as museums operate as attractors in these networks bringing together various elements, ideas, people involving different types of interactions, and as a border zone where different systems of representation meet.

Conclusion

So using Beck's thesis, what would museums as an institutional form look like, and how might institutions engage global risks such as climate change in new ways? Here an ethos of risk and uncertainty holds the potential for renewal and the development of new institutional forms. That is, by conceiving museums as complex, open systems, as part of networks in global flows, as platforms for interactions along with the idea of the reflexive, active, citizen.

One of the key themes is the intensified responsibility placed on the individual to define themselves, make choices and decisions about their lives in order to form their own biographies. In the past institutions were involved in shaping and reforming the individual by prescribing moral standards and forms of behaviour. Now institutions need to assist the "self interested" visitor in forming, planning and designing themselves as individuals on their own terms. The moralising and reforming frame might be conceived as more self-acting, through the production of information in a way that facilitates critical thinking and self action.

The notion of expertise and risk definition needs to become broader, away from solely rational scientific and economic perspectives to ones that engage culture and their competing definitions. Our research suggests that expert systems as knowledge resources, such as museums, are still important. There is, however, a need to acknowledge that museum expertise operates as one source that interacts with others according to their own rules, creating distinct properties and types of knowledge in the cultural order. Museums as part of a complex networked system can be conceived as a thought collective—part of a group performance along with other agencies in mapping out the social world around a given issue or event.

New modes of trust now exist in contemporary risk society. Because reflexive individuals form trust relationships based on mutual, reciprocal and active trust rather than trust that is passively accepted as in the past, institutions need to build on and reframe this trust relationship by adopting a more open, flexible and less hierarchical style of engagement and interaction. That is through reciprocity, exchange, dialogue and decision making. Controversy is seen as productive, as a means to generate and gather together a range of views around a given subject as an expression of an individual's self-politics rather than something to be controlled and minimised.

The museum sector has the opportunity to take advantage of networks and capitalise on their variability, interconnectivity and intercommunication as a means to contribute to contemporary debates and decisions—as trusted and respected information sources. There is an opportunity to view museum information as cultural and economic capital that can be used to activate, and contribute to discussions, gain currency and strengthen public-museum culture links. This might involve actively embedding museum information in debates, i.e., blogs and social spaces, and also harvesting information from the outside, i.e., news feeds etc into the museum space.

New political forms emerge according to Beck's thesis. Here institutions might consider how they can become part of sub-political movements and define what their interventions might look like within new political formations.

Climate change risk for example has the potential to build transnational communities and networks, and to activate a cosmopolitan imaginary. The seeds of these transformations can be seen with the Climate Change Youth Forum at the Natural History Museum in 2006 and the IGLO initiative. In a networked form, museums can operate as nodes in fluid networks and flows of information, people and resources and contribute to building communities by promoting public awareness of risk and by activating and connecting with others across borders over shared risk.

The advent of sub-political formations enables institutions to build new alliances with non-government organisations, experts and other grass-roots movements as part of these new political constellations. The question is where might institutions fit into these formations. Clearly our research so far suggests, for example, that institutions have a vital role in providing much needed information on climate change risk. Other interventions however involve connecting, networking, building alliances, developing fora for shared perceptions of risk, critiquing the policies of government and agendas of corporations, etc. Institutions are also required to become more self-reflexive and to make their positions transparent.

Interestingly, museums have new roles in risk human rights, that is, rights to information about risk and potentially to participate in decisions with transnational impacts. This could include the creation of transnational connections to activate discussions about risk allocation and inequalities in people's risk positions.

Institutions have a role with other agencies in public political culture to activate and broker cross-sectoral discussions and decisions with government, business, industry and communities around the larger systematic shifts about post-carbon futures, for example. The focus politically is on the carbon economy and protectionism, rather than looking to the longer term about how we might live. Sub-political movements of people developed out of climate change risk made public, can pressure these coalitions to bring about change and to collectively imagine an unknown future.

Institutions may have a role in networks for direct action and transnational protest by activating discussions, mobilising people, and by providing links to a range of information sources. They have a role in contributing to the socialisation of risk across generations, helping people to define their own biographical positions about what an imagined future might look like. Some of these ideas are challenging, involving radical reform for the sector. Potential interventions will vary between institutions. The challenge is to reconcile institutional forms and museum-public culture interfaces with the political settings institutions operate within.

The institution of second modernity heralds a new era in museology. This process of transformation and research into interventions and institutional forms as part of global risk society is the focus of the Australian Research Council international grant *Hot Science Global Citizens: The Agency of the Museum Sector in Climate Change Interventions*. The findings to inform this transition will emerge over the next three years.

References

Bauman, Z. 2007. *Liquid times, living in an age of uncertainty*. Cambridge: Polity Press.

Beck, U. 1999. *World risk society*. Cambridge: Polity Press.

Bennett, T. 1995. *The birth of the museum: History, theory, politics*. New York and London: Routledge.

Cameron, D. 1971. The museum, a temple or the forum, *Curator* xiv (1): 11–24.

Cameron, F. R. 2005. Contentiousness and shifting knowledge paradigms: The roles of history and science museums in contemporary societies. *Museum Management and Curatorship* 20: 213–233.

—. 2006. Beyond surface representations: Museums, edgy topics, civic responsibilities and modes of engagement. *Open Museum Journal* 8, http://amol.org.au/craft/omjournal/journal_index.asp (accessed October 8, 2008).

—. 2007. Moral lessons and reforming agendas: History, science museums, contentious topics and contemporary societies. In *Museum Revolutions: How Museums Change and Are Changed.*, Ed. S. Knell, S. Watson and S. Macleod, 330–342. London: Routledge.

—. 2008. Object-Orientated democracies: Conceptualising museum collections in networks. *Museum Management and Curatorship* 23 (3): 229–243.

Cameron, F. R., B. Dibley, C. Farbotko, C. Meehan and L. Kelly. 2009. Hot Science Global Citizens, online survey research findings, unpublished manuscript, Centre for Cultural Research, University of Western Sydney.

Castells, M. 1996. *The rise of the network society, the information age: Economy, society and culture vol. I.* Cambridge, MA, Oxford, UK: Blackwell.

Castells, M. 2004. Ed. *The network society: A cross-cultural perspective.* MA, US: Edward Elgar.

Chan, S. 2007. Tagging and searching—Serendipity and museum collection databases. Paper presented at *Museums and the Web,* April 11–14 2007, in San Francisco, California. http://www.archimuse.com/mw2007/papers/chan/chan.html (accessed 18 December 2009).

Contested Sites Exit Survey, Canadian War Museum, June 2003, unpublished manuscript, Centre for Cultural Research, University of Western Sydney.

—. Museum of Anthropology, Vancouver, June 2003, unpublished manuscript, Centre for Cultural Research, University of Western Sydney.

Contested Sites Omnibus Survey, Sydney, January 2003, unpublished manuscript, Centre for Cultural Research, University of Western Sydney.

Contested Sites Online Staff Survey, September–October 2003, unpublished manuscript, Centre for Cultural Research, University of Western Sydney.

Contested Sites Staff Focus Group Transcript CAN#c, 5 May 2003, unpublished manuscript, Centre for Cultural Research, University of Western Sydney.

__. USA#a, 17 September 2002, unpublished manuscript, Centre for Cultural Research, University of Western Sydney.

—. USA#b, 13 September 2002, unpublished manuscript, Centre for Cultural Research, University of Western Sydney.

Contested Sites Interview Transcript UK#b, 9 January 2003, unpublished manuscript, Centre for Cultural Research, University of Western Sydney.

Contested Sites Staff Web Survey, September–October 2003, unpublished manuscript, Centre for Cultural Research, University of Western Sydney.

Contested Sites Visitor Focus Group Transcript AUS#a, 11 November 2002, unpublished manuscript, Centre for Cultural Research, University of Western Sydney.

—. AUS#b, 12 November 2002, unpublished manuscript, Centre for Cultural Research, University of Western Sydney.

—. AUS#c, 12 November 2002, unpublished manuscript, Centre for Cultural Research, University of Western Sydney.

—. AUS#d, 19 November 2002, unpublished manuscript, Centre for Cultural Research, University of Western Sydney.

—. AUS#e, 20 November 2002, unpublished manuscript, Centre for Cultural Research, University of Western Sydney.

Ekberg, M. 2007. The parameters of the risk society: A review and exploration. *Current Sociology* 55: 343–366.

Ferguson, L. 2006. Pushing buttons: Controversial topics in museums. *Open Museum Journal* 8.

Hot Science Global Citizens Australian Online Survey, 2009, unpublished manuscript, Centre for Cultural Research, University of Western Sydney.

Hot Science Global Citizens Focus Group Transcript, Sydney adults, older families unpublished manuscript, Centre for Cultural Research, University of Western Sydney.

—.Focus Group Transcript, Sydney, adults, younger families unpublished manuscript, Centre for Cultural Research, University of Western Sydney.

—.Focus Group Transcript, Melbourne adults, older families unpublished manuscript, Centre for Cultural Research, University of Western Sydney.

—.Focus Group Transcript, Melbourne adults, younger families unpublished manuscript, Centre for Cultural Research, University of Western Sydney.

Jones, S. 2007. Building cultural literacy. Paper presented at *New Collaborations: New Benefits—Transnational Museum Collaboration*, International Council of Museums, July 26–27, Shanghai, China.

Reconceptualising Heritage Collections Designers Focus Group, 26 March 2008, Centre for Cultural Research, University of Western Sydney.

Reconceptualising Heritage Collections Powerhouse Museum curatorial focus group, 20 March 2008, Centre for Cultural Research, University of Western Sydney.

Tester, K. 2001. *Compassion, morality and the media*. Buckingham: Open University Press.

Thompson, J. B. 1995. *The media and modernity: A social theory of the media*. Cambridge: Polity Press.

Urry, J. 2003. *Global complexity*. Cambridge: Polity Press.

Notes

[1] The Australian Research Council and Canadian Museums Association funded international research project, *Exhibitions as Contested Sites: The Roles of Museums in Contemporary Societies* involved literature analysis of museological, theoretical debates and museum controversies; qualitative and quantitative research; phone and exit surveys; an online industry survey; and focus groups and interviews with staff, stakeholders and audiences involving 28 institutions in the US, Canada, UK, Australia and New Zealand. Quantitative research comprised 'phone surveys in Sydney and Canberra drawing on a sample of 500 respondents. We asked participants to respond to 16 topics that Australians might consider controversial and to a series of role positioning statements using a five-point Likert scale (strongly agree to strongly disagree). Exit surveys were conducted at the Australian Museum, the Australian War Memorial with 197 and 248 visitors respectively, and at three Canadian Museums, the Museum of Anthropology Vancouver, the Canadian War Museum and the Musée d'Art in Montreal with 286 visitors. Here participants were asked to respond to the range of questions comparable with the 'phone survey. Surveys were then analysed using SPSS (data analysis software) to compare data sets.

The qualitative phase involved five visitor focus groups (40 participants) in Sydney and Canberra. Here we discussed the findings of our quantitative research, museum visiting experiences, functions and activities, and the notion of authority, expertise, trust and censorship.

By comparison, we investigated the perspectives of museum staff, stakeholders and media using an online survey, in-depth interviews and focus group discussions with over 100 staff and stakeholders in 26 institutions in Australia, New Zealand, Canada, the US and the UK. Participants were asked to identify topics that were contextually controversial for their institution and country at the time to capture current thinking about museum roles and emerging controversies. Other questions related to museums and social responsibility, authority, expertise and censorship, controversies and their impact on institutional functioning, successful programming and funding arrangements. In comparing geo-political, social, cultural and institutional contexts we were able to illuminate the multifarious challenges, limitations and opportunities that institutions face in presenting contentious subjects.

[2] The Australian Research Council Linkage project, *Hot Science Global Citizens: The Agency of the Museum Sector in Climate Change Interventions* investigates the museum sector (natural history, science museums and science centres) currently and potentially as places to provide information, activate, broker discussions and decisions around climate change issues, locally and transnationally. The project is led by the Centre for Cultural Research, University of Western Sydney with partners Museum Victoria, the Australian Museum, Powerhouse Museum, Questacon, Liberty Science Center, New York and two universities, University of Melbourne and University of Leicester, Museum Studies involving an interdisciplinary team of 17 researchers.

The Hot Science Global Citizens Online Survey was conducted in December 2008 as part of a recently funded Australian Research Council grant, *Hot Science Global Citizens: The Agency of the Museum Sector in Climate Change Interventions*. This survey involved a general demographic of 1500 participants across four states in Australia: New South Wales and the Australian Capital Territory; Queensland; Victoria and Western Australia. The comparative US sample comprised a general demographic of 600 participants from New Jersey, New York State and New York City.

[3] Climate Action Network, http://www.climatenet work.org/ (accessed 18 December 2009)

[4] GetUp e-democratic network, http://www.getup.org.au/ (accessed 18 December 2009)

[5] International Action on Global Warming, http://astc.org/iglo/ (accessed 18 December 2009)

CHAPTER FOUR

EVOLUTION OF PURPOSE IN SCIENCE MUSEUMS AND SCIENCE CENTRES

EMLYN KOSTER

> Civilization is revving itself into a pathologically short attention span.[1]

> At its core, the greatest harm delivered by dogma is that it leads to a failure of imagination. We have been remiss in examining the intellectual premises of what museum contributions can and should be … It's time to reconsider the work of museums. (Glasser 2008)

> Engaging in continuous growth, renewal, and change—anchored in the context of our times and the continuity of who we are as individuals or organizations—is essential for leading both successful public lives and successful public organizations that make a positive difference in the world. (Luckow 2009)

The core issues

Examining the evolution of science museums and science centres through the lens of their purpose, against a cultural backdrop of societal and environmental trends is more instructive (e.g., Koster 1999; Lindqvist 2000; Ogawa et al. 2009) than the historically usual emphasis on the differing nature of experiences at these institutions—for example, static versus participatory exhibits (e.g., Danilov 1982). This point of view aligns with the axiom in architecture that form (the means) should follow function (the ends) as well as with the important distinction in business, and also in museums as Weil (2005) pointed out, between efficiency (doing things right) and effectiveness (doing the right things). In his refreshing study about the nature and purpose of leadership, Barker (2002) cites Aristotle's view that it should strive to be about the harmonious pursuit of positive consequences in the world. These principled approaches loom as imperative if the science museum and science centre field is to attain its optimum relevance to the pressing array of science-driven opportunities and challenges that surround society and the environment, now and into the future.

Unfortunately though, much valuable time was lost during what should have been a pivotal period of responsive action. It was during the closing decades of the twentieth century that the significant role of science to the intertwined futures of society and the environment became exponentially clearer. However, rather than pursuing their greatest possible purpose, the science museum and science centre field became overly enamoured with its invention of interactivity in exhibits and gradually also with the box office allure of blockbuster exhibitions and entertainment-minded film choices. The field also limited its potential scale of impact by focusing on the younger generation. Perhaps most critically (Davis et al. 2003), the field was reluctant to tackle contemporary, and therefore possibly controversial, issues with the result that voting adults were not being exposed to the science-driven issues that increasingly mattered. Further compounding the overall situation has been a relatively low incidence of research-informed approaches, planning horizons integrating regional and global scales, collaborative approaches with allied disciplines and, perhaps above all, of long term and relevancy minded leadership.

The scale of the problem now facing the museum field is increasingly the focus of urgent commentary. Given the uncertainties in the global economy, there has never been a greater need to define the principles and practices that will maximise the earned and contributed funding case for sustaining institutions in a mission-advancing way (Koster 2006a, 2009). Culminating his large body of work about making museums matter, the late Stephen Weil, emeritus scholar of The Smithsonian Institution, argued that the only dial on the museum's performance dashboard that ultimately matters is external usefulness (Weil 2002, 2005). He then lamented (Weil 2006, 4) that:

> The awkward fact remains that, for a variety of reasons, the museum field has never really agreed—and until recently, even sought to agree—on some standard by which the relative worthiness of its constituent member institutions might be measured.

Today's fractionalisation of the museum field across a spectrum of disinterest in, and orientation to, external relevance was reviewed by Koster and Falk (2007). Janes (2009) raises the bar on just how urgent the situation for museums has become in a context of what he frames as "a troubled world". Facing options of renewal, irrelevance or collapse, he argues that:

> … the majority of museums, as social institutions, have largely eschewed, on both moral and practical grounds, a broader commitment to the world in which they operate (13). It is only through confronting convention that museums will be able to create, invent and discover their futures as they go—the true hallmarks of an innovative organization. (17)

Other recent observers of the museum field have a more optimistic outlook. Looking ahead to the year 2020 from an urban planning perspective, Gijssen (2008, 46) visualises this enticing scenario:

> … the museum becomes critical to the long-range health of a place: central to think-tanks, planning initiatives and community transformations. It becomes one of those organizations a mayor calls upon when a crisis hits or new long range plans are being developed. It is an institution others actively seek for guidance and expertise, harvesting from its knowledge, communication methodologies, community connections, and relationships. In such an ecosystem, the museum's role does not have to be explained or rationalized; other NGOs embed it in their governance, research and educational programs. In this ecosystem, the museum is nimble, outward and future focused …

Contemplating the museum as a vital institution in the social and economic fabric of a city is not a new concept (American Association of Museums 1996), but the museum field has resisted embracing this outward state of mind. In a new forward-looking discussion guide for the US, Pastore (2009, 25) has this summary stance:

> From changes in information access, use, and preservation to advances in technology, shifts in society and community needs, and evolving learning and development methods—from economic considerations to changing metrics and the emergence of a new generation of professional leaders in the field—museums and libraries have the ability at this moment to remain relevant and dynamic institutions well into the future. This is an opportunity for these institutions to work with their communities in defining their relationships with the publics they serve and chart a course for success.

With respect to the purpose of this book to examine the immersion, or not, of the museum institution with any of the "hot topics" that pervade our increasingly complex world—many of which are, or need to be, rooted in science—the premise of this chapter is that both the internal barriers and the external opportunities for science museums and science centres must be tackled with a wholehearted, relevancy-driven, state of mind. These institutions need to be eminently useful places where all ages and stages of learning can turn disinterest into interest, interest into insight, and insight into action about the science-related matters of importance to the future of society and the environment, locally and globally. In this thesis, I agree with museum theorist and educator Eileen Hooper-Greenhill (2000). Embedded in this progressive state of mind must also be an embrace of new subjects that require public conversation for greater clarity around what is ultimately important (e.g., Leshner 2005). Increasingly, and leveraging every tool at their disposal, centres of science for the public need to be positioned as not only safe but also as ideal places for such roles. In the US, the National Research Council of the National Academies (2009) has completed a compelling synthesis on how informal learning environments are important places for all people of all ages and backgrounds to learn about the science in the world around them.

Generational developments

The grand science museums that opened during the 1800s and early 1900s in the cores of big cities across north-west Europe and the north-east and mid-western US were driven by missions of collection, research and display of artefacts to portray industrial and technological achievements, with some also offering apprenticeships and other training opportunities. The Deutsches Museum in Munich, Science Museum in London, Norwegian Museum of Science and Industry in Oslo, Franklin Institute in Philadelphia, and Museum of Science and Industry in Chicago are examples of this founding generation.

The 1960s became a pivotal decade: human population was increasing exponentially and there were mounting concerns about the future. Sir Fred Hoyle, the renowned British astronomer, had predicted in 1948 that "Once a photograph of the Earth taken from the outside is available, once the sheer isolation of the Earth becomes plain, a new idea as powerful as any in history will be let loose".[2] This moment came with NASA's momentous Apollo mission to the Moon in 1969. The resulting new appreciation for the fragility of our lonely blue-green planet gave rise to the anti-pollution movement and, over the next 30 years, to the addition of words such as environment, biodiversity, extinction, sustainable development, peak oil, climate change and sea-level rise to the public lexicon.

In terms of world exposition events, those spanning the 1960s in Seattle, New York and Montreal would become the last to portray an unbridled positive view of the world's future with respect to science and technology. The term "science centre" originated in Seattle where the popular science pavilion at the 1962 World's Fair became the Pacific

Science Center. Then the sudden advent of science centres in Berkeley, San Francisco and Toronto during 1968–69 with their focus on interactive learning about scientific forces, mostly physical ones, swept science museums into their second generation of development. Proliferating elsewhere in the Americas, to north-western Europe, the Asia-Pacific rim, Australasia, South Africa, and to parts of the Middle East, science centres eagerly pursued a role to increase scientific literacy in the new generation. In their retrospective assessment, Ogawa et al. (2009) argue that a close alignment by science centres with formal science education may have stifled their creativity in terms of impact.

Lacking collections in the traditional manner, science centres were initially seen as a misfit to the prevailing museum definition. Founded in 1973 and now with nearly 600 members in almost four dozen countries, the Association of Science-Technology Centers (ASTC) includes the science-and-society linkage as one of its strategic pillars. Since 1995, and mirroring the long tradition of the International Council of Museums (ICOM), the science centre field also holds triennial world congresses.

A poignant illustration of the growing disconnect between science and society, and of the role or lack thereof of science museums and science centres, arose from a headline newspaper article in the science section of the *New York Times* on March 19, 2005 that was titled "A New Screen Test for Imax: It's the Bible vs. the Volcano". The new giant screen film release entitled *Volcanoes of the Deep Sea* was unequivocal in its presentations of earth history and biological evolution. Initially rejected from theatre programs in several science museums because of concerns by religious fundamentalists, this stance then reversed in several institutions because a heightened consciousness of mission was spurred by this article. This development needs to be seen in the context of many wake-up calls about the "dumbed down" state of science education and public literacy in the US at the dawn of a critical century, as the following examples make clear. A national report by America's first astronaut John Glenn for the Federal Department of Education concluded that the state of science and mathematics teaching was "unacceptable" (National Commission on Mathematics and Science Teaching for the 21st Century 2000). An issue of *Scientific American* questioned the feasibility of human survival in an evocative issue titled "Crossroads for Planet Earth" (*Scientific American* 2005). And an issue of *Time* magazine ran a cover story with the question "Is America Flunking Science?" (Lemonick 2006). In spite of science museums or science centres being part of the educational landscape in just about every American city, the field was clearly facing both major challenges and opportunities at the formal / informal interface in science education and in the lifelong learning of the general public. The massive debate in the US about evolution, creationism and intelligent design that led up to the now famous 2005 case of *Kitzmiller et al. v. Dover Area School District et al.* in Pennsylvania has yet to make the teaching of evolution a straightforward matter (e.g., Volkers 2009).

The increasing focus in the science centre field on what relevancy entails leads to the purpose of third generation science centres being to illuminate how science—more broadly, the so-called STEM disciplines of science, technology, engineering, and mathematics—are integral to our culture and future. Indeed, society's STEM orientation is a new and important facet of culture. Driven by an ethos of social and environmental responsibility and a determination to make progress with impact evaluation, the third-generation state of mind needs to incorporate innovative approaches to a new activism around topical content, including what this book refers to as "hot topics".

Each successive generation continues to wisely learn from the entire history of the field, adapting and integrating the justifiably timeless features of each generation. Reflecting on the incremental evolution of the science museum and science centre field, the main purpose of the first generation was to chronicle technological and industrial developments through the collection, research and display of artefacts. From these museums, we ideally derive lessons to do with being a cultural destination, the educational power of iconic artefacts, and a mindset embracing workforce development. The contrasting main purpose of the second generation was to increase scientific literacy in the new generation, both in school and family settings, through participatory experiences. From these, we ideally derive lessons of new generation engagement, overall accessibility, integration of technology into experiences, and abundant partnerships, especially with formal education. And from third generation centres of science, we ideally need to sustain the emerging new conscience to be focused outwardly and toward the future as well as finding an astute balance between researched understandings of audience wants and needs. Summarising, Koster (2007a) suggested that the 21st century science centre is ideally a dynamic blend of first-generation prestige, second-generation engagement and third-generation relevance, and all infused with mission-accelerating partnerships across the public and private sectors.

Each and every decision by a science museum or centre towards bolder content evolves its brand position and makes further increments of evolution exponentially easier. The opposite of this tenet is equally important. For example, it is imperative for a science museum or science centre to realise that if its choices of touring exhibitions and giant screen films are light in educational content and / or bear no relation to pressing science-driven issues, then its external brand image and audience expectation will be shaped accordingly. Every step taken that is neutral or contrary to the greater good makes it that much more difficult for the museum to start or regain a strengthening reputation of relevance. So-called blockbuster exhibitions that are intended to attract much attention over limited periods, and sometimes with surcharged fees, may give the museum its biggest long-term challenges (Koster 2006b). They may be of questionable mission-advancing value from an ethical standpoint (e.g., Fras 2006) and some visitors may get into the habit of returning to the museum only when it hosts blockbusters. There is also the problem that if the museum's business model and its boardroom's preference come to depend on an ongoing supply of blockbusters, there can be no such assurance. But once in this frame of mind, a museum's easiest route may then be to book blockbusters that are increasingly at the periphery, or beyond, its fundamental purpose, thus causing an even greater degree of "mission drift".

Holistic intentionality

Exactly one hundred years ago, the visionary founding leader of The Newark Museum in New Jersey, John Cotton Dana, advocated that the museum should first learn what the community needs, then fit the museum to those needs (Peniston 1999). Although this ends-focused approach pinpointed the epitome of relevance for the museum field, the sector is only now beginning to overcome its internal inertia because of a rising crescendo of advocacy, the increasingly obvious myriad of opportunity contexts for institutional missions and, most importantly, perhaps because of a contributed revenue trend that is increasingly impatient for demonstrable outcomes. Barrett (1998) pointed out that while the attitudinal journey of any institution from self-interest to the greater good is preferably driven by a relentless desire to be more externally useful, transformations are often forced by adverse publicity and / or financial difficulty.

Starting in the mid-1990s and reflecting the rising conscience over usefulness, it started to become common to encounter the words "value" and "value-added" at conferences and in literature of the museum field. For example, at The Smithsonian's 150th anniversary symposium in 1995, this strong calling was issued (Skramstad 1997, 37):

> In the world of the future, every institution, including a museum, must be judged on its distinctive ability to provide value to society in a way that builds on unique institutional strengths and serves unique community needs.

At the recent centennial conference of the American Association of Museums, the strategist Michael Porter from the Harvard Business School was a keynote presenter. His call to action for the museum field was in the form of this forceful statement[3]:

> Museums should be clear about who they are, what makes them different, and why and how they exist as part of a value chain in society.

Porter (1985) had introduced the term "value chain" to describe how a product ideally passes through activities in an order and how, with each contributing activity, the product gains in value. The term "unique value proposition" (UVP), widely used in business as shown by the five plus million entries on the internet, was introduced to the museum field by Koster and Falk (2007, 194) who used these interrogative definitions:

> Unique: What sets the museum's offerings apart in terms of their discriminating features for each audience segment?
>
> Value: For each audience segment, what is the museum's intrinsic worth for its decision-makers at a competitive price?
>
> Proposition: What is the truthful and useful premise of the museum for each audience segment that is verifiable using quantitative and / or qualitative measures?

Like all nonprofits, museums need a mission to declare why they exist as well as "a systematic method that connects their callings to their programs" (Rangan 2004, 112). A UVP defines why a market segment should seek out, and expect to tangibly benefit from, a particular museum experience, whether that is provided by an exhibition, program or film or in an onsite, offsite or online mode. As examples, a museum seeking to be attractive to, and worthwhile for, teenagers might state its UVP as follows:

> To teenagers of diverse backgrounds, we offer programming and exhibitions that are engaging, multi-sensorial, interactive and technically cutting edge. We strive to fuel creativity among teens to stimulate their anticipation of the future and intentional consideration of career opportunities in the sciences. We are open-minded and inclusive in our approach to the learning process and respectful of your needs.

For teachers of school students, a UVP might read as follows:

> We are a unique full-service partner in the learning and teaching of science before, during and after school. For students in pre-K through middle school and of all backgrounds, we provide enriching curriculum-aligned experiences and resources well beyond those feasible in classrooms—onsite, offsite and online. For teachers of all backgrounds, we provide distinctive resources for professional development to foster more effective teaching. In both students and teachers, we encourage a practice of lifelong learning with new insights turned into meaningful societal and environmental actions. Our welcoming, professional and safe atmosphere offers excellent value in pricing, service and content terms.

A key point in this type of institutional thinking is that the development and marketing of museum experiences are most productively tailor-made for specific audience segments at the decision-maker level (Anderson et al. 2007). The most prolific metric of museum performance continues to be attendance yet, ironically, a total annual visitor count says nothing about the important subtotals of parents, school teachers, camp counsellors, and other group leaders who are actually responsible for decisions to bring groups of various sizes and for each of whom there is likely a particular UVP in play.

The thoughtful term "holistic intentionality" comes from the work of Korn (2007) who advances a view that a museum reaps its greatest external value if all of its resources and practices are aligned with a mission that expressly aims to bring about a positive difference in the world. There are two interrelated reasons why the quest for successful relevance is well served by the UVP concept. The first is that, by its very nature, a UVP is a precision approach to recruitment, content, services, marketing, communications, and development. The second is that a UVP is a business savvy approach that obliges a museum to optimise the alignment of its expertise with important external problems. Stated another way, and referring back to Skramstad (1997) who wrote about providing value in terms of unique institutional strengths and unique community needs, the UVP concept furnishes the critical flesh on the bones. Koster (2006a) provided a 10-point checklist of indicators to monitor progress towards a goal of institutional relevancy: he also listed suggestions of relevant content for natural history museums, human history museums, art museums, war museums, science museums, science centres, children's museums and aquaria / zoos. No museum can feasibly be all things to all people, and if it is trying to do so, it is destined to do nothing well.

A museum's choices of its short-duration content—whether these are touring exhibitions, films, programs, or events—are a conspicuous way to communicate a progressing commitment to the greater good. The 3–6 month duration of touring exhibitions can be 10–40 times faster than the turnover of whole galleries, which typically falls in a 5–20 year rotation cycle. Giant screen theatres commonly feature a concurrent program of several films with new additions at least twice yearly. As reviewed by Davis et al. (2003), science museums and science centres have started to add timely content in changing gallery and / or demonstration area(s). Seasonal programs, festivals, one-time special events, and evening dialogues at bars, for example, are among the museum's most flexible vehicles with which to experiment with new niche offerings, including with some risk-taking. Overall, the shorter and cheaper the offerings, the easier it is for the museum to pilot new approaches. Nowadays, the museum's toolbox contains abundant alternatives for the most powerful approach using a form-follows-function approach.

The attitudes and aspirations inside an organisation give shape to the rationale and direction of its decisions (Griffin et al. 2005). Lencioni (2002) distinguishes four types of internal values: non-negotiable, minimum behavioural standards for all employees; cultural cornerstones that guide actions, i.e., core values; aspirational values that are currently lacking but needed for success; and accidental values that may arise spontaneously and take hold over time. Of these, core values are pivotal in the development of a museum's brand profile with respect to its illumination, or not, of challenging or controversial subject matter. A cautionary note, however, is that an organisation's core values must never be a matter for executive dictate but rather the result of a deep soul searching across the entire enterprise.[4]

As non-profit institutions, museums should also draw inspiration from trends of thought and action across this wider context, and here too the pace of advocacy has recently been accelerating (Louria 2009). Colby et al. (2004, 26) urge non-profits to clarify "what success looks like" and Grant and Crutchfield (2008) present research on six practices shared by high-impact non-profit organisations. Bradach et al. (2008, 88) describe how nonprofits are "being much more explicit about the results they intend to deliver and the strategies and organisations they'll create to achieve those outcomes". In his message to the leadership of science centres, Luckow (2008, 5) also refers to the whole non-profit field. He stresses that impact is "the ultimate bottom line" and describes the new Noyce Leadership Institute[5] that focuses on "the need for greater effectiveness and public impact … at the crossroads of societal trends, global issues, and the cutting edge of informal science".

Controversy in science

It is an unsurprising aspect of debate about matters of societal and environmental progress that breakthroughs in understanding are often preceded by challenging or controversial moments (Issues Laboratory Collaborative 1995). Dictionary definitions for "challenging" are difficult, complex and ambitious and for "controversial" they include differing opinions, contentious and provocative. Public opinion around a hot topic can be visualised as a bell curve, or possibly a bimodal curve, that morphs over the time span of controversy, from left skewed to right skewed, ultimately to flatten out as acceptance grows, and often ultimately to disappear. Three everyday illustrations are wearing seat belts in vehicles, smoking tobacco in public places, and habitat protection for endangered species: initially controversial, such measures now enjoy wide public acceptance because they have come to be viewed by the vast majority as common sense. Citing the example of evidence versus non-evidence based medical treatments, Leshner (2007, 1326) observes that:

> A major source of tension in the science-society relationship arises from the increasing encroachment of science on issues related to core human values and strongly held beliefs.

Sometimes, and as shown by the example of the National Museum of Australia with its controversial coverage of indigenous Australians, it can take a very long time for polarised attitudes to subside (Casey 2001).

At what point—before, during, after, or never—does the museum responsibly become a stage for public engagement around a challenging or controversial issue? Certainly, the presentation and interpretation of such subject matter demands an extraordinary effort of innovative, sensitive and courageous effort to plan and implement the kind of coverage that will help its audience to gain a fuller perspective and greater understanding (Serrell 1998). Do the outcome rewards outweigh the input strains? And what, in any case, does an ethos of social and environmental responsibility behove the museum to think and do?

Science museums and science centres can learn some useful lessons from the zeal of aquaria, zoos and children's museums to evolve in response to the progressing needs of society and the environment. Spurred by both a changing internal ethos and media attention[6], there has mercifully been a pronounced trend away from barred concrete cages towards larger, more realistic, sometimes multi-species, enclosures with a conservation mission, plus there has been a rising concern over the scheduled performance of mammals in captivity. As covered by the *Los Angeles Times* on February 25, 2009, in an opinion titled "Loving Chimps to Death", Jane Goodall's famous lifetime of work plus a recent disastrous incident in Connecticut have led her to be vociferous against chimpanzees as pets or entertainers. For their part, children's museums are trying to tackle some of the most pressing issues affecting children's health, such as obesity. In 2003, the US-based Association of Children's Museums began a pilot study with four member institutions to examine how they could guide families along the path to health and well-being.

Recently in Helsinki, a "Science Engagement in Action" conference probed for the three most challenging issues facing humanity, the role of science in solving these challenges, and the role of science museums and science centres to engage people in the debate and action that are needed.[7] Climate change emerged as among the top-ranked issues. European science centres have been approaching this hot topic for some time already (Trautmann 2007). As a follow up, the CEOs of the 90 members of Europe's science centre association convened to try to resolve how best to communicate the science behind climate change and the risks that it poses (Hoeg 2009).[8]

The UNESCO-based International Social Science Council (ISSC)[9], whose role is to advance the practice and utilisation of the social and behavioral sciences to the problems we all face, offers a refreshing interdisciplinary approach. As one example, the International Union of Geological Science is using the ISSC to ascertain the next-generation science questions in earth system research.[10] Echoing a point in the opening of this chapter, this consultation process is founded on the philosophy that form should follow function—that is, focus first on the urgent questions and then determine and pursue the best approach that incorporates helpful collaborations. Science museums, science centres and their umbrella associations might well learn a great deal from this type of methodology.

In considering hot topics for our institutions, a distinction of those which are global from those which are local is important. Matters such as climate change, sea-level rise, peak oil, reduced biodiversity, and human evolution are, of course, of universal importance[11], but each region also poses its own set of pressing science-driven societal and environmental issues. Stimulated by the field's heightened consciousness to reach for maximum relevance and impact, every science centre at its chosen scale arguably has the potential to become a globally-mindful resource to living, learning and caring for, and working in, its own region.

A third-generation example

Situated next to the Statue of Liberty and Ellis Island on the Jersey City waterfront opposite Manhattan, Liberty Science Center has had an unprecedented history in the science centre field. Twelve years after its 1993 opening as a $68 million institution, it reopened in 2007 following a $109 million expansion and total renewal.[12] To prepare for this transformation, it relocated its administration and planning functions, together with a much reduced public operation, to several nearby locations for 22 months. This project enabled Liberty Science Center to shift gears in the quickest possible way from a second to third generation state in the meanings discussed earlier in this chapter. This project has already been described (e.g., Koster 2006b, 2007b; Koster and Schubel 2007; LaBar 2007; Osowski 2007; LaBar and Wood 2008) and has received accolades in both the museum field (e.g., Knapp 2007; West and Bossert 2007; Pes 2008) and with major news coverage. Nine months before reopening *The Star-Ledger* included this statement in an article on 4 October 2006 titled "Innovation and Inspiration: 'New' Liberty Science Center will be on the cutting edge of 21st-century museums":

> Most of all, what the planners of the 'new' Liberty Science Center want is for visitors to be inspired, to realize that science and technology are a part of their daily lives and to learn that it is within their power to take informed action on any scientific subject.

Three days before reopening on July 16, 2007, *The New York Times* expressed in its own editorial titled "Science for Big Kids" that:

> Gone is the beloved touch tunnel, but perhaps that's for the best. The updated Science Center … is shiny, new and high-tech, and does not condescend to its visitors … they've pulled the common denominator up … The new Center also tries to make science feel accessible, even local … To its credit, the center does not shy away from the things we wish were less real-world.

Liberty Science Center's stated mission is to engage diverse audiences in relevant issues that connect nature, humanity and technology and, through innovative and meaningful experiences, to inspire action that strengthens communities and advances global stewardship. Core values are expressed as trios of words under the three mutually-reinforcing stages of everyday work: the foundation—equity, integrity and sustainability; the approach—innovation, collaboration and entrepreneurship; and the impact—essential, influential and inspirational. Today, all exhibition, program and film choices address regional relevant issues in a global backdrop. An example is an exhibition titled *Infection Connection* that delves into the individual and collective responsibility to safeguard public health, and the coverage includes how our immune system can be compromised by sexual activity.

Before its opportunity to renew and expand, Liberty Science Center had evolved a socially responsible stance through the creation of programs that connect students' lives to cardiac bypass surgery through video-conferencing with a regional hospital, a novel state funding approach that provides systemic access for at-risk school districts, and advocacy for smoking cessation among youth (Koster and Baumann 2005). This stance was also manifest in the manner of Liberty Science Center's response in the aftermath of the terrorist attacks on the World Trade Center one mile away (Gaffney et al. 2002): and, the exhibition called *A Question of Truth* from the Ontario Science Centre[13], that only a handful of institutions ever booked, was featured during early 2002.

Since reopening, its orientation towards bold subject matter has continued apace. Travelling exhibition choices have included *Islamic Science Rediscovered* from MTE Studios in Cape Town and Dubai[14], *Race: Are We So Different?* from the Science Museum of Minnesota[15], and *The Science of Survival* from London's Science Museum[16]. Video-conferences with hospital operating rooms now also include globally-unique experiences with neurosurgery, kidney transplant surgery, and robotic and gynecological surgeries. Breakthrough exhibitions lasting 4–6 months have included the positions of the US presidential candidates on the main science issues and this provided for visitors of all ages to privately vote their preference with a public display of results. Catalytic workshops and conferences with corporate, government and non-profit parties have examined the progress in Botswana with combating HIV / AIDS (*The Star-Ledger* 2008), the rarely discussed crisis of hunger in America's cities, how acts of global terrorism can best be integrated with the school curriculum (Winkler and Riloff 2008), and solutions for coastal cities in light of the low frequency of catastrophic storms and the slow rise of sea level. Where possible, such collaborative events are approached in a manner that encourages acts of corporate social responsibility. Also, a growing consulting business seeks clients, both nationally and internationally, who have progressive aims for the museum field.

In 2008, a survey by *Parents Magazine* concluded that the new Liberty Science Center ranks in fourth spot of the top ten across the US, the first three in Boston, Columbus and San Francisco all having opened 40–50 years ago (Cicero 2008).

Boldly, but carefully, forward

The conclusion to this chapter echoes the summary of Koster and Schubel (2007, 119):

> Given the pressing issues that are germane to the missions of each museum type … it is a matter of accountability whether … institutions opt to be part of the solution or part of the problem … the search for greater relevance must never cease. Successfully heading in this direction depends on three facets of institutional culture being in place. The first concerns mission and vision—is there a clear and firm commitment to be of value to the societal and environmental problems we face? The second concerns leadership—is there a preparedness and competence to be an activist? The third concerns strategy—is there a relentless pursuit to be more externally useful and to nurture new perspectives in funding stakeholders?

The rising issue of hot topics accentuates the need for museums, and especially science museums and science centres, to be relevant but this course is not for the faint hearted. Should a museum that has yet to embark on a wholehearted journey of relevance plunge abruptly into the realm of controversial subject matter, it will surely do so at its public relations peril. On the other hand, for a museum that has been proactively on a journey increasingly relating to the important matters at hand, the majority of the audience will seldom be surprised over the latest step in its zeal to address topics of a challenging or controversial nature. Indeed a consistent profile of this nature will not only incrementally affirm the museum's chosen direction but also attract funders who increasingly seek outcomes that profoundly matter.

References

American Association of Museums. 1996. *Museums in the social and economic life of a city*. Washington D.C.: American Association of Museums.

Anderson, D., M. Storksdieck and M. Spock. 2007. Understanding the long-term impacts of museum experiences. In *In principle, in practice:*

Museums as learning institutions. Ed. J. Falk, L. Dierking and S. Foutz, 197–215. Walnut Creek, CA: AltaMira Press.

Barker, R. 2002. *The nature of leadership.* Lanham MD: University Press of America.

Barrett, R. 1998. *Liberating the corporate soul.* Burlington MA: Butterworth-Heinneman.

Bradach, J., T. Tierney and N. Stone. 2008. Delivering on the promise of nonprofits. *Harvard Business Review* December: 88–97.

Casey, D. 2001. Museums as agents of social and political change. *Curator* 44 (3): 230–234.

Cicero, K. 2008. The 10 best science centers. *Parents Magazine* September: 258–261.

Colby, S., N. Stone and P. Carttar. 2004. Zeroing in on impact: In an era of declining resources, nonprofits need to clarify their intended impact. *Stanford Social Innovation Review* Fall: 24–33.

Danilov, V. 1982. *Science and technology centers.* Cambridge MA: Massachusetts Institute of Technology.

Davis, J., E. Gurian and E. Koster. 2003. Timeliness: A discussion for museums. *Curator* 46 (4): 353–361.

Fras, B. 2006. Body Worlds 2: The anatomical exhibition of real human bodies. *Curator* 49 (4): 477–482.

Gaffney, D., K. Dunne-Maxim and M. A. Cernak. 2002. The science center as sanctuary. *Journal of Museum Education* Winter: 22–27.

Gijssen, J. 2008. Museums in 2020: Change and connectivity. *Canadian Museums Association, Muse* November–December: 44–46.

Glasser, S. 2008. Manifesto destiny. *American Association of Museums, Museum* November-December: 31–33.

Grant, H. and L. Crutchfield. 2008. *Forces for good: The six practices of high-impact nonprofits.* San Francisco CA: Jossey-Bass.

Griffin, P., L. Baum, J. Blankman-Hetrick, D. Griffin, J. Johnson, C. Reich and S. Rowe. 2005. Optimizing learning opportunities in museums: The role of organizational culture. In *In principle, in practice: Museums as learning institutions.* Ed. J. Falk, L. Dierking and S. Foutz, 153–165. Walnut Creek CA: AltaMira Press.

Hoeg, A. 2009. Our biggest challenge. *Attractions Management* 14: 18.

Hooper-Greenhill, E. 2000. *Museums and the interpretation of visual culture.* New York: Routledge.

Issues Laboratory Collaborative. 1995. *Communicating controversy.* Association of Science-Technology Centers.

Janes, R. 2009. *Museums in a troubled world: Renewal, irrelevance or collapse?* New York: Routledge.

Knapp, P. 2007. Walking the technology talk: At Liberty Science Center, visitors use technology and new media to interact with—and even change—museum content. *segdDESIGN* 22: 58–62.

Korn, R. 2007. The case for holistic intentionality. *Curator* 50 (2): 255–264.

Koster, E. 1999. In search of relevance: Science centers as innovators in the evolution of museums. *Daedalus, American Academy of Arts and Sciences* 128 (3): 277–296.

—. 2006a. The relevant museum: A reflection on sustainability. *American Association of Museums, Museum News* May–June: 67–80, 85–90.

—. 2006b. The attendance treadmill: Best gauge of science center fitness? *Association of Science-Technology Centers, Dimensions* May/June: 19.

—. 2007a. The public value of science museums: Past, present and future. *Museum Communication, National Museum of Science and Nature, Tokyo*. February 23–24. Program and Abstracts: 6–7.

—. 2007b. The reinvented Liberty Science Center. *LF Examiner* 10 (7): 1.

—. 2009. Sail and bail: Navigational aids for museums in economic turmoil. *Association of Children's Museums, Hand to Hand* 23 (1): 1–2, 11–13.

Koster, E. and S. Baumann. 2005. Liberty Science Center in the United States: A mission focused on relevance. In *Looking reality in the eye: Museums and social responsibility.* Ed. R. Janes and G. Conaty. 85-111. Canada: University of Calgary Press.

Koster, E. and J. Falk. 2007. Maximizing the external value of museums. *Curator* 50 (2): 191–196.

Koster, E. and J. Schubel. 2007. Raising the relevancy bar at aquariums and science centers. In *In principle, in practice: Museums as learning institutions.* Ed. J. Falk, L. Dierking and S. Foutz, 107–120. Walnut Creek CA: AltaMira Press.

LaBar, W. 2007. Exhibit commons: Liberty Science Center's new open source experiment. *Visitor voices in museum exhibitions.* Ed. K. McLean and W. Pollock, 140–144. Washington DC: Association of Science-Technology Centers.

LaBar, W. and A. Wood. 2008. Tall tales: A century of exhibiting tall buildings. Paper presented at the Council on Tall Buildings and theUrban Habitat, March 3–5 in Dubai, UAE.

Lemonick, M. 2006. Is America flunking science? *Time* 167 (7): 23–31.

Lencioni, P. 2002. Make your values mean something. *Harvard Business Review* July: 5–9.

Leshner, A. 2005. Where science meets society. *Science* 307: 815.

—. 2007. Beyond the teachable moment. *Journal of the American Medical Association* 298: 1326–1328.

Lindqvist, S. 2000. *Museums of modern science.* Nobel Symposium 112. Scientific History Publications and Nobel Foundation.

Louria, D. 2009. *reTHINK: A twenty-first-century approach to preventing social catastrophes.* Bernardsville NJ: LouWat Publishing.

Luckow, L. 2008. Leading for impact. *Association of Science-Technology Centers, Dimensions* September/October: 5.

—. 2009. Leading for continuity and change. *Association of Science-Technology Centers, Dimensions* November/December: 3.

National Commission on Mathematics and Science Teaching for the 21st Century. 2000. Before it's too late. US Department of Education www.ed.gov/americacounts/glenn (accessed 18 December 2009).

National Research Council of the National Academies, 2009. *Learning science in informal environments: People, places and pursuits.* National Academies Press.

Ogawa R., M. Loomis and R. Crain. 2009. Institutional history of an interactive science center. The founding and development of the exploratorium. *Science Education* 93 (2): 269–292.

Osowski, J. 2007. The Liberty Science Center will unveil its expansion and renewal project this summer: Bigger and better. *New Jersey Education Association Review* April: 12–14.

Pastore, E. 2009. *The future of museums and libraries: A discussion guide* (IMLS-2009-RES-02). Washington, DC: Institute of Museum and Library Services.

Peniston, W. 1999. *The new museum: Selected writings of John Cotton Dana.* Newark NJ and Washington DC: Newark Museum Association and American Association of Museums.

Pes, J. 2008. Space race: Liberty Science Center. *Museum Practice Magazine* Summer: 12–17.

Porter, M. 1985. *Competitive advantage.* New York: Free Press.

Rangan, K. 2005. Lofty missions, down-to-earth plans. *Harvard Business Review* March: 112–119.

Scientific American. 2005. Crossroads for planet earth. Special Issue, September: 10.

Serrell, B. 1998. *Paying attention: Visitors and museum exhibitions.* Washington DC: American Association of Museums.

Skramstad, H. 1997. Changing public expectations of museums. *Proceedings of Museums for the New Millennium.* 5–7 September, 1996. Center for Museum Studies, Smithsonian Institution, and American Association of Museums, 33-50.

The Star-Ledger. 2008. Global Health. Advertising Section. August 2.
Trautmann, C. 2007. Global warming at European museums. *The Informal Learning Review* 87: 1–4.
Volkers, N. 2009. The e-word. *Howard Hughes Medical Institute Bulletin* http://www.hhmi.org/bulletin/aug2009/upfront/word.html (accessed 18 December 2009).
Weil, S, 2002. *Making museums matter.* Smithsonian Institution Press.
—. 2005. A success / failure matrix for museums. *Museum News* January-February: 36–40.
—. 2006. Beyond management: Making museums matter. In *Study Series 12, International Council of Museums, International Committee on Management* 4–8.
West, R. and C. Bossert. 2007. Science museums face the 21st Century. *The Informal Learning Review* 87: 1–10.
Winkler, P. and Z. Riloff. 2008. Adding 9/11 to the curriculum. *New Jersey Education Association Review* September: 18–20.

Notes

[1] The Long Now Foundation, www.longnow.org (accessed 18 December 2009)
[2] http://earth.jsc.nasa.gov/ (accessed 18 December 2009)
[3] http://www.isc.hbs.edu/pdf/Strategy_for_Museums_20060427.pdf (accessed 18 December 2009)
[4] Lencioni (2002) notes that the core values of the failed Enron Corporation (http://en.wikipedia.org/wiki/Enron) had been stated as communication, respect, integrity, and excellence (accessed 18 December 2009)
[5] http://www.noycefdn.org/leadershipInstitute.php (accessed 18 December 2009)
[6] e.g. commercially successful films such as *Gorillas in the Mist* 1988 about the life of Dian Fossey and *Free Willy* in 1993 about a captive killer whale.
[7] Co-hosted on March 20, 2009 ASTC and Heureka, the Finnish Science Centre.
[8] Held on November 20-21, 2009 and hosted by ECSITE in Copenhagen.
[9] http://www.unesco.org/ngo/issc/1_about/1_introduction.htm (accessed 18 December 2009)
[10] http://www.icsu-visioning.org/ (accessed 18 December 2009)
[11] For a sample list of currently contentious issues, see http://www.idebate.org/.
[12] www.lsc.org (accessed 18 December 2009)
[13] http://www.ontariosciencecentre.ca/tour/default.asp?exhibitionid=11 (accessed 18 December 2009)
[14] http://www.americanarabforum.org/islamic_science_rediscovered.htm (accessed 18 December 2009)
[15] http://www.understandingrace.org/home.html (accessed 18 December 2009)
[16] http://survival.scienceof.com/12/partners/overview.html (accessed 18 December 2009)

CHAPTER FIVE

CURATOR: FROM SOLOIST TO IMPRESARIO

ELAINE HEUMANN GURIAN

> "... if the assumption is made that traditional curating follows a centralised network model, then what is the position of the curator within a distributed network model?"(Krysa, 2006)

> "Curators are stereotyped as dull pedants, alternatively talking down to visitors or discouraging them from even entering the curator's private realm, the museum. It is only natural that those trying to apply computers to the museum field would likewise choose curators as the enemy." (Hobbs 2002)

Setting the stage: the internet and our relationship to information

The use of the internet will inevitably change museums. How museums respond to multiple sources of information found on the web and who on staff will be responsible for orchestrating this change is not yet clear. The change, when it comes, will not be merely technological but at its core philosophical. The determining factors will be how directors conceive their museums' relationship to their audience and how that relationship should evolve.

Internet use is changing many aspects of our society—how we educate ourselves, judge the trustworthiness of information, collectively lobby for policy reform, do our work, determine where we live, and how we form real and virtual communities. People use the internet to find answers to their personal inquiries. At any time of the day or night anyone using a search engine can easily find multiple sites devoted to any topic. The located sites may be written by scholars, informed amateurs, or crackpots. The content may vary. The internet user must determine who s/he trusts amid all that available content. Some websites permit, even encourage, users to add and make changes to the information they view (Wikipedia, etc.). The browser need not be a passive recipient of text created by the originating writer / authority. And there is an increasing level of engagement (known as Web 2.0 or social networking) that results in groups of users bypassing authoritative control altogether and just talking to each other. In those social networking sites (i.e., Facebook, MySpace, Twitter, LinkedIn, etc.) organisations of all kinds, including museums, are now establishing their own accounts so that they might get attention.

Trebor Scholz in his article, “The Participatory Challenge”, characterises methods of person-to-person interchange as

> extreme sharing networks” “that include listservs, message boards, friend-of-a-friend networks, mobile phones, short message service/text messaging (sms), peer-to-peer networks, and social software such as blogs, autonomous social networks. [...] Extreme sharing networks are conscious, loosely knit groups based on commonalities, bootstrap economies, and shared ethics. They offer alternative platforms of production and distribution of our practice. (Scholz 2006)

Every museum visitor carrying a cell phone or MP3 player of some sort now has, or soon will have, access to subject-matter information not generated by the institution. The editorial control of information formerly the province of most institutions is quickly coming to an end because it is so easy to find additional or contrary views on the net.

Museums and information

Museums have created websites that contain a plethora of information and so believe they are taking advantage of the new technological possibilities. Most of this information however is written and promulgated by the museum itself and is therefore just an extension of the museum as authority. This chapter is not about the role of the museum’s website. Rather, it concentrates on two issues: the structural change a museum will have to make in order to intentionally share information not created exclusively or edited by museum personnel; and the integration of such information on the exhibition floor so that the visitor can find answers to their own self-generated queries while in the presence of the real object. In other words, I will focus on the control and flow of information within the exhibition space itself.

In contradistinction to information sharing found on the web, most museum exhibitions including topic choice and breadth and depth of topic exploration currently remain in the control of the institution. Typically the label copy of an exhibit is a synthesis of the information gathered and represents the institution's take on the matter. Some museums have experimented with allowing, even encouraging, input from others but this is generally reserved to specifically controlled sections of the exhibition in forms such as comment books or "talk back" walls. Even when museums use outside advisory committees who have disparate views on a topic, the museum's overall presentation is generally edited and thereby controlled by the museum itself. The degree of controversy and candour embedded in the exhibition creation is based on the museum's mission and not generally on the interest evidenced by the visitor. Topic choice and topic exploration are further determined by the institution's collections, position within the political firmament, the interest and belief systems of the staff, especially the curators, or conversely the availability of pre-packaged travelling exhibitions on offer. Obviously the more interest there is in creating dialogue with the audience and the more multi-voiced avenues are inserted within the exhibition, the wider and deeper the discussion can range. In other words "hot" topics can be more easily presented with both more balance and more opinionated passion when there are multiple avenues of input built into the exhibition.

Before I go further I must acknowledge that there are experimenters that fit neither the mould described above nor others suggested throughout this chapter. That is true for some individual curators and a few museums. Additionally there are other writers who predate me in speculating about this very issue. But before the reader dismisses the suppositions made throughout the chapter because they can think of individual exceptions, let me stress that the museum field generally, its curators, and those academic departments focused on training curators remain at the core philosophically unchanged despite their new websites and shiny new technological reference centres.

For the last century the museum staff member most responsible for creating and vetting information has been the curator. By job description, curators have been the acknowledged voice of museum authority. However, curators are beginning to find that visitors' easy access to internet information housed in handheld appliances sometimes compete for their attention and allegiance even while on the exhibit floor. And even authoritative curators have found that in presenting topics in which there are controversial viewpoints showcasing multiple authorities often lets the museum off the hook by offering the institution deniability.

Accordingly, curators (and the directors they work for) have a choice and an opportunity. They can decide to maintain their traditional position of being the authoritative source of information or they can become more involved in the distribution of multi-voiced information originating elsewhere. They can encourage their museums to participate in the growing appetite and expectations their visitors have for intellectual interactivity or they can persuade themselves that visitors have come to the museum for its exclusive expertise. Since I am not, and have never been, a curator I cannot predict how they will respond to these opportunities. The museum world is diverse and I am assured by others that the curatorial world reflects the same broad diversity of opinion as the field itself. I assume, therefore, that some / many curators will be interested in engaging in co-operative information sharing, following the pattern of change that is already surfacing in many other fields and in line with museums' evolutionary practices. We already see evidence of that in some, but not many, museum websites. But interested or not, changing the curator's position from the acknowledged unitary over-arching authority to serving as a conduit for information that is neither generated nor necessarily vetted by him or her is a big ask. It is a fundamental shift in the role itself. And the change, if it comes, must be cognisant of the curator's original motivation for wanting the job itself.

If curators came into their position out of genuine fascination for the subject matter, this new scenario will still provide a place for expertise and the opportunity to display the curator's knowledge as part of the informational mix. If the curator's pleasure in the job derives from the power that control of information gives him or her, then sharing the role of expert with others will feel like a diminishment of stature. Because for many sharing such authority will almost certainly feel like a profound and ill-conceived change, I believe that both museums (and their on-staff curators) will reject this transition and remain committed to their customary role as instructors. In the face of this opportunity, I believe the majority of museums will continue to feel strongly about maintaining their authoritative position and will choose to utilise only that portion of the new information technologies which, while looking modern, will not challenge their predilection for knowledge control.

At the same time the opening that the new technology brings, and which is already changing many other civic institutions, will, I believe, be embraced by experimental leaders in our field, who will create institutions more relevant to society's needs and ultimately more useful. Resistant or not, in the long run, I believe, the whole field will slowly evolve and in doing so will create positions that mediate among multiple voices and direct input by visitors. If curators do not lobby to become those people and get the training necessary to successfully rethink their roles, these new tasks will be offered to others bypassing curators and leave them in a less powerful (though still useful) eddy.

The curator's position

Curators come to their view as knowledge creators through tradition and training. A view of the etymology of the word curator gives some hint at the expectations museums had when the position was created: "Middle English curatour, *legal guardian*, from Old French curateur, from Latin cū rātor, *overseer*, from cūrātus, past participle of cūrāre, *to take care of*. [1]

The late 19th century museums were seen as benevolent and ennobling institutions that would reinforce the power of those already knowledgeable and transfer the canonical knowledge about the universe and aesthetics to those who could benefit from exposure to both objects and thoughts. While most museums are still convinced of the efficacy of this position, in the last century or so a number of museums have intentionally modified their position and have determined that their civic responsibilities lie more as fora for public debate than as institutions of information transfer. "Museums are now sites in which knowledge, memory and history are examined, rather than places where cultural authority is asserted" (Russo et al. 2008). This change is epitomised by the now classic Steven E. Weil journal article title "From Being about Something to Being for Somebody" (Weil 1999).

Even with this transition going on in parts of the museum sector, the job description of curator has most often remained tied to that original vision. And even more importantly the early assumptions of scholar, keeper, researcher of collections, and arbiter of taste, continues to inform the training of curators today. It is the training that will have to alter if we expect meaningful change in the future.

Curators under pressure

For the last fifty years or so, curators have been under pressure to defend or change their traditional position from those who have been agitating for change. Curators have, by and large, been successful in their resistance. As new permutations of more inclusive museums emerged, directors of some individual institutions have tried to redirect curators on their staff. Some institutions, taking extreme positions, have done away with the position altogether.[2] Inevitably the affected curator group could be counted on to protest.[3] In a certain number of cases they publicly resisted these incursions and asked for, and succeeded in causing, the removal of the offending director.[4] That victory, when it occurred, usually resulted in the return of the institution to the more "traditional" way of thinking, with the curators' position reinforced.

The tension between those who espouse the teaching of agreed canons and those who believe in a more relativist position of multiple viewpoints could be found within allied educational and civic institutions during these same periods. This schism remains as an ongoing debate in museums, universities, schools, libraries and granting agencies alike.[5] So this opportunity is just another in a series. The rift between proponents of canons and those who espouse relativism is often embedded in American political discourse known as the "culture wars". Simply put (though oversimplified) the political Left has espoused more inclusion while the Right has promoted "the grand narrative" of universal excellence. Within each camp there are people of goodwill who are convinced that their positions are best for society. While not suggesting that all individual curators are right wing (and they are certainly not), I am suggesting that the job of curator itself is traditionally based on a conservative position and is sometimes at variance with the internal philosophy and mission of the individual museum they work in.

The curators' job

From the time I began in the museum profession in 1969, the position of curator was considered the bedrock of museums and no "true" museum would consider functioning without them. Curators generally hold graduate degrees with a doctorate preferred in their area of specialty. They like to be considered experts in the academic sense and use university positions as their cognates. In museums, the curator has been seen as the resident intellectual expert as well as the recommender of additional acquisitions and research directions.[6] Additionally curators recommend de-accession of objects, write and promote collections policy, cultivate donors, write grants, participate in other fundraising activities, and engage in and present new research. It is often their personal cultivation of donors that leads to their job protection and sets them up as rivals to the director's power. In many museums, curators were (and are) the fulcrum on which decisions rest. Many directors (though fewer than when I started my career) come from their ranks. And even more directors defer to the wishes of the curators they supervise.

Changes

Over the last 50 years some profound changes have affected the curator's job, albeit slowly and unevenly. In large and mid-size museums, object care has been transferred from curators to specialised collections managers. This has meant that managers have become responsible for the physical care and technical record keeping of the object while curators retain their intellectual authority over the collection. This sharing of care has softened both the feeling of proprietary ownership and access in some but not all museums. "Formerly, senior curators (known as Keepers) had to be asked for permission by colleagues in other disciplines to view objects in 'their' collections" (O'Neill 2007).

The rise of the educator and public service

In the 1970s and 80s, when the American museum community became more dependent on earned income and faced pressure to increase admissions income, it was argued that museums needed to pay greater attention to the visitor's well-being. This led to the expansion and status of education and public program departments, charged with improving audience satisfaction. Educators often maintained that exhibitions created by curators were generally too scholarly and erudite to generate attendance. At that time (and in many cases still) curators proposed the exhibitions and controlled their content while all other staff members (educators, designers, etc.) were cast as supporting players. Educators argued that they could make exhibitions more responsive and understandable to visitors only if they had direct participation in the formative exhibition creation process.

Starting in the 1970s, as a counter-balance to curatorial control, some museums adopted a new exhibition creation paradigm known as the "team approach" which set up a decision-making group process that included educators and designers in addition to curators. The team approach became widely touted, taught and experimented with (Rounds and McIlvaney 2000, McIlvaney 2000, Roberts 2000, Gurian 1990, Lang 2003). It has been modified and remodified many times over the ensuing thirty years it has been in use. At base however, the team approach has had the intentional effect of diminishing the curators' dominance over exhibition content and interpretation wherever it was used.

When attendance figures began to be used as internal and external measures of success, some directors began to create new supervisory administrative posts within the museum hierarchy ("experience directors" and "vice presidents for public programs", etc.) charged with increasing the public's use of the museum. These new positions were organisationally placed at levels equal with curators and in positions to mitigate the curator's authority. Yet even in museums where such reorganisations took place, most institutions still expected curators to remain subject matter experts and to control the accuracy of content in exhibitions and on collections records.

First person interpretation

An additional attack on the curator's unitary control of content came when external stakeholders began to demand a voice in the creation of exhibitions. Many members of tribal cultures demanded to speak directly to the museum audience about objects made by their ancestors, bypassing the curatorial voice. Responding to this request became a leitmotiv for museums that housed cultural collections (National Museum of the American Indian (US) 1994, Gurian 2004, Anderson 1990). Allowing community members to speak directly to the visitor raised new curatorial problems. Believing in the tradition of presenting dispassionate "factual" information some curators were confronted with community members whose belief system differed and whose integration of "myth" and folklore was essential, they felt, to tell the necessary "truth". In some places first person labels or techniques such as co-curating exhibitions with community members proved to be a technique used to moderate disputes.[7]

In some museums there has been an increase in the number of curators of indigenous backgrounds who have the same scholarly credentials as their non-indigenous colleagues and whose expectations match the curatorial model. In other museums there has been an attempt to create positions where native knowledge is accorded parallel status with academic curators. Yet these accommodations are only successful in those museums where the curatorial staffs believe in them. The late Michael Ames, feeling that these adaptations were covering over the true intentions of the institutions wrote in 2005:

> Museums have typically preferred the Wizard of Oz technique: exhibits present the anonymous voice of authority, while in reality texts are constructed by one or more curators hiding behind the screens of the institution. As ideas about 'multi-vocality,' 'inter-textuality,' and 'hybridity' become more popular, more wizards may be added, including honorary Indigenous representatives recruited from outside the academy. Nevertheless museums continue in many cases to set the agendas, manage recruiting processes, and control the final editing and presentation of

exhibits. It is the nature of bureaucracies to protect their prerogatives. (Ames 2005)

Veracity and truthfulness

It can be argued that curators' reluctance to give up control is well grounded. Curators view their job as protecting the museum's reputation as intellectually trustworthy. Veracity is seen as a most important and central attribute for justifying the very existence of museums. Museums are trusted, curators argue, because they have "real" objects and present "truthful" information. But in cyberspace, curators argue, both the reality of objects and the reliability of information are under assault. Yet we all know that acknowledged scholars do not agree on many subjects, and making their contrasting arguments known does not diminish understanding, I would contend.

Many trusted organisations facing the same dilemma are creating electronic systems of multiple streams of responsive information that seem to enhance their reputation. A review of the *New York Times* electronic website with its multiple linkages can serve as an example. The rise of "open-source" academic journal websites might serve as another. The organisations that create informational formats that invite audience participation (i.e., Wikipedia) seem to have enhanced their usefulness and their importance. This is not without growing pains and limit setting but is intrinsically different from simple single source information found on labels in exhibitions.

So what's to become of curators?

Given this fast changing technological world that is challenging authoritative institutions, museums seem caught in a cross-road—to leave the museum in its traditional role as a unitary expert of civic trustworthiness or to decide to embrace the possibilities attendant to the role of knowledge gatherers, assemblers and responders, making museums into safe places for civic "fora". And even then, having made a decision to change (slowly or quickly) the director can still retain traditional curators as his / her knowledge experts, but in doing so the director will have to choose to assign the tasks of assembling multiple sources of information to the IT or the education department or both. I suspect this change will be gradual so that it feels organic. But assigning knowledge accumulation to others without changing the responsibilities of the curator as resident expert will diminish the power of the curator as knowledge tsar.

Interleaving the IT and education departments with the curators will open up old wounds and recent tussles. Museum educators and curators have had disagreements in the past about their respective roles and responsibilities and will have to clarify them again under these new conditions. Anticipating this problem, the code of ethics promulgated by the Association of Art Museum Curators in 2007 attempted to mediate the relationship and suggest that information presentation is a shared responsibility.

> Curators must accept the responsibility of addressing different audiences in their writing and speaking about their collections, whether a scholarly audience of their peers or a broader public without their specialised knowledge of the field. This responsibility extends to their writing, for museum publications as well as labels produced for the collection galleries or special exhibitions. In adapting their scholarship for a context extending beyond their immediate peers, curators can rely upon the expertise of educators in effectively addressing the general museum visitor.[8]

The person installed in this new museum position would answer questions and create the content base using a variety of internal and contracted expertise. The museum curator would become only one among a group of experts used by the information manager to provide content. The personality type best suited for this position would delight in locating a wide array of information (not exclusively self-generated), be well organised, have a naturally curious intellect and a responsive personality. They would view the location of controversial and oppositional information favourably and would enjoy creating multiple streams of disparate information.

The information manager job is somewhat analogous to "exhibition developers" who already exist in some museums. Developers create exhibitions by synthesising content from a variety of sources including staff curators. Hiring information managers would continue the curators' role of content generation as before, but curators would not determine which content becomes public or to what external sites the information was linked. The curator would become like a journalist who argues with the editor over placement of copy and length of text. Indeed, this already happens when a museum employs editors in the creation of label copy. The big difference between exhibition developers and information managers is the control of viewpoints presented. Developers conform to the museum's originating viewpoint even while using multiple sources of information. When representing controversial topics developers continue to present the direction laid out by the institution. Information managers would, on the other hand, have as a job description the location and presentation of a multiplicity of voices and would therefore make a much wider range of content available for the visitor to choose from. In fact, aside from creating formats and setting the protocol and etiquette surrounding the information, the information manager would most often refrain from editing allowing conversation and controversy to take place unhampered.

The technical opportunities of sharing authority

Linking exhibitions to outside sites with additional information, source material, and pictures of comparable objects, while technically easy to do so, takes a policy shift to allow the institution to broaden and share its authority. If the museum chooses to make such alternative information available to the visitor, should the curator be the funnel that determines how much and what kind of additional information the public database should contain, or will the museum just make the whole web available to be searched freely?

If the museum decides to include visitor input that too will raise a question: who on staff is the institutional responder, and what form should that response take? In other words, should answering public inquiry become integrated into the curator's job? And if the museum encourages levels of interactivity that bypass an institutional response and facilitate content that is person-to-person generated should quality control and monitoring of such exchanges become part of the curator's job as well?

Projecting current trends into the immediate future, I think electronic labels will soon be available for downloading on small hand-held hardware. This will make label changing and information customisation easy. It will also make current installations of three-dimensional objects into highly flexible armatures for many simultaneous, and different, exhibitions. Will the curator be involved in only one of these available streams or all of them?

It is the answers to these and similar questions that will determine the future job descriptions and relationships among, the curator, educator and information technologist. These are not merely administrative niceties. How these issues are resolved will go to the heart of the museum's philosophy—how it regards its role as trusted authority and how it defines its interaction with its audiences. And if the profession of curators collectively decides to embrace the new role of the knowledge gatherers and distributors then the curriculum of the graduate school and in-service training programs will need to be radically changed.

I can envision some curators enthusiastically taking on the public presentation of their already omnivorous intellectual selves because as trained scholars they in fact keep current by reading widely from multiple sources. Some curators may feel that this new role will be just as, or even more, rewarding than their current responsibilities as knowledge controllers and synthesisers.

Do curators need to stay on salary?

Given the changing world of information distribution described in this chapter, the question logically arises: "do we still need curators and if so, do they need to be on salary?" The answer will vary depending again on the central philosophy of the director. Without questions museums will continue to need access to content experts who will research objects, locate new collections, create information for the database, suggest and write collections policy, recommend individual accessions and de-accessions, and inform exhibitions—much as before. Yet the uses of that expertise will change.

Given the advantages espoused by those who promote outsourcing as a way to enhance an organisation's effectiveness, efficiency and flexibility, an institution's organisation chart might change considerably. While curators do not "own" the collection, their devotion and loyalty make them unique spokespersons for the institutional mission. They have credibility with donors and with the academic community. So destabilising their traditional position carries risk. Would the museum's content experts need to be curators? And if so, would they need to be on salary? Salaried curators are certainly not and never have been the only available knowledgeable scholars. Guest curators are already widely used. Offering to share access to university academics through joint appointments and paying portions of salaries exists as well. The benefit of outsourcing is organisational streamlining, keeping only those positions determined to be "core", and contracting out all other aspects of expertise as needed. What gets defined as core varies within museums. Some suggest that in service-providing organisations, only those who directly serve the public should be on salary. In addition, there is a case to be made that additional salaried positions should be held by the one senior supervisor in each of the other functions. Each of these senior supervisors serve as talent scouts and liaisons with groups of contracted experts in their field and are in charge of the distribution of needed work in a timely fashion. Such a combination of talent scout, work distributor and supervisor of incoming work product is seen increasingly as a job description for all salaried managers in many industries.

This job description is already evident in less sensitive areas of museum work, such as security and payroll. In order to extend this practice into areas of content, the museum would hire a chief curator who serves as the supervisor and distributor of needed contracted work to a network of experts selected to fit the specific museum in terms of expertise, interest and compatibility. It is the permanent "chief" curator who would be charged with carrying on the museum's mission and becoming the spokesperson for outside relationships. Some / many content experts themselves might prefer to be self-employed contract curators. Curators might like a work life that gives them access to a variety of collections and personal control of their time and interests. Museums might like that as well, deciding that they wish to have access to multiple points of view expressed by different curators, keeping the ideas presented to the public fresh and changing. There are already private companies of organised experts for hire in allied areas (registration, collections care, restoration, exhibition development, design and fabrication) some of which did not exist 25 years ago. It is not inconceivable that curators will also choose to amalgamate and become private advisors for hire.

In another model some museums have "wholly owned income generating subsidiaries" within individual museums that employ specific curators focused on research as needed by others.[9] These entities (mostly in the sciences) generate earned and grant income that cover costs and sometimes produce net revenue for their parent organisation. So keeping a whole group of curators on salary but hiring them out for others to use is not inconceivable either.

The training of curators to become directors

Curators have long been worried about changes to their job which include non-academic aspects like marketing, fundraising and cost accounting. Since museum directors were traditionally chosen from the curatorial ranks there has been a desire to "upskill" curators to keep them competitive. For example, an art foundation (The Center for Curatorial Leadership) has been set up to train art curators in gaining these needed skills in order to lessen the possibilities that directors would be chosen from business schools rather than academia. Speaking at the founding of the Association of Art Museum Curators in 2001, Philippe de Montebello, then Director of the Metropolitan Museum of Art, charged curators to consider as a high priority the crisis of the diminishing pool of future museum directors:

> If we are to win the battle of the "curator/director" over the administrator/director", a profile with which increasingly boards of trustees are instinctively more comfortable, and then it is essential to enlarge the pool of curators with the qualifications to be tomorrow's museum directors. It is essential, in order to reassure trustees that hiring curators as directors will not compromise the business-like running of a museums' affairs, in other words, their bottom line.[10]

The choice of directors in future may require even less knowledge of specific content and include more about methods of content interactivity. Where will this leave the curator with aspirations to direct museums?

Summary

This chapter is about the inevitable change in information availability caused by the net, and ways museums may choose to change their relationship with information access and control. It is further about the position of curator, because that is the role most closely linked with the museum's reputation as an authoritative institution. My fundamental assumption is that museums will soon need to shift from being a singular authority to a participant and encourager of intellectual and social engagement among its visitors. In doing so museums will have to look at the administrative assignments and responsibilities of staff in order to become this more responsive institution.

All this goes to the heart of the curator's job description as creator and producer of the information itself. Some will argue that changing the curator's position would not only be difficult but foolhardy. All museums must rely on content specialists whatever they do. However the current curator position could be transformed from today's unitary knowledge tsar to the enthusiastic distributor of knowledge gleaned from many sources and many points of view in real time. Curators have the option of becoming knowledge managers, light editors, an expert among experts, and an eager "includer". Or they can choose to remain the single-source one-way knowledge provider that many are today.

Any change will require new job descriptions, changed internal reporting structures, an altered training regimen and a different sense of self-worth. If curators choose to remain in an unchanged position, their museums will either have decided to ignore the interests of their future public, or given this important new responsibility to others. Put another way, to the extent that curators have been an impediment in holding back museums from becoming more candid about contested content, more responsive to their public and more catholic in their exhibition choice, then refocusing the curators' work to become eager distributors of views from multiple sources would help move museums to become the democratic and inclusive institutions many have long hoped for.

References

American Association of Musems.1991. Excellence and equity: Education and the public dimension of museums, a report. In *Task Force On Museum Education.* Ed. E. Hirzy. Washington, D.C., American Association of Museums.

Ames, M. M. 2005. Museology interrupted. *Museum International* 57**:** 44–51.

Anderson, C. 1990. Australian aborigines and museums, a new relationship. *Curator* 33**:** 165-179.

Blair; C., P. Glanville, F. Haskell, C.M. Kauffmann, S. Levey, D. Mahon, J. V. G. Mallet, J. Montagu and A. Radcliffe. 1999. Re-structuring at the Boston Museum of Fine Arts. *The Burlington Magazine.* 624.

Davis, A. B. 1980. A museum curator. *The Public Historian* 2: 97–99.

Gurian Heumann, E. 1990. Let us empower all those who have a stake in exhibitions. *Museum News.* March/April: 90-93

—. 1992. The importance of 'and'. *Patterns in Practice: Selections From the Journal of Museum Education.* Washington D.C.: Museum Education Roundtable, 88-89.

—. 2004. Singing and dancing at night. In *Stewards of the Sacred.* Ed. L. E. Sullivan and A. Edwards, 89-96. Washington D.C.: American Association of Museum in Cooperation with Center for the Study of World Religions, Harvard University.

Hobbs, S. D. 2002. The barbarians from poughkeepsie are in the museum: What now? A review essay on computers and museums. http://mcel.pacificu.edu/JAHC/JAHCV3/p-resources/hobbs.html (accessed 18 November 2009).

Krysa, J. 2006. Curating immateriality: The work of the curator in the age of network systems. In *Curating immateriality: The work of the curator in the age of network systems.* Ed. J. Krysa. Autonomedia (Data Browser 03).

Lang, W. L. 2003. Museum teams: Two exhibits and their lessons. *Anchorage Museum History Charrette.* Anchorage, Alaska: Anchorage Museum.

McIlvaney, N. 2000. Rethinking the exhibit team: A cyberspace forum. *Exhibitionist* 19 1: 8-15.

National Museum of the American Indian (US). 1994. *All roads are good: Native voices on life and culture.* Washington, D.C.: Smithsonian Institution Press in Association with the National Museum of the American Indian, Smithsonian Institution.

O'Neill, M. 2007. Kelvingrove: Telling stories in a treasured old/new museum. *Curator* 50**:** 379–400.

Roberts, L. C. 2000. Educators on exhibit teams: A new role, a new era. In *Transforming Practice.* Ed. J. S. Hirsch and L. H. Silverman, 89-97. Washington DC: Museum Education Roundtable.

Rounds, J. and N. McIlvaney. 2000. Who's using the team process? How's it going? *Exhibitionist* 19: 4–7.

Russo, A., J. Watkins, L. Kelly and S. Chan. 2008. Participatory communication with social media. *Curator* 51: 21–32.

Scholz, T. 2006. The participatory challenge. In *Curating immateriality: The work of the Curator in the age of network systems.* Ed. J. Krysa. Autonomedia (Data Browser 03).

Weil, S. 1999. From being about something to being for somebody: The ongoing transformation of the American Museum. *Daedalus.* 128**:** 229–258.

Notes

[1] see curator: http://education.yahoo.com/reference/dictionary/entry/curator (accessed 18 December 2009)

[2] In the 1970s the Boston Children's Museum created the role of Developer to replace Curator. The Developer job description was to organise exhibitions gathering information from many outside scholars and working with designers and educators. The role of Developer has become commonplace in many institutions.

[3] See Letters to the editor Blair, C., Glanville, P., Haskell, F., Kauffman, C. M., Levey, S., Mahon, D., Mallet, J. V. G., Montagu;, J. & Radcliffe, A. (1999) Re-Structuring at the Boston Museum of Fine Arts. *The Burlington Magazine.*

[4]http://mailman.nhm.ku.edu/pipermail/taxacom/1993-October/014412.html (accessed 18 December 2009) see public outcry of curators and other scientists against the then President of the Canadian Museum of Nature which eventually led to his dismissal in 1993.

[5] For example, the title of the American Association of Museum's statement on responsibility to its many publics—Excellence and Equity—reflected the tension of the participants who argued either for the primacy of scholarship (excellence) or inclusion (equity) and sometimes felt that there was no possible synthesis between the two.

[6] The current curator's job retains some variant of this original concept. An example is to be seen in the first sentence of the mission statement of the Association of Art Museum Curators written in 2001. "Curators have a primary responsibility for the acquisition, care, display, and interpretation of works of art for the benefit of the public". A similar version written for a different specialty and a decade earlier (in 1980) at the Smithsonian reads "The Federal Civil Service standards for a museum curator, as interpreted and applied by the Smithsonian Institution's National Museum of History and Technology, include four primary functions: collection of historical objects, exhibition, public service, and research." Davis, A. B. (1980) A Museum Curator. *The Public Historian,* **2:** 97-99.

[7] There are some directors and writers who are imagining new levels of activity. Geoffrey Lewis in "Memory and Universality: A UNESCO debate" attributes a description of "digital repatriation" to Bernice Murphy:

> Web 2.0 presents opportunities of interactive and co-creation of meaning which the museum world has only begun to explore. Digital repatriation is a powerful means of stimulating recuperative knowledge in source community. A reflexive museology should be developed through which new relationships can be established embracing all the communities involved. New projects and research should be commissioned.

[8] http://www.artcurators.org/members/aamc_professional_standards_practices.pdf (accessed 18 December 2009)

[9] See Museum of London Archeological Service for example

[10] www.curatorialleadership.org (accessed 18 December 2009)

CHAPTER SIX

LIQUID GOVERNMENTALITIES, LIQUID MUSEUMS AND THE CLIMATE CRISIS

FIONA CAMERON

Introduction

Climate change is a mobile collection of heterogeneous elements, events and effects. That is, from messages that urge us to reduce energy consumption to discussions at COP15 the Copenhagen meeting in December 2009[1] regarding the management of the atmosphere; to the calculations and data modelling of scientists about future scenarios; to heated debates between the Labor government and the Coalition in Australia about the implementation of an emissions trading scheme; to climate refugee immigration quotas and to an unseasonably warm winter. All these things, physical, cultural and social act on each other, are multi-scaled, none are separate. Clearly climate change governmentalities are hybrids of social and physical elements, dynamic, interactive, contested, always on the move, in the process of becoming, challenged and at once stabilised by various events.

Climate change governmentality is, however, framed as a problem on the basis of normative views around science and economics; managing populations, their habits and lifestyles, and neoliberal formations where climate change is cast as an economic issue, with market mechanisms offering cost-effective technological solutions. It is hardly surprising therefore, that Foucauldian governmentality "biopower / biopolitics", the analysis of the techniques and strategies used to manage humans as species bodies and populations and "advanced liberal or neoliberal government" the analysis of neoliberal governmental strategies, the market and the entrepreneurial individual as governmental mechanisms (Foucault 1991, Oels 2005) in their various iterations is widely and almost exclusively used by contemporary theorists to conceptualise and analyse contemporary climate change governance and policy development. These techniques are purposefully deployed across a range of disciplines in the analysis of climate change from cultural studies, anthropology, cultural geography and environmental planning. Because climate change has dramatically altered our perception of time in which the future has now displaced the past as an influence in the present, the risk concept and its social construction (Beck 1999, 137; 2006; Giddens 1999), has also been deployed as yet another governmentality as an attempt to control future events by anticipating how people are required to behave in the present to securitise an unknown future.

Considering that Foucauldian governmentality is so dominant in climate change analysis, one originally formulated on the analysis of the modern state and the regulation of their subjects (Foucault 1991), and in my search for a way to posit museums in broader climate change governmentality flows, I naturally turn first to cultural theorist Tony Bennett's (1995) formative work, the *Birth of the Museum*. Similarly, this work considers museums as institutional apparatus in the service of the early modern state. In my reworking of governmentality theory I also consider how a Foucauldian analysis of museums might work or not in terms of climate change governmentality flows in a complex, contemporary world.

In this chapter I discuss Foucauldian governmentality theory and to a lesser extent Beck's (1999) world risk society as dominant modalities used to conceptualise and analyse climate change governance, its limits and the roles of museums in these formations. I then pose a new theoretical form, "liquid governmentalities" based on systems theories; Zygmunt Bauman's (2007) liquid modernity; John Urry's (2003) global complexity; and Giles Deleuze and Felix Guattari's (1987) and Manuel DeLanda's (2006a) assemblages, as an alternative way of imagining climate change governmentality that more purposefully reflects the contemporary, complex, entangled, transnational climate change governmentality flows. I then link these ideas to the ways museums as governmental devices have been imagined, used and might be deployed in climate change governmentality.

Foucauldian governmentality theory and climate change

French philosopher Michel Foucault (1991, 100) defines governmentality as

> an ... ensemble formed by the institutions, procedures, analyses and reflections, the calculations and tactics that allow the exercise of this very specific albeit complex form of power, which has as its target population,

> as its principal form of knowledge political economy, and as its essential technical means apparatuses of security.

Foucault argues that the aim of these configurations of knowledge / power in the early modern state was "to secure the welfare of the population, the improvement of its condition, the increase of its wealth, longevity, health ..." and so forth (100). Here governmentality is articulated broadly as a purposeful collection of instruments, political subjectivities, forms of social control, control techniques, forms of knowledge undertaken by a multiplicity of authorities and agencies aimed to deliver a specific form of power over the population. That is, at once aimed to shape conduct, is anticipatory, future orientated and designed to produce a measure of securitisation.

According to "biopower" the dominant model of social change in climate change governmentality is to manage and discipline the population and the rational citizen through moralising and reforming behavioural economies, and the scientific surveillance and management of the atmosphere (Oels 2005). According to "advanced liberal or neoliberal government" the market acts as the predominant driver and organising mechanism for the state around climate change mitigation and adaptation through options such as carbon economies, green labour, financial products such as derivatives, all framed around the calculating, entrepreneurial individual (Oels 2005). These strategies are deployed through technologies of performance for example emission targets such as the Kyoto protocol and Copenhagen.

So according to a Foucauldian reading, climate change governmentality is shaped around a series of political rationalities and the circulation of power and knowledge. The instruments in which climate change governmentality is enacted operate through a series of apparatus, for example, governmental and educational institutions such as climate change ministries, schools, media, museums, the market, Kyoto, Copenhagen; forms of social control, and techniques such as policy and research; political subjectivities and technologies of self—the governing of our own conduct to promote attitudinal and behavioural shifts.

Governmentality and museums—the reforming and disciplinary apparatus

My research suggests very strongly that museums are linked into moralising and reforming behavioural economies around climate change likened to biopower, as pedagogic, disciplinary reformatories—places to shape the behaviour and habits of individuals and populations towards sustainable lifestyles on the basis of valued and authoritative information sources as a means of securitising life. The top five roles currently perceived for Australian museums and science centres in our online survey were: according to 76 per cent communicating leading edge climate change science; 75 per cent presenting a range of views on climate change; 73 per cent providing access to a range of resources on climate change and 71 per cent information on how individuals might change their lifestyles and consumer choices to reduce emissions (Cameron et al. 2009).

The findings also clearly articulate this double movement between the institution providing information as an influencing / reforming entity and individuals acting on themselves in changing their attitudes and conduct (Cameron 2007). Here 71 per cent of participants said that they use museum information to inform their own views, opinions and actions. The US sample (New York City, New York State and New Jersey) was similar, with one noticeable difference being that 70 per cent saw institutions as spaces to examine climate change as a broader, cultural, economic, technological, social as well as a scientific issue (Cameron et al. 2009).

The recent exhibition, *Climate Change, Our Future, Our Choice* at the Australian Museum explores the scientific and social outcomes of climate change by taking visitors on a journey into two very different futures. This simple binary invites the visitor to take one path "Do Something", encouraging the rational citizen to become green, to act now to reduce his or her carbon footprint as an actor capable of arresting climate change. The other "Do Nothing" shows how individuals acting irresponsibly perpetuate climate change through their behaviour and consumption habits, leading to inevitable climate catastrophe. Images of environmental destruction, receding glaciers, coal-fired power stations emitting greenhouse gases and coral bleaching link individual consumption to certain climate catastrophe. Messages to share, buy less and re-use around themes such as food, energy, transport and construction invite the visitor to assess their own carbon footprint categorising the individual as a carbon elephant or a carbon mouse.[2] A quote by German theologian and anti-Nazi activist, Dietrich Bonhoeffer is deployed purposefully to instill a sense of moral responsibility framed within the terms of future generations "The ultimate test of a moral society is the kind of world that it leaves for its children". Interestingly, climate catastrophe and the Holocaust become synonymous. The performance of moral responsibility is deemed a technique to avert a certain human catastrophe equivalent to the genocide of the Holocaust.

Museums are also seen as governing structures in flows of finance, capital and technology as part of market-based solutions, such as emissions trading and alternative energy sources. These governmentality flows are seen in the *Energy Quest* exhibition at Liberty Science Center, Jersey City, New York in which the various energy options for the future are detailed from fossil fuel (oil, coal, gas) to biomass, solar, wind and hydro to nuclear (fission, fusion) to wave and tidal to geo-thermal (hydro-thermal, hot dry rock and magma) sponsored by ExxonMobil Corporation.[3] In the exhibition *Waters of Tuvalu: A Nation at Risk* (Museum Victoria, Melbourne) market forces are seen as the solution to reduce emissions and as a mechanism to develop renewable energy in order to mitigate climate catastrophe—the problem of sea level rise, the disappearance of Tuvalu as a sovereign state and cultural loss.[4]

Risk, museums and uncertainty

Risk is another governmental form. Here risk acts as a technique for governing uncertainty and catastrophe—in which its assessment is used to manage and insure against the unknown (Ewald 1999, Beck 1999) as another governmental form to securitise life. To calculate risk is deemed a means of mastering time and disciplining the future. Risk has emerged as an important objective of contemporary market and governmental rationalities in climate change governance. To this end, museums are part of a wider collective of institutions from government, and agencies such as health, financial markets, statistics, insurance, science organisations and non-profit organisations as instruments for climate change risk management and minimisation.

Like the Foucauldian idea of discipline, understanding museums' role in risk, is one of an insuriantial or preventionist imaginary acting as risk spreading, responsibilisation and risk minimisation and securitisation mechanisms within these collectives. To this end, they are invested along with other institutions, in the identification, measurement and representation of these risk calculations through science—the primary means from which climate risk as a global crisis is formulated. A risk reading like Foucauldian discipline, also involves responsiblising the individual to manage climate change risk through their conduct. This resonates with Beck's (1999, 2006) neo-liberal individualisation thesis—a defining quality of risk society.

Unlike the discipline thesis however, the risk mode of address is different. The responsiblisation and individualisation process orients the individual's conduct toward the eventuality of climate change. That is, by expanding temporal horizons to the far future and "responsibilising" conduct itself through the assumption of a calculating, anticipatory regard for the future. This governmental technique highlights the consequences of an individual's decisions and at once exacerbates the anxieties and uncertainties of climate catastrophe. For example the *Waters of Tuvalu: A Nation at Risk* exhibition makes climate change threats real through images of high tides and flooding.[5]

Museums as a climate change risk governmentality entails the individualisation of a personal regard for the future, and the assumption of a unique mode of temporality—the necessity for action in the present for the future. This emphasis on risk future orientations and calculations and the apportioning of responsibility and individual decisions rather than just the consequences of events, can be seen in two exhibitions, the *Science of Survival* from the Science Museum in London, and also *Climate Change, Our Future, Our Choice* at the Australian Museum. Both use interactives that present future projections of climate scenarios. With the former, participants are invited to make informed decisions about new technologies, for example, producing safe drinking water in 2050.[6] The latter calculates the effects of sea level rise (from one to 14 metres calculated according to a temperature rise of up to four degrees) on Sydney Harbour and the New South Wales coastline based on scientific risk assessment scenarios. Here the viewer is challenged to reduce their carbon footprint to alleviate the effects of coastal attrition.

So here the temporal orientation of museums in programming is shifting. Within the risk and insurantial imaginary to which many science and technology museums and science centres are now engaged, the future of the planet is inscribed in the immediacy of the present. In terms of climate change governmentality, the future is orientated to mobilise individuals against certain risks in the interest of safeguarding their own futures. That is, by cultivating a reflexive awareness of their own agency within an extended time consciousness—the far future and accommodating them within a set of calculative practices relative to the future and its risks. In line with this, the aim is to induce the individual into a sustained form of life and mode of conduct in which the future appears as an object of reflexive calculation, available to calculative strategies of day-to-day conduct. Here museums act as moral technologies and reformatories making the individual responsible, as one that possesses the means to repair his or her effects.

Another feature of this orientation is the multiple responsibilisation of Australian citizens, families, households and communities, and indeed the developed world, for their own risks as part of a national and global citizenry. Clearly museums have a new role in the global anticipation and governmentality of catastrophe. This is clearly articulated in the *Waters of Tuvalu: A Nation at Risk* text,

> Tuvalu's greenhouse gas emission is miniscule in comparison to that of developed countries. Yet the geography, sovereignty and cultural heritage of Tuvalu are destined for extinction, unless world communities take responsibility for this issue.[7]

Here the nation has become subject to risk calculations, a direct reflection of the Intergovernmental Panel on Climate Change report on Small Islands vulnerability to sea level rise[8] based on scientific calculations and simulations (IPCC). Accordingly the museum intervention is based on a rational relation to nature, industrialised society and destruction—the loss of land and the extinction of culture, where risks become the object of scientific measurement and assessment subject to regimes of scientific causality and formal calculative rationality.

Re-working governmentality

Within the climate change governmentality stable Foucauldian governmentality has been reworked many times. New governmentalities have been formed around new subjects and rationalities out of contemporary discourses, and the range of actors has been extended in line with neoliberal formations and transnational movements. Political theorists Isabelle Lanthier and Lawrence Oliver (1999), for example, elaborate the theme of "biopolitics" to link issues of human life to the quality of air, water, urban space and the working environment to the normalisation of individual conduct through lifestyle practices and the emergence of environmental awareness (Darier 1999, 28). Environmental theorist Paul Rutherford (1993) extended Foucault's "biopower" concept as "ecopower / ecopolitics" to articulate the concern to adjust conduct to secure and manage all life forms for example the threat to biodiversity through climate change. Theorist Tim Luke's (1999) "green governmentality" globalises these concepts extending the notion of "biopower" to the whole planet where ecological problems become transnational security threats requiring political, economic or military interventions on a global scale. Ecological theorist Maarten Hajer's (1995) concept of "ecological modernisation" in its weak form draws the notion of a free market setting, technological innovation and both biopower and liberalism together focusing on the economic cost-benefit analyses of the various adaptation and mitigation options in which capital reorganises itself. "Civic environmentalism" is a newly defined resistive governmentality emerging from research on dominant governmentality regimes, green governmentality and ecological environmentalism (Bäckstrand and Lovbrand 2007). This governmental project sees the green movement as a governing entity. The green movement as a governmental apparatus according to Bäckstrand and Lovbrand (2007) encompasses on one hand, and in its extreme form, the discourses of anti-capitalist movements calling for the radical transformation of northern consumption and the free market towards a more eco-centric and just world order, and on the other a reform version in which a vital transnational civil society complements state centric practices therefore promoting increasing public accountability, deliberative participation and legitimacy (Bäckstrand and Lovbrand 2007,124).

Discursively speaking, museums are positioned in climate change governmentality as an institutional form that is primarily disciplinary working alongside others, where normative values and relations are expressed and legitimated, and as sites for managing citizen's actions and beliefs. The exhibition *Climate Change, Our Future, Our Choice* articulates all these governmentalities. For example, an extended biopolitics links a range of environmental resources such as air quality and dwindling water resources to individual consumption patterns and awareness raising around an emerging green citizenship. The notion of ecopower / ecopolitics links the need to save Australia's biodiversity and the protection of ecosystems through responsible consumption. Green governmentality, as articulated, links transnational security threats, for example, water and other resource conflicts, to the need for developed countries to change their lifestyles in order to project and delimit resource depletion. Ecological modernisation is linked to a series of future scenarios through TV newsbreaks detailing the cost-benefits of various energy options from solar to biofuels. The articulation of civic environmentalism is best described with reference to the problems of modernity and industrialisation and the capitalist system through images such as emissions from coal fired power stations and the problems of consumption indirectly through these moralising and reforming messages encouraging the development of a grass-roots environmental awareness. Carbon calculating mechanisms in which individuals determine their footprint link the exhibition to the market, carbon economies and future risk in which the institution acts as an economic instrument directed towards behavioural change. Here clearly the museum as an apparatus has become part of climate risk flows active in re-distributing "bads", the unintended consequences of industrialised society, through the calculating responsible individual combined and also linked to an earlier moralising and reforming treatise.

One of the main benefits of a Foucauldian, and indeed risk, reading is the ability to sharply focus the domination of certain governmental strategies, their disciplinary, calculative and anticipated future unknown effects, and competing subjectivities. These textual readings also detail neo-liberal discourses of the responsible individual, one well placed rightly or wrongly to divert climate catastrophe. However, these reworkings, although attempting to compensate for the inflexibility of existing forms, are still based on the same formula. All this does is conflate climate change governmentality and futures into a series of discrete, static, non-interacting concepts formulated around specific rationalities as detailed for discursive analysis. Here the textual analysis of exhibitions is deployed as a means of reading the dominant governmentality modalities and established relations of power, technologies of domination, the state, the market, and indeed the space in which the museum operates in the circulation of all these things. The production and legitimisation of these rationalities is borne out of a pedagogic legacy, an institution deemed as, after science organisations, the most trusted information sources on climate change (Cameron et al. 2009), and as apparatus to re-enforce the messages of reform and discipline. In terms of a risk reading, museums operate as a preventative mechanism, an apparatus for the administration of risk, dissemination and security. That is, one that is mobilised to securitise the unknown threat of climate catastrophe though the management of individuals and populations using techniques of reflexivity, risk calculations, individual responsibility and links to future scenarios. All these rationalities operate as attempts to produce certainty in a world that is uncertain.

Clearly these governmentalities and risk regimes fetishise what already exists in terms of governmental projects. The museum is read as a discursive text, and as an instrument for the circulation of these governmental concepts. A reading of governmental projects and likewise, the museum, involves the textual analysis of actual forms to discover their pre-determined properties, mechanisms and disciplinary effects. Moreover, there is an over-emphasis on the analysis of power and its deployment to imagine climate change as a cultural phenomenon, similarly with museums. Power and its circulation is just one aspect of climate change governmentalities and indeed museums as institutional forms.

A heavy reliance on social constructivist and discourse analysis limits a consideration of climate change in the cultural field to products of discursive struggles between subjectivities, around particular techniques and configurations of state and power. Movement and change and the emergence of other governmental alternatives is derived solely from what emerges in the in-between spaces within discursive struggles. For example, civic environmentalism emerged out of struggles between biopower, advanced liberal government and ecological modernisation rationalities within the Kyoto Protocol. If alternative governmental strategies are not evident in these discursive struggles, or indeed in the reading of a museum program, they are not visible.

Foucauldian governmentality are concepts where lines of enquiry are based on the analysis of a particular political rationality, where each of the elements to be analysed within his ensemble are concept dependent, a limiting frame for imagining both emergent and alternative governance strategies. These limiting frames also ensure that museums as read within a Foucauldian governmental frame as articulated by Bennett, and within climate change governmentality, are visible as primarily disciplinary. Clearly climate change governmentalities actual and potential cannot be captured in a stable concept.

Institutional visibility in climate change governmentalities emerges from their operation within a particular political rationality. Institutional analysis involves the tracing of the movement of knowledge / power and its resistive forces across these particular subjects, as well as double movements between technologies of domination, the museum, and technologies of self, force relations, tactics and disciplinary effects. In all these frames visitors are posited in a one dimensional frame, as rational and responsible citizens.

And finally how relevant is a governmentality thesis developed for the analysis of the rise of the early modern state to contemporary society and to contemporary museums, where these unities of composition are disappearing, in which mobility, complexity and uncertainty are defining elements?

Liquid governmentalities—the concept

Liquid governmentalities is a concept and method of analysis. It conceives of climate change governmentality, and indeed museums, as dynamic processes, as opposed to a search for the meaning, and the operation of existing forms through various techniques and apparatus. In his preface to *The Anti-Oedipus Papers*, Foucault suggests that Deleuze and Guattari (1972) answer questions less concerned with *why* things might be so, and more concerned with *how* to proceed (Kornberger and Ten Bos 2006). Here we shift our attention from the meaning of current climate change governmentalities to *how* to proceed and *how* museums can and might contribute, and their place within governmentality flows and spaces. Liquid governmentalities takes Foucauldian and post-Foucauldian govermentalities and Beck's world risk society along with others and reformulates them in a systems, assemblage frame.

Liquid governmentalities, and indeed liquid museums, engages a different ontology of the social and different spatial forms—the space of flows—complexity, liquidity, emergence and systems theory informed by Bauman's (2007) liquid modernity, Urry's (2003) global complexity, Latour's (2005) analytic of the social as hybrids of the human and non-human, Deleuze and Guattari's (1987) and DeLanda's (2006b) assemblages. It allows us to view the present and the future in different ways, to observe interactions between multifarious discourses as a creative process in the formation of climate change governmentalities, and to see the future as open and emergent. Liquid governmentalities also views climate change governmentality as interactions of the possible and the actual, and as a process of becoming.

Bauman's (2007) contribution to my re-formulation of Foucault's governmentality to one of liquid governmentalities as an ontological device, liquidifies governmentalites and furthermore liquidifies museums as apparatus. It also solves the problem of Foucauldian circulation based on one modality, power linked to specific rationalities, by emphasising the diverse modes and content of circulation, and movement, complex connectivity and relationality across bodies and entities.

Liquid governmentalities operate within flows—as spaces of energetic possibility exhibiting different intensities and stressors, that are non-linear, open, mobile and unpredictable. The space of flows operates on what Deleuze and Guattari (1987) call the strata. Flows in liquid governmentalities are made up of matter of different forms and shapes including human and non-human components and energy, the building blocks, each with their various properties, capacities and causalities.

It is within these flows that climate change assemblages actualise, or as DeLanda (2006a) suggests catalyse, as stable entities, for example, climate change science with collective properties acting as attractors and re-enforced through positive feedback loops. Here assemblages and their components, link, interact and emerge as well as dissipate.

Components in a liquid governmentality frame are linked by what Deleuze and Guattari (1987) call relations of exteriority, a dynamic machinic process, rather than a process of production. Here components, as material and expressive forms both human and non-human relating to climate change governmentalities, are concept independent. They are not bound within a particular concept as a political rationality such as biopower would suppose, nor are their properties pre-determined, but rather are free to move, interact, assemble and disassemble with others, a creative process in which new and different connections might emerge.

Climate change science, for example, is an assembly of material elements; networks of scientists involved in the techno-scientific surveillance of the planet, greenhouse gases, atmosphere, oceans, Arctic, Antarctic polar ice caps, computers, Kyoto protocol, transnational, national, federal and local government policy, populations, cultural institutions such as museums, expressive elements such as IPCC reports, data, climate modelling and simulations, media images, conversations, meetings, political lobbying and climate change sceptics. The properties of an assemblage such as this emerge through the interaction of these elements and is re-enforced or territorialised by material and expressive elements such as Al Gore's movie *An Inconvenient Truth*[9] for example and deterritorialised by climate change sceptics. Here the concept of change and constant movement can be conceptualised on the basis of this territorialising, assembling and deterritorialising, disassembling process.

One of the advantages of this idea is its ability to see climate change governmentality as mobile assemblages, and as a series of components that link across all scales. Local carbon emissions reduction initiatives link to the larger climate science assemblage to Copenhagen. The IPCC report, for example, plugs into and acts as a catalyst in the emergence of climate change economics through the Stern report[10] and to the Australian Garnault report[11]. The notion of space is not well conceived within the assemblage frame. Here Urry's (2003) distinct spatial patterns come into play in which the movement of matter, components and assemblages can be articulated, traced and scaled through distinct spatial and geographical markers. An assemblage can be thought of and mobilised around a concept, an expressive element or a material form. It has multifarious entry points.

In conceiving climate change governmentalites as assemblages, and their operation and means of analysis, I engage Deleuze and Guattari's (1987) notion of the plane of organisation and the plane of immanence. The plane of organisation is not dissimilar to Foucault's ensemble and the dimension on which his governmentality operates. Foucault views fluidity and unpredictability here and on this plane in terms of the circulation of particular rationalities and power. With a focus on machinic processes, however, the emphasis on subject / object breaks down. Foucault's governmentalities, techniques and risk as a governmentality therefore can be re-thought as both components and assemblages within themselves. The operation of power, calculations, tactics and the analysis of the "conduct of conduct" so central to Foucault becomes just one of the many capacities of the various components of an assemblage and indeed a museum.

By engaging Deleuze and Guattari's plane of immanence a new form of analysis emerges in climate change governmentalities and indeed museum analysis as an assemblage—the process of becoming, in the making, and emergence. That is, the analysis of the capacities and qualities of various components within these various assemblages, including affectual states, emotions, passions, etc. as well as thoughts, desires, beliefs, opinions and concepts. These are all produced virtually. They are in a state of being real but without being actual, as something in the making. These virtualities have an important directive role in any governmental and museum project, and have always been part of a component's duration, but regularly overlooked due to an emphasis on the Foucauldian actual.

Subjectivity is also reworked, no longer connected to disciplinary power and capital, but rather concerns change and movement through affect and desire, also giving rise to territorialisation and deterritorialisation, the strengthening or destabilisation of assemblages. Other key concepts include Deleuze and Guattari's (1987) multiplicites—the analysis of components as a multiplicity—forms and different states, the virtual and the actual on both planes rather than just the multiple.

Liquidifying the museum

Museums as institutional forms both new and old can be viewed as assemblages, liquid museums. The most dominant image of museums as an organisation is one of hierarchy, considered as a whole composed of parts, hierarchically organised and that operate together according to a central plan. That is, as an enclosed space, as a solid fixed entity, analysed as an apparatus in the service of a particular political rationality, and accorded a habitualised ordering of the social (i.e., knowledge / power, discipline and disciplinary effects, sign and interpretation, subject and subjectification, and as a striated relationship as a technology of domination against technologies of self). Rather here we consider museums also as a process, as a heterogeneous, fluid open system always on the move, in the process of becoming and made up of components of material (buildings, people, computers, exhibitions, collections, geographical location, funding) and expressive forms (expressions of legitimacy, trust, authority, networks, dispositions, aspirations, contracts, brand) and as mixtures exhibiting different capacities, linked to other assemblages as part of populations of other organisations, for example, climate change science. Here the organisation can never be reduced to its component parts as functional interdependencies. Rather an organisation can also be thought of in terms of the capacities and relations they embody as social actors with others as an open system, according to the notion of relations of exteriority (DeLanda 2006b, 10–11). Here these relations can be described as scaled, enfolded, interconnected and mobile. The former places emphasis on the actual acting as immobile patterns of thoughts and action inhibiting creativity and change (Patton 2006, 21). By considering institutions as dynamic processes, here relationships between its various components, their connections, interactions and links to wider public culture based on relations of exteriority broadens the ways institutions might be thought of, linked into and considered across various scales and analysed. Institutions might be considered, for example, as processes of, and as an integral part of, financial market assemblages around emissions trading and new energy options as seen through material and expressive elements in the *Energy Quest* and *Climate Change, Our Future, Our Choice* exhibitions. By considering museums as dynamic evolving processes and not as stable bounded entities it also offers a way of creatively exploring other options and alternative, unlikely relationships within other climate change governmentality assemblages beyond specific disciplinary and risk modalities. For example, how can institutions work with non-government organisations and other political entities in mobilising grass-roots movements, considering that they are viewed erroneously as apolitical; what are the opportunities and limits?

In considering museums as assemblages all the same criteria apply. They operate in the space of flows, on both planes. They are also subject to organising and disorganising processes, the latter has the capacity to disrupt the actualisation of processes and the boundaries of organisations (Thamen and Linstead 2006). Institutions for example are re-enforced through policy, notions of trust and legitimacy but also at once deterritorialised through developments such as Web 2.0 that challenge institutions as authoritative content producers. Moreover, it is still possible to study a modern hierarchical organisation as an assemblage given that the relations between its components are relations of exteriority (DeLanda 2006a, 258).

A Foucauldian disciplinary and a Beck risk reading of the museum in climate change governmentality is not precluded but rather thought of in new ways as a mobile and emergent process along with others. Moreover, a Foucauldian reading continues to be useful in interrogating the *why* of a different but also a complementary reading of the museum. At the individual level audiences are conceived as assemblages, as unique, historical and historically contingent, rather than as a one-dimensional rational citizen and as an object of discipline.

Conclusion

In summary, according to the liquid governmentality concept, climate change governmentality becomes a complex system of multi-scaled assemblages within global flows, both actual and in the making, made up of a heterogeneous mix of components comprising hybrids of physical, social and cultural elements, and material and expressive forms, such as actions and statements. Each of these components come together in various combinations, have their own properties, interact, compete, emerge and dissipate within transnational flows.

The combinational richness, openness, mobility and emergent qualities of liquid governmentalities allows the possibility of different governmental solutions to emerge. It allows us to view the present and the future in different ways, to observe interactions between the multifarious discourses as a creative process in the formation of climate change governmentalities, and to see the future as interactions of the possible, the actual, and as a process of becoming. Their capacities to affect and actualise, however, vary.

Conventional thinking in climate change governmentality and the roles of museums in these flows assumes that what is possible is always determined by what already exists. Engaging the idea of liquid governmentalities allows us to look beyond the established ideologies and relations between the state, science, the market and environmental politics to which museums form part, construct and legitimise, to consider, to offer some new alternatives and to see how others might be incorporated into the mix.

References

Bäckstrand K. and E. Lovbrand. 2007. Climate governance beyond 2012: Competing discourses of green governmentality, ecological modernisation and civic environmentalism. In *The social construction of climate change*. Ed. M. Pettenger, 123–141. London: Ashgate.

Bauman, Z. 2007. *Liquid times: Living in the age of uncertainty*. Cambridge: Polity Press.

Beck, U. 1999. *World risk society*. Cambridge: Polity Press.

—. 2006. Living in the world risk society. *Economy and Society* 35 (3): 329–345.

Bennett, T. 1995. *The birth of the museum: History, theory, politics*. New York and London: Routledge.

Cameron, F. R. 2007. Moral lessons and reforming agendas: History, science museums, contentious topics and contemporary societies. In *Museum revolutions. How museums change and are changed.* Ed. S. Knell, S. Macleod and S. Watson, 330–342. London: Routledge.

Cameron, F. R., B. Dibley, C. Farbotko, C. Meehan, L. Kelly. 2009. Findings of the Hot Science, Global Citizens Online survey. Unpublished manuscript, Centre for Cultural Research, University of Western Sydney.

Darier, E. 1999. Ed. *Discourses of the environment.* Oxford, UK and Malden MA: Blackwell.

DeLanda, M. 2006a. Deleuzian social ontology and assemblage theory. In *Deleuze and the social.* Ed. M. Fuglsang and B.M. Sorenson, 250–266. Edinburgh: Edinburgh University Press.

—. 2006b. *A new philosophy of society: assemblage theory and social complexity*. London and New York: Continuum.

Deleuze, G. and F. Guattari. 1972. *Anti-Œdipus*. Trans. R. Hurley, M. Seem and H. R. Lane. London and New York: Continuum.

—. 1987. *A thousand plateaus*: *Capitalism and schizophrenia* Minneapolis, MN: University of Minnesota Press.

—. 1994. *What is philosophy?* New York: Columbia Press.

Ewald, F. 1999. Foucault and the contemporary scene. *Philosophy Social Criticism* 25: 81–91

Foucault, M. 1991. *Governmentality*, trans. R. Braidotti. In *The Foucault Effect: Studies in Governmentality.* Ed. G. Burchell, C. Gordon and P. Miller, 87–104. Chicago, IL: University of Chicago Press.

Giddens, A. 1999. Risk and responsibility. *Modern Law Review* 62(1): 1–10.

Hajer, M. A. 1995. *The politics of environmental discourse: Ecological modernization and the policy process.* Oxford: Oxford University Press.

Harman, G. 2008. 'DeLanda's ontology: Assemblage and realism. *Contemporary Philosophical Review* 41: 367–383.

Kornberger, R. and Ten Bos, R. 2006. In *Deleuze and the social.* Ed. M. Fuglsang and B. M. Sorenson, 250–266. Edinburgh: Edinburgh University Press.

Lanthier, I. and L. Oliver. 1999. The construction of environmental awareness. In *Discourses of the environment.* Ed. È. Darier, 63–78. Oxford, UK and Malden MA: Blackwell.

Latour, B. 2005. *Reassembling the social: An introduction to actor-network theory*. Oxford, New York: Oxford University Press.
Luke, T. 1999. Evironmentality as green governmentality. In *Discourses of the environment*. Ed. È. Darier, 121–151. Oxford: Blackwell.
Oels, A. 2005. Rendering climate change governable: From biopower to advanced liberal government? *Journal of Environmental Policy and Planning* 7 (3): 185–207.
Patton, P. 2006. Order, exteriority and flat multiplicities in the social. In *Deleuze and the social*. Ed. M. Fuglsang and B. M. Sorenson, 21–38. Edinburgh: Edinburgh University Press.
Rutherford, P. 1999. The entry of life into history. In *Discourses of the environment*. Ed. È. Darier, 37–62. Oxford: Blackwell.
Thamen, T. and S. Linstead. 2006. The trembling organisation: Order, change and the philosophy of the virtual. In *Deleuze and the social*. Ed. M. Fuglsang and B. M. Sorenson, 39–57. Edinburgh: Edinburgh University Press.
Urry, J. 2003. *Global complexity*. United Kingdom: Blackwell.

Notes

[1] See http://en.cop15.dk/ for details on COP 15, the United Nations Climate Change Conference in Copenhagen, 7th–18th December 2009. The aim of this conference is to establish a new post-Kyoto protocol on greenhouse emissions.

[2] http://australianmuseum.net.au/Climate-Change/ (accessed 18 December 2009)

[3] http://www.lsc.org/lsc/ourexperiences/exhibits/energyquest (accessed 18 December 2009)

[4] *Waters of Tuvalu: A nation at risk*. Immigration Museum, Museum Victoria, catalogue.

[5] *Waters of Tuvalu: A nation at risk*. Immigration Museum, Museum Victoria, catalogue, 10.

[6] http://survival.scienceof.com/ (accessed 18 December 2009)

[7] *Waters of Tuvalu: A nation at risk*. Immigration Museum, Museum Victoria, catalogue, 9.

[8] Intergovernmental Panel on Climate Change, Working Group II Impacts, Adaptation and Vulnerability,
http://www.ipcc.ch/ipccreports/tar/wg2/index.php?idp=621 (accessed 18 December 2009)

[9] http://www.climatecrisis.net/ (accessed 18 December 2009)

[10] Stern Review on the Economics of Climate Change.
http://www.hm-treasury.gov.uk/sternreview (accessed 18 December 2009)

[11] Garnault Climate Change Review.
http://www.garnautreview.org.au/domino/Web_Notes/Garnaut/garnautweb.nsf (accessed 18 December 2009)

CHAPTER SEVEN

FROM "COLD" SCIENCE TO "HOT" RESEARCH: THE TEXTURE OF CONTROVERSY

MORGAN MEYER

> In the last century and a half, scientific development has been breathtaking, but the understanding of this progress has dramatically changed. It is characterised by the transition from the culture of 'science' to the culture of 'research.' Science is certainty; research is uncertainty. Science is supposed to be cold, straight, and detached; research is warm, involving and risky. Science puts an end to the vagaries of human disputes; research creates controversies. Science produces objectivity by escaping as much as possible from the shackles of ideology, passions and emotions; research feeds on all of those to render objects of inquiry familiar. (Latour 1998, 208–209)

How did the transition from "science" to "research" described by sociologist and philosopher of science Bruno Latour materialise in the world of science museums and science exhibitions? This question lies at the heart of this chapter. My aim is to examine the changing roles of science exhibitions from places of "cold" science, where secure, closed and fixed knowledge is communicated, to places that increasingly engage with "hot", controversial research and open debates. The examples discussed are European ones (from the UK, France and, above all, Austria) and I will be focusing on the display of controversies, rather than on displays that cause controversy. In the first part of the chapter, I discuss how controversies have been studied in the field of science studies. In the second I examine the recent evolution of (some) museums from cold to hot. Then, in the third part, I look at two recent exhibitions that dealt with the controversial nature of science.

I will argue that while the cold way to exhibit science is through stabilised objects, the hot way works through relationality, that is, through highlighting the multiple relationships between visitors and objects, and between the positions of the various contenders in the controversy. The chapter develops the concept of a "texture of controversy" to make sense of exhibition arrangements focused on positions, relationships and processes, rather than stabilised products and objects. In displays about controversies we encounter an object that is open in many ways: to be flexibly interpreted, to be engaged with, to be questioned, to be challenged. Such an object materialises a number of symmetries (and tensions): between various actors, between art and science, and between right and wrong. Two examples from the city of Vienna—the *Gallery of Research* and *the true/false inc.* exhibition—will shed light on how controversial science can be exhibited and some of the challenges of doing so.

The study of controversies in science studies

One way to make sense of the shift from cold science to hot research comes from the field of science studies (often interchangeably referred to as "science, technology and society" or "science and technology studies" or STS for short), a field that studies science within its wider social and cultural contexts. Those who study science from a social science perspective have observed that "science is at least as rich in discordance and uncertainty as it is in the settled harmony of consensus" (Thomas 2009, 131). Hence, the study of controversies has become a tradition in science studies, especially since the early 1980s onwards.

Certainly, evidence suggests that controversies are becoming more common. According to some, there has been a proliferation of controversies in recent years (Nelkin 1992, Brante 1993). What is more, by placing science in its social, cultural and political context, science appears much more open to conflicts and disagreement:

> Focusing on science in its relations with each of them [social realms] almost inevitably introduces elements of controversy. For it thus ceases to be simply a question of how the physical world works, and instead becomes a matter of how groups of people relate to each other—colleagues and rivals, sponsors and governors, reporters, critics and politicians, etc. (Arnold 1996, 74)

In the social studies of science, there has been an increased focus on "science in the making". In his book *Science in Action* (1987), Latour argued that controversies are "a way in" in order to study science in the making (rather than "ready-made" science) (4). Since the late 1970s and the beginning of the 1980s, it has become common in science studies to examine controversies in science and technology, be it food, global warming, nuclear energy or biotechnology. A current research project looks, for instance, into the controversies around flooding.[1]

Besides this, STS, and the social sciences more generally, have witnessed a "participatory turn" in recent years (Lengwiler 2008). In the realms of science this translates into rethinking the relationship between science and society and providing ways and fora for the public to engage in and debate with science and scientists. One example of this from the UK is the House of Lords report (2000) that stresses the need for debate between science and the public. Across Europe, in the past decades a wide array of fora have emerged to cater for just these new debates. To cite but a few: the Cité des Sciences in Paris, which opened in 1986; the first consensus conferences in Denmark in 1989 (Andersen and Jaeger 1999); the first scientific café in the UK in 1998 (Grand 2009); the Science Museum's Dana Centre in London, opened in 2003; and the London Natural History Museum's Darwin Centre, which opened in 2009. Not only is science becoming hotter both in academic texts and in terms of the proliferation of controversies, we also see a proliferation and professionalisation of institutionalised forums for dealing with this new hotness.

Why study controversies?

Why should we study hot topics, such as controversies? Controversies have the advantage that the contending disputants make social processes, which are usually not visible to outsiders, explicit. Processes normally hidden in laboratories or offices are brought into open and public view. In her preface to *Controversy,* Nelkin (1992) writes: "in the course of disputes, the special interests, vital concerns, and hidden assumptions of various actors are clearly revealed" (vii). By bringing these into public view, assumptions that are normally implicit are challenged, routine procedures are scrutinised and arguments are attacked (Brante 1993). It can therefore be rewarding to look at controversies for they are usually "data-rich" events. "Controversy studies make manifest the processes that lead to scientific knowledge and technological artifacts. In the midst of a controversy, participants often make claims about the stakes, strategies, weaknesses, and resources of their opponents" (Sismondo 2004, 100). A similar point is made by Vinck (1995) who argues that controversies are "privileged sites of observation for the sociologist" since they make "appear the different actors, as well as what they mobilise" (116).

In academia, conflicts in and around science have been studied for various reasons, for example, to gain insight into the science policy making process; in order to learn more about the various roles of scientists and non-scientists in policy making; to identify the ways in which the public might participate in decision making; to understand how controversies arise, how they are contained within the scientific community or expand into the public domain, how they are brought to a close, or why they persist; or to analyse the social construction and negotiation of scientific knowledge claims by disputing scientists (Scott et al. 1990, Martin and Richards 1995). Controversies reveal, in other words, the politics and the social fabric of science. From both an epistemological and methodological point of view, controversies therefore have a lot to offer. With this chapter I want to contribute to current debates by offering a more spatial reading of controversies in museum settings, thus further outlining a "geography of controversies" (Allagier 2007, 44).

How to study controversies?

Various approaches have been developed to study controversies (Callon 1981, Markle and Peterson 1981, Engelhardt and Caplan 1987, Dascal 1998).[2] A positivist approach towards investigating controversies accepts the dominant scientific view and takes it as a starting point. Analysing those who are deemed to be "wrong", finding out the reasons why and trying to locate truth—which is usually to be found in (the) nature (of things)—are the guiding principles of this perspective. Another approach, the so-called "group politics approach", looks at the various groups involved in controversies. Here, controversies are seen as a process of conflict and compromise involving various groups contending in a political marketplace (Martin and Richards 1995). Both of these approaches usually assume that science is a relatively neutral endeavour. This is contrary to the approach that has emerged from the sociology of scientific knowledge, of which the central tenet is that what becomes truth is not given by nature, but is rather the product of social processes and negotiations. The principle of symmetry (Bloor 1976) is the key principle for this perspective, suggesting that knowledge claims on both sides of the controversy need to be analysed. The analyst needs to treat the conflicting claims of the disputants symmetrically, or impartially. This means that the sociologist or historian of science must attempt to explain adherence to all beliefs about the natural world, whether they be perceived to be true or false, rational or irrational, successful or failed, in a symmetrical way. For this approach the "truth" or "falsity" of scientific claims is considered as deriving from the interpretations, actions and practices of scientists (Raynaud 2003, 50). The benefit of the principle of symmetry is neutrality. But the problem with this principle—if taken to its full potential—is that it prohibits any evaluative or judgmental role of the analyst. More so, there are instances in which researchers can become a "captive" of a controversy and in which symmetry does not provide a special mechanism for avoiding partisanship (Scott et al. 1990). Furthermore, "[s]ymmetrical analysis is almost always more useful to the side with less scientific credibility and authority. Epistemological symmetry often leads to social asymmetry or nonneutrality" (Scott et al. 1990, 490). Apart from the concept of symmetry, there are two other terms worth mentioning here, "interpretative flexibility" and "closure". The concept of "interpretative flexibility" pertains that facts are debated and interpreted in radically different ways by the parties in the controversy (Pinch and Bijker 1984). The closure of scientific controversies becomes an object of study as well. How do controversies come to an end and what are the processes through which this happens? Mol argues that the closure of controversies is a social phenomenon,

> [s]omething that depends on power, force, numbers. Whatever. Reason is never decisive, the reasonable is an outcome. The closure of a controversy means ... that one truth wins and the arguments in its favour retrospectively become those that are reasonable. (Mol 2002, 93)

Controversies in museums

Controversies are an increasing phenomenon in the museum world, both in terms of displays that cause controversies and in terms of displays about controversies (see, for instance, Cameron 2005). It is not unusual for museums nowadays to display contentious themes. This, however, has not always been the case. Throughout their historical development, museums "came to figure more as graveyards of scientific history, or less morbidly, as its trophy chests" (Arnold 1996, 58). Museums became mausoleums, and the science therein became "frozen" (60). The conservation and display of cold objects to the public, often in glass cases, was to be most closely associated with the common image of a museum. In recent years, however, there has been something of a (r)evolution, in some museums at least, towards displaying more hot topics. Since the mid 1980s, many museums have tried to move away from a rather old model of displaying science (Arnold 1996, Hein 2000).[3] Interactivity in the museum setting is therefore now a widespread trope—both as a discourse and as an architectural and material arrangement (Barry 2001, Witcomb 2006). Consequently, what we have witnessed over the past decades is a change of what museums display, and *how* they do so (Macdonald 2009).

The shift comes in different guises. It comes in a material form, with calls to move from a "conference architecture" towards an "architecture of interaction" (Yaneva et al. 2009). The bodily encounter between visitor and museum changes: a shift from a passive look and a rather immobile encounter towards new forms of interaction and hands-on exhibits. We witness changing paradigms in learning with an increased focus put on interpretative communities (Hooper-Greenhill 2000). Visitors are positioned differently as they are encouraged to interact with displays and increasingly written into museum exhibits (Macdonald and Silverstone 1990, Macdonald 2009). At the same time, there is an ongoing shift from a public understanding of science towards a public understanding of research (Lewenstein and Bonney 2004); and a move towards debating and representing unfinished science (Durant 2004). What is more, the museum object resonates differently: moving from an object of celebration towards a more ambiguous and "messy" object. Overall, therefore, the science museum has become a place increasingly concerned with displaying science in the making, rather than science already done. It has become a place that is not afraid of showing the uncertainties and ambiguities of science. To put it this way: if in the past, the museum displayed cold science, it now increasingly deals with hot research.

An enthusiasm for interactivity is not unique to the twenty first century, having arrived in Europe in the mid-1980s (Barry 2001, 137). Some often-quoted examples of interactive science museums or science centres in Europe are the Science Museum in London and the Cité des Sciences et de l'Industrie in Paris. Also worth mentioning are the Exploratory in Bristol, the Deutsches Museum in Munich and the Zentrum für Kunst und Medientechnologie in Karlsruhe. Let me just give a little more detail about the most well known of these examples here: the Science Museum and the Cité des Sciences. The director of the Science Museum describes its Dana Centre (which opened in 2003) as "a working laboratory for science dialogue"; scientists and members of the public are supposed to meet in order to discuss "on equal terms" (quoted in Salkie 2003). Various, often unexpected, formats are used: puppet shows about genetically modified foods, talk shows, pub quizzes about science, as well as debates open to the general public. The main purpose of the Dana Centre lies in "generating dialogue" (McCallie et al. 2007). Importantly, this dialogue is to be *symmetrical* (Davies et al. 2009).

Another example is the Cité des Sciences in Paris. Here too, a wide array of formats deal with science in the making, for example colloquia to permit citizens to intervene in the debates about the place of the technosciences in society, a blog on which people can debate about the controversies around global warming, and articles about controversial topics on its "Science Actualités" websites. One of the thinkers behind the Cité des Sciences describes it as a science museum of the "third generation"—the first generation displaying old objects, like a natural history museum, and the second generation having moved to the display of themes and scientific disciplines (Gsteiger 1994). The third generation of science museums, Gsteiger argues, brings together various disciplines and is concerned with the relationship between humans and technology and the environment.

There is a rise in efforts to engage the public in scientific controversies (Mazda 2004, 128). In a certain way, hot topics are about perspective, about vision. Put bluntly, there is simply *more to see*. The "Gläserne Forscherlabor" ("glass research laboratory") at the Deutsches Museum is an example where visitors can literally observe researchers in action and ask them questions. A similar example is the Darwin Centre at the Natural History Museum in London, where visitors can also, through glass windows, observe researchers at work in the museum. The museum's "greater epistemic transparency" reveals the urge to "create new performative and generative possibilities between experts and lay people" (Waterton forthcoming). Exhibiting controversies also means that there are *different things to see*. "Topics of global importance that challenge, upset, intrigue and attract are now legitimate areas for museological investigation" (Cameron 2005, 213). Gone is the simplistic linear approach to scientific change; in comes a view that regards controversies as an essential part of science (Mazda 2004, 129–30).

Having discussed in the previous section the benefits of *studying* controversies in science, what are the benefits (and the problems) of *displaying* controversies? It has been argued that exhibiting controversies can make ordinary subjects more interesting (Mazda 2004, 130). Visitors allegedly enjoy hearing other visitors' point of view and hardly see exhibitions as neutral. Exhibiting controversies might thus lead to "a more interrogative spirit in which to approach exhibitions" (Macdonald 1998, 234). More so, by displaying controversies museums can "introduce social issues and raise visitors' awareness of the political, economic, and environmental angles to current scientific debates" (Mazda 2004, 130). Yet, despite these benefits, the display of controversies does not come without its difficulties. The display of "hot topics … has made the business of science museums increasingly difficult and politicised", some argue (Stewart 2004, 43). Another difficulty for museums is that "museum displays traditionally take a long time to put in place and then they themselves remain fixed for a long time: they are thus not well suited to the often rapid position changes of controversy" (Macdonald 2009). After all, museum displays are normally located in buildings, and "buildings, other than artworks and scientific objects, *occupy a stable location*, they are *singular* and they are *used*" making them "mutable immobiles" (Guggenheim 2009, 46).

Finally, communication between the museum and its visitors becomes an issue as well. In their study of an exhibition in London's Science Museum, Macdonald and Silverstone argue that while the "exhibition strategy of single, unambiguous aims and questions may have been [useful] for aiding the clarity of communication, then, it was not necessarily well suited to dealing with controversy, which is essentially a matter of antagonistic or clashing information" (1990, 82). More so, visitors might want or expect "hard facts" in a museum (Macdonald 2009), rather than opinions and insecure knowledge; they too can appear to be "immobile" in the sense of not being familiar with encountering controversies in a museum.

Displaying controversy—two examples from Vienna

The Gallery of Research

I now turn to two exhibitions that explicitly dealt with controversies in science—what we could call "exhibition experiments" (Basu and Macdonald 2007).[4] The first example I want to discuss is the *Gallery of Research*, a gallery that was due to open in 2006 in Vienna. The idea for a gallery of research was first proposed by the then-president of the Austrian Academy of Sciences. A listed building of the University of Vienna was to be renovated to accommodate the exhibition. But the original idea—to have a rather classical display about "great" achievements of Austrian science—was soon transformed into a more daring one that was "staged as an experimental event that aimed at testing different ways of communicating scientific controversies" (Yaneva et al. 2009, 81). Here is how the gallery was described on promotional material to advertise the first pilot event in the (unfinished) gallery:

> The Gallery brings together scientists and artists from Austria and abroad, and engages them in a reflection on alternative ways of communicating scientific results to a larger public of non-experts. The public debate on GM food is only an occasion to talk about new forms of science communication. A purpose-built installation will confront the visitor with the complex ethical, social and political dilemmas of the food controversies (Gallery of Research 2005a).

In a report issued after this first event we further read that the Gallery's purpose was:

> to tackle not only successful scientific findings, but also challenges, unpredictable turns, pitfalls, failures and aberrations in research; to make citizens consider the social, ethical, moral and political implications of these issues, and the ways they become the basis of technological and political decisions. (Gallery of Research 2005b)

The project tried to experiment with a new architecture of display, drawing on art installation and science, in order to create a forum in which various groups could debate, and where art and science could be brought together (Yaneva et al. 2009, 81–82). The exhibition included, amongst other things, a video installation showing an anti-GM demonstration, an art installation with empty tins with labels of GM crops, a wall with keywords (in different size and colour, depending on their significance in the controversy), a timeline of the GM history, and a souvenir card stand. The exhibition was described as a "blend of art installation, original scientific research and live performance aimed at positioning the visitor in a simulated public space, where the variety of protagonists in the debate was made present" (Yaneva et al. 2009, 83). According to the gallery director, the whole installation provided a "setting that is reminiscent to the atmosphere created by the controversy. In addition, the tensions in the debate were also reproduced by the irregular geometry of the installation—one enters the setting and feels the tensions by following the lines on the floor".[5] So how did the audience react to the exhibition? The director of the gallery recalls:

> The audience was curious to see fresh research outcomes presented to a larger audience as the public is used to black-boxed representation, to cold science in the museum spaces rather than to unfinished, tentative results. It is hard to say that there was one public. Rather there were different groupings within the public and they all had different reactions. The nuances of the reactions varied: enthusiasm… curiosity …[6]

However, one of the problems was that the invited scientists were not at ease with their new, more performative roles. In addition, the public, it was argued "is not yet comfortable enough to explore new methods of science communication, based on art installation techniques, simulation and fair, i.e. to stroll, to ask questions to the presenters, to engage in communication, to question … to look behind the scenes" (Yaneva et al. 2009, 86).

The gallery was to open in October 2006, but eventually never did. After the president of the Austrian Academy of Sciences who initiated the project retired, the project did not get the same amount of support, and much less autonomy was given to the gallery.[7] The displays shown during the first pilot event also caused some agitation: the press found the event "strange" and "elitist"; the Austrian Academy of Science wanted the concept to be rethought and did not approve of a reworked version; and, after two years of work, the director of the gallery eventually quit her job and took on a lectureship post at a university.[8] Paradoxically enough, the project to map and exhibit controversies did itself become part of a disagreement.

Die wahr/falsch inc.

A second example, also from the city of Vienna, is the *die wahr/falsch inc.* exhibition (the true/false inc.), developed by a group of four curators. Several of these curators are also involved in the group called Xperiment!. One of this group's previous exhibitions was "Good bye tomato—good morning rice" an exhibition about "golden rice" which was displayed in Zurich and in Vienna (Xperiment 2007). For *die wahr/falsch inc.* exhibition, which took place in summer 2006, the curatorial team selected 11 hot spots,[9] that is, controversial topics (such as doping, the end of oil, life on mars, or allergies—see Figures 7.1 and 7.2).[10] These topics were exhibited as 11 modules in 11 different locations in the city of Vienna, along the pathway of U-Bahn (underground) number 1. Noteworthy are the presence of so-called "Modulbetreuer" (trained persons who were present at—and took "care" of—the different modules during the exhibition in order to engage in a dialogue with the public) and the use of a wide range of formats to interact with the public (guided tours, walks, discussions, roundtables, workshops, activities for schools, etc.). The exhibition was advertised as follows:

> Eleven small exhibitions ... deal with sensitive issues on the relationship between science and society. What is true and what is wrong? "Die wahr/falsch inc." raises questions in the form of images, installations, radio plays and discussions, that put science into question. ... In doing so, "die wahr/falsch inc." does not deliver answers, because science—like art—only ever asks new questions. ... Essential is the role of the visitors who, with their knowledge and their questions, become part of the "wahr/falsch inc." [author's translation]. (Die wahr/falsch inc. 2006)

Figure 7.1. Display from the module *SPeak Oil*, a module concerned with the scarcity of petrol and the question: How long can the world go on like this? (Photomontage by Elisabeth Kopf).

Figure 7.2. Installation from the module *I've Got Something*, a module concerned with the theme of allergies and advertised as follows: "The Allergy Playground invites children and adults to explore caves, delve into anecdotes, comments and facts, build their own allergy story, or simply to play in the mud and pick up what seems interesting on the hill!" (Picture by Dittrich, at the Museumsplatz in Vienna).[11]

The exhibition makers used what they called an "expanded mix of methods" for the displays and wanted to make sure that "during the exhibition, things can happen", i.e., that visitors did not encounter an already finished exhibition.[12] The original catalogue produced for the exhibition, begins with a humorous and playful dialogue:

> TRUE: I am wondering if it was FALSE to do this exhibition. People are confused, and nothing but losses. Science can't be told, not be criticised and not be understood.
>
> FALSE: Not at all, why, then, have we assembled the material here? Readers and viewers make their story in their head, the material is only ever suggestion and enticement.
>
> Thread: Or not. The line between incomprehensiveness and coherence is narrow. Someone has to hold the things together. Without narrator, without an element that connects, yes, without poetry, nothing goes. My life consists of nothing else: holding things together.

> TRUE: Don't forget, we are dealing with science here. Which you can't narrate; you have to understand it. If we don't make this clear for people, then they will think that they are being told fairytales… [author's translation] (Guggenheim et al. 2006, 11)

This passage nicely illustrates some of the characteristics of controversy from a sociology of science perspective: the multiplicity of voices and arguments; the attempt for symmetry between positions, such as right and wrong; the uncertainty and ambiguity of any scientific project. The passage also points to one of the inherent challenges when exhibiting controversy: to try to reveal the messiness and complexity of science without confusing visitors too much. One visitor comment, for instance, holds: "only point of criticism: unfortunately mediation is deficient" [author's translation] (Die wahr/falsch inc. 2006a). "You had to spend some time to engage with the exhibits, that was probably a point of criticism made by those who were looking for easily digestible food, as much as there was enthusiasm from intellectually and artistically ambitious people", one of the curators recalls [author's translation].[13] The weekly Austrian newspaper *Falter* wrote the following comments about the exhibition, which to their mind was "partly more a research project than an exhibition: clever and creative on the level of content, deficient in terms of communication" in which they judged some elements of the exhibition "impressive" and an "eye-opener", but "too demanding" overall.[14] Nonetheless, the final report of the exhibition stresses that overall "interest in the themes that were shown and the discussions that were offered was very big" and that especially teachers and pupils reacted very positively to the exhibition [author's translation] (Die wahr/falsch inc. 2006b, 88).

It proves difficult to compare the *Gallery of Research* and *die wahr/falsch inc.* since they were different events in many respects. For instance, the *Gallery of Research* only resulted in a pilot project that brought together between 40 and 50 invited persons whereas *die wahr/falsch inc.* was an exhibition visited by 13,600 people. There are some commonalities nevertheless. The *Gallery of Research* and *die wahr/falsch inc.* were exhibitions that brought together a range of different actors, stressed the uncertain and unstable nature of science, and had to deal with some difficulties to communicate their message. This reminds us of what Basu and Macdonald (2007) call the second age of experimentalism and experimental ethnographic writing in its "presentation of multiple voices and positions, and as unfinished and contingent" (6–7). While revealing the unfinished character of research and the multiplicity of positions in controversies, these exhibitions operate two kinds of shifts:

from a display that answers to a display that questions and from an exhibition that represents existing matters to an exhibition that performs, creates, and experiments with new ones. These kinds of shifts turn exhibitions into hot situations. "In hot situations", Callon (1998, 260) argues,

> everything becomes controversial ... These controversies, which indicate the absence of a stabilised knowledge base, usually involve a wide variety of actors. The actual list of actors, as well as their identities, will fluctuate in the course of the controversy itself.

Not only did the two exhibitions represent hot situations, they also, to a certain degree, became hot situations themselves, for they did not close or cool down the number and roles of the actors involved, the uncertainty and messiness of the science on display; they even experimented with the very essence of exhibitions, communication with the public.

On the texture and politics of controversy

The examples discussed in this chapter are by no means representative of museums in general, and I am not arguing that all science museums and science exhibitions are now displaying science in the making, rather than already finished science. Yet, it seems fair to say that over the past two decades there has been an increase in the display of controversial topics in science museums and science exhibitions. Furthermore, the examples considered here were temporary ones, which suggests further questioning the temporality of exhibitions about controversies. Are they, by their nature, to be short-lived? Or can we imagine more permanent settings? While the two Viennese exhibitions discussed here were of a short life span, the London Science Museum's Dana Centre is, for example, a more permanent structure. Those museums and exhibitions that do choose to focus on controversies, seem to have a few elements in common: they tend to use new representational strategies, in particular through borrowing and adapting strategies from the art world; there are different things to see and different ways these things are put on display; and they bring together a wider group of actors, thus distributing expertise and authority more widely and more symmetrically.

The display of controversy can be seen as a new way of assembling, as something that is "textured" differently. A controversy is not only something that brings together various actors and interests; it also takes place in a different kind of place and time than the display of cold science. So what can we say about the "texture of controversy"? First, that a controversy typically decentres the single object as the primary focus in an exhibition and concentrates instead on the positions and relationships between actors and objects. The move from cold science to hot research means that a process, rather than a product, is now on display. We could argue that while the cold way to exhibit science is through stabilised objects, the hot way works in relationship: through highlighting the multiple relationships between visitors and objects and between the positions of the various contenders in the controversy. The display of controversy brings together various kinds of methods, actors, materials, etc. Hence, symmetry (and tension) comes in different guises: between art and science; between right and wrong; between various voices, views, interests, etc. The efforts deployed to make exhibitions more symmetrical create an object that is open in many ways: to be flexibly interpreted, to be engaged with, to be questioned, to be challenged, to be misunderstood.

However, there can be a tension between, on the one hand, a well-intended interpretative flexibility of exhibits and, on the other, the inherent authoritative message and durability for which museums usually (are expected to) stand.[15] The two examples from Vienna mentioned in this chapter operated outside the confines of any museum. Yet, the problems that seem to arise with such exhibitions—the difficulty for some visitors to make sense of and engage with the displays—are relevant also for museums. Exhibition makers therefore have to negotiate a position between a politics of moderation and a politics of controversy. In their study about the controversy around food poisoning at the Science Museum in London, Macdonald and Silverstone (1990, 84) observed that the museum took a "moderate line". Perhaps, this holds true for museums in general. Museums, especially science museums, are significantly determined by such a politics of moderation. Conversely, there are many "cooling devices" in a scientific institution such as a museum that eventually frames displays and texts to be moderate and cold. Science and history museums are usually seen as "calm", "safe", "impartial", "civil", and "apolitical" places (Cameron 2005, 2007). These politics of moderation stand in stark contrast to a "politics of controversy", a way to exhibit more commonly found in contemporary art exhibitions.

A final thought. Heat, the common definition says, is a form of energy, not a substance contained in an object; it moves from one place to another in different ways (through conduction, convection, or radiation). A hot exhibition about controversy is all about movement: the bringing together of a mix of methods, of various actors, of different views, of colliding arguments, etc. How can a museum—an institution that is rather immobile, an institution that stabilises, orders, classifies, frames, freezes—

display hot topics, that is, topics that radiate in so many directions? Is a museum well equipped to *contain* any kind of controversies? Or are there some topics that are "too hot to handle"? If so, where and how do we draw the line between hot and *too* hot? These are but some of the burning questions that need further exploration.

References

Allgaier, J. 2007. *Representing science education in UK newspapers: A case study on the controversy surrounding teaching the theory of evolution and creationism in science classes*. PhD Thesis. Milton Keynes: Open University.

Andersen, I. and B. Jaeger. 1999. Scenario workshops and consensus conferences: Towards more democratic decision-making. *Science and Public Policy* 26 (5): 331–340.

Arnold, K. 1996. Presenting science as product or as process: Museums and the making of science. In *Exploring science in museums*. Ed. S. Pearce, 57–78. London: Athlone.

Barry, A. 2001. *Political machines. Governing a technological society*. London: Athlone.

Basu, P. and S. Macdonald. 2007. Introduction: Experiments in exhibition, ethnography, art, and science. In *Exhibition experiments. New interventions in art history*. Ed. S. Macdonald and P. Basu, 1–24. London: Blackwell.

Bloor, D. 1976. *Knowledge and social imagery*. London: Routledge.

Brante, T. 1993. Reasons for studying scientific and science-based controversies. In *Controversial science: From content to contention*. Ed. T. Brante, S. Fuller and W. Lynch, 177–191. New York: State University of New York Press.

Callon, M. 1981. Pour une sociologie des controverses technologiques. *Fundamenta Scientae* 2: 381–399.

—. 1998. An essay on framing and overflowing: Economic externalities revisited by sociology. In *The laws of the markets*. Ed. M. Callon, 244–69. Oxford: Blackwell.

Cameron, F. 2005. Contentiousness and shifting knowledge paradigms: The roles of history and science museums in contemporary societies. *Museum Management and Curatorship* 20: 213–233.

—. 2007. Moral lessons and reforming agendas: History, science museums, contentious topics and contemporary societies. In *Museum revolutions. How museums change and are changed*. Ed. S. Knell, S. MacLeod and S. Watson, 330–342. London: Routledge.

Dascal, M. 1998. The study of controversies and the theory and history of science. *Science in Context* 11: 147–155.

Davies, S., E. McCallie, E. Simonsson, J. L. Lehr and S. Duensing. 2009. Discussing dialogue: Perspectives on the value of science dialogue events that do not inform policy. *Public Understanding of Science* 18 (3): 338–353.

Delicado, A. Forthcoming. Scientific controversies in museums: Notes from a semi-peripheral country. *Public Understanding of Science*.

Die wahr/falsch inc. 2006a. *Die wahr/falsch inc. Presseinformation*. Vienna: Science Communications.

—. 2006b. *Die wahr/falsch inc. Abschlussbericht* (final report). Vienna: Science Communications.

Durant, J. 2004. The challenge and the opportunity of presenting 'unfinished science'. In *Creating connections. Museums and the public understanding of current research*. Ed. D. Chittenden and G. Farmelo, 47–60. Walnut Creek: AltaMira Press.

Engelhardt, H. T. and A. L. Caplan. 1987. *Scientific controversies: Case studies in the resolution and closure of disputes in science and technology*. Cambridge: Cambridge University Press.

Gallery of Research. 2005a. *Mapping controversies. The Gallery of Research / Galerie der Forschung. The case of genetically modified food* (flyer). Vienna: The Gallery of Research.

—. 2005b. *Mapping controversies. The Gallery of Research / Galerie der Forschung. The case of genetically modified food* (event report). Vienna: The Gallery of Research.

Gsteiger, F. 1994. Die vielbesuchte Cite des Sciences in Paris zelebriert lustvoll den Fortschritt. Im Technik-Tempel. *Die Zeit*, September 9.

Grand, A. 2009. Engaging through dialogue: international experiences of Café Scientifique. In *Practising science communication in the information age. Theorising professional practices*. Ed. R. Holliman, J. Thomas, S. Smidt, E. Scanlon and E. Whitelegg, 209–226. Oxford: Oxford University Press.

Guggenheim, M. 2009. Building memory: Architecture, networks and users. *Memory Studies* 2 (1): 39–53.

Guggenheim, M., B. Kräftner, J. Kröll, A. Martos and F. Oberhuber, ed. 2006. *Die wahr/falsch Inc. Eine Wissenschaftsausstellung in der Stadt* (exhibition catalogue). Vienna: Facultas.

Hein, H. S. 2000. *The museum in transition: A philosophical perspective*. Washington: Smithsonian Books.

Hooper-Greenhill, E. 2000. Communication and communities: Changing paradigms in museum pedagogy. In *Museums of modern science*. Ed. S. Linquist, 179–188. Canton: Watson Publishing International.
House of Lords. 2000. *Select committee on science and technology. Third report*. London: House of Lords.
Latour, B. 1987. *Science in action*. Cambridge: Harvard University Press.
—. 1998. From the world of science to the world of research? *Science* 280 (5361): 208–209.
Lengwiler, M. 2008. Participatory approaches in science and technology—Historical origins and current practices in critical perspective. *Science, Technology and Human Values* 33 (2): 186–200.
Lewenstein, B. V. and R. Bonney. 2004. Different ways of looking at public understanding of research. In *Creating connections. Museums and the public understanding of current research*. Ed. D. Chittenden and G. Farmelo, 63–72. Walnut Creek: AltaMira Press.
Macdonald, S. 1992. Science on display: The representation of scientific controversy in museum exhibitions. *Public Understanding of Science* 1 (1): 69–87.
—. 1998. Afterword: From war to debate. In *The politics of display: Museums, science, culture*. Ed. S. Macdonald, 229–236. London: Routledge.
—. 2002. *Behind the scenes at the Science Museum*. London: Routledge.
—. 2009. Exhibition experiments: Publics, politics and scientific controversy. Paper presented at the conference *Exposer des idées, questionner des savoirs*, January 29–30, Université de Neuchâtel.
Macdonald, S. and R. Silverstone. 1990. Rewriting the museums' fictions: Taxonomies, stories and readers. *Cultural Studies* 4 (2): 176–191.
Markle, G. and J. Petersen. 1981. Controversies in science and technology: A protocol for comparative research. *Science Technology and Human Values* 6 (1): 25–30.
Martin, B. and E. Richards. 1995. Scientific knowledge, controversy, and public decision-making. In *Handbook of science and technology studies*. Ed. S. Jasanoff, G. E. Markle, J. C. Petersen and T. Pinch, 506–526. Thousand Oaks: Sage.
Mazda, X. 2004. Dangerous ground? Public engagement with scientific controversy. In *Creating connections. Museums and the public understanding of current research*. Ed. D. Chittenden and G. Farmelo, 127–144. Walnut Creek: AltaMira Press.
McCallie, E., E. Simonsson, B. Gammon, K. Nilsson, J. L. Lehr and S. Davies. 2007. Learning to generate dialogue: Theory, practice and evaluation. *Museums and Social Issues* 2 : 165–184.

Mol, A-M. 2002. *The body multiple: Ontology in medical practice*. Durham: Duke University Press.

Nelkin, D., ed. 1992. *Controversy. Politics of technical decisions*. London: Sage.

Pinch, T. J. and W. E. Bijker. 1984. The social construction of facts and artefacts: Or how the sociology of science and the sociology of technology might benefit each other. *Social Studies of Science* 14: 399–441.

Raynaud, D. 2003. *Sociologie des controverses scientifiques*. Paris: Presses Universitaires de France.

Salkie, R. 2003. Heard the one about peat fibre? *Times Higher Education Supplement*, December 5.

Scott, P., E. Richards and B. Martin. 1990. Captives of controversy: The myth of the neutral social researcher in contemporary scientific controversies. *Science, Technology and Human Values* 15 (4): 474–494.

Sismondo, S. 2004. *An introduction to science and technology studies*. Oxford: Blackwell.

Stewart, L. 2004. *La buona e non mascherata filosofia (or the exhibitionists)*. In *Creating connections. Museums and the public understanding of current research*. Ed. D. Chittenden and G. Farmelo, 29–46. Walnut Creek: AltaMira Press.

Thomas, J. 2009. Controversy and consensus. In *Practising science communication in the information age. Theorising professional practices*. Ed. R. Holliman, J. Thomas, S. Smidt, E. Scanlon, and E. Whitelegg, 131–148. Oxford: Oxford University Press.

Vinck, D. 1995. *Sociologie des sciences*. Paris: Armand Colin.

Waterton, C. Forthcoming. Experimenting with the archive: STS-ers as analysts and co-constructors of databases and other archival forms. *Science, Technology and Human Values*.

Witcomb, Andrea. 2006. Interactivity: Thinking beyond. In *A companion to museum studies*. Ed. S. Macdonald, 353–361, Oxford: Blackwell Publishing.

Xperiment! (B. Kräftner, J. Kröll, and I. Warner). 2007. Walking on a story board, performing shared incompetence. Exhibiting 'science' in the public realm. In *Exhibition experiments. New interventions in art history*. Ed. S. Macdonald and P. Basu, 109–131. Oxford: Blackwell.

Yaneva, A., T. M. Rabesandratana and B. Greiner. 2009. Staging scientific controversies: A gallery test on science museums' interactivity. *Public Understanding of Science* 18 (1): 79–90.

Acknowledgements

Most of this chapter was written during my stay at the Department of Social Studies of Science at the University of Vienna in January and February 2009. I kindly thank all the members of this department. Joachim Allgaier, Maximilian Fochler, Veronika Wöhrer and Michael Strassnig have provided useful comments. Judith Kröll has given a lot of her time to answer my queries and read through earlier drafts. Thanks also to Albena Yaneva for her comments. Special thanks to Sharon Macdonald without whom this chapter wouldn't even exist and to Kate Woodthorpe for proofreading it.

Notes

[1] http://knowledge-controversies.ouce.ox.ac.uk/project (accessed October 7 2009)

[2] Some universities even deliver courses on controversies in science: the Ecole Nationale Supérieure des Mines de Paris (now called MINES ParisTech) has since the early 1980s developed a course called "description of controversies" (see: http://controverses.ensmp.fr) and the University Louis Pasteur (Strasbourg) and the University Diderot (Paris) deliver a course called "staging scientific controversies". Since spring 2009, a course called "mapping controversies" is being taught at 7 institutions across the globe (Sciences Po and MINES ParisTech in France, the University of Oxford and the University of Manchester in England, the Ecole Polytechnique Fédérale de Lausanne in Switzerland, the Ludwig-Maximilians-Universität in Munich, Germany, and the MIT in the US. See: http://www.demoscience.org).

[3] This is, of course, not a general trend. See Delicado's study of science museums in Portugal (Delicado forthcoming).

[4] Bruno Latour himself has been involved in the making of two exhibitions at the Zentrum für Kunst und Medientechnologie in Karlsruhe that brought together science, art, and religion/politics ("Iconoclash" in 2002 and "Making Things Public" in 2005). The two examples discussed in this chapter are relatively closely related to Latour and science studies: the first director of the *Gallery of Research* was a former PhD student of Latour at the Ecole des Mines in Paris; and the Xperiment! group, which was involved in *die wahr/falsch inc.* exhibition, presented some of their work at the "Making Things Public" exhibition.

[5] Yaneva, e-mail communication.

[6] Yaneva, e-mail communication.

[7] Yaneva, e-mail communication.

[8] http://www.falter.at/web/heureka/blog/?p=20 (accessed September 18 2009)

[9] Judith Kröll, Interview. 3 February 2009, Vienna.

[10] Here are the titles (and questions) of the modules: *International Park* (Must researchers stop at state borders when nature doesn't?), *Caring for Body and Soul* (How do people live in Permanent Vegetative State?), *Stained Perception* (They all

see it. It comes and goes. Could it be that it's alive?), *Who with Whom* (Should we prevent hereditary diseases?), *I've Got Something* (Why do more and more children have allergies?), *Gene Doping* (When does performance-enhancing become doping?), *Office for Scientific Flotsam and Jetsam* (How do scientists live as asylum seekers?), *Peer Reviews* (How does one recognise good science?), *SPeak Oil* (How long can the world go on like this?), *Self-Service* (How do we know what we want to ingest?), *Science Traffic* (What are the consequences of scientific globalisation?).

[11] http://www.wahrfalsch.com (accessed October 7 2009)

[12] Kröll, Interview. 3 February 2009, Vienna.

[13] Kröll, e-mail communication.

[14] http://www.falter.at/web/heureka/blog/?p=21 (accessed September 18 2009)

[15] To put it this way: the interpretative flexibility of displays ends where the interpretative rigidity of institutions, or institutionalised practices, comes into play.

CHAPTER EIGHT

A PERSISTENT PREJUDICE

RICHARD SANDELL AND STUART FROST

In 2006 a small exhibition at the British Museum took as its focus a remarkable and beautiful object, a silver vessel, created early in the first century AD, decorated with explicit sexual scenes between males and acknowledged as a masterpiece of Roman art (Williams 2006a). *The Warren Cup: Sex and Society in Ancient Greece and Rome* took an interpretive approach that directly addressed the subject of changing attitudes to sexuality and deployed techniques that sought to encourage visitors to make connections and comparisons between the social mores of the past and present day attitudes to same-sex love and desire. While the Museum's acquisition of this object in 1999 had stirred considerable interest in the UK's press (on account not only of the depictions around the sides of the Cup of a man and youth, and a youth and boy, engaged in sexual acts, but also the price—£1.8m—the museum paid to secure it), the subsequent 2006 exhibition appeared to pass with neither formal visitor complaints nor moral outrage in even the most conservative of newspapers.

This brief example, to which we return later in the chapter, suggests that the capacity for museums to engage with the topics of sex, sexuality and sexual and gender identity is markedly different today compared with even a decade ago. Indeed, further evidence of shifts in thinking and practice is offered by the increasing number of temporary exhibitions in the UK taking same-sex relationships as their main focus. *Hidden Histories* at the New Art Gallery Walsall in 2004 was the first show of its kind to focus solely upon the work of artists who had male same-sex relationships, such as Francis Bacon, Derek Jarman, Jasper Johns and Andy Warhol (Petry 2004). In 2006, both the Museum of London (*Queer is Here*) and the Discovery Museum (*Private Lives, Public Battles*) in Newcastle upon Tyne presented temporary exhibitions to coincide with lesbian, gay, bisexual and transhistory month[1]. In 2007 the Merseyside

Maritime Museum, part of National Museums Liverpool, hosted a small temporary exhibition—*Hello Sailor! Gay Life on the Ocean Wave*—which, through objects, audio reminiscences and filmed interviews with sailors, explored life on board passenger and merchant ships from the 1950s to 1980s.

Although these examples suggest that the topics of sexuality and sexual identity are no longer as taboo as they once were, museum practice nevertheless remains highly uneven with pockets of innovation and experimentation amongst widespread wariness, uncertainty, ambivalence or disinterest. Indeed, the fact that the vast majority of public museums still neglect the experiences of lesbian, gay, bisexual and transgender (LGBT) people is testament to the ongoing sensitivities surrounding the representation of sexual minorities[2].

At this time of change, this chapter seeks to open up the topic for greater debate and to begin to explore some of the issues surrounding the representation of sexual minorities and the challenges and opportunities created by museums' attempts to redress their marked absence in collections and display narratives. What factors account for museums' neglect or avoidance of these communities and topics? What approaches to representation and interpretation have museums begun to deploy in their attempts to develop more inclusive narratives pertaining to sexual and gender diversity? Focusing for the most part on the UK, where there has been an especially marked increase in the number of exhibitions specifically exploring the lives of lesbians and gay men, and drawing on a range of examples, this chapter addresses these timely questions and, in doing so, aims to contribute to broader debates about the potential for museums to engage visitors in thinking about contemporary (often challenging) rights-related issues.

Figure 8.1 *Hello Sailor!* Merseyside Maritime Museum, 2007. Copyright National Museums Liverpool.

A persistent absence

A number of writers have highlighted the paucity of exhibitions that include material pertaining to sexual or gender identities (Műller 2001, Vanegas 2002, Liddiard 2004, Sandell 2002, 2005, 2007). In 2002, drawing on her study of British social history museums, Angela Vanegas (2002), for example, argued that while there were increasing numbers of museums displaying material pertaining to lesbian and gay identities the vast majority of social history museums had still done little or nothing to represent lesbians and gay men within their exhibitions. The curators she interviewed cited the possibility of losing their jobs or funding, the lack of material in their (existing) collections, fear of audience complaints and the perceived inappropriateness of sexuality as a suitable topic for family audiences, as reasons for excluding reference to sexual minorities in their displays. Similarly, a decade ago Klaus Műller suggested that,

> in their label texts museums often struggle with a language that hides as much as it indicates. Rarely do curators include reference to lesbian and gay history in mainstream exhibitions, though extensive historical studies on the topic have been produced in recent decades. (2001, 36)

Nevertheless, the last ten years have seen some significant signs of change. A growing openness to redress the invisibility of lesbian and gay lives within collections and displays is evidenced by the marked increase in the number of exhibitions specifically dealing with issues linked to same-sex love and desire (and, to a lesser extent, gender transgression)[3]. Indeed, more of these exhibitions have opened in the UK in the last five years than in the previous half century (Frost 2008). There is increasing professional and academic interest in the potential for museums to promote human rights and counter prejudice and a minority of specialist museums, whose missions are built around these social goals, have purposefully included material and exhibits intended to challenge homophobia or heterosexism (Sandell 2007). In addition, there is a growing professional and academic debate exploring the issues involved in tackling this relatively uncharted territory (Vanegas 2002, Sandell 2007, Fraser and Heimlich 2008).

Museums then, have become increasingly interested in these topics but nevertheless have a long legacy of suppressing histories of sexuality, particularly those that have challenged heteronormative social mores[4]. Here we present a range of factors that help to explain the persistent and ongoing lack of engagement with (or acknowledgement of) sexual minorities in museums' public programmes.

Changing attitudes: Secret museums and the Victorian legacy

The reaction of museums to representations of sexuality in the art and material culture of ancient Greece and Rome provides a particularly fruitful lens with which to consider the impact of shifting social mores of tolerance towards sexual and gender differences.

In the late eighteenth century, excavations of the towns of Pompeii and Herculaneum, covered in antiquity by the eruption of Mount Vesuvius, began to uncover large quantities of Roman artefacts many of which were decorated with sexually explicit scenes and offered evidence of different attitudes to sexual behaviour. Wall paintings were discovered which revealed men and women engaged in sexual acts in a variety of athletic positions. Similar scenes were found depicted on terracotta lamps and ceramic tablewares. Priapic figures, phallic motifs and symbols were widespread. These archaeological finds offered striking visual evidence suggesting that attitudes to sexuality had varied significantly in the past—a suggestion that the guardians of public morals in the 19th and 20th centuries found particularly challenging (Kendrick 1997). While acquisition by museums of objects such as these was possible—their public display was certainly not. Even storing the material alongside more orthodox material was deemed problematic by some institutions. By 1795 the Herculaneum Museum in Portici, for example, had a ”secret room” for artefacts that were considered obscene (Grant and Mulas 1997). Similarly, by 1823 a ”cabinet of obscene objects” or ”reserved cabinet” had been created in a private room within the Royal Bourbon Museum (Museo Borbonico, the predecessor of today's National Archaeological Museum of Naples) to contain ”disreputable monuments of pagan licentiousness” (de Caro 2000, 23).

By the 1830s, some antiquities at the British Museum were being segregated from the main collections in store and from public displays on the basis of their obscene nature. During the 1840s and 1850s, other accessioned objects joined them in a secret museum, the Museum *Secretum* (Gaimster 2000, 2001). When Sir Charles Newton (Keeper of Greek and Roman Antiquities at the British Museum, 1861–1886) gave a fragment of a Roman cameo vessel (or *skyphos*) that depicted sexual scenes between a male youth and a boy to the Museum, the piece went straight to the obscurity of the Museum *Secretum* (Williams 2006b). It remained there until it was finally formally registered in the collection in 1956. Although formal secret museums were rare the reluctance to acknowledge the explicitly sexual aspects of classical art and other cultures or to make it easily available for study was widespread and continued well into the 20th century[5].

Substantial parts of E. P. Warren's large collection of classical artefacts were acquired by the Museum of Fine Arts, Boston. The Warren Collection of Erotica of Greek, Etruscan and Roman Art was received quietly by the Museum in 1908 but was not officially accessioned and catalogued until the 1950s (Sox 1991). Warren retained, for his own personal enjoyment, the silver cup (now owned by the British Museum) decorated with two scenes of male-male lovemaking. For decades after his death in 1928 the cup remained too controversial to find a buyer. The cup was offered to the Metropolitan Museum of Art in 1953 but was refused entry to the US by customs on the grounds of immorality (Williams 2006b). It was only in 1985, while the cup was still in private ownership, that is was displayed publicly for the first time at the Antikenmuseum, Basel.

Legislative constraints

Homosexuality was illegal in England and Wales until 1967 so it is not surprising that references to love, desire and sex between men were written out of the interpretative and intellectual frameworks of museum and gallery displays in the UK prior to this date. Indeed, the notion that a museum might openly and directly acknowledge to visitors the sexual orientation of, for example, an artist, a prominent local figure or a collector, is unthinkable prior to legalisation of homosexuality and before the gay rights movement gathered momentum.

Although in the decades between 1967 and the present day, social attitudes can generally be characterised as increasingly tolerant and accepting of sexual and gender differences, this trend has not proceeded evenly and without setbacks or complications. The introduction by the Conservative government of the UK, on 24 May 1988, of (the now infamous) Section 28 of the *Local Government Act*, operated to effectively deter local authority museums from addressing lesbian and gay-related themes in their exhibitions. This controversial amendment stated that a local authority "shall not intentionally promote homosexuality or publish material with the intention of promoting homosexuality"[6] and was widely attacked by critics as a discriminatory and regressive piece of legislation. The act was subsequently repealed more than a decade later on 21 June 2000 in Scotland, and on 18 November 2003 in the rest of the UK, and its impact in relation to museums is difficult to evaluate. While Section 28 had a powerful restraining effect on any attempts to increase the visibility of gay and lesbian history and culture in UK museums and galleries, it also undoubtedly had the effect of mobilising and inspiring many individuals, groups and organisations to challenge it. Indeed, some museum services, like Croydon Clocktower (in South London) and the Museum of London succeeded in introducing LGBTQ themed displays at that time[7]. Indeed, the website that accompanied *Pride and Prejudice: Lesbian and Gay London* at the Museum of London included the following statement;

> In 1988, Section 28 of the Local Government Act banned the 'promotion' of homosexuality by local authorities. This was the first piece of anti-gay legislation to be passed for 103 years, and the first to legislate against lesbians. The Museum of London is risking prosecution under Section 28 by putting on this exhibition in which it aims to celebrate the diversity of lesbian and gay life in London, to examine the enduring appeal of London to lesbians and gay men from around the UK and the world, and to explore the systems of oppression that lesbians and gays face.[8]

Nevertheless, challenges to the law of this kind were far from widespread and Section 28 undoubtedly constrained and delayed experimental practice in this area.

Media controversies and censorship

Attitudes to alternative lifestyles, sexualities and sexually explicit imagery have undeniably become more relaxed and tolerant in recent decades, a shift that has been reflected in mainstream popular culture in myriad ways. Nevertheless, the last 20 years has seen a number of controversies over exhibitions containing works with powerful sexual imagery, almost all of which have arisen over contemporary art works in galleries rather than historic objects in museum exhibitions.

The exhibition of a body of photographic work by Robert Mapplethorpe, which included a small number of sexually graphic images of men and sadomasochistic imagery, generated widespread debate in the American media when the Corcoran Gallery of Art in Washington D.C cancelled the exhibition *The Perfect Moment* in June 1989 (Kendrick 1997). The media storm sparked a fierce debate and the funding of the display through the National Endowment for the Arts brought the Federal Government into the furore. Despite the obvious artistic merit and intention of Mapplethorpe's work, the controversy led to the airing of misguided and predictably sensationalist views from some politicians about the use of taxpayers money to fund "homosexual pornography" or "the promotion of homosexuality" (Kendrick 1997, 245–247).

The factors which contribute to media controversies are complex, contingent upon context and not always easy to predict or unravel. In 2001, police raided the Saatchi Gallery in London to investigate photographs in the *I am a Camera* exhibition, that Tierney Gearon had taken of her own young children playing. Some complaints had been made that the nudity in the images was inappropriate and the police investigated to see whether they might contravene the 1978 *Protection of Children Act*, which makes it illegal to take or display indecent photographs of children. Nan Goldin's *Thanksgiving 1999*, an installation of 149 prints, was part of the same exhibition. Some of these photographs depicted drug taking and female and male nudity, including a man holding his erect penis and a post-coital man lying naked on a bed. The fact that Golding's work at that time received no attention from either the media or the police illustrates how sensitivities have changed over time. However, in 2007, the display of Nan Goldin's work at the Baltic Art Gallery in Gateshead was cancelled after controversy about a single print in the installation. The photograph in question was one of her own children titled "Klara and Edda Belly Dancing". The police were asked to investigate whether the picture placed the gallery at risk of prosecution under the terms of the *Protection of Children Act 1978.* After the withdrawal of the photograph by the Baltic Art Gallery the lender of the entire body of work for the exhibition felt the integrity of the artist and her work had been so unfairly compromised that he felt the entire show should close rather than go ahead without the contested image.

Against this background of heightened sensitivity to any artwork that features children (a growing trend that has been described by one art critic as paedophobia—an irrational fear about the threat posed by paedophiles)[9] it is interesting to note that the British Museum's carefully considered approach to interpreting the Warren Cup and its sexually explicit scenes between male youths and boys has not resulted in any hysterical media frenzy. Museum exhibitions and contemporary art galleries clearly operate within different parameters and it appears that both the media and public recognise this. Nevertheless the fear that a museum exhibition might attract hysterical media attention, threatening funding through central or local government, has no doubt been a significant factor in explaining the infrequency with which sex and sexuality have been addressed by museums in the past. Many museums were, perhaps, unwilling to take a risk on curating a display that might have offended key stakeholders or funding bodies. Moreover, a controversial exhibition might significantly damage the career prospects of those involved in its development.

Censorship exists in many forms and is not always the result of external concerns or media controversies. Indeed, more subtle forms of self-censorship regularly occur in museums and galleries, although—due to political sensitivities—this rarely gets reported. There is relatively little research in this area but the authors are aware of instances in the UK where, for example, an LGBTQ themed exhibition—one that contained no sexually explicit material at all—was nevertheless rescheduled by senior museum management to avoid being displayed at the same time as an exhibition aimed at family audiences. Self-censorship of this kind may be easily explained by the fears that museum staff have surrounding controversies but highlight a problematic lack of confidence in engaging with issues relating to LGBTQ rights and hint at a rather more sinister institutional homophobia to which we return later in the chapter.

It is understandable that many individuals and institutions have adopted a cautious approach to curating exhibitions with an explicit LGBTQ theme even though, with carefully and thoughtfully crafted interpretation, these displays have proved unlikely to provoke a media storm on the scale of *The Perfect Moment.* The reaction to exhibitions like *Pride and Prejudice: Lesbian and Gay London* at the Museum of London (1999), *Celebrate!* at Croydon Clocktower (2001) and other exhibitions referenced elsewhere in this chapter, suggest that museums in the UK might be more confident in their ability to successfully represent sexual minorities without attracting negative publicity—and more ambitious in this regard.

Irrelevant, unrepresentative or unprovenanced collections

Museums are extremely varied institutions and the extent to which LGBTQ themes and histories relate both to the mission of an individual institution and its collections differs widely. Science museums, natural history museums, and art and design museums have, of course, very different collections and priorities. The ability of a museum to adopt a more inclusive approach to sexual minorities through object-based displays is clearly influenced—at least in part—by that particular organisation's holdings, the depth of institutional knowledge about its collections and the willingness of its senior management and staff to think creatively about interpretation and audience engagement.

Serious collections-based study of sexuality has not, to date, been a priority for the majority of museums but there are recent signs of change with regard to this. In most cases, knowledge of relevant artefacts within collections is incomplete, which makes it less likely that sexual minorities will be represented in new permanent displays and temporary exhibitions. The assumption that museums do not hold material in their collections that reflect alternative sexualities (or that allow them to be addressed meaningfully) should, we would argue, be challenged and interrogated rigorously. In any case, the notion that LGBTQ histories can only be addressed by museums if they have extensive holdings of objects that have a direct, visible and immediately tangible connection with alternative sexualities in their collections is questionable and arguably betrays a lack of imagination or creativity.

The Museum of London has been one of the most active UK museums in looking at what material it has in its collections and in re-examining its collecting policy. It has disseminated knowledge of its LGBTQ holdings through exhibitions, events and the web[10]. The development of exhibitions like *Pride and Prejudice* at the Museum of London and *Celebrate!* at the Croydon Clocktower (which involved the acquisition of oral testimonies of lesbians and gays) also demonstrates that exhibition development can provide museums with the opportunity to make new acquisitions.

A number of museums have used events programming as part of a strategy for engaging LGBTQ communities and extending debates about alternative sexualities with their audiences. The British Museum, for example, highlighted attitudes to same-sex desire in Renaissance Italy through interpretative panels in their exhibition of Michelangelo's drawings in 2006 and then extended the debate with a lecture in the accompanying events programme. Historian Michael Rocke drew on his groundbreaking research (Rocke 1996) to explore Michelangelo's life and work in relation to the culture of same-sex desire in Florence.

The use of layered interpretation also offers opportunities for a more nuanced approach to engaging with these issues. The *Road to Byzantium* exhibition at Somerset House included a single bust of Antinous accompanied by a standard object label (Athaus and Sutcliffe 2006, 139). The restrictions of the label format limited what could be said about the object, however the provision of a free hand-held audio-guide allowed the curators of the exhibition to provide a thoughtful discussion about Hadrian and Antinous' relationship as lovers. Through the audio-guide, visitors were presented with the opportunity to learn more about the culture of same-sex relationships in ancient Greece.

Institutional and individual homophobia

The number of recent exhibitions that have represented LGBTQ communities or addressed LGBTQ themes could be taken as an indication that it has become easier for museum staff to successfully propose and develop these types of display. However, it would be unwise to assume that sexual identity has completely lost its power to provoke strong, negative and hostile reactions—*within* the institution as well as with external constituencies. Exhibition development is a complex process that often requires input from a range of individuals, each with their own views, values and perspectives. A number of writers have discussed institutional conservatism (Liddiard 1996, Vanegas 2002, Sandell 2007) and informal discussions at professional seminars and conferences have revealed anecdotal information (generally not publicly available given the legal and political sensitivities involved) related to individual practitioners' reluctance to work on LGBTQ themed projects in their employing museums. Rather worryingly, the authors are aware of more than one publicly-funded museum where a member of staff has expressed a desire not to work on an LGBTQ themed project because of their religious beliefs.

The development of exhibitions that acknowledge sexual minorities has very often required the initiative, drive and commitment of determined and resilient individuals. Michael Petry, for example, has written at length of the difficulties he encountered in curating *Hidden Histories* at the New Art Gallery Walsall in 2004. The exhibition included artwork solely by male same gender lovers (Petry 2004). Petry's account describes the difficulties he encountered with the local council who owned the Museum building and who insisted on having final approval of each artwork that was to be included and the label caption that accompanied it. Most of the works were on open display to all but a small number were restricted to a room where children under 15 had to be accompanied by an adult and three other works (including a drawing by David Hockney) were displayed in the Library where access could be controlled and restricted to visitors aged 18 and above.

Michael Petry's original title for *Hidden Histories* at Walsall Art Gallery was to be *Mad About the Boy*, the title of a Noel Coward song where Coward sings in heterosexual terms that were understood rather differently by same-sex lovers. Petry intended the title to be a reference to a secret being known but not directly spoken about or confirmed. However, Petry felt that, "ugly stereotypes about same-sex lovers being paedophiles was at the heart of the name change, regardless of the fact that the song was not about children, nor were there any images of children in the exhibition" (Petry 2007, 125). A conceptual work by Gonzales-Torres that consisted of an arrangement of wrapped sweets in the corner of the gallery that shared the same weight as the artist's lover, was excluded "as the [Council] official thought it would encourage paedophilia". The local newspaper, the *Walsall Express and Star* (April 5, 2004) ran a predictably hysterical story—*Fears as 'porn' art planned for gallery*—but despite all these difficulties the show enjoyed a successful run (Petry 2007). For Petry, the Council's behaviour and censorship of the exhibition was a clear example of institutional homophobia.

Audience responses (real and imagined)

Curators and managers sometimes invoke the reactions (both real and imagined) of audiences as reasons for not addressing issues that they believe may cause offence. In reality, audience responses are, of course, highly variable and sometimes unpredictable.

In an investigation of the ways in which visitors responded to exhibitions purposefully designed to counter prejudice, Sandell often found entirely different (sometimes opposing) responses by visitors to the same part of an exhibition. While many visitors to the Anne Frank House in Amsterdam, for example, expressed support for the museum's temporary exhibition, which highlighted contemporary forms of discrimination against a range of groups (women, faith groups, disabled people and gays and lesbians), one visitor nevertheless took exception to the exhibition's support for lesbian and gay rights to equality, writing in the museum's comments book "What a shame that you would manipulate the tragedy that was this girl's life into a defense [sic] of deviant sexual behaviour" (Sandell 2007, 95).

While the organisational culture in many museums remains risk averse and generally uncomfortable with receiving complaints and attracting public and media controversy, there is nevertheless increasing interest amongst practitioners and museum studies researchers in the value of actively and *purposefully* engaging visitors in debates around contentious topics (Sandell 2007, Cameron 2007), an approach that will inevitably generate responses such as those expressed at the Anne Frank House. From this perspective then, controversy might be viewed as not, in itself, entirely undesirable, but rather a part of the process of promoting more progressive understandings of difference.

Taking a clear stand on moral issues, especially those (such as gay rights) that have the capacity to invoke opposition from powerful constituencies, requires careful handling and a strong sense of organisational mission and purpose. Nevertheless, there are a growing number of examples of institutions that have successfully negotiated this field of practice and clearly (directly or indirectly) articulated their support for equal rights for sexual minorities without generating a media circus. Sandell (2007), for example, has discussed the strategies put in place at the United States Holocaust Memorial Museum from 2004, which enabled them to develop, present and tour the exhibition, *Nazi Persecution of Homosexuals 1933-1945*, even though public debates about the rights of sexual minorities in the US were particularly prominent at the time. In the preceding year, gay marriage had become one of the 'hot-button' issues in the Presidential election campaign and news media regularly featured stories in which gay rights activists were pitted against Republicans and Christian conservatives.

Although the evaluation of the exhibition, *The Warren Cup: Sex and Society in Ancient Greece and Rome*, did not specifically examine visitors' attitudes towards homosexuality, it nevertheless found that, what was arguably one of the more experimental, imaginative and challenging approaches to acknowledging differences presented by the British Museum, was also the most popular of a series of exhibitions held in that gallery up to that point (British Museum 2006). Moreover, it is interesting to note that Sandell's prior study (2007) evidenced the agency of such interpretative approaches in framing the ways in which visitors and society more broadly, perceived and debated rights-related issues.

Inclusive futures?

This brief survey of factors which have militated against the representation of sexual minorities in museums suggests that contemporary practitioners have inherited a difficult legacy from their nineteenth and twentieth century predecessors. Oppressive social mores—sometimes embodied in discriminatory legislation—combined with anxieties surrounding media controversy and censorship, have operated to restrict experimentation until quite recently. Where historic objects that might attest to gender and sexual diversity have survived in museum collections, their study has been discouraged by often inappropriate and anachronistic associations of sexually explicit material with modern notions of pornography or obscenity; or hampered by inadequate cataloguing that has failed to capture the object's significance.

Today, an increasing number of display initiatives are challenging the notion that museums have simply been unable to address attitudes to sex, sexuality and gender through exhibitions because of a lack of material in institutional collections. Moreover, a recent survey conducted by Proud Heritage which encouraged UK museums to revisit their collections to reveal material linked to LGBTQ histories, revealed wide ranging and often surprising holdings in diverse types of collection (Gilbert 2006, 2007). It also confirmed that, despite recent developments, many challenges remain:

> Very few museums or galleries have really addressed the enormity of their failure to properly collect, frame and interpret the lives and experiences of LGBT people … The number of institutions that have integrated any material into their permanent exhibitions still remains extremely low. (Gilbert 2007)

We would argue that relevant objects can be found in many collections around the world but where they are displayed they are often inadequately and inappropriately interpreted in galleries leaving visitors with little, if any, appreciation of their significance to LGBTQ history.

The decriminalisation of homosexual acts in England and Wales in 1967 reflected a substantial change in social attitudes to same-sex relationships but the long legacy of stigmatisation and omission, could not be redressed easily or quickly. Despite the liberalisation of attitudes to sex and sexuality, exhibitions that explicitly addressed either in their interpretative frameworks were rare throughout the 1960s, 70s and 80s. While publications exploring sex and sexuality through objects have became more widespread, public exhibitions exploring similar themes remained infrequent and unusual. References to relationships between same-sex partners in exhibitions continued to be omitted from the biographies of LGBTQ artists, and descriptions of their work continued to be misrepresented through what Michael Petry has termed a heterosexual lens.[11] From the late 1990s onwards, the inclusion of themes related to sex and sexuality, and the acknowledgement of same-sex histories and biographies within the interpretative frameworks of temporary exhibitions have become more common. Temporary exhibitions that have addressed aspects of sex and sexuality as their main theme have also become more frequent and, in fact, most of these have focused entirely on LGBTQ (rather than heterosexual) experiences. There are numerous reasons for this trend.

Central and local government has encouraged museums to continue to become more focused on reaching under-represented or marginalised audiences by acknowledging diversity and difference in their exhibitions and displays. The LGBTQ community has been particularly effective in encouraging museums to represent their interests and to adopt a more inclusive approach. Organisations like Proud Heritage, Pride Legacy and Our Story Scotland have played an influential role in encouraging and helping museums to adopt more inclusive approaches and the recent establishment of LGBTQ History Month has provided a focus for planning for those museums who have embraced it. Without the commitment of LGBTQ staff within museums and galleries and colleagues who share their values and perspectives on social justice issues, many of the exhibitions that are referred to in this chapter would not have come to fruition.

The last part of the chapter takes a closer look at three different exhibitions presented by UK museums and galleries in recent years, each of which represents different approaches to engaging with the theme of sexuality and same-sex love and desire.

Queer is Here

Queer is Here at the Museum of London (4 February–5 March 2006) reflects a number of common characteristics of recent exhibitions about sexual minorities. The display focused on modern LGBTQ history and placed a particularly strong emphasis on lesbians and gays with transgender and bisexual experience having a less prominent role. The exhibition was timed to coincide with LGBTQ month, was on a relatively small scale, and included comparatively few objects.

The exhibition was constructed around a large free-standing two-sided graphic panel. One side featured a "gay history time line" highlighting key moments in the history of London's LGBTQ communities from the passing of the *Sexual Offences Act* in 1967 to the passing of the *Civil Partnerships Act* in 2004 to the present day. The other side was divided into sections with headings such as Public Life, Homophobia and Bullying, Civil Partnerships, and The Rise of the Pink Pound. It highlighted gay activism and the campaign for equality, coming out, homophobia and bullying in schools, as well as the experience of gay people in the workplace and in the public eye.

Figure 8.2 *Queer is Here!* Museum of London, 2006. Copyright Museum of London.

The display featured a limited number of objects from the Museum's collection, grouped together in small display cases to illustrate some of the exhibition's main themes. Black and white photographs by Peter Marshall, documenting over ten years of Gay Pride events, were presented in rotation via a small TV screen. The exhibition included oral history recordings from the Museum of London's oral history collection and the Hall Carpenter Archive. These extracts were provided to individualise the displays and to reflect the impact of legislation on the lives of real individuals.

The exhibition reflected the Museum of London's strategic aim to explore and reassess cultural diversity through the Museum's collections and to reflect more effectively London's culturally diverse communities. The exhibition gave London's LGBTQ community a prominent position in the Museum building and demonstrated a clear and genuine commitment towards representing London's diversity (McIntyre 2007).

Temporary exhibitions such as *Queer is Here* play an important role in redressing the absence of LGBTQ narratives in museums. Though temporary, they are often relatively high profile, prove effective in engaging LGBTQ communities (as both co-producers and visitors) and provide a platform through which the institution can directly and explicitly advocate support for equal human rights. However, it is helpful to acknowledge the potential limitations of this kind of approach. Historian Robert Mills has argued that the interpretative frame deployed in *Queer is Here*—which documented manifestations of discrimination and sexual repression against a "narrative of progressive outness, visibility and liberation"—privileged certain kinds of experience over others (Mills 2008, 43). He further argued that:

> … an unquestioning reliance on the outness-repression dialectic, which disguises the complex and varied ways in which sexuality operates historically, potentially restricts the stories that can be told. It is a script that pushes certain dimensions of queer experience to the background, notably sexualities and gender identifications that refuse to chart a neat course to or from homosexual identity and being.

For Mills, exhibitions of this kind potentially reinforce the "homo-hetero binary calculus", the idea that individuals are either completely homosexual or entirely heterosexual. Moreover, the terms "heterosexual" and "homosexual" originate in the nineteenth century and can be problematic categories to apply to the more distant past where understandings of same-sex love and desire were sometimes very different. The approach taken by exhibitions such as *Queer is Here*, Mills suggests, may inadvertently reinforce visitors' assumptions about sexual identity rather than operate to challenge underlying assumptions about LGBTQ people or history.

The Warren Cup—Sex and Society in Ancient Greece and Rome

Definitive confirmation that the era of the secret museum was over at the British Museum came in 1999 when the Museum acquired a beautiful Roman silver cup made between AD 5 and 15 for £1,800,000. The small vessel, around 11cm in height, has become known as the Warren Cup after previous owner Edward Perry Warren. The exterior of the cup features two scenes, each of which depicts a pair of males engaged in penetrative sex (Williams 1999, 2006b). One of the two scenes features an older male who is distinguished by a beard and wears a wreath. He is the active partner. His passive partner is clearly younger, a beardless youth. On the opposite side of the cup, the active lover is a beardless youth, crowned with a wreath, while his partner is clearly a boy. The figures are probably Greek. The musical instruments, wreaths and mantles, like the beard, have been interpreted as signifiers of a Hellenised setting. These scenes were created by a highly skilled artist who raised them by hammering them into the thinner outer-casing of the Cup.

Between May and July 2006 the Cup was the centrepiece of a small exhibition, *The Warren Cup: Sex and Society in Ancient Greece and Rome*. The display occupied only a single room but it had a prominent location to the right of the main Museum entrance. One aim behind the series of small exhibitions held in this space was to explore different, experimental approaches to interpretation with a view to informing display practices that might subsequently be utilised in permanent displays throughout the building. The cases included a small number of objects, which were more heavily interpreted than those in the permanent galleries. Fewer objects encouraged visitors to engage more deeply with each in turn and with the Warren Cup in particular.

Figure 8.3 *The Warren Cup: Sexuality in Ancient Greece.* British Museum, 2006. Copyright The Trustees of the British Museum.

The display explored ancient Greek and Roman views of sexuality. The displays included Greek ceramics to illustrate attitudes to sex and sexuality in ancient Greece, and to highlight how influential these ideas were in the culture of ancient Rome. The cases included objects which allowed the curators to raise questions about attitudes in the Greek and Roman world to love between women, as well as love between men and heterosexual lovemaking (Williams 2006b, 7). Unusually for the British Museum, the interpretation offered opportunities to explicitly link the Cup's significance to the more recent past and to present day attitudes to same-sex relationships in the West.

The exhibition challenged or destabilised modern assumptions that sexual behaviour and attitudes have always been the same across culture and across time. A reproduction of an eighteenth century Dutch print, which we would view today as homophobic, highlighted more recent European attitudes to same-sex relationships. A still of a scene from the film, *Brokeback Mountain*, one of very few Hollywood films to focus on love and desire between male characters, created the opportunity for visitors to reflect on current attitudes to gay relationships. A reproduction of a Japanese print from 1830–1840 was used to highlight that sexual relationships between men had been accepted in Japan's past. A publication, lectures and a series of gallery talks supported the display and explored more widely attitudes to same-sex desire in ancient cultures.

Family Album

A recent temporary exhibition at the Graves Gallery in Sheffield (10 January–21 March 2009) explored the meaning of "family" in contemporary society through a selection of works that showed how family life has been represented in art from the 1600s onwards. The painted portraits included one of Sir Walter Raleigh and his son dating from the early seventeenth century and a painting of the five children of King Charles I, after Sir Anthony van Dyck. Photographs included one of Ringo Starr's wedding to Barbara Bach and an informal photograph of Sir Winston Churchill with his wife and grandchildren. The exhibition provided an opportunity to discuss changing notions of family in response to trends such as increasing divorce rates and recent landmark legislation, such as that enabling civil partnerships for same-sex couples in Britain.

Less than a decade ago, the vast majority of museum displays exploring the issue of family would have excluded any reference to same-sex relationships. In *Family Album*, however, the inclusion of an oil portrait of Sir Peter Pears and Sir Benjamin Britten by Kenneth Green allowed the interpretative framework of the exhibition to include same-sex relationships on equal terms. The exhibition label reads;

> **Sir Peter Pears and Sir Benjamin Britten, 1943**
> **Kenneth Green**
> **Oil on canvas**
>
> This portrait shows the composer, Benjamin Britten (1913-76) with his life-long partner, musical collaborator and inspiration, Peter Pears (1910-86). They met in 1934 and the first of Britten's ten operas, 'Peter Grimes' (1945), was written for Pears.
>
> They established the Aldeburgh Festival together in 1943 and founded the Britten-Pears School for Advanced Musical Studies in 1972.

Male homosexuality was illegal in Britain until 1967, when it became permitted for consenting adults over 21 unless they were in the armed forces. The age of consent was lowered to 18 in 1994. The Civil Partnerships Act of 2004 gave same-sex couples legal recognition and similar rights to married heterosexual couples.

National Portrait Gallery, London

Visitors to the exhibition were invited to offer their own response to the question "What does family mean to you?" by writing or drawing on a blank postcard and then adding the card to a wall-mounted display near the entrance. This approach encouraged visitors to actively reflect on their own ideas about family and also acknowledged that concepts of family are personal, diverse and sometimes contested. The inclusion of this single painting with a carefully written label significantly altered the approach of the exhibition. It demonstrates that a more inclusive approach to sexual minorities does not always require a large number of objects or a separate, specifically-themed exhibition. This approach to interpretation, which potentially permits multiple forms of difference to be represented and often provides opportunities to engage visitors in debates relating to contemporary issues, it has been argued, can powerfully operate to inform and enrich the ways in which visitors think about difference (Sandell 2005, 2007).

The acknowledgement of alternative sexualities within mainstream exhibitions with a broader more general theme like *Family Album* is becoming more common. Like *The Road to Byzantium: Luxury Arts of Antiquity* (Somerset House), the *Hadrian* exhibition at the British Museum acknowledged the sexual relationship between the emperor and Antinous and contextualised it in a meaningful way. Recent exhibitions about Simeon Solomon at the Birmingham Museum and Art Gallery (1 October 2005–15 January 2006) and David Hockney at the National Portrait Gallery (12 October 2006–21 January 2007) in London included relevant information about the impact and influence of the artists' sexuality on their work and careers. The recent *Jack Kerouac: Back on the Road* exhibition (ended 28 January 2009) at the Barber Institute of Fine Arts in Birmingham acknowledged the homosexual experiences of the Beats and also the way in which passages that described same-sex encounters in Kerouac's original scroll typescript were revised and moderated for the publication of the novel *On the Road* in 1957.

Prejudice in decline?

The recent exhibition at the Barbican Art Gallery, *Seduced: Art and Sex from Antiquity to Now* (12 October 2007–27 January 2008) arguably went as far as any museum or gallery in the UK has gone in terms of displaying sexually explicit artwork and material. The exhibition included photographs and films from the collections of the Kinsey Institute that depicted explicit sexual acts, including scenes of intercourse between men (Wallace 2007). Although the exhibition attracted a great deal of media interest this was, for the most part, characterised by serious discussion and debate rather than a hysterical media frenzy about 'pornography'. The exhibition was limited to visitors aged 18 and over and accompanied by warnings which minimised the risk of visitors being shocked or surprised by what they encountered[12]. However, the fact that this exhibition took place without major incident could be taken as an indication of how far attitudes have changed to sexually explicit material culture. The exhibiting of material illustrating sex between men, such as that included in *Seduced*, would not have been possible even a few years ago.

Signs of an increasing openness within the museum profession to engaging with LGBTQ themes and the increasing use of interpretative frames that (explicitly or implicitly) articulate support for the rights of sexual minorities are encouraging. It is, however, worth remembering that the inclusion of sexual minorities in permanent displays is still relatively rare and the majority of institutions still present exclusively heteronormative narratives in which sexual and gendered difference are denied. In some instances this may be the result of what might be understood as passive conservatism—a belief that museums should be free to operate in ways which take no account of shifting social attitudes and contemporary inequalities—while in others, there may be more worrying factors at play. Indeed, while attitudes towards sexual minorities may have become more open, accepting and respectful in general, it would be naïve to suggest that these are universally held.

In December 2005 a questionnaire survey was sent out to members of the UK's Museums Association by the organisation Proud Heritage, asking participants to identify material within their institution's collections which had links with the lives and histories of gay, lesbian, bisexual or transgender individuals and communities. Amongst the many positive responses received, the following was also returned.

> What is there to be proud of?
> a. Bringing AIDS to the world
> b. Destroying families and marriages

c. Population decline
d. Dividing church communities
e. Bringing down the wrath of Islam on the west?

What made this viciously homophobic anonymous response all the more worrying was that it came not from a random member of the public but from an individual active within the museums profession. The response continued:

> Please stop forcing your disgusting sickness in our faces. This isn't what I pay my MA [Museums Association] subscription for—the Association is to support the Museum profession, not to promote filthy perversions among the young and impressionable.

This disturbing response stands at odds with the more progressive developments that have taken place within museums in recent years. However, it serves as a reminder that although museums have an important role to play in actively shaping attitudes and challenging prejudice, they are also—to a degree—reflective of dominant social mores and can be constrained by them. Just as prejudiced individuals can be found within the communities that are served by museums; they can also be found within the museum itself.

References

Althaus, F. and M. Sutcliffe. 2006. *The road to Byzantium.* London: Fontana.

British Museum. 2006. *Warren Cup: Sex and society in Ancient Greece and Rome—Visitor responses. Executive summary.* London: Unpublished.

Burdon, N. 2000. Exhibiting homosexuality—Pride and prejudice: Lesbian and gay London. *The Newsletter of the Social History Curators Group—SHGC News*, 16 (April): 13–15.

de Caro, S. 2000. *The secret cabinet in the National Archaeological Museum.* Napoli: Electra.

Cameron, F. 2007. Moral lessons and reforming agendas: History museums, science museums, contentious topics and contemporary societies. In *Museum Revolutions.* Ed. S. Knell, S. MacLeod and S. Watson, 330–342. London and New York: Routledge.

Donnelly, J. 2003. *Universal human rights in theory and practice.* Ithaca and London: Cornell University Press.

Fraser, J. and J. E. Heimlich. 2008. Where are we? *Museums and Social Issues: A Journal of Reflective Discourse* 3 (1): 5–14.

Frost, S. 2008. Secret museums: Hidden histories of sex and sexuality. *Museums and Social Issues: A Journal of Reflective Discourse* 3 (1): 29–40.

Gaimster, D. 2000. Sex and sensibility at the British Museum. *History Today* September: 10–15.

—. 2001. Under lock and key—Censorship and the secret museum. In *Sex*. Ed. S. Bayley, 124–139. London: Cassell Illustrated.

Gilbert, J. 2006. National pride. *Museums Journal* February. 23.

—. 2007. Comment. *Museums Journal* October: 19.

Grant, M. and A. Mulas. 1997. *Eros in Pompeii: The erotic art collection of the Museum of Naples*. New York: Stewart, Tabori and Chang.

Kendrick, W. 1997. *The secret museum.* London: University of California Press.

Landesman, C. 2007. Naked fear on display. *The Sunday Times,* September 30, News review, 7.

Liddiard, M. 1996. Making histories of sexuality. In *Making histories in museums*. Ed. G. Kavanagh, 163–175. London: Leicester University Press.

—. 2004. Changing histories: Museums, sexuality and the future of the past, *Museum and Society* 2 (1): 15–29.

McIntyre, D. 2007. What to collect? Museums and lesbian, gay, bisexual and transgender collecting. *The International Journal of Art & Design Education, Special Issue: Lesbian and Gay Issues in Art, Design and Media Education* 26 (1): 48–53.

Mills, R. 2008. Theorising the queer museum. *Museums and Social Issues*: A *Journal of Reflective Discourse* 3 (1): 41–52.

Műller, K. 2001. Invisible visitors: Museums and the gay and lesbian community, *Museum News* September/October: 34–39, 67–69.

Petry, M. 2004. *Hidden histories—20th Century males same sex lovers in the visual arts.* London: Art Media Press.

—. 2007. Hidden histories: The experience of curating a male same sex exhibition and the problems encountered. *The International Journal of Art & Design Education, Special Issue: Lesbian and Gay Issues in Art, Design and Media Education,* 26 (1): 119–128.

Rocke, M. 1996. *Forbidden friendships—Homosexuality and male culture in renaissance Florence*. New York: Oxford University Press.

Sandell, R. 2002. Museums and the combating of social inequality: Roles, responsibilities, resistance. In *Museums, society, inequality.* Ed. R. Sandell, 3–23. London and New York: Routledge.

—. 2005. Constructing and communicating equality: The social agency of museum space. *Reshaping museum space: Architecture, design, exhibitions*. Ed. S. Macleod, 85–200. London and New York: Routledge.

—. 2007. *Museums, prejudice and the reframing of difference*. London and New York: Routledge.

Sox, David. 1991. *Bachelors of art. Edward Perry Warren and the Lewes House brotherhood.* London: Fourth Estate.

Vanegas, A. 2002. Representing lesbians and gay men in British social history museums. In *Museums, society, inequality*. Ed. R Sandell, 98–109. London and New York: Routledge.

Wallace, M., M. Kemp and J. Bernstein. 2007. *Seduced. Art and sex from antiquity to now*. London: Merrell.

Williams, D. 1999. The Warren Silver Cup. *British Museum Magazine* 35: 28.

—. 2006a. Cup of love. *British Museum Magazine* 54: 7.

—. 2006b. *Object in focus: The Warren Cup* London: British Museum Press, 2006.

Notes

[1] See http://www.lgbthistorymonth.org.uk/ for further information (accessed 10 March 2009)

[2] The language used to explore these topics is fraught with sensitivities and different terms are used in different settings. "Queer" is used by some writers and activists to encapsulate the widest array of differences and individual identities related to gender, sexuality, desire and expression (Fraser and Heimlich 2007). "Sexual minorities", though not unproblematic, is a more inclusive term than gay or lesbian, "being open to any group (previously, now, or in the future) stigmatised or despised as a result of sexual orientation, identity, or behaviour" including gay men, lesbians, bisexuals and transgender people (Donnelly 2003: 229). The acronym LGBT (or sometimes GLBT or GLBTQ) is widely used by community groups and organisations campaigning for equal rights for lesbian, gay men, bisexual and transgender individuals.

[3] Sandell (2007) specifically highlights the limited presence of representations of transgendered people, despite the growing number of museum projects that draw on lesbian and gay experiences.

[4] Heteronormativity refers to contexts in which alternatives to the heterosexual norm are either not acknowledged or where they are regarded as unacceptable deviations (Fraser and Heimlich 2008, 9).

[5] Formal secret museums were not common because other museums had fewer objects to deal with and these could be easily confined in a keeper's office. Before and after accession objects were sometimes subject to censorship through the

removal or covering of the genitals. Sexual organs depicted on Greek vases were occasionally painted over. Emasculation of figures in ethnographic collections and even taxidermy specimens is also documented.

[6] www.opsi.gov.uk/acts/acts1988/Ukpga_19880009_en_5.htm (accessed 10 March 2009)

[7] *Celebrate* in *Lifetimes* at the Croydon Clocktower ended Sunday 25 November 2001. *Pride and Prejudice* ran at the Museum of London 2 July–22 August 1999 (Burdon 2000).

[8] www.museumoflondon.org.uk/archive/exhibits/pride/index.htm (accessed 10 March 2009)

[9] Cosmo Landesman, "Naked fear on display," *The Sunday Times*, September 30th 2007, 7.

[10] See "Reassessing what we collect—The LGBT Community in London" at: www.museumoflondon.org.uk/English/Collections/OnlineResources/RWWC/Themes/1161/ (accessed 10 March 2009)

[11] Petry (2004) provides a number of more recent case studies that demonstrate the different ways in which same-sex histories have been written out of exhibitions and catalogues.

[12] Signs at the entrance to the gallery read "Over 18s Only. The exhibition contains work of a sexually explicit nature including images of heterosexual and homosexual intercourse."

PART TWO:

ENGAGEMENT

CHAPTER NINE

CONTROVERSIES IN CONTEXT: COMMUNICATION, HOT TOPICS AND MUSEUMS IN CANADA

JENNY ELLISON

Tony Bennett's path-breaking *Birth of the Museum* (1995) argues that museums have been sites for the transmission of power and knowledge; disciplinary spaces where dominant discourses are communicated to visitors as expert knowledge. Bennett's text is part of a much broader challenge to museum practice that began in the late 20th century. This resulted in a many-faceted shift in museum practice, toward a more audience centred approach, as well as a discursive shift in the understanding of museum authority. As both Stephen Weil (1999) and Eilean Hooper-Greenhill (1994) have suggested, the focus of museums is shifting away from the care and storage of their collection toward serving and collaborating with their audience. This observation led Hooper-Greenhill to suggest that museums should be understood as media for communication. Understanding museums as a medium for communication has many ramifications for museological practice: it demystifies museums as sources of knowledge, truth and facts in favour of being places about ideas, information and dialogue. This approach also opens up the possibilities of what museums can do in their exhibition spaces and public programming. Recent technological developments in Web 2.0, including social media and smart phones, not to mention the digitisation of museum collections, are evidence that the communicative possibilities for museums are only expanding.

Controversy has sometimes arisen as a consequence of museums' attempts to be more inclusive and less authoritative in their approach to audiences (Bothwell et al. 2008, Butler 2008). Although there are no singular explanations for why particular topics or approaches become controversial, controversies seem to most commonly result when audience expectations come into conflict with museum practices. As principal researcher for *Contested Sites Canada* (Canadian Museums Association 2003), I conducted research on the causes and consequences of controversies in Canadian museums.[1] Data on Canadian audiences, journalists and museum staff was based on the methodological framework and research practices established for the international *Exhibitions as Contested Sites* project. This project considered how institutions can deal effectively with mounting exhibitions on controversial issues and sensitive topics. The Canadian research confirmed many of the findings of the international study: that audiences are open to the presentation of a wide variety of topics, as long as museums do not push a particular viewpoint and audiences are able to have their say. These findings show that audiences and potential audiences are prepared for museums to take on the role of civic actors, to be social spaces for research and debate about important issues. One wonders, however, how all of this excitement about the possibilities for museums as a medium of communication plays out in practice? Does it mean that museums can go full steam ahead and explore the sexy, evil and dark sides of their collections?

Contested Sites Canada data suggests that the variety and complexity of museum-stakeholder relationships has made the presentation of "hot" topics very challenging. Previous Canadian controversies have shown that the power and knowledge complex within which museums are situated extends beyond the museum walls to the community, political climate and cultural context in which exhibitions and public programs are mounted. Some museums report feeling beholden to their stakeholders and unsure of how to handle contentious topics (Dubin 1999, Contested Sites Staff Focus Group transcripts 2003). People we might not initially think of as stakeholders identify with the museum, as national or community institutions, because of their race, gender, religion and so on. Journalists, special interest groups and even politicians feel they have a stake in what and how hot topics are presented in museums: multiple "special" interests factor into the museum exhibitions. In this chapter, interviews with museum staff and journalists and a quantitative survey of museum audiences in Canada will be used to explore the risks, causes and perceived consequences of presenting hot topics in a museum. It will show that hot topics are shaped by the social and political context within which museums operate.

Methods and frameworks

This research began as an investigation into the relationship between the media and museums. Analyses of museum-related controversies have tended to suggest that the media oversimplifies and exacerbates these debates (Butler 2008).[2] For example, in *Displays of Power: Controversy in the American Museum from Enola Gay to Sensation,* Steven Dubin (1999) claims that the controversy over *Sensation* at the Brooklyn Museum of Art was a "pseudo-event," conjured up by the media's hunger for a good story. While the author concedes that the media are rarely responsible for "launching these events", he suggests the media amplify and sustain them by giving controversies more coverage than they warrant. After reading media coverage of a number of controversies, I was sceptical of the claim that the media exacerbated museum controversies. A content analysis of two different controversies, *Body Art*, an exhibition on tattoos and body piercings at the Australian Museum in Sydney and *The Lands Within Me*, an exhibition of Arab-Canadian art at the Canadian Museum of Civilization (CMC) in Gatineau, Quebec, revealed that museums and other stakeholders play a significant role in generating controversies in the first place. Museums often became newsworthy as a consequence of their own communications strategy and decision making, rather than the media's amplification of these stories (Ellison 2003b). After reviewing the evidence I concluded that the notion that newspapers or journalists can incite or fan the flames of controversy was insufficient to explain the variety of media coverage and potential responses to any museum-related story.

Focusing on the media did, however, provide a starting point for thinking about how controversies play out between museums and their stakeholders. I decided to look at the media as an "intervening public" to consider how museums in Canada are communicating and how they could be communicating (Smalley 2002). An intervening public can be understood as a person or institution who passes information on and acts as an opinion leader for the "key public" (audiences) that museums hope to reach (Rawlins 2006). Looking at hot topics through the lens of the mass media offers another way of thinking about the character and possibilities of museums as a medium for communication and the museum / audience relationship.[3] This approach to "the media" and "museums" is meant to move beyond questions of who is to blame for controversies toward a discussion of how communication shapes museum controversies (Strinati 2000). I will review Canadian museums' responses to controversy through the lens of the institution, audiences and journalists, and discuss their views on the risks and rewards of presenting provocative topics in museums. These observations will be drawn from focus groups at three Canadian museums (Museums A, C, and E), interviews with journalists and communications managers at Canadian institutions, and a survey of

300 visitors to Museums A, E and F. To conclude, I look at the role communication and new media might play in making museums hot in the future. People "read" museums much like they consume other forms of popular culture and knowledge of this fact may help us to better engage audiences of the future.

Institutional stakeholders

Interviews with staff at several major Canadian museums reveal that there is a lot of uncertainty around the presentation of hot topics because of a fear that provocative exhibitions will be interpreted in the wrong way. A great deal of this uncertainty was based on major Canadian museum controversies of the past, most notably *The Spirit Sings: Artistic Traditions of Canada's First People's* which opened at the Glenbow Museum in Calgary, Alberta in January 1988 and *Into the Heart of Africa* at the Royal Ontario Museum (ROM) in Toronto, Ontario in November 1989. *The Spirit Sings* was part of the Arts Festival of the 1988 winter Olympics. It was intended to be a showcase of Canadian native art and artefacts developed in collaboration with experts and members of native communities from across the country. The expensive task of drawing artefacts together from across Canada and Europe was funded with a grant from Shell Oil Canada as well as funding from the provincial and federal governments. The Lubicon Lake Cree nation campaigned against the exhibition because Shell was drilling for oil in an area they considered their traditional land. A media campaign against *The Spirit Sings* was part of efforts by the Lubicon to draw attention to an unresolved land claims and first nations' issues in Canada (Harrison 1988; see also Chapter Two). The boycott was supported by a number of members of the Canadian Ethnology Society as well as well-known members of the Canadian museum community (Harrison 1988, Trigger 1988). The *Into the Heart of Africa* exhibition examined the representation of African museum collections through a post-modern and post-colonial lens. The ironic tone of the exhibition was intended to expose the colonial worldview of collectors of African material culture, but the exclusion of African voices from the exhibition drew the ire of the local black community. The Coalition for the Truth About Africa (CFTA) was formed in response to the exhibition. The CFTA accused the ROM of racism and held regular information pickets outside the institution. The exhibition was also drawn into a controversy over the shooting of two black youths by Toronto police around this time, and the systemic social and economic inequalities experienced by black people (Mackey 1995, Mensah 2002). The *Into the*

Heart of Africa debate continues to resonate with the Canadian public: it was the subject of editorial comment in November 2007 when Shelley Butler's book about the show was reissued in paperback (Fulford 2007; Butler 2008).

The Spirit Sings and *Into the Heart of Africa* clearly shifted how Canadian museum staff understand stakeholders and their perception of the risks of engaging with sensitive subjects. Both exhibitions were described as having transformed community consultation practices. A staff member at Museum E in British Columbia (Contested Sites Staff Focus Group CAN#e 2003, 2) observed that they:

> rippled through and changed practice across the country, maybe in different ways depending on your relationships with communities … not just in terms of protocol agreements … but just in terms of how you might approach things … [T]hat particular exhibit also point out something to curators—curators became very nervous after that exhibit because clearly the way things were being done was not the way things were going to be done in the future … And the curator of the exhibition was targeted as the person responsible for it.

Into the Heart of Africa, in particular, had a direct impact on the way that Museum E worked with their stakeholders. A task force is now established for each exhibit, consisting of members of the curatorial team and representatives from the (primarily) aboriginal communities that are represented in the institution (Contested Sites Staff Focus Group CAN#e 2003, 2). Museum E staff felt that their relationships with stakeholders had become primary and noted that they would not risk these relationships, even if it would "draw useful dialogue or debate" (Contested Sites Staff Focus Group CAN#e 2003, 4). Curators at Museum A in Ottawa and Museum C in Toronto also expressed a desire to prevent an *Into the Heart of Africa*-type controversy. They admitted that they avoided pursuing anything too edgy and tended instead to take a "folk art" approach to community and culture (Contested Sites Staff Focus Group CAN#a 2003, 7). As a consequence, exhibitions in these institutions made little mention of some controversial and dark issues in Canada's past, in favour of a "celebration of the culture" of different ethnic groups (Contested Sites Staff Focus Group CAN#e 2003, 2).

Into the Heart of Africa and *The Lands Within Me* did not seem to catalyse debate within museums in Canada so much as create a chilly climate among curatorial staff. The commentary by museum staff about their fear of alienating stakeholders is also evidence of what Eva Mackey (1995) has called a "crisis in representation" in Canadian museums as staff struggle to find new ways to interrogate the past. This observation reflects focus group commentary from Canadian museum staff, who expressed a number of concerns about engaging with controversial topics. These included fear of reprimand from local, provincial and federal funding bodies, fear that the media will misinterpret or misrepresent the museum's intentions and fear of angering or misrepresenting key stakeholders (Contested Sites Staff Focus Group CAN#c 2003). Although these fears are clearly grounded in the precarious funding situation of cultural institutions in 21st century Canada, they also seem to be grounded in fear of controversy itself. As Peter A. Cramer's (2008) analysis of museum controversies suggests, the term tends to be used to denote "a large-scale, amorphous event involving ill-defined parties". Cramer argues that controversy is a rhetorical term used to classify events that do not fall easily under the categories of "debate" or "argument" and do not clearly originate from *either* the cultural context *or* the institutions involved. An examination of communication between the museum, the media and stakeholders in Canadian museums controversies supports Cramer's claim that controversies are complex and inter-discursive events.

The CMC's handling of *The Lands Within Me: Expressions by Canadian Artists of Arab Origin* illustrates that a defensive and "closed lip" communication strategy can actually make a controversy worse. The September 25, 2001 decision to postpone the opening of *The Lands Within Me* in the wake of the 9/11 terrorist attacks in the US was met with widespread dismay by the Canadian public and media. There was a sense that "now, more than ever" this exhibition featuring Arab-Canadian artwork was needed. The most prominent complaint came from then-Prime Minister Jean Chrétien, who received an all-party standing ovation in the House of Commons when he condemned the CMC's decision to cancel the show (Abu-Laban 2002). Yasmeen Abu-Laban argues that the government of Canada used every opportunity possible in the post-9/11 period to assert that Canada was a multicultural nation and the true defining characteristic of modern, secular Canada. Not surprisingly, the CMC bowed to this pressure and *The Lands Within Me* opened to further controversy, when it was revealed that the exhibition included a video art installation of a Palestinian woman who supports the Intefadeh against Israel because she was tortured in an Israeli jail (Ellison 2003). The revelation of this video cast doubt on the CMC's original claim, that they postponed *The Lands Within Me* in order to add context to the exhibition in light of 9/11.

The controversy over *The Lands Within Me* stands in sharp relief to *The Spirit of Islam: Experiencing Islam Through Calligraphy* exhibition that opened at the Museum of Anthropology (MoA) in British Columbia in October 2001. In response to 9/11 the museum held a series of community consultations where they found that the public and the media were interested in anything that would help them deepen their understanding of Islam. Where the CMC alienated part of the community of Arab-Canadians who had participated in the exhibition, the MoA gained the support of the Vancouver Arab community who arranged to have English-language translations of the Koran available free to visitors (Contested Sites Staff Focus Group Transcript CAN#a 2003). A Vancouver arts journalist recalled the MoA's handling of *The Spirit of Islam* favourably. He found that it was otherwise difficult to get an arts story on air in the fall of 2001 and the exhibition allowed him to bring a new angle to the dialogue on Islam at that time (Contested Sites Interview Transcript CAN#a 2003). Journalists in Ottawa saw *The Lands Within Me* as a good story for different reasons after realising something was amiss when the CMC cancelled their show. Paul Gessell (2001a), arts reporter with *The Ottawa Citizen* described the CMC's initial cancellation of the show a "public relations disaster". Gessell's subsequent coverage of the exhibition called into question the CMC's explanation for the cancellation and delay, as well as the absence of CMC Chief Executive Officer Victor Rabinovitch from the show's opening. Those who were present at the opening looked nervous and failed to mention the controversy. Gessell (2001b) described the scene as "one of those situations in which a foul smell is in the room but no one wants to admit it's there".

In attempting to be cautious in their approach to a sensitive subject, the CMC's fear and mishandling of *The Lands Within Me* became palpable to audiences and to local journalists. *The Lands Within Me* became a juicy story about the CMC, rather than a fresh angle on Islam because the CMC itself did not have a clear angle on what the show meant. Controversy was fearful for museum staff because they sensed its unpredictability and uncertainty about what might generate a negative. Our focus groups with museum staff confirmed Eva Mackey's (1995) observation that a lot of the focus in major Canadian institutions has been placed on figuring out what went wrong and avoiding media controversies, rather than on finding new ways to represent the experiences of different social, political and ethnic groups. In the next two sections of the chapter I will examine audience and journalist commentary on controversies. These stakeholders have their own ideas about how sensitive subjects should be communicated to the public.

Audiences and (as?) stakeholders

Contested Sites Canada audience research suggests that, to a certain extent, there may be a disconnect between what museums *think* will upset their audience, and the audiences own expectations and experiences with museums. Visitor surveys were collected at three Canadian Museums in June and July 2003.[4] Visitors were asked to respond on a five-point Likert scale (strongly agree to strongly disagree) on the extent to which museums should be engaging with, challenging and resolving controversial issues. Visitors were not comfortable with the notion that museums should "push" a particular viewpoint. When asked if museums should "Lead public opinion about controversial topics, by pushing a particular view," 34 per cent disagreed and another 13 per cent strongly disagreed. Similarly, 50 per cent of respondents disagreed or strongly disagreed with the notion that museums are "places that should take an active political role to bring about change". Respondents were significantly more likely to agree and strongly agree with statements suggesting museums should challenge or critically examine important topics. Nearly 90 per cent of respondents agreed that museums are "places for critical examination of important topics" and a further 71 per cent agreed or strongly agreed that museums "should challenge generally accepted views on important topics". Audience enthusiasm for "critical engagement" closely paralleled their desire to be able to make comments on the topics being presented, with 90 per cent of all respondents saying they wanted to be able to give feedback. It is clear that audiences are uncomfortable with the idea that a museum might favour a particular viewpoint. Instead, museums are meant to be places which challenge, discuss or critically examine important topics.

Museums were overwhelmingly seen to be a source of reliable information by respondents. A total of 84 per cent of respondents (55 per cent agreed, 29 per cent strongly agreed) that "the information presented in museums is reliable". A further 14 per cent of respondents were unsure or disagreed that museums are a reliable source of information. Only one per cent of respondents disagreed with the statement that museums are reliable sources of information. These numbers may explain why it is that audiences trust museums to deal with controversial and contentious issues. A second series of questions, based on the kinds of issues which should be discussed in museums, suggests that audiences are open to almost any topic being presented in a museum. Potentially contentious issues, including "Terrorism", "Globalisation", "French-Canadian Nationalism"[5], "Canada's Native People", "Immigration to Canada" and "East and West Coast Fisheries" had a total of 70 per cent or more respondents saying they agreed or strongly agreed such topics should be examined in museums. Topics such as "racism", "drugs", "religion" and "death" were affirmed at a rate of between 60 and 70 per cent agreeing or strongly agreeing. "Cloning" at 59 per cent, had the lowest level of approval among all the issues suggested to the visitors.

Audiences' apparent openness to debate and dialogue within museum spaces in Canada seems in line with the general spirit of museological practice aimed at making museums civic spaces and media for communication. Our focus groups with museum staff revealed, however, that museums do not necessarily know this about their audiences. This is because audience research and visitor feedback has taken a back seat to community consultation because of cost and time constraints. Museums A, B and C made attempts to collect feedback from visitors, primarily through comment books. Once comments are collected, however, they tend to end up in the archives, "sitting there for students to write masters degrees on them" (Contested Sites Staff Focus Group Transcript CAN#e 2003) rather than with a curator or interpretive planner. As a consequence, audience research "doesn't really penetrate to the actual practical workings of the museum" (Contested Sites Interview Transcript CAN#c 2003). The audience research gap raises the question of whether or not museums in Canada see their audiences as key publics. While Museums A, B and C had protocols in place for dealing with the communities whose artefacts are represented in their institutions, there were no protocols in place for representing the broader local, provincial or national communities they represented. Museums must keep in mind that people we might not think of as stakeholders do identify with the museum and this sense of ownership can generate conflict (Dubin 1999).

Controversies over the representation of Canada and Canadians have arisen as a consequence of museums' misreading their local and national audiences. *The Lands Within Me* offers an example of such a controversy, because Canadians felt that the CMC had gone against the Canadian value of multiculturalism in their decision to cancel/postpone the show.[6] Audiences bring their baggage with them to the museum and they expect museums, particularly national museums, to represent them (Cameron 2003). The CMC, more than most other Canadian museums, is a national institution that has the cultural authority to represent Canada to itself and to the world. Although the museum is funded at arms-length by the government, the tone of exhibitions like *The Lands Within Me* is in line with public policy since the 1970s, which has claimed a multicultural and multi-ethnic history for Canada. At their best, multicultural approaches are used to incorporate non-British people into the historical narrative and public face of Canada. Less enthusiastic interpretations of multiculturalism have suggested that this policy has been used to develop a narrative of Canada as an overwhelmingly good country with good intentions, thereby neutralising racism and inequities of the past (Bannerji 1996). Either way, multiculturalism has become more than a public policy with its incorporation into public celebrations such as Canada Day, museum narratives, school textbooks and public service announcements such as the Charles R. Bronfman Foundation's "Heritage Minutes" (Cameron 1995, Mackey 1999). The idea that Canadians are united in their differences has shaped discussions of national identity in the last few decades.

Our survey of Canadian museum visitors indicates that multicultural discourses complicate Canadian museums' communication abilities. There is a tension between people wanting to learn the "facts" from museums and wanting to see something affirming or uplifting along the lines of the multicultural history narrative (Ferguson 2006). This tension between fact / affirmation and learning about / from the past played out over the Canadian War Museum's (CWM) interpretation of "bomber command" (see chapter two). "Bomber Command" was a panel in the Second World War section of the CWM's permanent exhibition space. The original panel suggested that Allied Bombers "strategic" bombing attempts had a limited impact on German War production and that the aim of the air raids was to "crush civilian morale" (Bothwell et al. 2008). The Royal Canadian Legion spoke out against this interpretation of the past because they felt that it denigrated their members' by implying that the veterans participated in a war crime. The museum convened a panel of academic historians to discuss this matter and to help arbitrate the situation. The panel was split in their decision, with two members agreeing with the CWM's interpretation of Bomber Command and two disagreeing. The federal government became interested in this controversy and formed a Senate subcommittee to investigate. They ruled that the CWM reword the panel to reflect that this was a subject for debate and to make it less insulting to veterans (Bothwell et al. 2008). Robert Bothwell et al. argued that the public's willingness to side with the veterans, evidenced by coverage of public reaction in the media, shows that there is a deep reluctance among Canadians to learn from the past and "admit the *truth*" about bomber command. Bothwell et al. argue that the CWM is not "about recreating the minutiae of lived experience" but about "the evolution of the war and its strategic consequences".

While the rhetoric of the Royal Canadian Legion may have been overblown, Bothwell et al.'s comparison of "experience" to the "truth" muddies the situation even further. What the public debate on Bomber

Command reveals is concern that the museum was not adequately representing the experiences of veterans. As *Contested Sites* survey data demonstrated, Canadians indicate a keen interest in seeing "different sides of the story". Rather than seeing support for the veterans as a reactionary and anti-modern attack on the museum, we might see it as an assertion of the importance of "lived experience" to museum audiences. How else can museums make history real to their audiences than through the prism of lived experience? The perspective of people who were present during historical events is one part of the overall picture of such events. Experience is not minutiae which runs contrary to the truth about the past, it is central to the way historical actors and writers of history interpret the past. In dismissing the role that experiential knowledge (of stakeholders or audiences) might play in a museum exhibition, Bothwell et al. follow those before them who have dismissed experiential knowledge as "emotional", "soft" and "subjective" and therefore not generalisable in a way that yields "truth" (Code 1991, 1995). Experiential knowledge, including the "local" knowledge of audiences should be considered relevant to museum practice, particularly because it is shaped by the same "cultural and political institutions and ideologies" as museums themselves (Code 1991). Bomber Command is evidence that Canadians expect so-called special interest groups to get a fair shake in museum spaces.

The media: An intervening public

The media does not necessarily see museums as an intervening public in the museum community, and will only go after a museum story if it is newsworthy. Like many other institutions, there are unwritten rules that govern the way news is gathered and disseminated. For example, television newsreaders are expected to look at the camera when they talk and audiences expect news programs to begin with the most newsworthy item of the day. News stories themselves have "relevance structures" that usually dictate the way a story is laid out (van Dijk 1985). Known as the inverted pyramid model, news reporting usually begins with the conclusion or the "crux of the story", followed by the less significant and timely details. Thus, print media stories are edited from the bottom up (Tapsall and Varley 2001). Unwritten rules likewise apply to the information that is selected as newsworthy for the audience. News values or news angles are a basic guideline of journalistic practice used to gauge the newsworthiness of their subjects. These values include the potential impact and prominence of a story on the audience, its timeliness and proximity to the community, the amount of conflict or unusualness in the story and finally, the overall currency of the topic, whether or not it is something the audience is already talking about.

For museums, an understanding of what is newsworthy is important, both from a public relations and an exhibition planning perspective. As "Samir" an arts reporter from Vancouver put it:

> the idea is to get people in the door. How are you going to get people in the door? It's just like me, when I do a story, like, sometimes I recognise I've got to give them a bit of candy. I can't give them medicine and say eat this, its good for you. No one is going to buy that, you've got to give them something, right? And that's the reality, you can not, no one is above the fray anymore, no one. (Contested Sites Interview Transcript CAN#a 2003, 6)

As this quote from Samir indicates, being newsworthy is not the same thing as being worthy. An important scientific finding, a significant object or new idea will not get news coverage unless it includes "a bit of sauce" (Contested Sites Interview Transcript CAN#b 2003, 2) "Sauce" is not necessarily sex, controversy or sensationalism. Rather it means asking "what can I tell people today that they didn't know yesterday?" For "Peter" a newspaper arts reporter from Ottawa this means finding the "human interest … in a story … an appeal to human emotions" (Contested Sites Interview Transcript CAN#d 2003, 9). "Andrea", a radio host from Toronto, described human interest as "something that the listener will identify as affecting them" (Contested Sites Interview Transcript CAN#b 2003, 1). Note here that the journalists are talking about an emotional, rather than an intellectual engagement with their audience. The question at hand is not, "why does this matter" but rather "why does this matter to me and my community?"

As the media landscape changes and the resources available to traditional journalists diminish, it is increasingly important for museums to communicate effectively with the media. "Jaclyn", the communications manager at a Canadian university museum felt that her local media outlets did not express much enthusiasm for the exhibitions. She found the local media rarely challenged the issues or subjects in the exhibition, saying she felt a lot of museum coverage wasn't "very good or insightful" (Contested Sites Interview Transcript CAN#c 2003, 8). Conversely, one of the journalists working in Jaclyn's market told me in his professional experiences with her museum, he didn't

> get the sense that they are open to the public in a very sort of welcoming way. It's like they are begrudgingly open to the public and it's almost like

> whatever they do in terms of research is more important than a dialogue with the public at large. (Contested Sites Interview Transcript CAN#c 2003, 2)

This sort of he-said-she-said dialogue is evidence that museums may not have a good understanding of how the media is structured or of news values. Rarely will there be a budget for someone to be assigned to museums exclusively or to offer in-depth reviews of museum exhibitions (McDonald 2002). Nor will museums be able to control media messages and guarantee good publicity. Expecting journalists to do the leg work and getting frustrated and angry when they don't deliver "can lead to misunderstanding and bad relationships" (Smalley 2002). As Canadian controversies such as *The Lands Within Me* and *Into the Heart of Africa* have shown, it is also important to have a coherent message about the museum and special exhibitions. The media and the public very easily catch on when there is a gap between "what is actually said in public and what appears to be happening behind the scenes" (McDonald 2002).

"The story" that interests the media may require the museum to link an exhibition to core news values of timeliness, topicality and links to the local community. In order to explain the distinction, I will include here an excerpt from my interview with Andrea, a Toronto radio host, describing how news values shaped her coverage of the Royal Ontario Museum's *Elite Elegance: Couture Fashion in the 1950s* (2003):

> I went around with one of the society ladies who had donated many of her haute couture gowns to this exhibit and what we talked about was how we have lost that sense now of dressing up for an occasion. And what that means and whether it matters. Because, well, the old way of looking at it was, "oh things are going downhill and nothing is like it was and everything was so glamorous back then". But she actually took the view that, frankly, back in those days, she didn't mind spending that much money on dresses. But she has a different view now, she'd rather be giving that money to the charity if she is going to a ball, why should she spend four thousand dollars on a dress to look good for the one night, when she could give four thousand dollars to the charity and look maybe not quite so dazzling, but you know, be a humbler person for the experience.

So, it was, the story became about the transition of values over time and with the journey, wisdom. And the hook, was the couture exhibit at the Royal Ontario Museum (Contested Sites Interview Transcript CAN#b 2003, 6–7).

Andrea's view of the story behind *Elite Elegance* was not necessarily the same as the curatorial focus of the show. Objects are understood by

Andrea to be the beginning of a conversation about the contemporary world, rather than a story in themselves. Andrea's commentary on *Elite Elegance* tells us a few things. It reminds us that the contemporary narrative as well as the history of an object can be relevant to the audience. More relevant to the discussion of the relationship between the media and museums is to consider what Andrea's anecdote tells us about creating good stories *for* the media.

Conclusions: Making museums hot

Journalists, audiences and museum staff all agree that museums should be engaging civic spaces. This chapter has demonstrated that realising the goal of museums as a civic space is a complicated and often political undertaking that can challenge public perception, inflame institutional politics and throw funding into question. Recognising the potential constraints museums face when trying to work with controversial subjects, I will conclude with a brief discussion of successful approaches to media and communications recently undertaken by Canadian institutions. There are some lessons about the character and possibilities of museums in contemporary society to be found in these examples of the incorporation of traditional and new media into exhibition spaces.

Effective communication with museum audiences can generate discussion about a museum exhibition without generating controversy. The key is to generate debate and discussion about a museum without attaching the museum to any particular position on this topic. Canadian institutions have been able to do this by involving experts from outside their institutions—authors, academics, journalists, and artists—to participate in public programming about their exhibitions. In addition to keeping the museum at arms-length from potentially contentious issues, this approach has the advantage of allowing the museum to link the exhibition to current issues and events. For example, the Vancouver Museum offers "Secrets in the City" tours with thematic links to permanent and upcoming exhibitions. Led by a local author, this program includes guided walks through Vancouver's "lost" neighbourhoods, past sites of historic interest and into places that might otherwise be off limits, or outside the purview of the average city dweller. The novelty of the program, combined with the popularity of the walks led Shaw Cable in Vancouver to approach the Museum to do a series of "Secrets of the City" television segments. The Vancouver Museum has been able to extend its reach into the local community and generate discussion about the changing urban landscape, without risking its own reputation.

Probably the most interesting and cost effective options for museums looking to extend their capacity to communicate with their audience are new media and Web 2.0 technologies. The ROM in Toronto combined new and older approaches to programming in their preparation for a Dead Sea Scrolls exhibit that opened in June 2009. The museum's Institute of Contemporary Culture, a unit through which curators engage with current events, hosted a series of talks on the ten commandments and commandments for the 21st century. The museum hosted Christopher Hitchens, author of *God is Not Great: How Religion Poisons Everything*, Camille Paglia, author of *Sexual Personae* and a lecturer on religion at the University of the Arts in Philadelphia, PA, and A. J. Jacobs author of *The Year of Living Biblically: One Man's Humble Quest to Follow the Bible as Literally as Possible.* This is an example of making a historical topic relevant to contemporary questions and concerns. The ROM series generated discussion and press among journalists in Toronto and the authors were also guests on national talk shows.[7] Perhaps most interestingly from a new media perspective, the institution has posted the talks online as a series of podcasts so that people outside of Toronto can listen in on the discussion.

In reviewing the question of hot topics, it is necessary to consider how multiple interests factor into the reception of museum exhibitions. The ideal for museums is to provoke conversation in a way that is thoughtful and honest; to purposefully connect audiences, while relying on depth and material resources that museums have to offer. The examples and case studies above are evidence of the complexity of these questions, but also of the creative possibilities available for institutions to serve and collaborate with their audiences.

References

Abu-Laban, Y. 2002. Liberalism, multiculturalism and the problem of essentialism. *Citizenship Studies* 6 (4): 459–482.

Bannerji, H. 1996. On the dark side of the nation: Politics of multiculturalism and the state of 'Canada'. *Journal of Canadian Studies* 31: 103–128.

Bennett, T. 1995. *The birth of the museum: History, theory, politics.* New York: Routledge.

Bothwell, R., R. Hansen and M. Macmillan. 2008. Controversy, commemoration and capitulation: The Canadian War Museum and bomber command. *Queen's Quarterly* 115: 367–387.

Butler, S. 2008. *Contested representations: Revisiting into the heart of Africa.* Peterborough, Ontario: Broadview Press.
Cameron, E. 1995. Heritage minutes: Culture and myth. *Canadian Issues* 17: 13–24.
Cameron, F. 2003. Transcending fear, engaging emotions and opinion: A case for museums in the 21st century. *Open Museum Journal* 6: 1–46.
Code, L. 1991. *What can she know: Feminist theory and the construction of knowledge.* Ithaca: Cornell University Press.
—. 1995. How do we know? Questions of method in feminist practice. In *Changing methods: Feminist transforming practice.* Ed. S. Burt and L. Code, 105–125. Peterborough: Broadview Press.
Contested Sites Interview Transcript CAN#a, 10 June 2003, unpublished manuscript, Centre for Cultural Research, University of Western Sydney
—. CAN#b, 11 June 2003, unpublished manuscript, Centre for Cultural Research, University of Western Sydney.
—. CAN#c, 11 June 2003, unpublished manuscript, Centre for Cultural Research, University of Western Sydney.
—. CAN#d, 2 June 2003, unpublished manuscript, Centre for Cultural Research, University of Western Sydney.
Contested Sites Staff Focus Group Transcript CAN#a, 16 May 2003, unpublished manuscript, Centre for Cultural Research, University of Western Sydney.
—. CAN#e, 16 May 2003, unpublished manuscript, Centre for Cultural Research, University of Western Sydney.
—. CAN#c, 5 May 2003, unpublished manuscript, Centre for Cultural Research, University of Western Sydney.
—. CAN#e, 5 May 2003, unpublished manuscript, Centre for Cultural Research, University of Western Sydney.
Cramer, P. A. 2008. Controversy as a media event category. In *Rhetoric in detail: Discourse approaches to politics, society and culture.* Ed. B. Johnstone and C. Eisenhart, 279–305. Amsterdam: John Benjamins Publishing Company.
Dubin, S. C. 1999. *Displays of power: Memory and amnesia in the American museum.* New York: New York University Press.
Ellison, J. 2003a. Front page challenge: Museums and the media. *Muse: The Voice of Canada's Museum Community* 21: 36–39.
—. 2003b. Revisioning the media, museums and controversy: A preliminary case study. *Open Museum Journal* 6**:** 1–27.
Ferguson, L. 2006. Pushing buttons: Controversial topics in museums *Open Museum Journal* 8. 1–38.

Fulford, R. 2007. Into the heart of political correctness. *The National Post.* November 24.

Gessell, P. 2001a. Arab art show gets off to rough start: Videotaped interview with Lebanese woman jailed by Israel triggers probably the most politically charged art exhibition opening Ottawa has ever seen. *The Ottawa Citizen.* October 19.

—. 2001b. Museum pulls plug on Arab-Canadian art exhibit: Museum of Civilization's response to attacks leaves artists angry and insulted. *The Ottawa Citizen.* September 26.

Harrison, J. D. 1988. "The spirit sings" and the future of anthropology. *Anthropology Today.* 4: 6–9.

Hooper-Greenhill, E. 1994. *Museums and their visitors.* London: Routledge.

—. 2000. *Museums and the interpretation of visual culture.* New York: Routledge.

Mackey, E. 1995. Postmodernism and cultural politics in a multicultural nation: Contests over truth in the *Into The Heart of Africa* controversy. *Public Culture* 7**:** 403–431.

—. 1999. *The house of difference: Cultural politics and national identity in Canada.* London: New York: Routledge.

McDonald, J. 2002. *Working the media: Both sides of the showcase symposium.* Sydney: Museums and Galleries Foundation of New South Wales.

Mensah, J. 2002. *Black Canadians: History, experiences, social conditions.* Halfiax: Fernwood Publishing.

Rawlins, B. L. 2006. *Prioritizing stakeholders for public relations.* Gainesville, Florida: Institute for Public Relations.

Smalley, D. 2002. *Working the media: Both sides of the showcase symposium.* Sydney, Australia: Museums and Galleries Foundation of New South Wales.

Strinati, D. 2000. A*n introduction to studying popular culture.* New York: Routledge.

Tapsall, S. and C. Varley. 2001. *Journalism: Theory in practice.* Melbourne: Oxford University Press.

Trigger, B. 1988. Reply by Bruce Trigger to Julia Harrison's article "The Spirit Sings and the Future of Anthropology". *Anthropology Today,* 4**:** 6–9.

Van Dijk, T. 1985. Structures of news in the press. In *Discourse and communication: New approaches to the analysis of mass media discourse and communication.* Ed. T. van Dijk, 69–93. Berlin: Walter De Gruyter.

Weil, S. E. 1999. From being about something to being for somebody: The ongoing transformation of the American Museum. *Daedalus* 128: 229–258.

Notes

[1] *Contested Sites Canada* was funded by a research scholarship from the Canadian Museums Association. It was conducted in partnership with *Exhibitions as Contested Sites, the Roles of Museums in Contemporary Societies.* Focus group interviews in Canada were carried out by Lynda Kelly and Fiona Cameron. Audience research and journalist interviews were conducted by Jennifer Ellison.

[2] Butler suggested that the media tended to polarise debates about *Into the Heart of Africa*, though she also concedes that the main players in the controversy contributed to the debate.

[3] As Hooper-Greenhill notes, the reorganisation of the museum/audience relationship is one of the greatest challenges facing museums.

[4] A total of 287 surveys were collected at three Canadian institutions, B, E and F. English-speaking respondents represent 76% of the total number of people surveyed, with another 12% being French-speaking. A further 10% of people answered in English, but identified their first language as something other than English. Of the 287 people surveyed, 57% were male and 43% were female. The majority of respondents (46%) were between the ages of 35 and 64, with another 36% under the age of 34 and 20% over the age of 65. Approximately 1 in 10 museum visitors was approached on weekdays and weekends. More than half of those questioned had visited a Canadian museum in the previous 12 months. The survey was offered in French at two institutions where operations are bilingual. Museum B is in Ottawa, Ontario. Museum E is in Vancouver, British Columbia. Museum F is in Montréal, Québec.

[5] "French-Canadian Nationalism" here refers to the separatist movement in the province of Quebec.

[6] See for example letters to the editor from this period, such as Kibbins, G. (27 September 2001) Art show should open (letter to the editor). *The Globe and Mail.* Toronto, Wong, K. (15 October 2001) Support Arab artists by attending exhibit (letter to the editor). *The Ottawa Citizen.* Ottawa, Ontario.

[7] CBC RADIO (18 June 2009) Q. Toronto, Ontario.

CHAPTER TEN

ENGAGING MUSEUM VISITORS IN DIFFICULT TOPICS THROUGH SOCIO-CULTURAL LEARNING AND NARRATIVE

LYNDA KELLY

It has long been recognised that learning plays a central role in people's lives and is essential to our humanity (Confucius undated, Dewey 1938, Bowen and Hobson 1987, Claxton 1999). Learning is an individual and social process in which humans are constantly engaged, both consciously and unconsciously. Dewey stated that true learning has "longitudinal and lateral dimensions. It is both historical and social. It is orderly and dynamic" (1938, 11). Dewey also suggested that learning was:

- the capacity to act intelligently in new situations through exercising personal judgment
- the interplay and interaction of objective (external) and internal factors
- a transition between individuals and their current environment
- a lifelong process of growth
- social—a shared common experience
- flexible, yet directed.

More recent learning theories have focused on the conjunction between the individual learner and the socio-cultural context of the learning, with an emphasis on the individual as an agent of change (Rennie and Johnston 2004, Fosnot 2005). Current theories of learning also focus on the meanings individuals make based on their experience—alone, within a social context and as part of a community (Falk and Dierking 1992, 2000, Matusov and Rogoff 1995, Hein 1998, Leinhardt and Knutson 2004). Museums are unique contexts for learning, often called "free-choice" learning environments (Falk and Dierking 2000). Museums have the opportunity to shape identities—through access to objects, information and knowledge visitors can see themselves and their culture reflected in ways that encourage new connections, meaning-making and learning (Falk and Dierking 1992, 2000, Silverman 1995, Weil 1997, Hein 1998, Bradburne 1998, Hooper-Greenhill 2000, Falk 2004).

Museums have developed from being repositories of knowledge and objects to having a "multifaceted, outward looking role as hosts who invite visitors inside to wonder, encounter and learn" (Schauble et al. 1997, 3). Falk and Dierking suggested that museums "need to be understood and promoted as integral parts of a society-wide learning infrastructure" (2000, 225) as they are an important part of a broader educational environment and complement other forms of learning.

Museums have always seen themselves as having an educational role. The earliest museums were founded on the premise of "education for the uneducated masses" (Bennett 1995), "cabinets of curiosities" (Weil 1999) established to "raise the level of public understanding … to elevate the spirit of its visitors … to refine and uplift the common taste" (Weil 1997, 257). The past ten years have seen a conceptual change from thinking about museums as places of education to places for learning, responding to the needs and interests of visitors (Falk and Dierking 1995, 2000, Bradburne 1998, Weil 2002, Falk 2004, Rennie and Johnston 2004). Weil stated that museums need to transform themselves from "being *about* something to being *for* somebody" (1999, 229).

Literature about why people visit museums has revealed that the overwhelming reason given was for some type of "learning experience", usually described as education, getting information, expanding knowledge or doing something worthwhile in leisure. Often the word "learning" was used, which was linked to higher-order fulfillment of personal needs and enhancing self esteem (Kelly 2007). Falk reported that people who visited museums valued learning, sought it in many ways and were usually better educated than the general population:

> The primary reason most people attend museums, whether by themselves or with their children, is in order to learn. … [Therefore they are] likely to see museums as places that provide opportunities for them to expand their own and their children's learning horizons. (1998, 40)

Prentice's research into recollections of why people visited museums found that "motivations of 'to learn' and 'broaden general knowledge' were reported irrespective of visitors' educational level, social class or age" (1998, 53). Jansen-Verbeke and van Rekom's study of visitors to Rotterdam, specifically the Museum of Fine Arts, demonstrated that the central motivation for visiting the art museum was "… to learn something" (1996, 367). Similarly, Combs (1999) discovered that people visited the Winterthur Museum, Gallery and Garden (in the US) primarily for learning and recreation. Mitchell's (1999) study of family visitors to the Australian Museum, Sydney found that while many factors triggered the decision to visit, the most important reason cited for family groups was "to learn" closely followed by "entertainment". Results from surveys of 413 visitors to the Australian Museum demonstrated a number of factors that motivated museum and gallery visits, with the principle ones (in order of choice) being experiencing something new, entertainment, learning, family interests and doing something worthwhile in leisure (Kelly 2007).

The practice of education in museums has a long history (Hooper-Greenhill 1994, Roberts 1997, Hein 1998). Whichever theory was foregrounded by scholars and practitioners was largely dependent on both their epistemological position; their background and training; and their beliefs about how knowledge was created. As Hein (1998) argued, whether knowledge was acquired independently of the learner or constructed in the mind by the learner was an important component of how learning was viewed and what epistemological path was followed. Hein also emphasised constructivism as an approach to developing and assessing museum learning experiences. Constructivism is a theory of learning that focuses on the learner and the meanings they make based on their prior experience, knowledge and interests. Constructivism had a major influence on the ways that museums thought about learning during the 1990s and was widely adopted in museum practice. Museum learning experiences provided under a constructivist framework encourage learners to use both their hands and their minds to experiment with the world and reach their own conclusions, through choosing what they want to attend to (Hein 1998). Many of the principles underpinning a constructivist approach to learning have now been captured within socio-cultural theory, which is being increasingly seen as a more holistic approach to thinking about and designing museum learning experiences, especially those dealing with difficult or contentious subject matter.

Given the key role learning plays in museums, this chapter considers socio-cultural theory as a conduit for engaging visitors with difficult topics and assessing their museum experience. A socio-cultural approach to explaining visitor learning is applied through analysing summative evaluation of visitors to an Australian Museum exhibition that tackled the difficult topic of death, titled *Death—The Last Taboo*. The place of narrative in museum exhibitions is also considered through analysing visitor responses to the confronting aspects of the exhibition. In considering these two areas it is recognised that curatorial decisions play a key role in developing exhibitions, however these will not be addressed here as the focus is solely on visitors' responses and how that relates to their own experience.

Socio-cultural theory and museums

Socio-cultural theory is becoming increasingly prominent in current museum learning literature as a framework for research (Schauble et al. 1997, Leinhardt et al. 2002, Ellenbogen 2003a, 2003b). Socio-cultural theory is based on the idea that human activities take place in cultural contexts through social interactions that are mediated by language and other symbol systems and shaped by an individuals' historical development (Matusov and Rogoff 1995, Ash 2003, Sedzielarz 2003). It also understands, accounts for and makes explicit the "… unplanned intersection of people, culture, tools and context" (Hansman 2001, 44), emphasising the importance of culture, environment and history in every learning context and event (Schauble et al. 1997). Socio-cultural theory emerged from Vygotsky's work, who proposed that learning is a socially-mediated process where learners, both adults and children, are jointly responsible for their learning (1978).

Falk and Dierking suggested that " who we are, what we are, and how we behave are products of the socio-cultural context in which we are immersed" (2000, 38). They concluded that learning was essentially an individual construct: "The socio-cultural context defines both who we perceive ourselves to be and how we perceive the world we inhabit" (2000, 39), as well as a social experience where "meaningful learning results when a person is able to actively construct and find personal meaning within a situation. Virtually all such learning is either directly or indirectly socially mediated" (2000, 41). They further argued that

> … all learning is situated within a series of contexts … an organic, integrated experience … a product of millions of years of evolution, an adaptation that permits an ongoing dialogue between the whole individual and the physical and socio-cultural world he or she inhabits. (2000, 10)

Falk and Dierking proposed the contextual model of museum learning to account for factors they identified in their earlier work (1992), however with a more holistic view that recognised the long-term nature of learning (Figure 10.1).

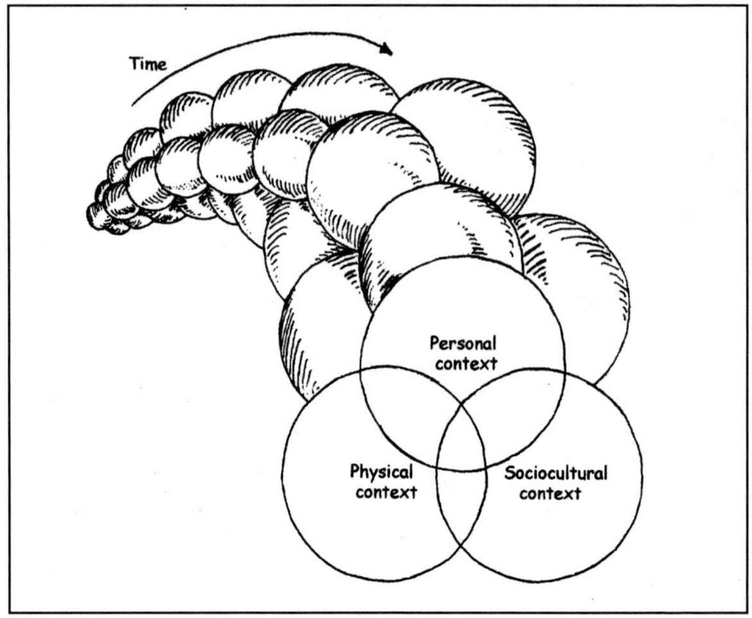

Figure 10.1 The contextual model of learning. (Source: Falk and Dierking 2000, 12)

In this model the physical context consists of the tools and settings of the museum, including architecture, design, objects and subsequent reinforcing events and experiences outside the museum. The personal context includes motivations and expectations, prior knowledge, experience and beliefs, interests, choice and control; as well as how these are perceived, filtered and ultimately incorporated into memory and learning. Finally, the socio-cultural context accounts for within-group mediation, facilitated mediation by others and cultural mediation (Falk and Dierking 2000). It was suggested that knowledge is constructed through social mediation across members of a group, both as an individual process and through participation in a community of practice.

A range of other practitioners have explored socio-cultural theory in a museum context (Matusov and Rogoff 1995, Schauble et al. 1997, Falk and Dierking 2000, Leinhardt et al. 2002, Paris 2002, Ellenbogen 2003a, 2003b). From an analysis of this literature four interlinked elements that underpin socio-cultural theory can be identified: individual, culture, environment and historical development, illustrated in Figure 10.2.

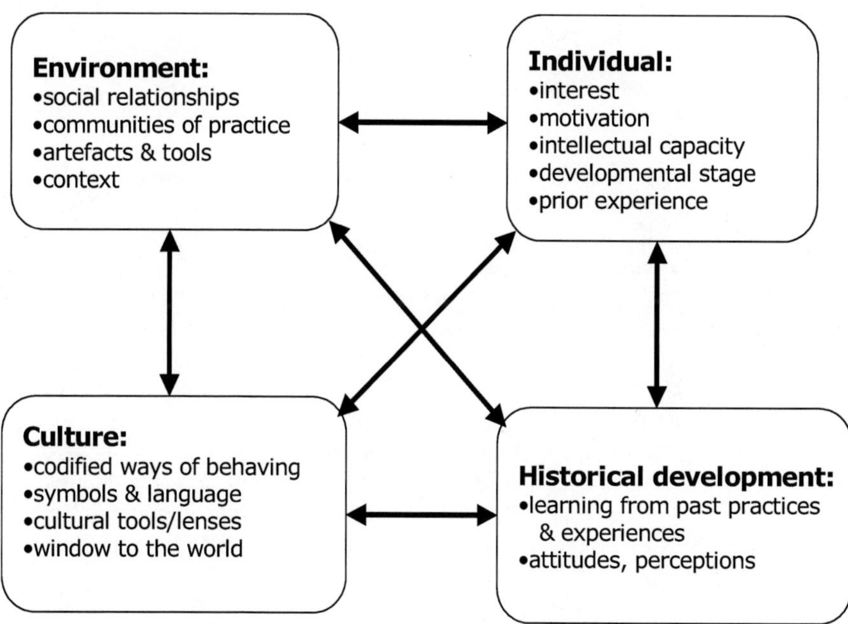

Figure 10.2 Socio-cultural theory. (Source: Kelly 2007, 56)

Several aspects of socio-cultural theory relate to the individual, including interests, motivation, intellectual capacity and development. Initial approaches to museum learning were often focused on the learner as an individual. Although knowledge, learning and meaning-making is essentially an individualised process, the social context and tools provided at the time are key factors in both what is learned and why it is learned, based on a person's interests and motivation. The important role of individuals, their intellectual capacity and level of development need to be acknowledged, coupled with the recognition that individuals also function within a socio-cultural framework (Wenger 1998).

Culture refers to a person's adaptive way of life, which is formed through customary ways of behaving; sets of codes and signals; use of artefacts and tools; participation in formal and informal institutions; and within a set of social relations. These, in turn, are codified through language (Ogbu 1995, Falk and Dierking 2000). A set of underlying assumptions make customary behaviours meaningful within a particular culture:

> Culture is the framework or 'window' through which members of the population see the world around them, interpret events in that world, behave according to acceptable standard, and react to perceived reality. (Ogbu 1995, 80)

As children develop they learn the appropriate behaviours and social norms of their culture that make customary behaviours meaningful within that culture. Falk (2004) points out that culture also plays a strong role in shaping an individual's identity.

In socio-cultural theory environment encompasses the physical context, including the artefacts and tools that are provided, as well as social relations within a group and communities of practice (Lave and Wenger 1991, Matusov and Rogoff 1995). In a museum context a community of practice is comprised of the interplay between the mediation provided by the museum environment, in terms of objects, interpretive tools and texts, and individuals and their participation in a community, such as a family, a school or a group of friends. These ongoing social interactions with artefacts and tools are where meaning is made and learning happens.

The historical development dimension in socio-cultural theory accounts for cultural practices, as previously discussed (Ogbu 1995), as well as lived histories and experiences within multiple communities of practice. The role of prior knowledge and interests (Roschelle 1995) that shape attitudes, values and learning are also accounted for in historical development. Perceptions and expectations of museums, as well as previous experiences with them, are key historical factors impacting on the individual. Research has continually found that the characteristic with the most impact on adult museum visits is whether they were taken to museums as children and the types of experiences in which they engaged (Falk and Dierking 1997, Ellenbogen 2002).

Leinhardt et al. proposed the following definition of museum learning derived from socio-cultural theory:

> learning as meaning construction, a socially mediated phenomenon that was a consequence of dialogue among the curatorial premise, the supporting tools of signage and other symbol systems, and the visitors themselves … learning as a conversational elaboration [where] the language becomes enriched by specific details of objects and themes from the museum and reflects the affective and personal connections to the museum in a way that goes beyond simple statements of like or dislike or identification. (2003, 25)

It has been recognised that museums are sites where a socio-cultural framework could be applied to learning since most people visit in some type of social group and come with specific prior interests and knowledge (Schauble et al. 1997, Leinhardt et al. 2002, Paris 2002). Museums are mainly free-choice, providing a wide range of tools which visitors use to make their own meaning, both as an individual and part of a community (Hein 1998, Falk and Dierking 2000). Paris (1997) outlined the way that socio-cultural views of learning could be integrated into a theory of museum learning. He stated that to facilitate meaningful learning museums need to create environments that encourage exploration and enable meaning to be constructed through choice, challenge, control and collaboration, leading to self-discovery, pride in achievements and learning, where visitors "may 'learn' more about themselves and their experiences through reflection" (Paris 1997, 23).

Museums and the role of narrative

The potential of narrative approaches to learning have been explored more recently by museums. It is recognised that humans are natural storytellers—since ancient times humans have been using stories that represent an event or series of events as ways to learn (Abbott 2002). Bruner (1986) suggested that humans employed two modes of thought—paradigmatic (or logico-scientific) and narrative. He described imaginative narrative as leading to

> good stories, gripping drama, believable (though not necessarily 'true') historical accounts. It deals in human or human-like intention and action and the vicissitudes and consequences that mark their course. It strives to put its timeless miracles into the particulars of experience, and to locate the experience in time and place. (1986, 13)

Roberts (1997) used the framework of narrative to explain the shifts in museum education theory over time, and suggested a narrative approach to educational practices as a way to enhance the ways visitors engaged with museums. Museums are ideal places where stories can be told that encourage visitors to make their own meanings and learn from them. Bedford noted that:

> Stories are the most fundamental way we learn. They have a beginning, a middle, and an end. They teach without preaching, encouraging both personal reflection and public discussion. Stories inspire wonder and awe; they allow a listener to imagine another time and place, to find the

> universal in the particular, and to feel empathy for others. They preserve individual and collective memory and speak to both the adult and the child. (2001, 33)

Ideas about narratives have been developed and applied to museums by a range of writers and researchers. Allen (2004b) researched the use of narrative tools as ways for visitors to make meanings about science. Allen defined narrative in a museum context as taking the personal perspective, involving a series of events, containing emotional content and authentic in origin, with someone telling the story. Allen (2004a) also drew attention to the problem that the museum sector still does not clearly understand how the power of narrative could be used to enhance visitor learning, specifically about scientific principles. McLean (2003) described the ways visitor experiences could be constructed in different types of learning environments, using the analogy of "the campfire, the cave and the well" as ways to demonstrate how humans have been storytellers for a very long time—such as yarning around a campfire, sharing experiences in a cave whiling away the long winters and gossiping around the village well.

Bedford (2001, 2004) and Rounds (2002) considered that narrative was a powerful way that cultural and social history museums, in particular, engaged visitors, with Bedford proposing that storytelling was the "real work" of museums. Bedford argued that stories aided humans in defining their values and beliefs and allowed the listener to project their own thoughts, feelings and memories onto the story and "make connections between museum artifacts and images and visitors' lives and memories" (Bedford 2001, 30).

Socio-cultural theory and narrative: *Death—The Last Taboo* exhibition

Research conducted as part of the *Exhibitions as Contested Sites* project found that museums were considered trusted places for gaining information about difficult and contested topics: "People who have discovered the value of museums use them as one of a wide range of information resources" (Kelly 2006, 2). Data from that study suggested that museums were related strongly to trust, reliability, credibility and authority, as well as places for education and researching subjects of interest to visitors. It was suggested that the educational role of the museum could be to "… provide visitors with information about issues that museums are best equipped to deal with in an open, honest and truthful way through providing object-rich learning experiences" (Kelly 2006, 6).

In 2003 the Australian Museum staged an exhibition on the difficult and potentially confronting topic of death, called *Death—The Last Taboo*. The aims of the exhibition were, in an overall sense, to talk about a subject that was not often discussed while answering many questions people are reluctant or scared to ask. Other purposes of the exhibition were to demystify death, especially as it is so sanitised in a Western society and to provide an opportunity for people to consider death at a time and place removed from it. The Museum project team chose to focus on the practical aspects of what happens after a person dies, the choices people have about these and to make the experience as real as possible through providing full, factual details about the processes that occur after death. An important decision early in the planning was to make the exhibition object-based using the Museum's collection as much as possible.

The topic of death had the potential to be controversial, however, given the research cited above, the Museum felt it was the appropriate venue for such an exhibition and that the topic could make use of the Museum's extensive cultural collections and scientific expertise. In the early stages of exhibition development, care was taken to identify what information was required from potential visitors through a front-end evaluation[1]. Five focus groups were undertaken with visitors to museums to understand their general attitudes towards death; gauge interest and expectations in the topic of death; and provide guidance about content and presentation. An important aspect was to test how far the Museum could go in showing objects and visual material that could be considered "gruesome".

Overall, it was found that the target audience for the exhibition was adults, and that visitors expected the exhibition to have both a scientific and a cultural focus. Most felt that showing confronting objects and visuals within the context of the Museum and its collections was essential for visitor engagement and learning, rather than just for morbid curiosity. Potential audiences were also interested in stories surrounding death and how attitudes have changed both across cultures and over time.

The summative evaluation of the exhibition encompassed both qualitative and quantative studies with visitors to *Death—The Last Taboo*. The aim of these were to provide an overview of visitors' responses to the exhibition, specifically to obtain a visitor profile, motivations for attending, what they most liked / disliked, and other general information about the exhibition such as key messages and design aspects. A quantitative survey of 151 visitors was conducted over two weeks in June 2003. The data showed that visitors to the exhibition were predominantly females visiting in groups. A sizable proportion (46 per cent) were new visitors. There was a very high satisfaction with the exhibition, with 86 per cent of visitors rating it highly; 95 per cent stating they would recommend the exhibition to others and 88 per cent of visitors thought it met or exceeded their expectations. The data also demonstrated that visitors were easily able to articulate that the main messages of the exhibition were: different ways of dealing with death (52 per cent of respondents); demystifying death (28 per cent); death is a part of life (24 per cent); and to increase general understandings about death (12 per cent).

From these interviews people were recruited to participate in one of four focus groups held during the last week of August 2003 (towards the end of the exhibition showing). As part of the process, visitors were taken on a tour back through the exhibition and asked how they remembered feeling and thinking at various sections of it. Responses to some of the more confronting material in the exhibition were also explored in detail.

As noted earlier, socio-cultural theory is underpinned by four essential elements: *individual, culture, environment* and *historical development.* The outcomes of the focus group aspect of the evaluation have been identified as resonating with the four elements of socio-cultural theory. In relation to the *individual* component it was found that personal responses to death were based on an individual's experiences and prior experiences with death: "I'm coming to terms with death as an old lady and coming to this was part of that, accepting it and so on". Another visitor, when reminiscing about the mortuary section, commented that "I spent a long time on the instrument cabinet looking at the explanation of what they use on what part of the body. You'd never see anything like this. Then you think this is someone's job…". Others thought that death was a thought-provoking topic that was well executed: "It made sense of something that's hard to make sense of". Visitors also stated that the exhibition demystified death and made it part of the everyday for them: "We all know we are going to go, but very few people can talk about it the way we're talking about it now". They also felt that the exhibition provided good, factual information presented in a sensitive way: "It was trying to create understanding, death is something that happens, this is how you can deal with it".

Visitors demonstrated an interest in how death was treated across different *cultures*, with the realisation that a Western view of death could be quite narrow, and an appreciation of what we can all learn cross-culturally. This is closely related to the *environment* aspect of socio-cultural theory, where visitors were also keenly interested in the idea of death as a social practice across a wide range of cultural contexts, as well as the artefacts and tools employed across these different contexts:

> I find it interesting that we have these fairly rigid cultural experiences that are the norm for us, but all the cultures are so different and what we do is so different. For some people it's a huge celebration, others have a huge mourning period. The way we deal with it is so different and it's usually defined by our culture.

This comment from a visitor about the crematorium section of the exhibition demonstrates the understanding gained by visitors about the processes after death: "When you're at the crematorium the curtains close and that's the end of what you see and you always wonder what happens now? This shows you what happens behind the curtain".

Finally, the *historical development* component of socio-cultural theory was manifest from the focus group data where visitors discussed how practices have changed over time, and expressed views about practices that may seem "quaint" today were part of deeply held values from past eras. One of the most popular exhibits was a series of showcases showing Victorian mourning attire and objects. Not only were many visitors not aware of these practices they were amazed that many of these have become inherent in modern responses to death, such as in wearing black and some of the formalities of Western death rituals: "It's weird how they wore mourning dress for something like two years. The wife does this long and the children do this long etc. Where does two years come from? It just shows the formality of that generation I guess. I wonder where that stuff went?" As well as the idea that history was not very long ago and therefore "odd" practices can be appreciated within the context of that era: "They had the photos families took of people when they died and they used to keep them in their lockets because it reminded them of that person. That's really freaky and that only happened 100 years ago. It's odd but it's what they did".

As mentioned earlier, narrative is a key way that visitors engage with museum exhibitions and can be a very powerful tool to assist visitors in dealing with difficult and contentious topics. One area of the exhibition that was particularly confronting for visitors was the final section that contained six personal stories, each consisting of a simple showcase with objects and text. The evaluation showed that these stories were extremely powerful for visitors, with the narrative approach taken considered both respectful, interesting and very moving. Two exhibits in this area in particular evoked strong responses. The first consisted of a shoebox given back to a family with the charred personal effects taken from the handbag of their mother, who had died in a car accident. The other showcase contained a pair of boots worn by a suicide victim alongside the original suicide note. Visitors reported that this section was easy to engage with because of the real stories and objects from people: "I found that last part poignant and moving because they were contemporary deaths and the objects in the showcases were so evocative. I was drawn back to them several times, I couldn't leave the exhibition because of that, I kept circling around them". Visitors were both surprised and moved at how candid people could be about their feelings and in doing so learned about how others approached and dealt with death, as well as prompting some to think about how they might mourn loved ones: "… [the personal stories section] was fascinating and so unexpected to see in an exhibition. It showed what you actually get reduced down to and it was reality. It was somebody's story…". This area had particular resonance for those who had experienced a death recently: "I lost my partner only a few years ago and I was captivated by those images and the sense that they reflected a person that had lived and loved with other people and that was the remnants of them apart from memory". As this was the final part of the exhibition visitors felt it was a good way to end their visit, with most saying they left feeling calm and thoughtful, having had a rewarding and moving experience.

Socio-cultural theory, narrative and museum exhibitions

Socio-cultural theory has been suggested as an appropriate theoretical framework for museum learning as it accounts for meanings made within a social context, rather than facts learned (Schauble et al. 1997, Jeffery-Clay 1998, Leinhardt et al. 2002, Ellenbogen et al. 2004, Falk 2004, Rennie and Johnston 2004). In discussing museum learning Matusov and Rogoff stated that "Museums, as educational institutions, provide opportunities for people to bridge different socio-cultural practices and, through this process, to bridge different institutions and communities" (1995, 101).

When applied to a museum exhibition socio-cultural theory demonstrates that visitors come to understand the context of the world they live in through strong, individual and shared personal connections. In terms of *Death—The Last Taboo*, the way the exhibition was approached provoked thought and discussion: "It spurred me on to think about death because at my age we don't think about death. I never really considered what kind of casket I'd like". Overall, the exhibition added to public understanding about a very important topic: "I think I'm more capable of dealing with death now than what I was before I went in there just because I know so much more about it".

As also discussed in this chapter, narrative is a key way for visitors to engage with topics that are difficult and confronting. The power of narrative when applied to such topics is best summed up by two visitors' responses to the exhibition: "I liked the part where the guy killed himself and they actually showed a picture of where he did it and the lady who was killed in a car crash and the charred remains of her belongings and how her relatives didn't know what to do with them...". Museum exhibitions can be profoundly moving for people and can encourage visitors to respond to a difficult topic as well as being very thoughtful and reflective on their learning and how these topics relate to their everyday lives: "... I loved the way they told people's stories. It made it real and you could think what if that was my mother or brother. You started thinking well what's in my pockets when I walk out the door—what would be in my box?"

References

Abbott, H. 2002. *The Cambridge introduction to narrative*. Cambridge: Cambridge University Press.

Allen, S. 2004a. Designs for learning: Studying science museum exhibits that do more than entertain. *Science Education* 88 (Supplement 1): S17–S33.

—. 2004b. *Finding significance*. San Francisco: Exploratorium.

Ash, D. 2003. Dialogic inquiry and biological themes and principles. *Journal of Museum Education* 28 (2): 8–12.

Bedford, L. 2001. Storytelling: The real work of museums. *Curator* 44(1): 27-34.

—. 2004. Working in the Subjunctive Mood: Imagination and Museums. *Curator* 47(1): 5–11.

Bennett, T. 1995. *The birth of the museum: history, theory, politics*. London: Routledge.

Bowen, J. and P. Hobson. 1987. *Theories of education: Studies of significant innovation in western educational thought* (2nd ed.). Brisbane: John Wiley and Sons.

Bradburne, J. 1998. Dinosaurs and white elephants: The science centre in the 21st century. *Museum Management and Curatorship* 17 (2): 119–137.

Bruner, J. 1986. *Actual minds, possible worlds*. Cambridge: Harvard University Press.

Claxton, G. 1999. *Wise-up: The challenge of lifelong learning*. London: Bloomsbury Publishing.
Combs, A. 1999. Why do they come? Listening to visitors at a decorative arts museum. *Curator* 43 (3): 186–197.
Confucius, trans D. Lau. 1979. *The Analects*. London: Penguin Classics.
Dewey, J. 1938. *Experience and education*. New York: Kappa Delta Pi.
Ellenbogen, K. 2002. Museums in family life: An ethnographic case study. In *Learning conversations in museums*. Ed. G. Leinhardt, K. Crowley and K. Knutson, 81–101. Mahwah: Lawrence Erlbaum Associates.
—. (Ed.). 2003a. Sociocultural perspectives on museums part 1. Washington: Journal of Museum Education.
—. (Ed.). 2003b. Sociocultural perspectives on museums part 2. Washington: Journal of Museum Education.
Falk, J. 1998. Visitors: Who does, who doesn't and why. *Museum News* 77 (2): 38–43.
—. 2004. The director's cut: Toward an improved understanding of learning from museums. *Science Education* 88 (Supplement 1): S82–S96.
Ellenbogen, K. and L. Dierking. 1992. *The museum experience*. Washington: Whalesback Books.
—. (Eds.). 1995. *Public institutions for personal learning: Establishing a research agenda*. Washington: American Association of Museums.
—. 1997. School field trips: Assessing their long-term impact. *Curator* 40 (3): 211–218.
—. 2000. *Learning from museums: Visitor experiences and the making of meaning*. Walnut Creek: AltaMira Press.
Fosnot, C. 2005. *Constructivism: Theory, perspectives, and practice* (2nd ed.). New York and London: Teachers College Press.
Hansman, C. 2001. Context-based adult learning. In *The New Update on Adult Learning Theory*. Ed. S. Merriam, 43–52. San Francisco: Jossey-Bass.
Hein, G. 1998. *Learning in the museum*. London: Routledge.
Hooper-Greenhill, E. (Ed.). 1994. *The educational role of the museum*. London: Routledge.
—. 2000. *Museums and the interpretation of visual culture*. London: Routledge.
Jansen-Verbeke, M., and J. van Rekom. 1996. Scanning museum visitors. *Annals of Tourism Research* 23 (2): 364–375.
Jeffery-Clay, K. 1998. Constructivism in museums: How museums create meaningful learning environments. *Journal of Museum Education* 23: 3–7.

Kelly, L. 2006. Museums as sources of information and learning: The decision-making process. *Open Museum Journal* 8.

—. 2007. *Visitors and learners: Adult museum visitors' learning identities*. PhD, University of Technology, Sydney.

Lave, J., and E. Wenger. 1991. *Situated learning: Legitimate peripheral participation*. Cambridge: Cambridge University Press.

Leinhardt, G., K. Crowley and K. Knutson (Eds). 2002. *Learning conversations in museums*. Mahwah: Lawrence Erlbaum Associates.

Leinhardt, G., K. Crowley and K. Knutson (2003). Museum learning collaborative redux. *Journal of Museum Education* 28 (1): 23–31.

Leinhardt, G., and K. Knutson. 2004. *Listening in on museum conversations*. Walnut Creek: Altamira Press.

McLean, K. 2003. In the cave, around the campfire, and at the well. Paper presented at the ICOM-CECA Annual Conference, Oaxaca, November 2–6.

Matusov, E. and B. Rogoff. 1995. Evidence of development from people's participation in communities of learners. In *Public Institutions for Personal Learning*. Ed. J. Falk and L. Dierking, 97–104. Washington: American Association of Museums.

Mitchell, N. 1999. *The buying decision process of families visiting the Australian Museum–A focus on problem recognition and information search* (unpublished report). Sydney: Australian Museum.

Ogbu, J. 1995. The influence of culture on learning and behaviour. In *Public Institutions for Personal Learning*. Ed. J. Falk and L. Dierking, 79–95. Washington: American Association of Museums.

Paris, S. 1997. Situated motivation and informal learning. *Journal of Museum Education* 22: 22–27.

—. (Ed.). 2002. *Perspectives on object-centered learning in museums*. Mahwah: Lawrence Erlbaum Associates.

Prentice, R. 1998. Recollections of museum visits: A case study of remembered cultural attraction visiting on the Isle of Man. *Museum Management and Curatorship* 17 (1): 41–64.

Rennie, L., and D. Johnston. 2004. The nature of learning and its implications for research on learning from museums. *Science Education* 88 (Supplement 1): S4–S16.

Roberts, L. 1997. *From knowledge to narrative: Educators and the changing museum*. Washington: Smithsonian Institution Press.

Roschelle, J. 1995. Learning in interactive environments: Prior knowledge and new experience. In *Public Institutions for Personal Learning*. Ed. J. Falk and L. Dierking, 37–51. Washington: American Association of Museums.

Rounds, J. 2002. Storytelling in science exhibits. *Exhibitionist* 21 (2): 40–43.

Schauble, L., G. Leinhardt and L. Martin, 1997. A framework for organising a cumulative research agenda in informal learning contexts. *Journal of Museum Education* 22: 3–8.

Sedzielarz, M. 2003. Watching the chaperones: An ethnographic study of adult-child interactions in school field trips. *Journal of Museum Education* 28 (2): 20–24.

Silverman, L. 1995. Visitor meaning making in museums for a new age. *Curator* 38 (3): 161–169.

Vygotsky, L. 1978. *Mind in society: The development of higher psychological processes*. Cambridge: Harvard University Press.

Weil, S. 1997. The museum and the public. *Curator* 16 (3): 257–271.

—. 1999. From being *about* something to being *for* somebody: The ongoing transformation of the American museum. *Daedalus* 128 (3): 229–258.

—. 2002. *Making museums matter*. Washington: Smithsonian Institution Press.

Wenger, E. 1998. *Communities of practice: Learning, meaning and identity*. Cambridge: Cambridge University Press.

Notes

[1] Both the front-end and summative evaluations were conducted by the author in conjunction with Robyn Hayes, from Vivid Qualitative Research, Sydney.

CHAPTER ELEVEN

MAKING CHOICES, WEIGHING CONSEQUENCES: PEDAGOGY AND POLITICS OF TRANSPORTATION IN *AMERICA ON THE MOVE*

MARGARET A. LINDAUER

Introduction

"Transportation is choice and consequences. It's had an impact on daily life and on the environment. It's had an impact on work, and it's been important for immigration and migration", explained one of the exhibit development team members of *America on the Move* (AOTM), the reinstallation of the transportation hall at the National Museum of American History in Washington, DC.[1] The exhibition, which opened in November 2003, replaced a teleological display of technological changes with a more complex representation of transportation history, presenting selected choices that individuals and government agencies in the US made over the course of 125 years (from 1876 to 2000). The exhibition noted how these choices have variously shaped and been shaped by economic, industrial, demographic and cultural changes that occurred in dynamic relationship to one another. For example, construction of cross-continental railroad transformed the agricultural industry, which affected migration and immigration, which in turn was affected by political developments such as the 1868 *Chinese Exclusion Act* that suspended Chinese immigration.

Like transportation, exhibit development fundamentally involves choices and consequences—making choices about what stories to tell and how to tell them while weighing anticipated consequences in terms of how those stories will be received. While AOTM exhibit development team members shared a clear sense of the overarching exhibit theme—changes in transportation have affected and been affected by changes in communities, commerce, landscapes and individual lives—they did not have a prescription for what visitors *ought* to receive from the exhibit. In the words of one curator,

> We were very clear [during the development process] that we wanted people to learn things. That's our job. But we were also very clear that we didn't want to hit them over the head didactically and make them learn anything [in particular], because they come here of their own volition.

Another team member noted that people attend museum exhibitions for various reasons, not all of them educational, and what visitors get out of a show relates to their already established interests, social agendas and previous experiences. In other words, as this team member noted, visitors engage in "free-choice learning", a term coined by John Falk and Lynn Dierking to refer to "learning experiences that occur in and from places like museums, as well as those that occur while watching television, reading a newspaper, talking with friends, attending a play, or surfing the internet" (Falk and Dierking 2000, xi).

At the same time that AOTM exhibit development team members expected visitors to engage in free-choice learning, they hoped that visitors would discern the overarching theme and consider its relevance to their own lives. In the words of one team member,

> We were trying so hard to make points about landscapes, commerce, communities, people. It's about people [and] it's about transportation systems co-existing at the same time … I would hope that if we teach them things, we teach them things that actually have to do with that.

Another team member expressed hope that AOTM would prompt visitors to consider the potential consequences of their own transportation choices in relationship to past and present economic, environmental and cultural issues: "The point is … to try to get people to think about the choices they've made, or that the government has made, and why they make the choices they make".

In this chapter, I argue that "free-choice learning" appropriately accounts for the wide range of educational outcomes among visitors, but it was an insufficient conceptual model for developing an exhibition that would prompt visitors to consider the relevance of the exhibition to their own lives. I suggest that "critical pedagogy", an educational philosophy aimed at engaging learners in analysing social issues (Freire 1995), would have been compatible with curatorial hopes for visitor reception. However given the socio-political context in which the exhibit was developed, application of critical pedagogy would necessarily have been quite limited. I accordingly offer concrete suggestions for how it could have been judiciously applied in the final section of the exhibit.

Research methods

Before presenting my analysis and proposal, I am compelled to acknowledge that my research was not motivated by an interest in exploring the concept of free-choice learning but rather an intellectual curiosity in applying interpretivist evaluation methods to a summative exhibit evaluation. I began the project with two overarching questions in mind: What is the range of educational experiences that the exhibit accommodates or elicits among visitors? And in what ways does that range compare to team members' expectations and hopes?

Data collection began with interviewing 13 exhibit development team members (curators, educators and design manager), asking each person to recount her / his role in the project and to describe what she / he would like to know from visitors. I asked these open-ended questions in order to discern team members' curatorial and educational intentions, i.e., the historical research they felt was important to impart and what they expected and/or hoped visitors would glean from the exhibit.[2]

From interviews with team members, I identified key issues or topics to include in my interviews with visitors.[3] I began each interview by asking individual or groups of visitors to tell me generally what they thought of the exhibition. My intention was to establish at the outset of the conversation that I was interested in hearing about their visits in their own terms (as opposed to pre-determined response categories). Thus, before introducing topics or questions gleaned from my interviews with team members, I re-stated visitors' replies, asking them to confirm and / or elaborate upon my account of their remarks. After the general "what did you think?" conversation-starter, I typically asked visitors if there were some areas of the exhibit where they lingered longer than in other areas, and if so, why they lingered there. I also asked, "If you were going to describe the exhibit to someone who hasn't seen it, is there a theme or idea you would tell them about?"

Once it seemed that I had sufficiently elicited visitors' responses to these questions, I posed more pointed, though still open-ended, questions related to exhibit team members' expressed hopes. For example, I asked if the exhibit made visitors think about any current issues related to transportation and / or ways in which historical changes in transportation have affected their own lives. I also asked if during their visit they thought about both good and bad consequences resulting from changes that historically have occurred in relationship to transportation. Then, after noting that curators had hoped to recount past events or issues that were historically political or emotional without telling visitors what to think, I asked visitors if they thought curators were successful.

Any given interview did not necessarily include all these questions, but rather proceeded as if it were a natural conversation that unfolded in response to visitors' opinions and assertions. These interviews lasted anywhere between five and 45 minutes, depending upon visitors' schedules, comfort levels and interest. This free-flowing, conversational and non-systematic interview style is a typical feature of interpretivist evaluation, which seeks to elicit a range of participant opinions and accounts of their experiences and does not rest on statistically computing systematically collected data that focuses on predetermined behavioural, cognitive or affective variables (Guba and Lincoln 1989).

Interpretivist research designs are often iterative, meaning that they take shape as research proceeds. Data analysis invokes an inductive reasoning process, working from multiple readings of transcribed interviews to generate data categories (as opposed to working with categories determined in advance of data analysis). Thus there is not a singularly correct method for assessing ways in which a given exhibition functions educationally. Invoking Falk and Dierking's theory of free-choice learning is one possible approach among many, which, in the case of AOTM, is justified by the fact that team members referred to it as they recounted the exhibit development process.

Free-choice learning outcomes

Falk and Dierking (2000) explain that free-choice learning "tends to be non-linear, is personally motivated, and involves considerable choice on the part of the learner as to what to learn, as well as where and when to participate in learning" (13). Thus predicting exactly what a visitor will learn from a particular museum experience is difficult because "it requires knowing something about who is visiting, why they are visiting and with whom, what they are doing before and after the visit, what they see and do in the museum, and how these factors interact and interrelate" (13). To conceptually organise these various factors, Falk and Dierking propose a "contextual model of learning". In their words, learning is "the process /

product of the interactions … [between] three overlapping contexts: the personal, the sociocultural, and the physical" (10).

The personal context is constituted by the ways in which new experiences transform attitudes, thoughts and memories of a visitor's prior knowledge, interests and experiences. As one AOTM team member asserted, "My feeling is most people [who] go through history exhibits, their first take on things is a personal one. So, you know, 'my father used to have a car like that', is by far the most common comment that we'll get". This kind of personal connection may be considered nostalgic rather than educational, however, as another team member explained, a nostalgic experience can be educational, "if it makes you self-reflexive, if it makes you examine your relationship to the [exhibit] content and make a connection".

My conversations with visitors illustrated her point. For example, a retired man from Illinois gleefully told me, "There was a 1950 Buick [in the exhibit] … That was one of the first cars I ever drove. Unfortunately the first time I drove it, I ran into the back of somebody else 'cause I didn't know what I was doing". He chuckled as he proceeded,

> And the Buick hit the Chevrolet that was in front and crunched it, just crumpled it up. And there wasn't even a scratch on the Buick. I mean, it was built so well. All that chrome. The chrome didn't even chip on that car. And it cost me about a hundred bucks to fix the other guy's car.

He paused, reflecting briefly, and added, "But it was a learning experience".

I used his comment about a learning experience as an opportunity to note that lots of visitors seem to have nostalgic experiences in AOTM, and I asked him if he thought a nostalgic experience is also a learning experience. He answered without hesitation,

> Oh yes, because, well, you look back and you remember, but now you see those things differently … It's like, you have these memories but then you also see your memories sort of in relationship to other things that you hadn't thought of before.

Other visitors offered similar explanations of how they connected personal memories or histories to a larger historical context. For example, a man from Maryland referred to a section of the exhibition that focused on the inter-relationship of public transportation systems, suburban isolation and social history, as he explained,

> I was interested in the part about Park Forest [Illinois]. I used to live not too far from there, so that was kind of interesting. I always thought about Park Forest as … an older suburb … 'cause I was growing up in the 60s and 70s and it's been around since the late 40s. But this [exhibit] was showing it as a brand new subdivision and I hadn't thought of it that way. I thought of it as an older area, where newer subdivisions were further out. And I was thinking about how those newer places, the ones further out, those didn't have the same kind of [racial] tensions when they developed.

This visitor was referring to the display in AOTM of a memo from the Social Action Committee of the Park Forest Unitarian Church that was addressed to village employees. The memo offered directives for dealing with the tensions that had arisen during the integration of African American families into Park Forest. The AOTM visitor was not merely reminiscing about where he grew up but rather saw his memory of a place through a new perspective, which in turn sparked a question in his mind, "Why didn't later suburbs experience the same tensions?"

This multi-faceted learning experience—recalling personal history, relating it to a broader history, and articulating a question for possible investigation—corresponds to one exhibit team member's remark that "We're not here to give people facts, facts, facts, information, information, information. We're here just to get them interested, a little spark … [And from that] they might want to find out some more". It also corresponds to the socio-cultural context of learning.

As Falk and Dierking (2000) explain, exhibitions are "created … with the intention of communicating, that is, 'conversing' with the reader" (41). As such, exhibits can contribute to "people's efforts to negotiate personal and cultural meaning … actively making sense of the interpretation presented and attempting to relate it to their own experience and world view" (46). For example, a woman visiting from New York with her sister and nephews referred to a section of AOTM that focuses on changes in the shipping industry, and she noted that it unexpectedly answered questions they had recently pondered:

> We just drove through New Jersey on the way here, and we were talking about longshoremen yesterday. We saw these huge cranes in New Jersey. And I thought it was really interesting that there was an exhibit there [in AOTM] about how it's different [now], you know, with how many tonnages are moved, because I was looking at those cranes [yesterday] and I was thinking about all the longshoremen who lost their jobs [in the 1960s]. I think that was an issue that started when I was young, and … so then here it … saying how much tonnage, how much more they move now with so many fewer laborers.

Her comment not only exemplifies how learning occurs through social interaction but also how difficult it would be to predict or control the factual knowledge that visitors will acquire from an exhibition. Each person brings a unique personal history and set of interests that will influence what she / he learns.

In their discussion of the socio-cultural context, Falk and Dierking cite research by psychologists Lev Vygotsky, who coined the term "zone of proximal development" (Vygotsky 1978), and Mihaly Csikszentmihalyi, whose research has focused on the psychological state of "flow" (Csikszentmihalyi 1990). Vygotsky's early 20th century research (which was suppressed by the Soviet Union until the 1960s) focused on the development of increasingly complex cognitive skills among children. He found that a child's skills are most effectively advanced when an adult guides that child to engage in an activity that is slightly beyond the skills the child has already mastered. In other words, the activity falls within that particular child's zone of proximal development. Vygotsky noted the significance of language and conversation between adult and child, as the child is coached to complete tasks that she / he would not be able to accomplish on her / his own. Furthermore, Vygotsky stressed the importance of looking at each child as an individual whose pace of development is distinct from that of other children.

Csikszentmihalyi similarly emphasises variation among individuals in his research findings regarding the psychological state of flow—an "optimal experience … that is an end in itself" generated from activities "done not with the expectation of some future benefit, but simply because the doing is itself the reward" (Csikszentmihalyi 1990, 67). As an individual's skills, knowledge and experiences expand, activities that once led that person to a state of flow may no longer be sufficiently challenging. Thus conditions for "flow" will not only vary from one person to the next but also change over the course of a person's life.

Ideal educational or "flow" activities are therefore designed in response to an assessment of an individual's (or group of individuals') skills, knowledge, interests, abilities, preferred learning styles and types of intelligence. This is, of course, an impossible endeavour in a museum setting that sees thousands of visitors each week. Falk and Dierking (2000) accordingly recommended that exhibits—the physical context of learning—incorporate various means for imparting information (188), as is exemplified by *America on the Move*.

In the words of one AOTM team member, "the exhibition was really, very, very committed to different learning styles . . . [because] from the Smithsonian's point of view, learning styles are accessibility issues". The commitment to accommodate various learning styles is reflected by the combination of various media—traditional didactic panels and object labels, computer-narrated text, documentary-style films, manipulative devices (crates that can be opened and text panels that can be rotated, spun or flipped), interactive computer games / activities, etc.

However, for visitors to AOTM who are not cognisant of their own learning styles or of the fact that several exhibit components are designed to accommodate other accessibility issues, the resulting experience is a sight-and-sound extravaganza that does not readily accommodate contemplation and analysis (e.g., "flow"). For example, one family described how perplexed they were to find audio components that, when activated by visitors, repeated adjacent printed information. The father rhetorically asked, "Do they [the exhibit curators] think we can't read?" He was not aware that these audio components were meant to accommodate people who are visually impaired.

The immersive environments (theatrical settings that feature cast figures engaged in conversation and activities) also reflect institutional standards. As one AOTM team member noted, "The Secretary and his Undersecretary have been very vocal about cutting edge in design in exhibits and multimedia … and money is coming in with a mandate … [for] exciting immersive exhibits". However, as another team member cautioned, while an "immersive environment hopefully prods people to think about their place [in relationship to the past] … it can be overwhelming. And it's noisy … it might be too over-stimulating". Indeed, a museum visitor who lives in the Washington DC area and was visiting the museum with his wife validated this concern. He said, "It's overwhelming, I mean there's so much, it's hard to see one thing and focus on it for very long, before you're drawn away".

A study conducted by the Smithsonian Institution Office of Policy and Analysis (2005) that tracked and timed 149 visitors as they traversed through AOTM found that 76 per cent of those visitors spent less than 30 minutes in the exhibition, and the average time was 11:39 minutes. Precious little historical information can be absorbed—let alone applied to contemporary issues associated with transportation (as team members had hoped)—while traversing a 27,000 square-foot (2,500 square-metre) exhibition in that amount of time. In the words of a man from San Jose, California, visiting with his eleven-year-old son:

> There's a lot of people nowadays that are limited on time, where mentally they think, "Oh you know I want to go in there for an hour and get out, and get something out of it." And you can't … For example, you've got the car in the mud, you know, they're pulling it out, and you think, "Well yea,

> what did that mean to me?" You know, it's nice to see … [but] it's a lot of stuff that you just kind of recognize. You know there's a trailer, you know some people are camping, there's a little girl there, and that's nice to see, but you just see it very briefly and then you walk away, you know.

I asked him if he was able to find information whenever he was looking for it. He replied,

> Well that's just it, you see, there's just so much there you don't know where to look. I mean, there's plenty of information and you can see, I saw the labels, and I saw that I could read about different things, but I wanted to know why it all was there. What were they trying to say with all of these different things?

As this visitor implied, despite opportunities to read text panels, watch videos, listen to narratives, play computer games, manipulate interactive devices and walk past (or through) reconstructed historical settings, visitors are not engaged in an explicit pedagogical program that asks them to consider the transportation choices they make in their everyday lives, the consequences of which will contribute to future economic, industrial and cultural developments. In other words, visitors are cast as witnesses rather than participants in making history by their everyday decisions and actions.

The limits of free-choice learning

If Falk and Dierking's contextual model of free-choice learning is invoked as a measure of educational outcomes, then AOTM is to be lauded as a terrific success—the exhibition sparked memories, invoked previous knowledge, and compelled some visitors to want to learn more. However team members also espoused more specific educational objectives. As one person stated:

> We were trying so hard to make points about landscape, commerce, communities, people. It's about people [and] it's about transportation systems co-existing at the same time … I would hope that if we teach them things, we teach them things that actually have to do with that.

He elaborated that he didn't expect people to come out saying "lives, landscapes, commerce, communities" but rather to pick up the sense of relationships.

As I noted above, I initiated my interviews with visitors by asking them what they thought of the exhibit and where they lingered. Later in the interview, when I asked, "If you were going to describe the exhibit to someone who hasn't seen it yet, is there a theme or idea you would tell them about?" numerous visitors indicated that the exhibit referred to relationships among historical changes. For example, upon reflection, a man from Denver, Colorado, said that the exhibit showed "how it [transportation] evolved in so many different ways and how that shaped culture, culture shaped it". He paused briefly and then remarked, "The modes of transportation in the United States have changed over time. Sometimes the government's been involved in those changes [and] sometimes it's been economic".

However, most visitors remarked that the exhibit was primarily about change over time. For example, a man from South Dakota explained the exhibit is about "different ways of moving across the country at different times, how you start with horse-and-carriage, move to the steam engine, to a train, to an automobile and semi-[truck]". I asked him if the exhibit showed ways in which changes in transportation affected people's lives or communities, he replied, "I guess you could say that, but it's not something I was thinking about".

Some people who characterised the exhibit theme as "change over time" also noted that historic changes in transportation have improved people's lives. In the words of a man from El Salvador, "It's about getting from one place to another, easier and faster. How technology keeps making it better and easier". His remark invoked an entrenched story of progress, which was not necessarily anathema to the exhibition, but rather incomplete. As one curator explained,

> We did everything we could … to not play to the obvious strength of … transportation as this wonderful metaphor for progress. It's a story that I think transportation has been used for a long time. But, it's not that it's not a true story. Immigration and migration is about people heading out to a new territory for a better life, and often times, that's what they get. And so, you don't want to not do that, but it's not the only story either.

Team members also hoped that visitors would think about historical changes in relationship to current transportation-related issues affecting their lives and communities. In the words of one team member, "The point is … to try to get people to think about the choices they've made, or that the government has made, and why they make the choices they make". Unfortunately, most visitors said no when I asked, "Did the exhibit make you think of ways in which changes in transportation have affected your life?" and "While you were in the exhibit, did you think about any current issues related to transportation?" Indeed, one man explained, "I actually think goin' in there kinda helps you forget about current issues and concentrate on a simpler time."

While the exhibition rarely compelled visitors to associate historical developments with current issues, my interview questions prompted some visitors to tell me about problems that affect their lives. For example, a man from Norfolk, Virginia, replied,

> It [AOTM] didn't really relate to current things. But it could have. I mean, we're in Virginia, where it's a car culture. And it's just constant, you know. Everyone's going in the same direction. It's just insane to me … you know, emitting all these things, these greenhouse gases … I think the guys who are making money off the steel, the gas and the rubber, could do the same off of trains. What's the difference?

And a woman from New Jersey said,

> They could have made things more pronounced. Like the bicycle, it just said they [bicycles] gained popularity rather quickly . . . But the bicycle could have played a more important role in the exhibit … I think there are ways that they could make it more thought-provoking towards, you know, things we're facing. I didn't really see anything that was sort of, you know, asking big questions.

Among the handful of visitors who indicated that knowledge of the past represented in AOTM relates to understanding the present, a man from Leesburg, Virginia, said that the exhibit "pointed out that back then, we had to evolve to mass transportation. And it made me think we may need to do it again". He then referred to a film depicting conversant commuters in the 1950s, which was created for AOTM and projected on a screen installed on the inside, front end of a subway car from Chicago. He said,

> You know, looking at … the conversation that was going on, on the train, about having to commute and stuff like that, and not driving into town. It kind of made me think about where we're going … I think we're getting to the point now where traffic is very heavy in the inner cities and we gotta go back to public transportation … because, you know, the areas are just getting so populated that there's no place for cars anymore.

A man from Florida who described himself as a bicycle commuter tacitly shared this sentiment, though also remarked that the exhibit did not sufficiently refer to current issues:

> There was this thing about the urban streets and the pollution in Chicago. That I thought was pretty well done. And they discussed the cutting of the Congress Street expressway and how that affected Chicago. And that was good. But nothing about, for example, junk yards all over the country or nothing about environmental pollution caused by leaking gas tanks, nothing about the inability to re-use strip shopping centers which were the result of the expressways and the growth of the suburbs …. or areas of the city that are too near the interstate, and gas stations that have closed ... There was nothing about the manufacturing process either, now that I think of it. Missing was the oil fields or, um, the junk yards, the disposal of all this transportation.

I asked him if he felt the museum had a responsibility to include some of those things. He said,

> Yea, I do. I do … The way it is now, it's like a chamber commerce thing where it's very much a celebration of America on the move … I felt like … it didn't make us pause, which is what I think a well-curated show would do, on this subject.

Critical pedagogy and the politics of exhibiting transportation history

The curators' hope that visitors would think about current issues in relationship to historic changes associated with transportation resonates with Paolo Freire's commitment to teach people to "read the world" at the same time that they learn to "read the word" (Shaull 1995). The overarching objective of his teaching practice was social justice. Learners would ideally extend their awareness of cultural, socio-economic and political mechanisms through which some people maintain socio-cultural, political and economic dominance other groups of people (Freire 1995).

With Freire's teaching philosophy as foundation, teachers and scholars have conceptualised critical pedagogy in response to questions: What knowledge will be produced and disseminated? Who decides? How are those decisions made? Particular responses to these questions will vary among educational settings, though critical pedagogues generally concur that social justice depends upon presenting learners with provocative critical content and allowing them democratically to construct knowledge from multiple perspectives. Teachers therefore call upon learners to articulate the personal knowledge that they bring to a learning experience. From the exchange of information, anecdotes, opinions and interpretations, learners then build new (non-prescribed) knowledge.

Critical pedagogy is typically cast as having a leftist political objective insofar as it validates the perspectives of people who historically have not been empowered (or equipped) to contribute to negotiations that effect social, economic and cultural changes. In this sense, it resonates with current trends in new museum theory, but it has not been widely applied in museum practice (Lindauer 2007). Indeed because of its explicit political-pedagogical objective, it would not have been possible for AOTM members to apply it broadly to the entire installation.

"In the last four or five years in the Smithsonian", one team member explained, "everything has been very politicized", resulting in heightened scrutiny from members of Congress, journalists and the general public. Furthermore, he noted, "Senior Smithsonian administrators and donors seemed to embrace the notion of transportation as this wonderful metaphor for progress" and therefore expected the exhibition to be "a show about progress and transportation technology with an overlay of mobility and upward mobility". Thus they scrutinised and disputed the appropriateness of an exhibition script that wove transportation history into American history writ large, including discussion of race, gender and socio-economic issues associated with historical trends and events. As one curator noted,

> The things you take for granted in academia are much more difficult to do in a museum … We're not saying anything that shocking [in AOTM]. We're saying that the railroads, the trolleys, [and] the roads reflected the social and cultural hierarchies of the United States. But for some reason that's a lot more shocking in this context, at least to senior managers and donors.

AOTM curators accordingly made a deliberate choice to present information dispassionately and to describe both sides of historically contentious issues, allowing visitors to think what they will about those issues (which is not the same as articulating one's thoughts and opinions to one another—as critical pedagogy prescribes).

AOTM visitors also seemed to want and / or expect dispassionate text that presented undisputed facts. For example, a woman visiting from Illinois explained, "Not everybody agrees with the same things. You know, facts are universal but interpretations, people's opinions, they're different for everybody". According to another visitor, dispassionate didacticism corresponds to historical accuracy:

> It's one thing to describe what has been, you know, we **did** extend Route 66; people **did** take it to California when they were escaping the

> Depression; there **were** roadside cabins and a lot of them were not open to Black people. These are historical facts that are going to be hard to deny.

If the exhibit had explicitly invited people to think about current transportation issues, the Smithsonian, in the words of this visitor, "would have been skating on thin ice".

Despite administrative scrutiny and visitor expectations / preferences, critical pedagogy could have been applied, albeit as a relatively small component of AOTM. Indeed, the final section of *America on the Move*, "Going Global", represents an appropriate size, placement and overarching theme, though the installation style would need to change. Like other sections of the exhibition, "Going Global" alludes to a specific time and place in which transportation plays a significant role in socio-economic changes. A satellite map of the southern California coast extends the length of one wall (perhaps 30 feet [9 metres]), while the year 2000 is represented by news headlines continuously looping across an equally long electronic billboard on the opposite side of the room. Below the electronic billboard, three video screens are evenly dispersed. Each screen features a pastiche of photographs, films and narratives presented in jump-cut collage and representing an aspect of globalisation, e.g., the development of fusion food or the inter-continental clothing industry. At the same time, a selection of rock songs, including "Californication" by the Red Hot Chili Peppers, plays loudly and continuously.

This section of AOTM, in the words of one team member, "puts you in the middle of heated political controversy" and ideally "give[s] people the tools for them to look at this and say, 'Oh, okay, I really like the fact that I can get cheap clothes, but I guess that has consequences that I didn't really think about'". However, according to visitors' remarks, the installation does not draw people into such analysis or self-reflection. A woman from Seattle explained,

> We were watching the video, which is riveting … [but] I was trying to do two at once—the Los Angeles one and the, uh, globalization one … I found them interesting, but I think there was too much going on … I mean there was the, uh, the messages going across the top and the three screens, music, and trying to listen … I can't quite figure out was the end has to do with America on the move.

A twelve-year-old boy from Manhattan who struggled to make a connection between this section and the rest of the exhibition said,

> The last part had, like, screens all around, and it showed, like different weird things or something. But then the three screens would show, like, Japanese food or Chinese food, and I didn't really get it. Is it the car that shipped it? Is that the transportation? Or were they focusing on, "Oh, a zipper should go here and here" and "this is how the eel is cut"? And it's kinda like, "What's this got to do with transportation"?

In other words, presentation techniques obscured the overarching theme of the "Going Global" section: fast and inexpensive global transportation systems influence changes in commerce in the US (and around the world)—what people buy, the clothing they wear, the food they eat and the range of jobs that they might have.

The multimedia techniques could be repurposed, according to the principles of critical pedagogy, to engage visitors in debating the good and bad socio-economic consequences of globalisation. It could also prompt visitors to consider relationships between past and current issues associated with changes in transportation. For example, computer stations that cast as critical thinkers could offer a menu of topics and a range of facts followed by provocative questions through which visitors would indicate their perceptions of "good" or "bad" consequences of globalisation. The computer stations could be interconnected so that visitors engage in an electronically facilitated discussion, wherein people would respond to and / or compare their opinions to those of other visitors. The section could also include opportunities for visitors to record personal stories and beliefs about how their own lives and communities have historically been affected by transportation systems.

This approach would enact three principal features of critical pedagogy (Gore 1993) if it: 1) offered critical content that explicitly demonstrates how people's lives are variously shaped (positively and / or negatively) by changes in transportation systems; 2) enacted democratic teaching techniques with questions that prompt visitors to articulate how their own actions and behaviours relate to broader socio-political, cultural, environmental and economic issues; and 3) invited visitors to share curatorial authority by contributing their own stories, opinions and interpretation of facts to the production of historical knowledge represented in a national museum. The overarching objective would be to avoid directing visitors to a predetermined conclusion, while also prompting to cultivate a habit of analysis regarding multi-faceted choices and consequences that politicians, business people, families and other citizens have faced as they enact changes in transportation.

References

Csikszentmihalyi, M. 1990, *Flow: The psychology of optimal experience*. New York: Harper & Row.

Falk, J. and L. Dierking. 2000. *Learning from museums: Visitor experiences and making of meaning*. Walnut Creek, CA: Altamira Press.

Freire, P. 1995 [1970]. *Pedagogy of the oppressed*. New York: The Continuum Company.

Guba, E. and Y. Lincoln. 1989. *Fourth generation evaluation*. Newbury Park, CA: Sage Publications.

Gore, J. 1993. *The struggle for pedagogies: Critical and feminist discourses as regimes of truth*. New York: Routledge.

Lindauer, M. A. 2007. Critical museum pedagogy: A conceptual first step. In *Museum revolutions: How museum change and have changed*. Eds. S. K. Knell, S. MacLeod, and S. Watson, 303–314. London: Routledge.

Shaull, R. 1995. Foreword to *Pedagogy of the oppressed*, 11–16. New York: The Continuum Company.

Smithsonian Office of Policy and Analysis. 2005. Multiple perspectives on *America on the Move* at the National Museum of American History. Washington DC: Smithsonian Institution.

Vygostky, L. 1978. *Mind in society: The development of higher psychological processes*. Cambridge, MA: Harvard University Press.

Notes

[1] I ethically am bound to respect the confidentiality of AOTM exhibit development team members, as I promised at the outset of the evaluation. Thus team members whom I interviewed are not named as their comments are cited.

[2] I conducted these interviews, each of which lasted approximately 60 minutes, over the course of two weeks, approximately three months after AOTM opened to the public.

[3] I conducted 76 interviews over the course of five days, speaking with 125 visitors. My sampling method was opportunistic (as opposed to systematic); I stood immediately outside the exhibit exit and invited visitors to share their opinions as they left the exhibit hall. When visitors accepted my invitation, we walked to a nearby table and chairs where we could comfortably sit. I interviewed a wide range of visitors in terms of social group (visiting alone, as a couple, or in a group of family or friends), age, ethnicity, and geographic residence (local, regional, national and international). Thus interviewees as a whole loosely typified a Smithsonian audience but were not intended to be demographically representative, in a scientific sense.

CHAPTER TWELVE

HAILING THE COSMOPOLITAN CONSCIENCE: MEMORIAL MUSEUMS IN A GLOBAL AGE

PAUL WILLIAMS

Globalisation and the re-energising of memorialisation

Significant research now exists about the relation between national atrocities, collective memory, and public memorialisation. As a primary focus, post-war German practices of forgetting, remembering and commemorating the Holocaust have by now generated a substantial body of writing (see, for example, Young 1994, Huyssen 2003, Till 2005). As the German case attests, the relation between a populace prepared to confront terrible events and governments and organisations willing to provide for public memorial spaces is normally imagined as a national affair—even in the face of the erasure of Jews from the national body through annihilation and displacement. Similarly, whether in the attempts to face Armenian or Cambodian genocides, or the search for truth about Argentinean or Chilean state terrorism, the collective memory of violent harm is generally conceived as national memory. Accordingly, constructive public remembering is assumed to be beneficial largely for the civic health of the nation concerned.

The question of how globalisation, with its attendant increasingly diasporic populations and an emerging public with transnational identifications, has affected these connections has been only occasionally discussed, and little theorised. This chapter aims to remedy the lack of critical attention to two connected facts that have become patent over the past twenty years: an unprecedented flow of instantaneous mediascapes and tourists crossing borders (Appadurai 1996), and a near-worldwide "memorialising moment" realised in the creation of, and popular interest in, inert memorial structures, that also shows no sign of slowing (Williams 2007).[1] This correlation is not especially intuitive; while it can be posited that both the international media and tourism industries help people to learn about others' diverse personal histories, thereby encouraging transnational identification and empathy, it does not necessarily follow that an increasingly globally aware public would seek out physical memorial museums. After all, while a tenet of globalisation holds that new technologies contribute to a cultural *milieu* characterised by speed, emphemerality and spectacle, the concrete, memorial museum might be seen as outmoded, operating at the opposite pole from the stream of sound-bite digital media.[2]

This chapter, however, will describe how globalisation and physical memorials can be understood as complementary. The key lies with a growing post-nationalist public that identifies with what I call "cosmopolitan conscience". The concept is reminiscent of "cosmopolitan citizenship", or the "world citizen", which has long been a utopian ideal, dating back to Ancient Greece (Linklater 2002, 317). Cosmopolitanism is particularly pertinent to memorial museums, since they generally detail crimes against greater humanity and their contravention of international legal instruments and conventions. Prominent examples include the Nuremberg Conventions, the *1948 Convention on the Prevention and Punishment of the Crime of Genocide*, the *1948 Universal Declaration of Human Rights*, and the *1984 Convention Against Torture, and other Cruel, Inhuman, or Degrading Treatment or Punishment.* Cosmopolitan conscience also has much in common with Levy and Sznaider's term, "cosmopolitan memory", which they use to describe popular responses to globally historic events, and the Holocaust in particular (Levy and Sznaider 2002). I differentiate my term on the grounds that "conscience" has the benefit of avoiding complicated debates over how memory is constituted—in individual, collective and "imaginary" terms—and connects directly to the moral impetus of memorial museums.

As an enacted identity, cosmopolitan conscience requires some kind of embodied performance that enables those interested in it to achieve self-recognition. Memorial museums, I posit, provide an apposite environment for this act. The observations about visitors that follow are not drawn from a qualitative survey of individuals at museums, but are instead based, looking top-down, on how institutions hail their audience through narrative constructs and physical environments that invoke cosmopolitan conscience. This chapter will posit that memorial museums play a key role in actualising this emerging identity by providing sensuous, haptic experiences that establish its common contours. A variety of examples will show how exhibition tactics at memorial museums, combined with their expressive meta-themes—those of love, family, loss, trauma, bereavement, and memory—provide a universal frame with which people from many walks of life can identify.

Memorial museums and the performance of conscience

Globalisation and its ensuing diversification and splintering of social allegiances shifts, to a degree, the understanding of collective memory from the unified, chronological narratives of nationhood to the episodic, affective narratives of groups. The awakening, through media and travel, of a cosmopolitan conscience has helped to produce what Barbara Misztal (2004) calls the "sacralization of memory" (67). Misztal is interested in how "the decline in the role of national and religious memories as stable sources of identity reopens the space for search for both authentic identities and useable pasts" (68). Misztal's description of the search for personal identity reflects a shift from "an imagery of dwelling", most suited to a period when nationalism felt self-evident and secure, to an imagery of journeying, "which is conducive to our present unsettled times" (2004, 68). Journeying, for Misztal, is not simply reflective of current travel, but metaphorical; the search for a sense of self, she suggests, is increasingly conducted through explorations of different social, cultural and spiritual identities.

In practical terms, the ability to travel to memorial museums in distant places is, of course, facilitated by tourism. At present, tourism continues to grow—the World Tourism Organisation predicts that the tourism sector will surpass one billion international travellers by 2010 (White 2001, 9). Cultural tourism is a segment outpacing tourism overall, and visitor numbers at sites that fall under the rubric of memorial museums are also increasing (Williams 2007, 7–20). It remains, of course, that political and economic factors mean that global tourism, and visitation to memorial museums, is asymmetric, and remains a predominantly Western privilege. This has important implications for visitor expectations and, in a feedback process, the experience (including facilities, languages, and interpretation) provided by museums. While we remain far from the spread of global interchanges that true cosmopolitanism might require, there is significant energy in the exchanges that take place. As Jean-Didier Urbain notes:

> Engaged to various degrees in the planetary ethnography of our modernity, travelers and tourists participate in a vast movement of observation and reconnaissance. They are carried forward by the same current that ceaselessly feeds and reconstitutes our vision of the world. Tourism is not the degrading massification of travel. Rather, it is the *generalisation of a way of knowing*. (Urbain 2002, 120)

Rather than simply homogenising or flattening experiences, this common "way of knowing" may involve the tourist's greater grasp of our shared human lifeways. This may lead to an ensuing appreciation that, to various extents, historical tragedy has inflicted all societies, and a natural desire to visit places that relate meaningfully to such experiences.

Precisely because globalisation has seen the increasing reproduction of historical signifiers in a great variety of arbitrary, often commercially-focused locations, memorial museums, by contrast, are valued for offering authenticity in abundance. Given that the very nature of history involves its lapsed temporality, the fixing and retracing of an event in site-specific geographies is a surviving method for imparting its essence. Authenticity, it should be noted, is conceived here as less a matter of an impeccable edifice, and more as one related to visitor *experience* (McCannell 1992). We understand that most places and the objects that claim objective authenticity can be critiqued as being (re)constructed as such through architectural, design, and curatorial interventions (and such pointed non-interventions as the "arrested decay" approach). Visitors, normally arriving at memorial museums with a heightened state of receptivity to the topic at hand, are ultimately those who judge whether or not a site is authentically expressive. An experience-based notion of authenticity places the definition in the hands of the beholder, or in, as Ning Wang puts it, "a potential existential state of Being which is activated by tourist activities" and involves the "disintegration of pretension" (Wang 2003, 221). This can occur in interpersonal interactions in the museum, and in heightened internal reflections that are less often found in the routines of everyday life. While authentic experiences are difficult to objectively define, an experiential sense of some shade of existential transformation is known when it is felt.

Visitors to memorial museums, bearing diverse cultural and historical identities, respond individually to the "moral education" at the heart of memorial museums—the cluster of ideas concerning personal culpability, victimhood and responsibility. They are faced with exhibitions that frame questions such as: which groups suffered? Who was to blame? Are we / they still suffering? Are we / they still to blame? For their part, visitors may counter: how does the memorial museum narrate group experiences within its interpretation? How does this accord with my own sense of the event? If I have little investment in, or knowledge of, this catastrophe, am I simply a spectator, a voyeur? In the social environment of an exhibition, narrative design can both quell and magnify anxieties about one's perceived social identity: how am I being judged? Am I viewed by other visitors within one of the museum's victim or perpetrator categories? Alternatively, how can I prove my commitment to the message at hand?

It is notable that memorial museums have flourished during this global age that sees the entrenchment and naturalisation of "identity politics". By this I refer to the group feeling associated with social movements, the members of which unite around common cultural practices and experiences of actual or perceived injustice. Identity lies at the heart of memorial museums, since their core topics (genocide, terrorism, political persecution, displacement and suchlike) involve certain people being singled out based on their presumed group affiliation. The idea that identity can often be established—no matter how accurately—through physical appearance, language and custom makes visits to memorial museums especially charged, since people will arrive with a keen sense of their own identity-appearance. Memorial museums receive visitors whose identities span a range of affiliations—including survivors, their families and friends, perpetrators and their families and friends, those from the affected region or social group, those from regions, social groups or nations that inflicted the harm, the larger national demographic, concerned international visitors, and the more general realm of sightseeing tourists. Notions of "involved", "implicated", "affected", "neutral" and "unmoved" are relative and relational as historical-geographic categories, and also exist in an affective sense: the ways we attach ourselves to and distance ourselves from histories are not always predictable.

Rather than approach memorial museums through a normative museum studies approach that foregrounds exhibition narratives, I propose that their visceral, kinesthetic, haptic and intimate qualities are equally vital (Kirshenblatt-Gimblett 1998, 194). Increasing attention to the architectural and design elements of museums helps to enrich this focus. Daniel Libeskind's use of architectural "voids" in the Jewish Museum, Berlin, is a case in point. The museum's affective power lies not just in its content, but also in the experience of its awkward, foreign, claustrophobic spaces. Its off-kilter interiors produce an experience in bodily uncertainty; the key motif is the spatial indecision of one's own movements, and watching others in the act (and having them watch you). When a docent locks a door behind you in the 30-metre high "Holocaust Tower", the immediate impression is only of darkness and disorientation.

Figure 12.1. Holocaust Tower, Jewish Museum, Berlin. Image taken by author with permission.

As one's eyes adjust, the imprisoning effect of the concrete space becomes evident—and abjectly alienating. Visitors together tend to instinctively gaze upwards towards a single high slit that gives a glimpse of the sky. The only comfort is the sense that others are sharing the same tall, empty, unheated space.

Memorial museums increasingly attempt to provide such evocative common spaces. Similarly, at Berlin's Memorial to the Murdered Jews of Europe, Phnom Penh's Toul Sleng Museum of Genocidal Crimes, and the Kigali Genocide Memorial Centre, the visitor's own movement and accompanying sense of fear, grief, bewilderment or calmness is as much the focus as physical objects themselves. On the grounds of the Bergen Belsen Memorial visitors will find the "House of Silence", an architecturally sparse, diamond-shaped room with wooden pews and a table at one end, on which tributary pebbles are laid. Standing at the rear of the space and gazing upwards, one notices that the points of the semi-transparent roof make the shape of a cross. I raise this example because, in terms of a sense of communal conscience, a useful analogy that illuminates the sensory experience of memorial museums is churchgoing. At both places, people may attend not only to learn information (such as historical facts or the details of scriptures), but because they wish to be in a total environment where they can rehearse and affirm a sense of *being in place*. Both memorial museums and churches make concrete the notion of sacred ground and congregate people around a single topic. (There are, perhaps, other related parallels: both teach in a moral tone, emphasising our common propensity for sins and terrible acts toward others and advocate the need for ongoing self-examination.) My attention rests on the slippery topic of an individual's *quality of feeling* that stems from being in a certain place, and around others interested in exercising the same moral concern. An accent on the physical is in line with the idea, central to the study of trauma, that we remember not so much in a cognitive, declarative fashion, but in one that is bodily and sensory. This is especially pertinent when the themes related to us by memorial museums are those of physical discomfort, pain and alienation.

As physical structures, memorial museums provide effective containers for the *global emplacement of memory*. Consider, for instance, how Auschwitz's "Arbeit Macht Frei" gates have become a globally recognised icon and point of entry for other more complex histories associated with the Holocaust. Such images of atrocity are recognised, reproduced, and circulated in an ever-growing array of media: print, television, film, and the internet—where one's own uploaded images can join a global collection of tagged memories. An associated shift in history museums from artefact-based and collection-driven to being immersive, experiential and narrative-driven inevitably affects how memory is constituted. Discussing the US Holocaust Memorial Museum, Alison Landsberg writes: "the mass media has begun to construct sites, which I will refer to as transferential spaces, in which people are invited to enter into experiential relationships with events which they themselves did not live (Landsberg 1997, 66). These spaces "might instill in us 'symptoms' or prosthetic memories through which we didn't actually live, but to which we now, after a museum experience or a filmic experience, have a kind of experiential relationship" (82).

Indeed, memorial museums are often *reminders*, rather than primary frames, for what we have collectively already pictured and conceived via mass media. For visitors, authenticity may be prized precisely because it is slow, embodied, reflective and offers a sense of unique, individual experience—qualities that instantaneous media cannot provide. In the case of the 9/11 terror attacks, for instance, it may be that the televisual version provided, for some, an inadequate way of coming to terms with the event (even though it was, for nearly all, the authentic initial mode of experience). Hence, we see an intriguing paradox: visitors remain especially attracted to performing a pilgrimage towards artefacts resting in a physical museum space, even as those museums themselves cite the experiences of globally dispersed subjects as the true referents for "what an event meant". Consider, for instance, *September 11, 2001: A Global Moment*, shown at the Memorial Pour La Paix in Caen, Normandy, to date the largest museum exhibit on the topic. "Where Were You on September 11 2001 at 8:46am?" is the marketing strapline promoting the exhibit. "Where were you?" is premised on round-the-clock worldwide media. This framework, based on not just "what happened to them?" but *you,* shifts the visitor from the outside observer of history to its central subject. The experience and feeling of the global visitor is tantamount.

A focus on the responsibilities of the global citizen is made explicit in the Los Angeles Museum of Tolerance's "Tolerancenter". On entry to the multi-subject, technologically rich, performance-oriented space that precedes its Holocaust exhibition, visitors are confronted by a speaking character in a ten-foot-high video display called the "Host Provocateur". After spouting an assortment of biases, he asks whether visitors sympathise with anything he has said. Denied any real opportunity to respond, he directs visitors to "enter the door marked Prejudiced, because you are". Visitors turn to two closed doors, one bright red, marked "prejudiced", the other "unprejudiced" in a more soothing green. Those who persist and try the green door find it is locked. Similar experiences follow, as Oren Baruch Stier describes:

> Wandering among a total of thirty-five 'hands-on' exhibits with titles such as 'Images that Stay With Us', 'It's So Easy to Misjudge', 'Me…A Bigot?' and 'What We Say, What We Think', we explore, at our own pace, the relationship between words, images, and intolerance, responding interactively to a series of colorful and even entertaining displays. Such relationships are also addressed in the 'Whisper Gallery', a dark, winding corridor where racial epithets and hateful slurs ('camel jockey', 'jungle bunny', 'greasy dago', 'bulldyke bitch', 'loudmouth kike', and the like), assault us (Stier 1996, 840).

The Host Provocateur returns to occasionally goad visitors, before final screens in the gallery ask: "Who is responsible?" The multi-lingual answer is "You are". The idea is that discrimination lies within everyone, and that those who cannot admit this are simply not trying hard enough. The question of the scale of behaviour—from an offensive ethnic joke to mass murder—is one that is little acknowledged. Or rather, the sliding continuum is exactly the museum's point—Nazis and other tyrants are there to show that if we do not check ourselves for private thoughts, terrible actions can easily follow. In this, specific histories are not themselves the focus of concentration and remembrance, but are instead devices in the museum's pedagogical toolbox.

A related museological tactic is the issuing of identity cards. Initiated by the US Holocaust Memorial Museum, visitors receive an identity card on entry that describes the life history of someone who suffered through or perished in the Holocaust. The idea is that each life was as meaningful and precious as one's own—and that it is only luck or circumstance that separates their fate from ours. At Johannesburg's Apartheid Museum, visitors are asked to choose from two sets of identity cards according to their racial identity. They are then directed to one of two turnstile doors—one for blacks, one for whites.

Figure 12.2. Entrance to Apartheid Museum, Johannesburg. Copyright Adam Carr (released to the public domain).

In the passage for blacks the walls are covered with faded photos from old passbooks they were forced to carry in the days of white rule. Waiting at the end of the hallway are life-sized photographs of four white men, members of the Race Classification Board that assigned identities by studying the kink of hair, the width of noses, the fullness of lips, and gradations of skin color. While white visitors pass through a hallway covered with their own identity cards, they can glimpse the black visitors through a metal grid. The two groups remain separated until the passages rejoin, and all visitors meet at the foyer of the main exhibits (Swarns 2001, E1). Such museum tactics aim to have the visitor *feel*, as an antidote to the cold intellect associated with Nazism and apartheid that produced decisions about the course of others' lives. If political histories can be understood through a sensual process, visitors might remember (or conjure) the *experience* of prejudice, these museums wager. As spaces of performance, the US Holocaust Memorial Museum and Apartheid Museum produce a sense of ourselves in the company of tyrants. Our emotional response to this experience is an indicator of conscience.

Empathy and media affect

The real and perceived distance between the geopolitical status and identity of the observer and that of the casualties being observed may be held to test the limits of the cosmopolitan conscience. Can hundreds of thousands killed in, for instance, Darfur ever mean as much to New Yorkers as the 2,603 killed at the World Trade Center? The six murdered in its 1993 bombing? Clearly, this question is not resolved objectively; the impact of any event is formed subjectively, and is heavily influenced by its media prominence, itself governed by factors such as its size and scope, its ease of understanding, clearly defined roles of good and bad, the involvement of women and children as victims, and any lateral, circumstantial connections to the observing society. Despite the contemporary emphasis on the role of media in the sparking and dampening of sympathy, musing on the issue of compassion towards suffering distant people is not new. In the 18th century, thinkers such as Balzac, Diderot and Rosseau presumed that geographic, ethnic, and socio-economic likeness to oneself largely determined the degree of human compassion (Dean 2003, 89). Ever since, when sympathy was first posited as an essential component of the Enlightened Self, there has been an accompanying debate about whether images or other representations of suffering stimulate our sensitivity to it, or instead produce indifference, numbness or (in contemporary terms) "compassion fatigue".

The issue of gaps in understanding, and the impossibility of picturing or feeling violence completely, relates to Dominick LaCapra's notion of "empathic unsettlement", in which "emotional response comes with respect for the other and the realisation that the experience of the other is not one's own" (LaCapra 2001, 40). This effect disrupts the supposed link made by many memorial museums that a close understanding of the past can aid the avoidance of future atrocities. Empathic unsettlement suggests that remembrance is a "difficult return"—offsetting the redemptive notion that the future will be improved if we remember. Learning through "empathetic unsettlement" can occur on two levels: on the one hand, one learns the details about what happened to others in another time and space. On the other hand, one learns "within the disturbances and disruptions inherent in comprehending these events" (Simon et al. 2000, 3). That is, we learn about the lives of others that we can no longer touch, and at the same time come to understand the limits of this learning experience. The distance between these is not necessarily debilitating and, in fact, draws important attention to how the idea of personal transferability (the "could've been me" effect) is disturbed by historical, political, cultural, social and economic distances of all kinds.

Memorial museums, in pursuing the role of agents of social rehabilitation in the aftermath of violence, position human connectivity as a key to healing. For instance, following 9/11, representatives from the Smithsonian National Museum of American History and the Museum of the City of New York wrote that, "it is critical that we respond to those challenges thoughtfully and positively, embracing the opportunity to help our visitors understand these tragic events and contributing to the nation's healing" (Gardner and Henry 2002, 52). Similarly, Oklahoma City National Memorial spokesperson Nancy Coggins has stated:

> Timothy McVeigh wanted to blow up a government building and create anguish so great it would never heal. Yet, just the opposite occurred. One man's evil act didn't tear us apart; instead it brought us together. The Memorial is about courage and compassion. It isn't about McVeigh. He's barely mentioned at all. (Quoted in Stein 2006)

The museum's therapeutic dimension is encapsulated by its Children's Area, where young visitors are encouraged to express their feelings about the tragedy by drawing on chalkboards in an art space.

Memorial museums increasingly make dialogue between visitors an essential component of their programs. At Cincinnati's National Underground Railroad Freedom Center, it was decided that the racially charged nature of its subject meant that a physical space should be provided that could safely discharge agitated feelings. Out of concern that people might exit the exhibition galleries with unresolved feelings of guilt, anger and resentment, the centre offers "The Dialogue Room" for discussion. Trained facilitators encourage visitors to examine their feelings and share them in a controlled environment. Similarly, New York's Lower

East Side Tenement Museum includes a "Kitchen Conversation" component where, after a tour, visitors gather for a facilitated conversation about immigration and struggle. Each visitor introduces his or her own ethnic roots and family history as a way of comparing and contrasting stories of hardship, triumph, and immigration issues today.

Through such programs the "memorial" aspect of these museums may be tipping them away from being institutions that, after some balanced consideration, provide a factual account of what was endured, and towards those that intervene earlier to act as agents of social repair. Memorial museums have evolved within a period when public grieving—from Princess Diana to 9/11—has become a media event (see Kear and Steinberg 1999). As Erika Doss has argued, "Oklahoma City and Colorado's [Columbine High School massacre] memorials elided the historical realities that produced them, largely because of contemporary assumptions that grieving, in and of itself, is a prescriptive political practice" (Doss 2002, 69). Victimhood too has shifted from a literal to a poetic interpretation, taking in broader categories of people. Consider the inscription on the granite memorial fountain dedicated to the 1993 World Trade Center bombing, erected in 1995 and destroyed on 9/11: "On February 26, 1993, a bomb set by terrorists exploded below this site. This horrible act of violence killed innocent people, injured thousands, and made victims of us all". The distinction between the "victim could have been me", popularised in the aforementioned identity-card style exhibition tactics, and "me as victim" in such memorial attributions blurs the lines that once separated the historical subject and the observing visitor.

Historical intertextuality and entanglement

The moral invocation to say "Never Again", adapted from Elie Wiesel's sparse lament in *Night*, has been widely embraced in the past 40 years by memorial museums worldwide. As a general statement of permanent remembrance and the continued need for vigilance against potential future atrocity, the oath now enjoys a currency that overflows the Holocaust and has become part of a global lexicon. From the official document detailing Argentinean disappearances (*Nunca Mas*) to its most recent invocations towards Darfur, referencing atrocities in relation to one another has become commonplace over the past 20 years. The transformation of the Holocaust from memory bound to local ethnic, and national identities to a global collective memory has been widely noted (Levy and Sznaider 2002). As Harold Kaplan wrote: "Whatever we say of a great crime and its punishment, the true universality of the Holocaust lies in its legacy to conscience" (1994, xiii).

Since they rely partly on the availability of documentary visual evidence (especially in the form of photography and film), massive political atrocities, I posit, only gained a readily recognisable shape from the mid to late nineteenth century onwards. However, it is now certain that most acts of atrocity will never again lack for recorded evidence. The dissemination of historical atrocities as textual and audio-visual information has undoubtedly contributed to their emergence as hybrid signifiers. These have been difficult to miss: after 9/11 there was talk of it being a new generation's Pearl Harbour. Madrid's Atocha train station bombing was named "3/11"; the London bombing quickly became "7/7"; the Bali bombings are sometimes called "Australia's 9/11". Similarly, the world's most recent genocide in Darfur is reflexively related to those in Rwanda, former Yugoslavia, Cambodia, Armenia, and the Holocaust. Argentina's "dirty war" disappearances are compared to those in Chile, and to a lesser degree, Bolivia, Uruguay, and Peru. The messages conveyed by memorial museums are also influenced by ongoing world events (in the way, for instance, that the 9/11 attacks gave Pearl Harbour's USS Arizona Memorial a re-energised sense of mission and consequence) (see White 2004). The Caen Peace Memorial has a rolling roster of epochal events, adding a 9/11 display to existing exhibits depicting the D-Day beach landings and the fall of the Berlin Wall.

In a revealing study of visitors' remarks left in the comments books at the US Holocaust Memorial Museum shortly after 9/11, Michael Bernard-Donals describes how in many entries American visitors registered an association with Holocaust-era European Jews on the basis that they too had seen group members killed on the basis of identity—because of "who we are". As visual images, there was a felt resonance between the recent memory of 9/11 headshot photographs in New York and those of Holocaust victims. In comments, visitors extended Hitler's personal qualities as the embodiment of "pure evil" to Osama Bin Laden (and, to a lesser extent, Yasser Arafat). Connections between the Holocaust and contemporary events (sometimes only very tangentially related to it) reveal how it has come to form an essential yet potentially dehistoricised frame of reference upon which to project all manner of atrocities.

The interplay between *repetition* and *recollection* is key to any consideration of the relationship between personal memory and the way it becomes attached to history. Patrick H. Hutton (1993) conceptualises repetition as "the moment of memory through which we bear forward images of the past that continue to shape our present understanding in unreflective ways". These moments of memory are like "habits of mind" that are readily attached to existing cultural representations (Hutton 1993, xx). The problem with the display of overlapping stories of victimhood is that normative frameworks of likeness that permit the proper and properly outraged assessment of injustice might be obscured (Dean 2003, 98). Could it become possible that identifications of commonality are causing unique events to be collapsed into a kind of museums-of-conscience genre? As Jeffrey Feldman (2003, 839) writes:

> Museum representations of September 11 have exhibited a 'tyranny of usage' at work in the commemoration of tragedy, wherein the content of a specific tragedy has been expressed through structures and principles of expression emergent from previous memorial concerns. How does one distinguish between form and content in museum exhibitions?

Indeed, if museums eventually accede to a common mode of display and narration, might an event-specific institution lose its sense of singular focus and purposefulness?

Contrary to this position, Michael Bernard Donals argues that the shift from the here-and-now of personal circumstance to the museum's then-and-there of lessons—no matter how media-oriented—can promote great awareness:

> Visitors' use of contemporary events as screens for their understanding of the Holocaust is due to what I will call "forgetful memory", in which aspects of events seen but not remembered insinuate themselves into individual and cultural memories so well wrought as to be (presumably) hermetic. It is this memory effect that may provide the viewer with a kind of memorial agency that – contrary to what Stjepan Mestrovic calls a "post-emotional inertia" in the face of the culture (or memory) industry – prevents a conflation of memory from becoming an endless cycle of memorial repetition, in which the Holocaust becomes 9/11, and atrocities simply stand in for one another. (2005, 74)

Recent years have seen many studies that investigate the ways that memories represent and make present a past. Many fewer, however, have paid attention to how aspects of memory that are actively and imperfectly formed in museums intervene in, and make possible, a more progressive future.

Conclusion: intimate histories and global publics

The idea of cosmopolitan conscience described in this article is quite distinct from the notion of civic responsibility we associate with the era of modern nation-building, where societies typically aimed simply to forget negative events and mythologise glorious ones. The lamenting of negative events has an increasing currency that can demonstrate positive personal and communal traits: of individual tolerance, social diversity and transnational identification. Tragedy, put simply, can be unifying. Barbara Misztal, for instance, states that, "remembering crimes against humanity is essential for sustaining solidarity and nourishing mutual care" (2005, 1327). Museums situated on authentic sites of destruction that offer evidence of crime and tragedy both feed a desire for, and nurture, a public that sees historical misdeeds as vital moral coordinates for contemporary life. Of course the question of how conscience is awakened and enriched by the museum, and where it takes effect after the visit, is a provocation I can only raise here.

This chapter is, then, motivated by an issue of timeliness: the ongoing proliferation of memorial museums may soon make them a conventional part of civic life and tourist routes. It is patent that there has been an upsurge in memorial museums—one critic is almost certainly right to claim recently that "more memorial museums have been opened in the last 10 years than in the past 100" (Jenkins 2005, 22). It remains to be seen whether this broadens the popular appeal of "performing conscience", or, if they become less novel, the loosely conceived public that currently accounts for their surge in popularity wanes. Indeed, the identification of a public holding a "cosmopolitan conscience" may be tempered by doubt. Part of the issue of identifying any new sense of "public" lies with defining its parameters: people come and go, and shifts in terms of national, ethnic and cultural allegiance both drive and follow historical developments. At a more concrete level, attempts to accurately identify visitors to memorial museums will always be an imprecise science. What does seem clear is that the parameters outlined herein—which cite the importance of tourism and media in the shaping of a globally aware subject—help to explain the viability and growth of conscience-oriented institutions, and contribute to the characteristics through which such museums conceive of their audience. Among museums of all kinds that increasingly focus on the visitor, memorial museums that broach themes of community, its ruin, and its memory are currently at the forefront of activating and coalescing an especially vibrant new sense of the museum public.

References

Appadurai, A. 1996. *Modernity at large: Cultural dimensions of globalization*. Minneapolis: University of Minnesota Press.

Dean, C. J. 2003. Empathy, pornography, and suffering. *Difference* 14 (1): 88–124.

Donals, M. B. 2005. Conflations of memory or, what they saw at the Holocaust Museum after 9/11. *CR: The New Centennial Review* 5 (2): 73–106.

Doss, E. 2002. Death, art and memory in the public sphere: The visual and material culture of grief in contemporary America. *Mortality* 7 (1): 64–82.

Feldman, J. 2003. One tragedy in reference to another: September 11 and the obligations of museum commemoration. *American Anthropologist* 105 (4): 839–43.

Gardner, J. B. and S. M. Henry. 2002. September 11 and the mourning after: Reflections on collecting and interpreting the history of tragedy. *The Public Historian* 24 (3): 37–52.

Hutton, P. H. 1993. *History as an art of memory*. Hanover: University Press of New England.

Huyssen, A. 2003. *Present pasts: Urban palimpsests and the politics of memory*. Palo Alto: Stanford University Press.

Jenkins, T. 2005. Victims remembered. *Museums Journal* 105 (5): 22–25.

Kaplan, H. 1994. *Conscience and memory: Meditations in a museum of the Holocaust.* Chicago: University of Chicago Press.

Kear, A. and D. L. Steinberg Eds. 1999. *Mourning Diana: Nation, culture and the performance of grief.* London and New York: Routledge.

Kirshenblatt-Gimblett, B. 1998. *Destination culture: Tourism, museums and heritage.* Berkeley: University of California Press.

LaCapra, D. 2001. *Writing history, writing trauma.* Baltimore: John Hopkins University Press.

Landsberg, A. 1997. America, the Holocaust, and the mass culture of memory: Toward a radical politics of empathy. *New German Critique* 71: 63–86.

Levy, D. and N. Sznaider. 2002. Memory unbound: The Holocaust and the formation of cosmopolitan memory. *European Journal of Social Theory* 5 (1): 87–106.

Linklater, A. 2002. Cosmopolitan citizenship. In *Handbook of citizenship studies.* Ed. E.F. Isin and B. Turner, 317–332. London: Sage Publications.

McCannell, D. 1992. *Empty meeting grounds: The tourist papers Vol. 1.*, London and New York: Routledge.

Misztal, B. A. 2004. The sacralization of memory. *European Journal of Social Theory* 7 (1): 67–84.

—. 2005. Memory and democracy. *American Behavioral Scientist* 48 (10): 1320–38.

Simon, R. I. et al. 2000. Introduction: Between hope and despair: The pedagogical encounter of historical remembrance. In *Between hope and despair: Pedagogy and the remembrance of historical trauma.* Ed. R.I. Simon, S. Rosenberg and C. Eppert., 1–8, Maryland: Rowland & Littlefield.

Stein, S. Oklahoma City Monument and Museum, *ArtID*, November 13 2006. http://artid.com/members/shifrablog/blog/post/110 (accessed September 24 2009).

Stier, O. B. 1996. Virtual memories: Mediating the Holocaust at the Simon Wiesenthal Center's Beit Hashoah-Museum of Tolerance, *Journal of the American Academy of Religion,* 64 (4): 831–52.

Swarns, R. L. 2001. Oppression in black and white: South Africa Museum recreates apartheid. *New York Times*, December 10: E1.

Till, K. E. 2005. *The new Berlin: Memory, politics, place.* Minneapolis: University of Minnesota Press.

Urbain, J-D. 2002. *L'idiot du voyage: Histoires de tourists.* Paris: Payot.

Wang, N. 2003. Rethinking authenticity in tourism experience. In *Tourism: Critical concepts in the social sciences.* Ed. S. Williams, 218–29. London and New York: Routledge.

White, G. M. 2001. Public history and globalization: Ethnography at the USS Arizona Memorial. *CRM: The Journal of Heritage Stewardship.* (5): 9–13.

—. 2004. National subjects: September 11 and Pearl Harbor. *American Ethnologist.* 31 (3): 293–310.

Williams, P. 2007. *Memorial museums: The global rush to commemorate atrocities.* Oxford: Berg.

Young, J. E. 1994. *The texture of memory: Holocaust memorials and meaning.* New Haven: Yale University Press.

Notes

[1] A note about terminology is useful here. A memorial should be generally understood as an umbrella term for anything that serves in remembrance of a person or event—including non-material forms such as a holiday or a song. Monuments are best seen as a subset of memorials, characterised by their physical

appearance. A museum, as we know, is an institution devoted to the acquisition, conservation, study, exhibition and educational interpretation of objects with scientific, historical or artistic value. I use the term *memorial museum* to identify its dual foci: *commemorating* death and suffering of some kind, while also *explaining* its context.

[2] Online memorials to historical atrocities, especially those with tagging and social networking capabilities, deserve a separate analysis in terms of their patterns of use. It is also worth noting that a small number of memorial museums are beginning to include digitally interactive elements in their physical displays.

CHAPTER THIRTEEN

THE POLITICS AND POETICS OF CONTEMPORARY EXHIBITION MAKING: TOWARDS AN ETHICAL ENGAGEMENT WITH THE PAST

ANDREA WITCOMB

On a recent visit to London, on a cold, damp and windy Sunday in mid-December, I went to Dennis Severs' House in Spitalfields. I knew in advance that this was no ordinary historic house, either rich in decorative arts or a lesson in the life of a historic figure. Instead I was coming to a house that used the art of installation, to produce a range of sensory experiences to suggest the presence of an imaginary Huguenot silk weaver's family over three generations. In the process, the house told a history of family life, domestic space, leisure and work, as well as aesthetic sensibilities, while hinting at the wider social, economic and political processes that affected that household.

Nothing I had read about the house, however, quite prepared me for the powerful impact of having to remain silent in order to experience the atmosphere created by Dennis Severs in what was once his home. Unable to communicate my responses or indeed listen to those of others, I was forced to respond to my own reactions, to feel my way about, to let the house itself, its fabric, its light, its sounds, its smells, its contents, and the ghostly presence of its imagined inhabitants, take over my own subjectivity. Rather than imposing myself on the space, I had to let the space impose itself on me. I had to learn to feel, to sense, to imagine what made this installation hang together. In letting my own body respond to the space I began to follow the trail as if playing a game—an imaginative game in which I constructed a narrative about the house's inhabitants and the times in which they lived.

Indeed, it is the way in which you are invited to play a game that has struck commentators. In a review of the house, Jane Black (2005, 9), writing for the *Washington Post* recalls that

> As you enter, you're advised not to take anything too seriously. But for the house to reveal itself, you must be willing to play the game. You must actively suspend disbelief, forgetting that the sound of the passing carriage comes from a crudely hidden cassette tape. You must not look for explanations. Instead you must consciously use your senses to soak up the atmosphere and use your imagination to fill in the gaps.

Many would perhaps understand the experience provided by Dennis Severs' installation as escapist, nostalgic, or a trip back in time, particularly at Christmas time when the house comes alive with the smells of fruit mince, cloves in oranges and brandy soaked dried fruits waiting to be mixed with eggs, sugar and flour to make the Christmas pudding. However, I value the house for the way in which the art of installation is used to capture the feeling, as well as the aesthetics, of a range of periods—the extremely confined spaces in which women lived their lives in the 18th and 19th centuries, the patterns of middle class family life and the pathos of a family's rise and descent into financial ruin. Without using a single didactic label, Severs managed to convey an understanding of life in a different time, while conveying those experiences we all value—family life, the memory of the hearth, of good conversation, of companionship, of feeling safe from the world outside.

While an extreme example of the new turn to what might be called sensorial or affective forms of interpretation, the kind of "palpable" history that Severs created in his house has its parallels in contemporary forms of interpretation practice that seek to avoid linear, rational and didactic means of communication to impart information and meaning to visitors. In this chapter, I wish to analyse two examples as a means to explore the potential they offer for generating more complex understandings of the past and in particular for crossing the boundaries produced by cultural memories and identities.

There is, of course, a context for this new sensory turn that is far more complex than the association with immersive technologies and the power of the call for experience-based tourism, both of which animate contemporary museological activity (Kirschenblatt-Gimblett 2000). While museums increasingly have to compete with leisure industries by reconfiguring visitors as consumers whose "newly dominant practices of attention" are perceived to require "capturing" through more entertaining phenomena and illusionist techniques (Henning 2006, 52–3), there are also political and historiographical contexts for the new turn to sensory forms of interpretation. Here I want to outline just three of these.

The first is a growing dissatisfaction with available approaches to representing cultural diversity in both museological and academic contexts. The second is a concomitant realisation that public cultural institutions like museums need to address the problem of social cohesion as well as social inclusion. The third is a dissatisfaction with the limits of traditional approaches to making history which, it is argued, do little to engage imagination and empathy.

In previous work (Witcomb 2006) I argued that the increasing critical attention on the part of governments in western democracies to the ways in which museums have dealt with revisionist historiographies indicated a need to rethink how we deal with issues around cultural and social diversity. Both the culture wars in America and the history wars in Australia, to take two examples, pointed to the limitations of a pluralist approach to questions of representation. At the time, conservative governments questioned the public role of museums, strongly arguing that they should not take sides in political debates but instead present a consensual narrative about national identity. Whether enacted in the fiascos around the *Enola Gay* exhibition at the Smithsonian National Air and Space Museum (Zolberg 1996), *The West as America* exhibition at the National Museum of American Art (Wallace 1994) or in the National Museum of Australia 2003 Review (MacIntyre and Clark 2004), it became clear that revisionist historiographies and fragmented narratives were not welcomed by those who held the strings to the public purse.

At the heart of these critiques was a dissatisfaction with the lack of a coherent narrative that drew the community together. These exhibitions' foci on the representation of diversity, difference and alternative perspectives on the past were interpreted as not placing enough emphasis and importance on the need for public institutions to build social cohesion. As the *Review of the National Museum of Australia: Its Exhibitions and Public Programs* (Commonwealth of Australia 2003, 17) put it, the main weakness of the National Museum of Australia is a lack of coherence. There is, the review argued, "little narrative thread connecting a staccato of images, and snapshots of people who deliver their own fragment of opinion". In the wake of the "war on terror", these critiques have become even more important as governments everywhere look to ways of building social cohesion within the nation (Message 2007).

While it is easy to go on the defensive and dismiss these criticisms as motivated by political conservatism, it is increasingly obvious that those on the left are also asking questions about the implications of a radical pluralist approach. While the most prominent critics of pluralism have been self-identified conservatives, more voices on the left are lamenting the loss of an ability to imagine "common dreams" (Gitlin 1995). One of the problems with this pluralist framework was that little thought was given to relations between the different parts of the mosaic of national identity. In practice, the aim of representing cultural diversity often collapsed into the representation of single interest groups without much thought as to the dialogue between them (Witcomb 2003, 2006; Message 2005), creating what Ghassan Hage (1998, 157) has called "zoological multiculturalism". Along the same lines, other critics of multiculturalism have come to perceive it as responsible for creating a divisive "community of separate cultures" more interested in rights than responsibilities (Heywood 2006), adding to what is becoming a considerable literature on the shortcomings of multiculturalism by both conservative and left scholars (for example, Betts 1999; Hage 1998, 2006; Ang 2005).

The problem has also been noted at the practical level in terms of audience responses. For example, an audience study immediately after the opening of the Australian National Maritime Museum in Sydney found that the majority of visitors found the lack of a strong chronological framework disorienting (Witcomb 2003). For them, an accent on the plurality of voices equated with a lack of narrative. In the US, audiences perceived an accent on pluralism not as a representation of a democratic impulse but instead as an ideological critique that is against populist narratives of celebration. As Doering (2002) put it, "visitors don't generally expect their national museums to be debating the significance or meaning of their contents or to embody a wide range of viewpoints". These findings leave museums with a problem. As Ian McShane (2004, 14) put it,

> how does a museum construct a coherent and compelling narrative that gives voice to competing perspectives? How can museum programs resist declaring themselves for either consensus or pluralism, as if a simple choice between the two existed, but draw productively on both impulses?

It is not surprising therefore, that in the most recent scholarship there is an increasing interest in the potential of museums to contribute to dialogue across cultural differences (Peers and Brown 2003; Kreps 2003; Witcomb 2003, 2006; Newman 2005; Message 2006).

My interest lies in the potential connections between the identification of these problems with an increasing recognition of the power of materiality as a force for interpretation in its own right, one that extends traditional rational forms of interpretation. My particular interest is in the potential of these recognitions for a new form of history making, particularly in museological contexts. Like Ross Gibson (2008), I tend to think that non literary forms of making history may provide opportunities to "sense" or "feel" the presence of the past in the present and that these opportunities are what provides a space to engage in building historical imagination and empathy for the situation of others. For Gibson, the opportunity to "feel the past in your bones" is far more likely to lead to a "conviction" about the relationship between past and present and therefore what needs to be done in the future than a mode of history making that proceeds through reasoned argument. The significance of this for Gibson lies in the fact that

> the conditions of living and working in an aftermath-culture such as Australia are such that a great deal of the vital evidence is either missing or non-textual and the evidence that we do have is often partial, broken or obscured by denials. Which means that the conventional historiographical protocols often come up short when we try to get the fullest possible comprehension of the past that shaped our present. (Gibson 2008, 186)

Gibson's arguments can be supported by emerging themes in recent museological literature which are open to the potential of "palpable" forms of history making and representational practices. There is, for example, a growing literature on the experience of materiality in exhibition spaces (Dudley 2009), a recognition that museums are as much spaces for affective forms of encounter as rational ones (Clifford 1997; Kavanagh 2000; Storrie 2006; Henning 2006), where objects have a force of their own, having the power to impinge on our lives. Furthermore, much of this power lies in the way in which these experiences relate to the production and maintenance of memories, as Marcus Kwint et al. has explored (1999). As they put it, the question is not what objects represent that is important but what they can do to us, how they influence our behaviour and consciousness. These memory spaces, I want to argue, can work in terms of imaginary play, in which audiences momentarily inhabit other worlds and learn how to navigate them. That experience, I want to argue, requires them to suspend their own identity and imagine that of others, resulting in affective cross-cultural experiences.

This new attention to the affective power of objects is connected to a growing theorisation of affect on the part of art historians, anthropologists and cultural geographers. Influenced by the work of philosophers such as Deleuze (2000) and Merleau-Ponty (1968, 2002) and by actor-network theory (Latour 2005), there is now a body of literature which attempts to theorise and analyse the affective powers of objects and places. While the focus has been predominantly on the aesthetic, through the work of art, architectural and film critics such as Susan Best (2001), Jill Bennett (2001, 2002, 2005) and Brian Massumi (2002) there is also a growing realisation that places also have affective power (Wise and Chapman 2005; Van Leeuwen 2008). In all of this work there is an attempt to understand how material experiences, often registered through the body in intensely physical ways, can lead to deep emotional and cognitive experiences which can be profoundly life changing.

Before offering an analysis of how this might work, I want to briefly explore the usefulness of a notion of play in an exhibition context by appropriating the work of Steve Johnson (2005) on multimedia. Johnson is interested in building an understanding of contemporary media culture that is alive to what he calls its "cognitive workout" rather than judging it on whether or not it offers "a morality play" (Johnson 2005, 14). Motivated by a desire to argue against conservative critics who constantly attack popular screen culture, Johnson argues instead that contemporary forms of multimedia offer "a progressive story: mass culture growing more sophisticated, demanding more cognitive engagement with each passing year" (xi). He develops his arguments by looking at the narrative structures of these texts rather than their textual content, with his first example being video games. His analysis reveals the complex set of skills required of audiences to decode the texts, producing what he calls a "cognitive workout".

Johnson describes the nature of the activities required to decode the text as a search for clues, which then need to be interpreted and collated into a narrative. The first task that needs to be done is "seeking" (Johnson 2005, 37). "Seeking" is characterised by an openness to explore the world on the screen, looking for clues, actively piecing the puzzle together. At its base is a willingness to experience a certain sense of aimlessness or being lost. Control can only be achieved by interpreting the clues. This can only be done by what Johnson calls "probing" and "telescoping" (41). "Probing" involves experimenting, as the rules of video games are never a pre-given. They only become apparent as you play. Recognising them involves "detecting subtle patterns and tendencies in the way the computer is running the simulation" (44). Knowing which bits of the sequence are important and how to put them together is only possible by keeping in mind the larger objectives of the game and their relationship to immediate objectives. It is a process that involves recognising how the game involves a series of nests all nestled neatly into one another. Take one away and the sequence breaks. Understanding the objectives has a temporal dimension in which short term objectives are important because of the role they play in the long term ones. Managing all of these objectives and understanding the relationships between them is what "telescoping" is about. The narrative of the game, however, is only produced in retrospect, when all the tasks have been completed and the narrative has been produced. In video games, narrative is not a story to follow; rather it is the end product of engaging in the game, of interacting with the medium. "Probing" and "telescoping" are thus forms of cultural practice that encourage analysis and participatory thinking. They challenge you to think about the environment you are in and recognise the order within it.

Johnson's identification of "seeking", "probing" and "telescoping" as strategies of interpretation can be used to explore the ways in which contemporary forms of immersive exhibition designs play with affect to produce narratives in which relations between past and present are neither didactic in the conventional sense of wanting to impart particular bits of information to visitors nor embedded within a morality play that tells the visitor how to behave or what values to have. This is not to say that such exhibitions are not ideologically driven—the difference I suggest is that they focus on building a sense of an ethical rather than a moral relationship to the past and so do not come across as didactic. They work by producing feelings, senses and innate cultural memories, not by lecturing. Furthermore, the ways in which they build with their audiences an ethical relationship to the past is precisely what distinguishes them from their historical antecedents—dioramas, period rooms and various theatrical assemblages. Far more open and interactive than their predecessors, the meanings are not easily read but require work, imaginative play and physical interaction on the part of visitors. In an important sense, their narrative is only produced in the active engagement of the visitor in the space itself.

My first example comes from Greenough, a town just south of Geraldton, a major port on the mid-coast of Western Australia. Established in the nineteenth century but abandoned after a flood in the 1950s, the town is now owned by the National Trust of Australia (WA) and managed jointly with the local council and in consultation with the local community. While layers of the first interpretation done by the National Trust in the 1970s, which attempted to recreate the historical village, still exist, it is on the new layer of interpretation done by Mulloway Studio architects in consultation with Paul Kloeden from Exhibition Services, both from Adelaide, South Australia that I wish to focus. Because of shortness of space I will only analyse the entrance display through what was, at one time, the local store.

One of the visual characteristics of the landscape at Greenough is its emptiness and desolation. A windswept landscape, the trees are bent double. Other than the buildings on the main street, the settlement is widely spread, giving a sense of isolation. Visitors feel this isolation as the wind whistles across their faces, leaving its own visceral mark. The emotional impact is one of foreboding, of desolation, which stands in stark contrast to the initial expectation of visiting a historical village built on prior experiences of visiting "pioneer" villages. It makes for an evocative space that invites imaginative play precisely because of the sense of isolation and initial appearance of emptiness.

That sense of emptiness is reflected in the style of interpretation chosen for the entry to the site itself, via the original settlement store. The first thing we notice is the sparseness of the interpretation, the amount of space left empty and the stark whiteness of the space itself. The room we enter is not filled with text and images, or objects in glass cases. Nor is there an attempt to recreate the store. Instead there is a map painted onto the floor and wall in one corner, one extended text printed onto the wall, the odd sentence on the wall, a minimalist white boat with a few images in it and a few paint scrapes on the wall. The first impression is one of disorientation—what is this? What do I do here? To get anything out of it you have to take your time and explore the space engaging in what Johnson would call "seeking" and "probing". In the process you begin to immerse yourself in the space itself as part of the effort to generate a narrative about this particular building and more generally about the site as a whole.

What then are the clues available to the visitor to construct their own sense of what this place is about? What follows is my own reading of these clues, my own attempt to "seek", "probe" and "telescope" in an effort to construct a narrative that would make sense of the place. In the process, however, it is the affective nature of that experience, the way in which it works on my body, then on my consciousness and finally on my understanding of the place, in which the value of the "game" lies.

As I walked from the car park to the first building, I noted a red line painted onto the floor boards of the verandah. It seemed to provide a trail to follow as it continued beyond the heavy glass door I had to push to enter the building. Before I did so, I looked across to the main street of the settlement barred from me by a "ye olde" heritage gate. I could not help but notice that the door I was about to push open was not only new but a minimalist, clean and contemporary intervention into the heritage building. On entering, I was faced not only with a sense of emptiness but also of whiteness. It was clear to me that the building had been renovated. I was not therefore entering a reconstructed past. As I looked around me, somewhat disoriented, I decided to follow the red track on the floor, which clearly led to a large map at one corner of the room. To read it, I realised, I needed to step on it. It was only as I did so and began to look and read that I slowly realised I was becoming part of its meaning. For the map connects the location I was standing in—the old Greenough store to the wider landscape it sits in and to history. This forced me to ask about my own connection to that history. As I probed the map, looking at its detail I began to recognise white settler names and indigenous names for the same place. With a shock I realised that I had not just come to visit a pioneer village—I had come to a place where invasion had taken place for it was clear that there were inhabitants with a much longer relationship to that place than "the pioneers" whom I now recognise as colonists—that is as invaders.

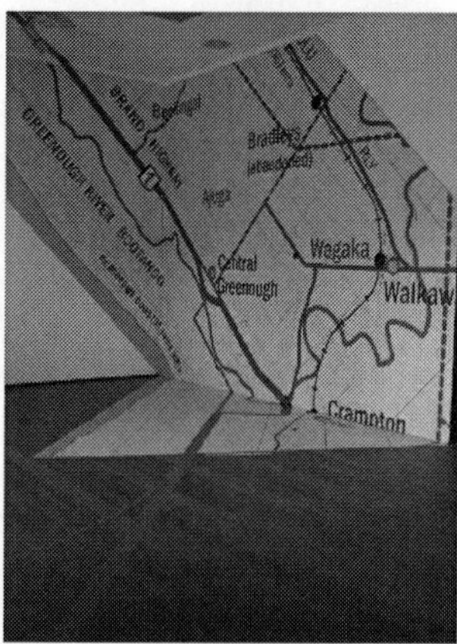

Fig. 13.1 Corner map in entrance area. Photographer: Kate Gregory with permission.

As I looked up I received confirmation of this discovery in a wall text to the left of the map which told me:

> A map is nothing more than a series of clues, clues as to where we are, where we have come from, and where we are going. Contour lines provide clues as to the natural landscape. Yamagi words provide clues as to the natural landscape. Yamagi words provide clues to the indigenous occupation of the land, their meeting places and yam grounds. Survey lines, roads, fences and building markings provide clues as to how it was settled by Europeans. But these are only clues. The reality lies beyond the map, all around us.

My own place within this location came from my physical interaction with the map. As I approached it, stood on it and read it, I replicated the position of the mapper/explorer. Unlike the earlier explorers however, I could not hide under the pretext of *Terra Nullius* for the map signals the presence of the indigenous people loudly and clearly, implicating me within this history. My gaze was not simply that of the tourist—I too have a role in the production of this history by the simple fact of whether or not I recognised the tension embedded in the map. The point here is that I am not being told what to think. Instead, I am positioned in relation to the past and the present in a manner that demands an ethical response. The two temporalities, I realise, are not disconnected.

Hints of the white history of the place emerged as I sought the other clues in the room—one line sentences on the wall that mark the dates of various occupations, paint scrapes that show the passage of time and the height of the flood that led to the abandonment of the settlement, some introduced shelving with photographic evidence of the site's former history as a store. As I began to manipulate the various clues available to me I began to make a story—a story about what must have been a clash of cultures, about hardship and isolation, about the role of the store as a centre for the community. I could not actually fill in the content of this story; I just had its bare contours. As I passed through what was once a doorway but is now simply an opening in the wall, I entered another room with a few more clues. For here, alongside the minimalist "graffiti" lines on the wall that informed me of various periods of occupancy by different inhabitants of the store itself, there were four props displayed on plinths with individual lighting from above as if they were art objects. These props, on closer examination, extended the insights provided by the map in the first room. The props required a high degree of "probing", however, to reveal their message.

Fig. 13.2 "The Prop Gallery". Photographer: Kate Gregory with permission.

The first prop appeared to be a dress pattern for an old-style dress. On closer inspection however, the pattern turned out to be by "Buckaroo Bobbins" © 2003 with a "Bonus Pattern for making your own sandbags ideal for protecting your home against rising floodwaters" with a little diagram of water lapping against sandbags. A sense of humour was at play with a reference to the flood that led to the settlement's abandonment. The second prop offered a joke at the expense of the National Trust itself and its past approaches to the interpretation of heritage. The prop consisted of two bars of soap (Fig. 13.2). Their labels, which form their wrapping, read: "This soap is Sarah's Conservation Soap" with the words "Sanitises before public display", "Try it on your site", "Extraordinary cleansing powers", "Removes all unsightly buildings and stories", "Produces absolute cleanliness on heritage sites". Two Union Jack flags make up the brand emblem. Not everyone would be able to decode the text here as it requires some awareness of past modes of heritage interpretation and a critical perspective on them. For those with the required literacy, however, the bars of soap alert the visitor to the constructed nature of all heritage sites. They warn the visitor not to take everything at face value but to read beyond the immediately obvious. They are, in fact, an instruction on how to approach both the site itself and its interpretation.

Almost as if by way of example, I was immediately presented with the value of reading beyond the obvious. For the next prop was some coiled barbed wire fencing, appearing to all intents as if still in its original wrapper. Initially thinking that the wire served as a reminder of settlement, indicating the history of this place as a farming community I bent over to read the label on the wrapper. It read: "Settler's own ideal for disrupting nomadic lifestyles and keeping people out". In a Benjaminian moment, I recoiled, almost in horror at the matter of fact way in which this simple prop was made to stand for the process of colonisation. The shock lay in the realisation of how simple it was to prevent people from entering their traditional lands. From a physical, visceral response to this object then, I experienced an affective experience in which shock, registered first of all as a physical reaction manifested in the activity of recoiling away from the object, became an emotional state and finally cognitive understanding. My sense of history had become intensely "palpable". It was also this palpability that gave me the ability to begin to construct a narrative. For by then, in noting the relationship between the various clues, I had began to produce a narrative by "telescoping" the various clues into a series of nests that gave me a narrative about the process of so called settlement.

The last prop, a tin with a wrapper around it read: "Extract of rust—for debility and impoverishment. Free for all wheat farmers after 1865". Despite being "the granary of the colony" for a time, rust was a disease that affected the Greenough crops of wheat and sent many farmers into ruin. One needs to know what rust is and make the connection that it affected this settlement relatively early on in its history. The affective power of this prop, compared to the last one was, however, minimal. I just had one more clue as to the history of this settlement.

Quite clearly the clues we are given require some prior knowledge and a willingness to work at decoding them. But whether or not we have the prior knowledge to connect the clues into a narrative of invasion, settlement and disaster, it is obvious that we must work to read the landscape. All of these clues tell the visitor that there is more to this site than meets the eye. It is not possible to remain blind and continue to read it within a framework that produces a romanticised nostalgia for the pioneer past by cloaking it in warm images of a close community. As if to reinforce the clues we walk out through a passage with an inviting red leather bench on which visitors can sit. As I did so I was confronted with a wall of text. Reading it, I realised I was reading an extract from explorer George Grey's diary for 1839. The extract represents perhaps one of the earliest Aboriginal accounts of European exploration in Western Australia in which Grey recorded Noongar man Warrup's description of the journey he took when looking for the men that Grey had left behind, only to find them dead. In a final act of "telescoping", the words in front of my eyes crystallised my thoughts and confirmed, through their documentary status, that which white Australians have always found difficult to face—that pioneering was in fact the process of invasion. I now have a narrative, produced by my by own hard work in "seeking", "probing" and finally "telescoping" the clues on offer. I do not have an enormous amount of detail, but I have an approach to the site, an indication of the historical themes that it embodies and, most importantly, an indication that I too am implicated in history by the way in which I respond to the strong suggestions embedded in the clues.

A less problematic example, in terms of its expectations from audiences, is a recent display on Little Lonsdale Street in Melbourne as part of the Melbourne Story exhibition at Melbourne Museum. It is of interest because it uses techniques of reconstruction to challenge received ideas about the past in ways that push beyond the simple production of nostalgia. Opened in 2008, this display aims to use an immersive environment to challenge received historical understandings of this part of working class Melbourne during its lifetime and after its redevelopment in 1948. Little Lon, as the area is known by Melbournians, was an intensely multicultural, working class area in the central area of the city. Its image in the popular imagination, however, was that of an inner city slum "riddled with poverty, prostitution and drug addiction" (Smith and Tout-Smith forthcoming). To challenge this image, the curators—Charlotte Smith and Deborah Tout-Smith—used a modern approach to the old technique of recreation. Not content to present their recreation in the mode of a period room, their approach relied on the use of embodied, sensory experiences to produce a powerful form of "palpable" history that challenged middle class understandings of the lives of the working class. They then supplemented this experience with a more traditional archaeological display that provided the "evidence" for their arguments.

The approach was undertaken knowing that audiences wanted immersive experiences. Evaluation studies

> repeatedly showed that visitors wanted to be more than passive observers: they wanted to enter into environments where they could touch things, open drawers, listen and smell, and where they didn't have to read too much. Visitors wanted to discover hidden histories and learn new information. (Smith and Tout-Smith forthcoming)

Moreover visitors expressed "a desire to experience a variety of emotions in the museum: shock, excitement, surprise, sadness and delight" (Smith and Tout-Smith forthcoming).

Hence, in this recreation, it is possible to walk through the space as if it was a heritage site, not simply to look at it behind glass. The attention to detail, such as the fabric used for construction, the presence of soil on the pavements against the two reconstructed houses, the use of smell as well as soundscapes makes the experience of walking through the display a powerful one. The soundscapes in particular evoke the presence of a community long gone and invite the visitor to linger a while and explore the space.

In its form and genealogy, the display could easily be accused of producing nostalgia through its evocation of a long-gone community in warm tones. However, these warm tones are exactly what counteracts the dominant impression in the public imagination of the area as a slum. What is produced is not so much nostalgia as an understanding that the image of the area as a slum cannot capture the full diversity of human experience in that place. What then are the clues that help you understand the display in ways that go beyond nostalgia?

I was attracted to the display first of all by the sounds of children's voices, playing in the streets. I eventually found their source, low down at street level. Bending down to catch what they were saying, I was surprised by the sense of community that their little familiar rhymes evoked. Not so much nostalgia for the past as recognition of the ongoing nature of human activities and a sensation of pleasure at this recognition. Standing up I heard another soundscape, that of an Italian man speaking. Moving towards the source of his voice, this time at my face level, I heard Mr Bracchi, an Italian migrant speaking about his experiences in Little Lon, setting up as an ice-cream vendor who eventually started his own ice-cream factory in the area. Looking around I noticed the hint of a cart behind the glass windows of a shed door. Peering, I recognised with pleasure that I was looking at his street cart. Even before I entered one of the cottages I already knew that this was a display about a community with a strong sense of pride in their achievements.

In peopling the place, the curators were of course attempting to present Little Lon as populated by actual people rather than the homogenised image of its inhabitants as slum dwellers and no-hopers (Smith and Tout-Smith forthcoming). By combining the results of an archaeological dig with historical archival research, they were able to populate the place with stories of people who had actually lived there. As they put it, this research shows quite clearly that while a working class area, Little Lon

> was a rich social environment, culturally and socially diverse with people from Ireland, England, Italy, Syria, India and China calling it home. The small area was crammed with schools, factories, shops, churches, meeting

> halls, pubs, brothels and houses—many owner-occupied. The laneways were public thoroughfares and communal spaces in which children played, women hung out their laundry, and families prepared meals. (Smith and Tout-Smith forthcoming)

The two cottage replicas, one of a very poor working class family and the other of an owner-occupied dwelling one step up the social scale, provide a rich immersive environment in which to extend the insights gained on the lane outside. Unlike conventional period rooms that only seek to provide a lesson in aesthetics, these recreations use theatrical means based on in-depth historical research to represent lived experience. Thus attention has been paid to getting the right lighting for the period, the exact scale of the dwellings based on archaeological and archival evidence, as well as using pictorial, archaeological evidence and oral history accounts of living in the area to furnish the interiors. The result is a visual, aural and physical experience that begins to give an impression of people's hopes and problems, their religious and cultural networks, the nature of their work and their memories and sense of attachment to the place.

Thus in the poor cottage I was struck by the attempt to decorate the place despite the obvious lack of money portrayed through the shabby condition of the house and the simple and heavily worn furniture. I was drawn to the decoupage on the walls with images taken from illustrated magazines. At almost the same time my eye was drawn to the hole in the ceiling where the wooden ceiling struts were showing through. I could feel the presence of the cottage's inhabitants by the presence of their worn clothes hanging on the door handle, while I gained an insight into their lives from a soundscape of Sister Esther, an Irish nun who worked in the area. The impression I gained is one of hardship combined with a strong sense of family and aspirations for a better life. These are not no-hopers, lacking in moral values.

Fig. 13.3 Living area of the "poor" cottage. Photographer: Ben Healley. Courtesy of Museum Victoria.

Likewise, in the second cottage I begin to understand that a number of Little Lon residents had respectable jobs, owned their own home and could even afford some of the better things in life. There are more decorations and a crocheted apron on the mantelpiece, samplers on the wall, better furniture, muslin instead of hessian curtains. Moreover, in Little Lon there was a real mixing of ethnicities, with Mary Hayes recalling as part of her childhood going over to the neighbours, the Bracchi family, to get spaghetti and homemade tomato sauce.

Fig. 13.4 Living area of "richer" cottage. Photographer: Ben Healley. Courtesy of Museum Victoria.

What both of these case studies show is that it is possible to use the experience of space, of materiality, and the senses, to engage visitors in an imaginative sense of play that builds upon received knowledge in order to challenge it. Furthermore, this can be done either through strategies of shock, such as at Greenough, or by playing on people's pleasure in nostalgic experiences. Unlike exhibitions that use labels and graphics to tell the audience about the past in a literal and didactic manner, these exhibitions use embodied forms of experience to encourage the visitor to look beyond the apparently obvious or known and thus actively construct a new subject position for themselves in relation to their experiences in the exhibition. Importantly, it is their active role in constructing these narratives that gives them an opportunity to develop an ethical relationship to the past by reassessing their own perceptions of it and recognising the continuities between such perceptions and the legacies of the past in the present.

References

Ang, I. 2005. The predicament of diversity: Multiculturalism in practice at the art museum. *Ethnicities* 5 (3): 305–320.

Bennett, J. 2001. Stigmata and sense memory: St Francis and the affective image. *Art History* 24 (1): 1–16.

—. 2002. Art, affect, and the 'bad death': Strategies for communicating the sense memory of loss. *Journal of Women in Culture and Society* 28 (1): 333–351.

—. 2005. *Empathic vision: Affect, trauma, and contemporary art.* Stanford: Stanford University Press.

Best, S. 2001. What is affect? Considering the affective dimension of contemporary installation art. *Australian and New Zealand Journal of Art* 2–3: 207–225.

Betts, K. 1999. *The great divide: Immigration politics in Australia.* Sydney: Duffy and Snellgrove.

Black, J. 2005. London's house of spirits. *The Washington Post*, June 26: 9.

Clifford, J. 1997. *Travel and translation in the late twentieth century.* Cambridge, MA: Harvard University Press.

Commonwealth of Australia. 2003. Review of the National Museum of Australia, its exhibitions and public programs, a report to the Council of the National Museum of Australia. http://www.dcita.gov.au/Article/0,,0_1-2_2-4_113158,00.html (accessed 12 December 2009)

Doering, Z. D. 2002. Serving the nation: Lessons from the Smithsonian. Paper presented at the Museums Australia National Conference, March 18–22 in Adelaide, Australia. Available at http://www.museumsaustra lia.org.au/events/htm (accessed 17 June 2004)

Deleuze, G. 2000. Proust and signs. In Vol. 17 *Theory out of bounds.* Trans. Richard Howard, Minneapolis: University of Minnesota Press.

Dudley, S. 2009. *Museum materialities: Objects, engagements, interpretations.* London and New York: Routledge.

Gibson, R. 2008. Palpable history. *Cultural Studies Review* 14 (1): 179–186.

Gitlin, T. 1995. *The twilight of common dreams: Why America is wracked by culture wars.* New York: Metropolitan Books.

Hage, G. 1998. *White nation: Fantasies of white supremacy in a multicultural society.* Sydney: Pluto Press.

—. 2006. We will fight them on the beach: Cronulla and the tensions of Australian multiculturalism. *Catalyst: Journal of the British Commission for Racial Equality* May.

Henning, M. 2006. *Museums, media and cultural theory.* Issues in Cultural and Media Studies Series. Maidenhead: Open University Press.

Heywood, L. 2006. National identity in spotlight. *The Courier-Mail*, 28 Nov.

Johnson, S. 2005. *Everything bad is good for you.* London: Allen Lane.

Kavanagh, G. 2000. *Dream spaces, memory and the museum*. London and New York: Leicester University Press.

Kirschenblatt-Gimblett, B. 2000. The museum as catalyst. Keynote address at the Museums 2000: Confirmation or Challenge conference, September 29 in Vadstena, Sweden http://www.nyu.edu/classes/bkg/web/vadstena.pdf. (accessed 12 December 2009)

Kreps, C. 2003. *Liberating culture: Cross-cultural perspectives on museums, curation, and heritage preservation*. London and New York: Routledge.

Kwint, M., C. Breward and J. Aynsley Eds. 1999. *Material memories*. Oxford: Berg.

Latour, B. 2005. *Reassembling the social: An introduction to actor-network theory*. Clarendon Lectures in Management Studies. New York: Oxford University Press.

Macintyre, S. and A. Clark. 2003. *The history wars*. Carlton, Victoria: Melbourne University Press.

McShane, I. (2004). 'Living dangerously' at the National Museum of Australia. *Museums Australia Magazine* 12 (3): 12–15.

Massumi, B. 2002. *Parables for the virtual: Movement, affect, sensation*. London: Duke University Press.

Merleau-Ponty, M. 1968. *The visible and the invisible*. Trans. A. Lingis. Evanston: Northwestern University Press.

—. 2002. *Phenomenology of perception*. Trans. Colin Smith. London: Routledge.

Message, K. 2005. Representing cultural diversity in a global context: The Museum of New Zealand Te Papa Tongarewa and the National Museum of Australia. *International Journal of Cultural Studies* 8 (4): 465–485.

—. 2006. *New museums and the making of culture*. Oxford and New York: Berg.

—. 2007. Museums and the utility of culture: The politics of liberal democracy and cultural well-being. *Social Identities* 13 (2): 235–256.

Newman, A. 2005. Social exclusion zone and 'the feel good factor'. In *Heritage, museums and galleries: an introductory reader*. Ed. G. Corsane, 325–332. London and New York: Routledge.

Peers, L. and A. K. Brown Eds. 2003. *Museums and source communities*. New York: Routledge.

Smith, C. and D. Tout-Smith. Forthcoming. Recreating place: Little Lon. *Journal of Museum Management and Curatorship* 25 (1).

Storrie, C. 2006. *The delirious museum: A journey from the Louvre to Las Vegas*. London: I. B. Tauris & Co. Ltd.

Van Leeuwen, B. 2008. On the affective ambivalence of living with cultural diversity. *Ethnicities* 8 (2): 147–176.

Wallace, A. 1994. The battle over 'The West as America'. In *Art apart: Art institutions and ideology across England and North America.* Ed. M. Pointon, 89–101. Manchester and New York: Manchester University Press.

Wise, A. and A. Chapman. 2005. Introduction: Migration, affect and the senses. *Journal of Intercultural Studies* 26 (1–2): 1–3.

Witcomb, A. 2003. *Re-imagining the museum: Beyond the mausoleum.* London: Routledge.

—. 2006. How style came to matter: Do we need to move beyond the politics of representation? In *South Pacific museums: Experiments in culture.* Ed. C. Healy and A. Witcomb, Melbourne: Monash University E Press. www.epress.monash.edu/spm.

—. 2007. 'An architecture of rewards': A new poetics to exhibition design? *Museology e-journal*, 4, http://museology.ct.aegean.gr/ (accessed 12 December 2009)

Zolberg, V. 1996. Museums as contested sites of remembrance: The Enola Gay affair. In *Theorizing museums: Representing identity and diversity in a changing world.* Ed. S. Macdonald and G. Fyfe, 69–82. Oxford: Blackwell Publishers/The Sociological Review.

CHAPTER FOURTEEN

"MYMUSEUM": SOCIAL MEDIA AND THE ENGAGEMENT OF THE ENVIRONMENTAL CITIZEN

JUAN FRANCISCO SALAZAR

Introduction

Museums and science / art centres continue to determine in great measure our understanding and social construction of societies' past and present. Increasingly, museums and science centres have also become key agents in the representation, speculation and simulation of possible futures, from the utopian to the dystopic. This chapter invites thinking into how museums and science centres can engage the technologies and practices of social media toward increased citizenship participation in relation to climate change. When examined through the lens of citizen epistemologies and ontologies, the range of contentious and contested topics with which contemporary museums engage elicits fundamental questions of cultural transformation and issues of access, participation, knowledge creation and ownership. In relation to the question of engaging publics in climate change action, there is still uncertainty as to how social media can play a more fundamental role beyond offering the illusion of participation, access and creative content production. Recent literature examines the emergence and impact of social media and social networking and how these new forms of communication open spaces for participation and co-creation. Yet very few analyses go beyond the new promises of networked socio-technical communities. The techno-evangelism of much of the recent social media discourse certainly contrasts with the political economy of the knowledge divide in the information society. This chapter provides a discussion on the use of networked digital media in museum contexts and on the role that citizens' media may play in specific instances, such as how climate change is communicated in museums and science centres.

The individualisation of the citizen

In a scene from Steven Speilberg's film *Minority Report* pre-crime unit police chief John Anderton (Tom Cruise) has detected that, in order to hide a murder case involving the highest police department director, the police force is enmeshed in a serious case of conspiracy and corruption. Fleeing through the cityscapes of Washington D.C in 2054 AD Anderton is assaulted in the subway system by interactive billboards that identify citizens / consumers by way of eye-scans that pierce the brains of passers-by with personalised and customised ads. The eye-scan system in Speilberg's film resonates with Roland Barthes' notion of the "punctum", those personal and private meanings that jump out of photographs to pierce the viewer (Barthes 1981) in the sense of the possibility of connecting visual technologies with human private repertoires of sensations, memories, tastes, and choices. At other times in the film, holograms detect what individuals have purchased, and ask for feedback and participation in virtual surveys. In the world of the near future imagined by Spielberg, eye scanners and holograms that allow for sophisticated surveillance, social control and entertainment, form a concealed network that surrounds individuals. Despite its obvious product placement purposes, the film does raise some interesting questions concerning social software and convergence. As Palmer points out in "this lurid scenario of surveillance-meets-marketing, advertisers explicitly customise their message to the individual by scanning the retina of the eye" prompting new questions about the "destandardisation, fragmentation and pluralisation of consumption" (Palmer 2003, 161).

In a similar way, the irruption of social media into the private spaces of the everyday come to demonstrate what Reguillo has called—in reference to de Certeau—"the clandestine centrality of the everyday" (Reguillo 2000, 77). Since the early 1990s, social theory accounts of global capitalism (Bauman 2001, Beck 2001) have suggested the emergence of systemic processes of individualisation and new forms of subjectification. These processes have certainly multiplied with the proliferation of social software and social networking technologies in the past ten years. The multiplication and mobilisation of social relations through social media applications coincide with a shift (some would argue a decline) in forms of social organisation. Social media give a face-lift to the everyday vernacular, instigating processes of "biographical liberation", discussed so eloquently by Beck (1992). This new mode of social relations is explained by

Wellman in the following terms: "the change from groups to networks means that rather than fitting into the same group as those around them, each person has his/her own 'personal community'" (Wellman 2001, 227). Social networks have come to customise the platforms where personal engagements take place. If the mass media have been the dominant form of content provision in the 20th century, social media shift the equation from providers of content to providers of platforms. Yet most definitions of social media / networking are technologically biased. They emphasise the technologies and technics employed, the mode of information, and the technological shaping of social life and institutions. New media theory has yet to come up with a significant new theorisation of social change, or how these new cultural transformations are framed and determined by the political economy of new media. Gumucio Dagron summarises this void by stating that "the web, which for many of us is a wonderful tool, is not even an object of curiosity for most of the poor of the world. It doesn't contribute at all to the solution of their daily problems, unless it is 'localised'" (Gumucio Dagron 2005, 11).

Social media and museums: the emerging MyMuseum space

As part of the "MySpace.com boom" of the mid 2000s, museums and science / art centres worldwide set up MySpace sites to connect in a different way with their visitors and audiences. By joining the "MySpace.com boom", cultural institutions intended to take advantage of social networking as a way of reaching deep into communities of interest and to tap into the consumer behaviour of technologically enabled groups, or "smart mobs" (Rheinhold 2003). Emerging research on social media in museums is looking at the relationship between social media, cultural institutions and digital participation (Watkins and Russo 2007, Russo et al. 2008). As knowledge apparatuses, many museums and science / art centres worldwide have shifted significantly in recent decades toward more participatory perspectives that validate, and occasionally even give prominence to, community content as authoritative cultural knowledge. Museums and science / arts centres are using social media to create or improve popular knowledge-sharing networks in which cultural participants share images, information and experiences throughout communities (Russo et al. 2008). For this reason, it is imperative to question how social media in fact extend and perpetuate dominant ideologies such as consumerism and popular culture, rather than challenge them.

Today, to produce their news content, commercial news networks employ community-driven models in which amateur audiences supply a wide range of images submitted via their phones, internet, or PDAs. Likewise, institutions such as museums and science / art centres incorporate community-supplied digital content, collected and exhibited via social media portals accessed by visitors through mobile cellular phones and iPods. Users might find advantages in using their own devices, such as bypassing restrictive museum schedules and distant locations. However, the fundamental question is if these uses of social networks truly affect citizen participation. Participation can be seen as a kaleidoscope-type process, as Alfonso Gumucio Dagron (2001) suggests. "[I]t changes its colour and shape at the will of the hands in which [it] is held". In fact, as Gumucio Dagron demonstrates through an extensive examination of a series of participatory communication initiatives worldwide, communication and participation are two words that share a common root. Etymologically, the Latin *communio* relates to participation and sharing and it is only during the past 50 years or so that the concept of communication has been equated, confused, and used interchangeably as with the word information (Gumucio Dagron 2001).

This first wave of social media used by museums and science centres has yet to produce a critical examination of social media that addresses the cultural politics of the digital divide. Much of the current research around new media in museums still fails to provide an in-depth analysis of civic-driven participation in the digital realm. Watkins and Russo (2007) have described a significant adoption of new communication technologies by museums in recent years, particularly the use of social media for self-publication, image sharing or online video. While these new engagement strategies may provide solutions for museums wishing to interact with communities and audiences in more creative and lasting ways, it still remains unclear how such media can be sustained within the museum, whether such initiatives are a valid response to the ongoing challenge of audience connection, and what issues are raised within the institution by a more participatory approach to cultural communication. A key issue remains the ways in which participatory processes are reduced to mere access and interaction, and therefore potentially "reducing the power equilibrium that is constitutive of participation" (Carpentier et al. 2009, 172). As Carpentier (2007) claims, in recent years the term participation has been stripped of its political connotation, and this has happened simultaneously with the slippage of the term interactivity. As Celia Lury (2007) also points out, interactivity understood as a responsive activity within programmed boundaries is radically different from interaction, understood as change and negotiation. In this sense, during this first wave, museums and science / art centres have emphasised interactivity rather than fostering interaction. For Jenkins (2006), interactivity is a property of the technology, while participation is a property of culture. In this regard it could be argued that social media perform what Manuel Castells (2001) has termed as "networked individualism", rather than fostering deep and transformative models of participatory communication that encourage publics to exercise the power of decision making and to become fully involved in the formulation of policies and plans of action (Jacobson and Servaes 1999). This type of participatory communication is absent in much of the decision-making processes of museums and science / art centres in relation to public culture. Conversely, further research is needed to understand how current uses of social networks by museums and science / art centres are intensifying "the isolating and stratifying impacts of new media" (Srinivasan 2006, 497), that may point to the importance of focusing on culture (participation) as much as on interactivity (technology). Some current examples may illustrate this further.

Numerous museums worldwide have developed online "Mymuseum spaces" where visitors can view and download images, insert their own tags on images and create online postcards. But access to information is still a world apart from a truly participatory model where *ownership* entails audiences having a voice in the process of content creation. In cases like Mymuseum, social networking says very little about grass-roots engagement in the processes of creating content and managing decisions. Many museums have also made use of Flickr's Commons initiative which has been taken up as a mechanism for opening up participation by allowing users to annotate and tag objects (such as images and artefacts) and therefore accepting, at a basic level, the relevance and authority of folksonomies. The Brooklyn Museum, for example, launched in early 2009 an innovative program titled *1stFans* as a way to develop a system that could "speak" directly to visitors in a personalised way. Combining the use of closed groups on Facebook and Flickr and a private Twitter feed featuring work by original artists, *1stFans* is "an attempt to turn the impersonal engine of museum membership into a relationship-based, community-centered interaction for two specific museum audiences."[1] However, social media engagements like these tend to demonstrate that current uses of social networking by museums and science / art centres have more to do with models based in networked short-term diffusion of persuasion-driven messages, rather than in models based in long-term processes of dialogue and debate to foster conscientisation, and ultimately, long-term social change. As Alexandra Juhasz (2008) reminds us,

"YouTube's reliance upon popularity serves to maintain the status quo in terms of who is actually heard, and what they are permitted to say, not to broaden these fields". As is the case with social media and networking in general, the question of access only offers a superficial understanding of participation. Access is not a goal in itself, but a step toward autonomous forms of ownership of the processes of communication and representation. Social networking platforms may be based on some principles of participatory communication; however, in their current uses, social media reproduce the fundamentals of hierarchical models of communication, such as promoting individual over social change. Internet-based social media are founded on social interaction rather than social participation. In reference to Latour's notion of "object-oriented democracy" (Latour 2005), Marres (2008) has referred to "object-oriented publics" to explain that publics not only exist to the extent that they are addressed by discourses circulating in media and / or institutional circuits, but are also held together by material and physical associations. And in this sense social media provide both a virtual and a material form of association, but unlike other participatory citizens' media forms of social networking, citizens become objects of change rather than agents of change.

Many questions remain around issues of how citizens may use social media to engage in critical scientific debates and decisions that affect their futures in the context of museums and science / art centres. Beyond opening opportunities for downloading or tagging photos and artefacts from museum collections, or commenting in museum blogs about the experience of their visit, the role that social media and networking can play in providing platforms for deep political and civic engagement is still unexplored. It remains to be seen how social media can move beyond the model of social marketing and customisation and offer real possibilities to open dialogue between the different knowledges and perspectives held by scientists and citizens (local and global). In their vision of the customised museum, Falk et al. (2007) argue that customisation requires significant changes in the role of the museum, shifting from an authoritative position of knowledge (content) provider to a position of partner (co-creator) and platform provider. This question of distributed creativity is an important building block of a more participatory culture. Does this mean that museums are shifting from being content providers to being platform providers? Current literature suggests that museums and especially science / art centres are changing from delivering knowledge to facilitating learning through participatory designs of experiences, and what is more relevant, from the distribution of information to a communicative engagement that revolves around posing key questions and engaging in hot topic debates and public culture (Falk et al. 2007, 85, see also Chapter Three).

Undoubtedly, many museums are beginning to reframe dominant expertise and to incorporate civil society's views, in ways that might question the very nature of expertise. These are significant steps that will certainly lead to the recognition of new synergies between expert and lay knowledge. The Virtual Museums of Canada for example, is a network actively fostering participatory engagement with First Nations' organisations in the work of museums and archives. Through social web applications, such as blogs and wikis, indigenous peoples are invited to question the authority of museums as they describe and define objects and artefacts. This focus has also been taken up by research projects looking at local knowledge databases and forms for decentering the museum through the sharing of information and co-creation of knowledge databases between cultural institutions, such as museums / science centres and indigenous communities (Boast et al. 2007, Srinivasan et al. 2009). Again, the problem needs to move from the question of access to the predicament of ownership. More specifically, how can museums and science / art centres develop or elicit fluid ontologies that can allow for adaptive structures for knowledge representation based on the involvement of communities as content co-creators? How can these organisations remain open to continual redesign based on community input? Non-hierarchical social structures also demand non-hierarchical technological infrastructures and solutions, which trigger a different set of queries about technology control, and who defines and redefines, configures and reconfigures technological objects and tools.

Emerging research demonstrates that, not satisfied with simply receiving information, people increasingly seek opportunities to engage, modify and transform content. In the context of museums and science / art centres people seek opportunities to co-create content and to engage in curatorship and management. How science and technologies are "narrativised" and presented to diverse publics becomes particularly problematic for museum and science / art centres that explore the option of co-creating content. While museums are starting to take advantage of social media opportunities, they have yet to acknowledge the social and cultural ramifications of the commercial imperative driving the implementation of new media (Lax 2007). Together with promoting user-generated content, museums and science / arts centres must enable cultural participants to be both critics and creators of digital culture (Russo et al. 2008). More importantly, museums and science / arts centres must engage with critical debates on the digital divide and develop strategies for inclusiveness, participation and access, as the "media worlds of welfare dependent, who queue at local libraries for free access … is worlds apart from the high-speed access increasingly being designed only for business" (Nightingale and Dwyer 2007). As Russo et al. (2008) claim,

> the widespread viability and sustainability of social media as tools for curatorial practice, participatory communication, and informal learning in museums, libraries, galleries, and archives remains to be determined. Any successful use of social media tools will need more effort than the download of free software and the hope that someone technically-minded in the organisation will implement and sustain a participatory communication program. (Russo et al. 2008, 25)

One area that is of particular sensitivity is database narratives, whose primarily non-linear, open-ended structure exposes or thematises the dual processes of selection and combination that lie at the heart of all stories (Kinder 2002). In this kind of storytelling model, the interactors can select any particular data or fragments of it from a series of databases or paradigms (events, myths, sounds, photographs, etc.) and recombine them according their own frames of reference. In line with Kristeva's notion of intertextuality—which conceives the origin of a new signifying system made up of the transpositions of formal elements between already existing sign-systems—Everett (2003) proposes that we look at new media as "a metasignifying system of discursive absorption whereby different signifying systems and material are translated and often transformed into zeroes and ones for infinite recombination" (Everett 2003, 7).

Brokering science: museums as science-citizen networks

Museums and science centres have an increasingly significant role to play in new emerging and controversial topics in public culture. Among these, climate change emerges as one of the most prominent challenges. It has been 20 years since the "Earth Summit" (United Nations Conference on Environment and Development) in Rio de Janeiro whose most important outcomes were two significant documents: the United Nations Framework Convention on Climate Change and Agenda 21. Since 1992, from Rio, through Kyoto and Bali, to Copenhagen, there has been a slow acceptance that climate change has become a fundamental form of political contest yet without a "politics of climate change" in place (Giddens 2009). Several decades of environmentalism have also given rise to a generation of environmental detractors, "a virulent hostile coalition of industrialists, right-wing commentators and conservative politicians" (Hamilton 2007, 147) in what has been termed the "invasion of the skeptics in the battle for public opinion" (Hamilton 2007, 147). The current political scenario leading to COP15 in Copenhagen in late 2009 demonstrates how scientific uncertainty has become politicised, and this politicisation is permanently framed through the mass media in very normative ways.

It would be difficult to disagree that the mass media (broadcast and print) constitute the main source of information, and also the most determining factor in the degree of conscientisation (awareness) and concern of people for climate change. More difficult is to concede up to what point the discursive construction and reproduction of scientific claims in the media is strongly entangled in ideological standpoints that legitimate "a program of action vis-à-vis a given social and political order" (Carvalho 2007), where ideology "works as a powerful selection device in deciding what is scientific news, i.e. what the relevant 'facts' are, and who are the authorised 'agents of definition' of science matters" (Carvalho, 2007).

The media are key elements in the mediation of the "relations of definition" (Beck 1992) between science, the public and the political spheres. It is somewhat striking to observe the frequency with which climate change media coverage takes the form of a social marketing campaign pointing to how citizens "address 'green' issues, and climate change in particular, and in that way fulfil their civic responsibilities" (Marres 2008) by simply changing a few domestic practices. Experience is an affective, subjective, and personal process and on that basis, environmental media campaigns and coverage are only targeted to the ways individuals can cut their "emissions at home", offering carbon calculators for households to measure their carbon footprint with the promise of saving energy and money. In this type of media coverage, the implicit model is based on the notion that social change is merely an aggregation of individuals making small changes to their daily routines. Climate change is mostly framed in the mass media through a particular linear logic that is performed through the very interaction with the information medium itself. This performative logic of the mass media refers to the "organisational, technological, and aesthetic functioning, including the ways in which media allocate material and symbolic resources and work through formal and informal rules" (Hjarvard 2007, 3 in Couldry 2008, 376). The blast of the news coverage of climate change in the mass media, particularly during 2009 in the lead to the UN COP15 Summit in Copenhagen, may be a reflection of an incipient shift towards a more sophisticated global political ecology. On the contrary, this increase in media coverage of climate change may be directly linked to a journalism logic of newsworthiness based on events and figures, such as timing, significance, proximity or prominence. In many cases, climate change is constructed as media-orchestrated events (Marres 2008). Also important is to note that climate change has been big news in the media of most OECD countries, but it is certainly not the case in many other countries. The bottom line remains unchanged: more information does not necessarily mean more or better communication, and certainly no more action, nor increased public engagement. In this context, how social media will shift from a paradigm of aggregated individualism to media that provide genuine and dynamic interfaces for science-governance-civil society dialogues is still to be seen. Mike Davies has poignantly asserted: "Our world, our old world that we have inhabited for the last 12,000 years, has ended, even if no newspaper in North America or Europe has yet printed its scientific obituary" (Davies 2008). The mass media have provided an over-saturated landscape of information (transmission of messages with or without feedback) often focusing on campaigns, yet in general terms fail to communicate (share knowledge and dialogue) about climate change. If it is not the role of the mass media to engage in long-term processes of change, then whose role is it? Certainly alternative, citizens' and community media play a significant role in the communication of climate change, by filling in the gaps between global and local understandings of climate change (adaptation and mitigation). Citizens' media reinstate the local dimension; they do not have to reach all audiences, they do not have to talk to everyone. This entails shifting the focus to empowering communities to themselves take action on climate change based on their own informed decision-making processes in a process of dialogue with climate change science and policy. In this regard citizens' media, from radio to digital social media / networking, provide a relevant platform to rethink civic action, and on the other hand, recognise the unacknowledged cultural contingencies of scientific knowledge (and by extension, how they are presented, for example, in museums or science centres). In this particular regard, science museums and centres may play a pivotal role in new ways of engaging citizens in climate change debate and action as brokers between science, policy-makers and the public. Considering that one of the main goals of Agenda 21 was to re-orient education towards sustainable development *and* to meet the challenges of a low-carbon or post-carbon economy, the ensuing lack of engagement with learning institutions, including museums and science / art centres is a significant shortcoming. Museums and science / art centres are uniquely positioned to become relevant sites of learning (Hooper-Greenhill 2007; Kelly 2007); thus, these institutions can play key roles in redefining modes of environmental literacy, shaping how we learn about environmental science, and how we build consensus toward new forms of environmental citizenship. Museums and science centres have a pivotal role to play in the engagement of the environmental citizen and social media ought to be considered as a tool of engagement within a larger framework of participatory media and participatory design.

Participatory media have been characterised as rhizomatic (Carpentier et al. 2009, Bosch 2010) as they cut across boundaries imposed by markets and states, and they are part of intricate webs of civil society networks acting as catalysts and meeting points for a variety of movements and organisations. And in this sense social media have still to fulfill their promise of a "network revolution" providing both a virtual and a material model of association, where citizens can become agents of change and no mere objects of change. Museums and science centres must continue to redefine their roles within the particular communities in which they are inserted and in order to be "agents of change" in climate change interventions they must rethink how they engage with larger rhizomatic civil society organisations. Many museums and science centre across the world have produced numerous exhibitions on climate change in recent years. This is of critical importance as a way of thinking on and about climate change that is not disembodied and abstract (as presented by the media), but rich in feeling, in intuition, in emotion, and connection to larger social, political, cultural and historical contexts. But how do museums move beyond the exhibition and the representation of science to a more performative role embedded in local and global cultural solidarities? As spaces for engagement for different knowledges to coexist, museums are strategically positioned as spaces where "people's fragmented, uncertain, incomplete narratives of agency …" on and around climate change for example "… can be valued, preserved and made available for exchange, while being related analytically to wider contexts of power" (Couldry 2006, 172).

An interesting example of a recent project attempting to connect those fragmented and incomplete narratives of climate change is *Superstruct*[2], a multiplayer online game launched in 2007 that in some ways attempted to address these issues. Based on "extreme-scale collaboration" played on fora, blogs, videos, wikis, and social media online spaces, the game was designed by Jane McGonigal, as part of a project developed at the Institute for the Future, a not-for-profit think tank based in California. The game aims to predict what the world might look like in 2019. In the game, players are known as SEHIs (Super-Empowered Hopeful Individuals) whose missions are to "save the world" by predicting through the telling of local stories, strategising with others, and "superstructing". The game creates a sense of an "imagined network". Drawing from Benedict Anderson's analysis of the nation as an "imagined community", Wendy Chun (2007) argues that we are witnessing the emergence of imagined networks that are both less and more than communities or nations, and which, contrasting to communities, "emphasise flow, movement and the constant adding and pruning of connections" (Chun 2007, 125), stressing fluid relations rather than fixed identities. It might be valuable to think the role of museums and science centres as an "imagined network", where social media becomes a means to an end rather than the end itself. It is important to note however, that while the game was played by over 7,000 individuals in ten or so countries, most of the of the players came from only three countries; over two thirds from the US, with the remaidner mostly from Canada and the UK. This aspect reveals problematic issues in the material and political economy aspects of the digital knowledge society. In this regard the citizens of these imagined networks could be constructed as "eventive publics" (Lash and Lury 2007) that exist only "as moving, dynamic, asynchronous entities that could not possibly exist in a static form" (Marres 2008).

Conclusion

Museums and science centres worldwide are increasingly employing social media tools to connect with audiences in new ways, to open up collections in digital and virtual forms, and engage with important debates in public culture. Social media networks offer many opportunities to think of new forms of engagement, at the same time that they pose concerns about the nature of participation itself. It is therefore necessary to think of a shift from the "mymuseum" to the "ourmuseum". Museums and science centres are one of many pools of information from where civics engage in public debates, and therefore their insertion within a rhizome of engaged institutions and social movements may place the museum in a different space for engagement. Thus, within a framework of communication rights and the political economy of a growing digital economy, museums and science centres must become relevant cultural brokers that contest current understandings of the complex interfaces and intersections between science, media and citizenship. Perhaps there is a role for participatory citizens' media models to inform how museums and science centres can engage with local communities. The role of connecting with local communities and forging assemblages of socio-technical networks of knowledge building is crucial for museums and science centres, especially when thinking of their role in engaging in north-south and south-south dialogues. In this context community and citizens' media might be better positioned to recognise that environmental knowledge, vulnerability and resilience to climate impacts, are embedded in local knowledge. Citizens' media allow social subjects to claim a space for their public voices as they correct the distortions and bias of mainstream media that would otherwise remain unchallenged. Citizens' media, "as fracturers of the symbolic" (Rodriguez 2001, 150), cultivate symbolic resistance and contestation. Citizens' media reinstate the local dimension; they don't have to reach all audiences, they do not have to talk to everyone. This entails shifting the focus from ratings and profit to empowering communities into taking action based on their own decision-making processes and in processes of dialogue with climate change science and policy experts. In this regard citizens' media can provide a relevant platform to rethink how museums and science centres present scientific knowledge and encourage civic action. Citizens' media participatory models of communication have the potential to move forward current uses of social media and networks, from surveillance and advertising and into co-creation of knowledge and shared decisionmaking and policy implementation.

References

Barthes, R. 1981. *Camera lucida: Reflections on photography.* New York: Hill and Wang.

Bauman, Z. 2001. *The individualized society*. Cambridge: Polity Press.

Beck, U. 1992. *Risk society: Towards a new modernity*. Newbury Park, CA: Sage.

—. 2001. *Individualization: Institutionalized individualism and its social and political consequences*. London: Sage.

Boast R., M. Bravo and R. Srinivasan. 2007. Return to babel: Emergent diversity, digital resources and local knowledge. *The Information Society* 23 (5): 395–403.

Bosch, T. 2010. Theorizing citizens' media: A rhizomatic approach. In *Making our media: Global initiatives toward a democratic public sphere* (vol. 1). Ed. C. Rodriguez, D. Kidd and L. Stein, 71–87. New Jersey: Hampton Press.

Carpentier, N. 2007. Participation, access, and interaction: Changing perspectives. In *New media worlds: Challenges for convergence.* Ed. V. Nightingale and T. Dwyer, 214–230. Melbourne: Oxford University Press.

Carpentier, N., L. De Brabander and B. Cammaerts. 2009. Citizen journalism and the North Belgian Peace March. In *Citizen journalism: Global perspectives.* Ed. S. Allan and E. Thorsen, 163–714. New York: Peter Lang.

Carvalho, A. 2007. Ideological cultures and media discourses on scientific knowledge: Re-reading news on climate change. *Public Understanding of Science* 16 (2): 223–243.

Castells, M. 2001. *The internet galaxy: Reflections on the internet, business and society*. New York: Oxford University Press.

Chun, W. 2007. Imagined networks: Rhetoric, poetics and politics in electronic communities and online networks. In *Sensor-census-sensor: Investigating circuits of information, registering changes of state*, 124–127. Delhi, India: The Sarai Programme and Centre for the Study of Developing Societies.

Couldry, N. 2006. *Listening beyond the echoes: Media, ethics, and agency in an uncertain world.* Boulder, Colorado: Paradigm Press.

Couldry, N. 2008. Mediatization or mediation? Alternative understandings of the emergent space of digital storytelling. *New Media & Society* 10 (3): 373–391.

Davies, M. 2008. Living on the ice shelf: Humanity's meltdown. http://tomdispatch.com/post/17494926 (accessed 10 July 2009).

Everett, A. 2003. Digitextuality: Theses on convergence media and digital reproduction. In *New media: Theories and practices of digitextuality.* Ed. J. Caldwell and A. Everett, 3–28. London: Routledge.

Falk, J.H, L. Dierking and S. Foutz, Eds, 2007. *In principle, in practice: Museums as learning institutions.* Plymouth, UK: Altamira Press.

Giddens, A. 2009. *The politics of climate change.* Cambridge: Polity Press.

Gumucio Dagron, A. 2001. *Making waves: Stories of participatory communication for social change.* New York: The Rockefeller Foundation.

Gumucio Dagron, A. 2005. *From the summit to the people.* http://www.scribd.com/doc/9576032/Upper-Floor-Lower-FloorI4D (accessed 12 December 2009).

Gumucio Dagron, A. 2008. Six degrees and butterflies: Communication, citizenship and change. In *Civic driven change: Citizen's imagination in action.* Ed. A. Fowler and K. Biekart, 1–10. The Hague: Institute of Social Studies.

Hamilton, C. 2007. *Scorcher: The dirty politics of climate change.* Melbourne: Black Inc Agenda.

Hooper-Greenhill, E. 2007. Education, postmodernity and the museum. In *Museum revolutions: How museums change and are changed.* Ed. S.

Knell, S. Macleod and S. Watson, 367–377. New York: Routledge.

Jacobson, T. and J. Servaes, eds, 1999. *Theoretical approaches to participatory communication.* Creskill Hill, NJ: Hampton Press.

Jenkins, H. 2006. *Fans, bloggers, and gamers: Exploring participatory culture.* New York: New York University Press.

Juhasz, A. 2008. 4 Lessons of YouTube for activists. Paper presented at the 7th OURMedia International Conference, Accra, Ghana, August, 2008.

Kelly, L. 2007. Visitors and learning: Adult museum visitor's learning identities. In *Museum revolutions: How museums change and are changed.* Ed. S. Knell, S. Macleod and S. Watson, 276–290. New York: Routledge.

Kinder, M. 2002. Hot spots, avatars and narrative fields forever—Buñuel's legacy for new digital media and interactive database narrative. *Film Quarterly* 55 (4): 2–15.

Lash, S. and C. Lury. 2007. *Global culture industry: The mediation of things.* London: Polity Press.

Latour, B. 2005. From realpolitik to dingpolitik or how to make things public. In *Making things public.* Ed. B. Latour and P. Weibel, 14–43. Cambridge: MIT Press.

Lax, S. 2007. Access denied: Arguments about equality and access to new media in the information society. In *New media worlds: Challenges for convergence.* Ed. V. Nightingale and T. Dwyer, 199–213. Melbourne: Oxford University Press.

Lury, C. 2007. Just do it: The brand as new media object. In *New media worlds: Challenges for convergence.* Ed. V. Nightingale and T. Dwyer 308–324. Melbourne: Oxford University Press.

Marres, N. 2008. The making of climate publics: Eco-homes as material devices of publicity. *Distinktion, Scandinavian Journal of Social Theory* 16: 27–46.

Nightingale, V. and T. Dwyer, eds., 2007. *New media worlds: Challenges for convergence.* Melbourne: Oxford University Press.

Palmer, D. 2003. The paradox of user control. Paper presented at the 4th Digital Arts and Culture Conference (DAC 2003), Melbourne, May.

Reguillo, R. 2000. La clandestina centralidad de la vida cotidiana. In *La vida cotidiana y su espacio-temporalidad.* Ed. A. Lindón Villoria. 77–94. Mexico City: Anthropos.

Rheingold, W. 2003. *Smart mobs: The next social revolution.* Cambridge, MA: Perseus Publishing.

Rodriguez, C. 2001. *Fissures in the mediascape: An international study of citizens' media.* Creskill Hill, NJ: Hampton Press.

Russo, A., J. Watkins, L. Kelly and S. Chan. 2008. Participatory communication with social media. *Curator* 51 (1): 21–31.

Srinivasan, R. 2006. Indigenous, ethnic and cultural articulations of new media. *International Journal of Cultural Studies*. 9 (4): 497–518.

Srinivasan, R., R. Boast, J. Furner and Katherine M. Becvar. 2009. Digital museums and diverse cultural knowledges: Moving past the traditional catalog. *The Information Society* 25 (4): 265–278.

Watkins, J. and A. Russo. 2007. Cultural institutions, co-creativity and communities of interest. Paper presented to the 2nd International Conference, Online Communities and Social Computing 2007, July 22–27 Beijing, China. Published in D. Schuler, Ed., *Springer Lecture Notes in Computer Science* 4564: 212–221.

Wellman, B. 2001. Physical place and cyberplace: The rise of personalized networking. *International Journal of Urban and Regional Research* 25 (2): 227–252.

Notes

[1] http://www.brooklynmuseum.org/ (accessed December 19 2009)

[2] *Superstruct Game.* Institute for the Future 2007. www.superstructgame.org/ (accessed December 19 2009)

CHAPTER FIFTEEN

FROM COMMUNITIES OF PRACTICE TO VALUE NETWORKS: ENGAGING MUSEUMS IN WEB 2.0

LYNDA KELLY AND ANGELINA RUSSO

Research has demonstrated that visitors appreciated the role museums could play as authoritative, trusted and credible sources of information, and that they were accessed by a wide range of people (Falk et al. 2001, Lake Snell Perry and Associates 2001, Ellenbogen 2002, Cameron 2006, Kelly 2006). In studies of museums and controversial issues it was found that visitors welcomed museums having exhibitions and programs on these kinds of hot topics as long as they could comment on them somehow (Kelly 2006). At the time that work was undertaken the internet was in early stages of development, with a Web 1.0 environment that had a primary focus on access to information (Seely Brown and Adler 2008). Since then, the internet has opened up a whole new way of engaging users, with Web 2.0 now giving access to people—where those with common interests can meet, share ideas and collaborate. Seely Brown and Adler argued that the most profound impact of the internet was "… its ability to support and expand the various aspects of social learning" (2008, 18), therefore enabling people to solve problems together and engage audiences in all aspects of museums' processes. The challenge is however, how to create and foster a Web 2.0 mindset among museum staff within a framework of communities of practice leading to creation of value networks between museums and their audiences.

Although communities of practice are very relevant to the work of museums they are less well understood across the sector, particularly as a way to engage staff in organisational change, such as that demanded by Web 2.0 and social media, given that "Web 2.0 puts users and not the organisation at the centre of the equation. This is threatening [for staff], but also exciting in that it has the potential to lead to richer content, a more personal experience" (Ellis and Kelly 2007).

This chapter explores the ideas surrounding communities of practice and how they could be applied in thinking about how to better engage museum staff with Web 2.0 at an institutional level. It considers how to encourage a Web 2.0 mindset through addressing issues surrounding organisational change, curatorial practice and learning through discussion of a series of case examples. The chapter concludes by discussing next generation 'value networks' as an extension of communities of practice. Value networks enable audiences to participate with museums on their own terms through drawing relevant information and engaging in discourse that is of value to them yet, in doing so, present a range of challenges for museums.

What are communities of practice?

Communities of practice are "self-organised and selected groups of people who share a common sense of purpose and a desire to learn and know what each other knows" (Hansman 2001, 48). As well, they "share expertise and passion about a topic and interact on an ongoing basis to further their learning" (Wenger and Snyder 2000, 3). Communities of practice as an approach has been applied across a diverse range of subject areas including adult learning (Merriam 2001), management theory and practice (Wenger 1998, Wenger and Snyder 2000) and museums' relationships with indigenous people (Kelly et al. 2006). From a visitor perspective social learning seen through the framework of communities of practice is a potentially powerful way to describe the learning that takes place during a museum visit and the practices inherent in the experiences that museums structure, and has been explored in young children's learning (Fasoli 2001), analysing museum learning through conversations (Abu-Shumays and Leinhardt 2002, Leinhardt and Gregg 2002) and in studies of visitor identity and learning (Paris and Mercer 2002, Kelly 2007).

Museum learning theories are intertwined with the notion of "communities of practice" where the importance of learning is not only central to the individual but within a process of co-participation within a social context (Kelly et al. 2006). Lave and Wenger first proposed the idea of communities of practice in 1991 as a way to explain the complexities of learning when studying apprenticeships, finding that the learning in these situations was not just in the heads of individuals, but occurred within a process of co-participation. They propose that learners should be active, contributing members of communities and that learning is made possible through involvement with, participation in, and acceptance into, a community. Their work has made a significant contribution to the discussion of the social dimensions of learning inspired by the work of Vygotsky and social constructivism (Vygotsky 1978, Daniels 1996). The idea was to think beyond learning as a cognitive process to concentrate on what kinds of social engagement provide the best contexts for learning. Lave and Wenger suggested that learning required involvement in a practice, not just as an observer but as a participant who also has a responsibility for the outcome: "Learning is a process that takes place in a participation framework, not in an individual mind" (1991, 15). They saw learners as active and contributing members of communities. Learners became learners through involvement with, participation in and, finally, full acceptance into a community: "learners inevitably participate in communities of practitioners and that mastery of knowledge and skills requires newcomers to move toward full participation in the socio-cultural practices of a community" (1991, 29).

Some questions this approach raises include could social media affirm learning experiences within dispersed museum audiences in an environment where it has traditionally proved difficult to sustain communities of practice? And, could new communities of practice be formed around the interplay between the mediation provided to audiences (for example, exhibits, public programs and events), their participation in a community of practice and their relationship with the museum?

Museums and Web 2.0 as social spaces

The social role of museums has changed dramatically in the last decade, but communication and design rationales are still catching up. Museums no longer fit the early modernist model of the 19th century museum, with its authoritative narratives, many now offer interactive and open-ended experiences (Russo and Watkins 2006). Social constructivist approaches to communication have helped museums to connect with the experiences, memories and understandings that visitors bring with them (Watkins and Mortimore 1999). They have also have enabled the deconstruction of grand narratives and have affirmed the role of audiences in social learning. Museums are more open to cultural diversity, local knowledge, popular memory and in dealing with contentious issues. These ideas have tapped a form of community intelligence and have created a path from modernist certainty and institutional centrality to social networking and demand-driven intellectual engagement with culture. In turn, this has changed the ways that museums respond to the challenges of increasingly democratised civic engagement and their audiences' desire for two-way interaction. Museums are now sites in which knowledge, memory and history are examined, rather than places where cultural authority is asserted (Hooper-Greenhill 2000, Kelly and Gordon 2002). Museums and visitors collaborate in the "making of meaning" whether, for example, visitors are local residents who lived through a particular period of time, school students working on problem-based research projects (Hooper-Greenhill 2000), creator communities seeking to reconnect with their cultural heritage (Kelly et al. 2006) or even community members seeking to use a museum's resources to take collective action on a topic (Leinhardt and Gregg 2002, Jensen and Kelly 2009).

Existing studies suggest that museums enable cultural participants to explore images of themselves, their histories and communities within a social context (Falk 2005). Where and how audiences interact with, create and share knowledge are critical issues within the educational infrastructure available to museum audiences. Falk (2006) advances the notion that museum audiences' identities, motivations and learning are intertwined, and proposes that many individuals attend museums to confirm and define identities in a prosaic way. Paris and Mercer (2002) argue that audiences use museums as vehicles for deconstructing deeply expressed identity and Kelly (2007) found that interactions with exhibitions could radically alter visitors' learning identities.

However, there has been little research on how social media and digital content creation can extend learning and build partnerships between museums and their various communities of interest. For example, highly successful commercial social media such as Flickr, Facebook and YouTube make it possible for individuals to upload personal content to widely accessed websites and add tags to enable others to search and review this content. These kinds of social media present opportunities for museums to research new roles in managing the relationship between cultural heritage and digital cultural content creation (Kelly 2009). Although it has been suggested that the web is essentially a social space (Bearman and Trant 2008), museums remain slow to recognise their users as active cultural participants in many-to-many cultural exchanges and, therefore, social media have yet to make a significant impact on museum communication models, which remain fundamentally one-way (Russo and Watkins 2006, Russo et al. 2008).

What then is social media and how can museums take advantage of it within a community of practice and progress to the next stage as a value network? Social media has been defined as the "term for the tools and platforms people use to publish, converse and share content online. The tools include blogs, wikis, podcasts, and sites to share photos and bookmarks"[1]. An important component of social media is the idea of social networking, which refers to "online places where users can create a profile for themselves, and then socialise with others using a range of social media tools including blogs, video, images, tagging, lists of friends, forums and messaging".[2]

Social media have both short and long term effects on museum learning and communication and in particular, how citizens can take collective action on issues that are critical to them. In order to realise the immediate opportunities afforded by social media, museums need to work with designers, communications experts and educationists to re-engage their many diverse communities. This strategy could encourage audiences to respond to what they discover and relate it back to themselves in ways which are meaningful to them. Holden and Jones suggest that the modern institution must "… draw from our common past and cultural heritage to create a diverse and grounded future" (2006, 6). Web 2.0 has the potential to capture this social value and assist in the exploration of ways of empowering audiences in a more participatory, multicultural and engaged society.

The tools provided by Web 2.0 also provide new ways to learn about audiences through interacting with them directly, where museum staff can act as stimulators and facilitators within a community of practice. Audiences can invest in and contribute their ideas, with the subsequent interactions informing and shaping their museum experience (Jensen and Kelly 2009). However, the challenge for the museum sector is the patchy uptake of these tools and many reservations about what Web 2.0 actually offers. A range of museums have been actively experimenting with social media, with many having established a strong online presence both on their own websites and in other spaces (Bernstein 2008, Russo et al. 2008), however, to date, little exploration has been undertaken into how these tools may influence the ways that museums work as organisations (Kelly 2009).

Why should museums participate in Web 2.0 initiatives?

Social media offer people many ways to shape both their own experiences and those of others through deliberate acts such as contribution, commenting, rating or re-mixing, or through other acts incidental to their use (such as through searching, subscribing, being counted toward most visited or other recommender systems). As O'Reilly

(2005) observes "One of the key lessons of …Web 2.0 is: Users add value. Web 2.0 companies set inclusive defaults for aggregating data and building value as a side effect of ordinary use of the application. [T]hey build systems that get better the more people use them". This is another manifestation of what Bricklin described as the "cornucopia of the commons" where "… the act of using the database adds value to it" (2000). In the Web 2.0 world "… to use is to contribute" (Russo and Peacock 2009).

To investigate the idea of participation, Web 2.0 and museums in more detail, an online survey of 2,006 participants across eastern Australia was undertaken asking about the kinds of online activities undertaken in the previous month, as well as where they accessed the internet, how comfortable they felt with technology and demographic information (Kelly and Russo 2008). The range of activities surveyed included watching videos, using social networking sites, participating in discussion boards and forums, reading customer reviews, reading, commenting and publishing blogs, tagging web pages, listening to podcasts, using wikis, uploading content such as images, videos and web pages and using feeds to pull content to email.

Participants were also asked whether they had visited a museum / gallery in the previous six months, with 41 per cent (n=829) having done so. The data from this group was then separated to compare against the rest of the sample to see if there were any differences in their online behaviour. The data showed that museum / gallery visitors participated at higher levels across all activities. Apart from using social networking sites, statistical tests revealed that these differences were highly significant across all categories. These findings suggested that, not only do those who visit museums participate in more online activities, they were engaging in activities that are participatory and two-way, such as posting and reading customer reviews, reading blogs, listening to podcasts and tagging content.

A one-day workshop held in November, 2007 (e-kids' college) with 24 students from nine schools across New South Wales looked further at some of these findings. Students were consulted on a range of issues encompassing their use of digital technologies in leisure and for learning. They undertook a behind-the-scenes tour of the Museum, spoke with a number of scientific staff and experienced the public areas of the Museum in order to provide feedback about the Museum's potential online offer. An important component of the research was to seek feedback and advice about how the Museum's research and collections could be better utilised through digital media to match their needs and interests. One outcome that emerged was the overwhelming interest by the students in the Museum's content, staff and the sensory engagement primarily through touch, but also the visual aesthetic. They were also very thoughtful about how the Museum could complement what was already available online and carve out its own place (Kelly and Groundwater-Smith 2009). One student, who had attended both the 2006 Kids' College and the e-kids' college in 2007, had this to say:

> Last time I came here [in 2006] we focused mainly on new technology and we were constantly saying we needed more screens, games and interactive displays, but since then I have been thinking: I can do that at home, I can watch movies, play games etc. at home. If I come to the Museum I want to be able to get information, read it and be able to learn from it. It is good to have these things (screens etc) but I guess, like all things, in moderation. The website needs to suit all audiences. I got the feeling that you were trying to find out what we want but we are not the only people that use the Museum. A section on the site, with bright colours, games etc could be good, but it is unlikely that the reason we are at a Museum site in the first place is to play the games. We can do that anywhere. If we are there we are probably looking for information of some kind.

As demonstrated in the quote above, museums are seen as key information sources. Research emanating from the *Exhibitions as Contested Sites: The Role of Museums in Contemporary Society* research project, found strong support in quantitative visitor surveys for museums being "Places to explore important issues". For example, 97 per cent of Australian War Memorial (Canberra) visitors; 91 per cent of Canadian museum visitors and 90 per cent of Australian Museum visitors agreed or strongly agreed with this statement. Museum staff who were sampled also accepted this idea, with 94 per cent of respondents also agreeing or strongly agreeing with this statement. Support for the statement museums as "Places that should provide information sources about important topics" was even higher, with 99 per cent of Australian War Memorial visitors, 96 per cent of Canadian visitors; 98 per cent of Australian Museum visitors and 94 per cent of staff respondents agreeing or strongly agreeing. When faced with issues of contention or difficulty, people are looking for reliable informed sources, and museums are seen as one of these (Kelly 2006, 2009).

Web 2.0 as a community of practice

The rise of museum studies in the past 30 years has applied the critical theories and key principles of semiotics and post-modernism to reframe the larger changes within which museums now operate (Pearce 1994,

Bennett 1995, Hein 1998). While the focus on post-modernism and semiotics has broadened the more traditional one-to-one communication focus of museum programs, these fields of discourse do little to contend with the realities of consumer-led changes to audience perceptions and user interaction with museum content. Therefore, establishing Web 2.0 as an instigator of community of practice falls within socio-cultural theory (see chapter 10) which is based on the idea that human activities take place in cultural contexts through social interactions that are mediated by language and other symbol systems, shaped by an individuals' historical development. It also understands, accounts for and makes explicit the "unplanned intersection of people, culture, tools and context" (Hansman 2001, 44), emphasising the importance of culture, environment and history in every learning context and event (Schauble et al. 1997). Social learning is considered an active process of reflection leading to self-awareness and change. It is facilitated by a wide range of tools and, as data by Kelly (2007) shows, is most successful when undertaken by choice.

In order to test a theoretical framework, from 2008 the Australian Museum has been working in partnership with Swinburne University on a grant project, *Engaging with Social Media in Museums*, funded by the Australian Research Council. The aims of the project are to:

1. Investigate innovative connections to social media networks by Australian and international museums, using digital content, multimedia design and communication strategies.
2. Advance creative engagement with curiosity-driven learners, information searchers and amateur content creators in the practice of collection and interpretation of the past in ways that build community use, understanding and enjoyment of museums.
3. Lead cross-disciplinary debate within museum studies through reference to design, audience evaluation and cultural communication.

One outcome of the project was building a community of practice among museum staff who were working together on social media pilots. The original grant application called for the development of a research network yet it appeared that this would be difficult to achieve without understanding who the main instigators of current museum research actually were. In the first instance, Museum 3.0[3] was established to create a community of practitioners engaged in discussions on issues related to the museum sector. At the time of writing (December 2009) the network has over 1,800 members. With this broad membership base, a survey was undertaken to explore the impact of the network on the professional lives of those working in the sector.

One unexpected outcome of the survey was the belief that Museum 3.0 could act as a space for developing new research projects. Several respondents commented on their desire to collaboratively develop projects with other members. As a result of this a new group has been added, "Project Central", a workspace for those interested in developing collaborative inter-institutional projects. However, the possibility for such a space to become inundated with conceptual rather than systematic projects is great. Therefore, to alleviate this, a two-step process is encouraged. First, potential members need to contact the conveners with ideas which will be vetted within the community in the form of blog postings. Second, those interested in engaging in the project will be then invited to collaborate within the workspace provided. This workspace is by invitation only and only open to those who are serious about developing projects, applying for funding and participating in a broader discourse. As a parallel measure, professionals from outside the network will be identified and invited to also contribute to the discussions.

Another project that emerged from *Engaging with Social Media in Museums* was to trial the use of social media as a front-end evaluation tool when developing content and themes for an exhibition at the Australian Museum on the topic of evil (Jensen and Kelly 2009). The *All About Evil* exhibition concept came to the Australian Museum from the Royal Tropical Institute (Tropenmuseum) Amsterdam after the success of their exhibition displayed in 2006. The exhibition was built from the Tropenmuseum's cultural collections and included over 900 items, including loans from European collections and private lenders. Given the potential controversial nature of the topic it was felt that extensive front-end evaluation needed to be undertaken to test out exhibition themes, stories and content. In the past, front-end evaluation studies would have been time-consuming, costly, and rather limited in the number and types of audiences that could be researched. Now, however, museums have the opportunity to use Web 2.0 tools provided by social media to interact more directly with a range of audiences on their own terms in a more equal, two-way relationship and, ultimately, to form multiple communities of practice.

In order to undertake the evaluation through interacting with potential audiences, an exhibition development blog was established using Blogger, a free online blogging tool[4]. A decision was taken to make the blog unmoderated and to not host it on the Australian Museum's website. This was risky but it was assumed that in being removed from the Museum respondents could be more free in their comments and participation. This proved to work well with no inappropriate comments posted, yet it was found that although there were up to 200 readers of the blog there were minimal comments being made.

In February 2009 an *All About Evil* Facebook group was created[5], in part to address the frustrations of little two-way activity on the blog, but also to test whether Facebook would provide a better vehicle for discussion on themes and possible content for a target audience of young people. The group proved to be popular, with over 750 members at December 2009 who are generating a great deal of activity and discussion between the Museum and members, as well as among members themselves.

When comparing activity on both the blog and Facebook sites it was found that the blog was more of a reader space rather than a commenting space, with Facebook providing more discussion and interaction and, therefore, a better example of a community of practice in action. There could be a number of reasons for this. First is the nature of the subject matter. Evil may be a "sexier" topic for a Facebook audience who tend to be aged around 20–30 years. Second, although an attempt was made to make the blog as conversational as possible, it still seemed to have a (somewhat) authoritative voice. In the Facebook environment discussions seem more free-flowing and casual. People are able to drop a few lines in a chatty way or write paragraphs if they really have something to say. Finally, it is speculated that the lesser amount of activity on the blog could be technologically-related. Signing up to use a blog is not necessarily easy and could be potential barriers to participation, especially if people aren't familiar with using online blogging applications such as Blogger or Wordpress.

The *All About Evil* case study is an example of an active engagement with audiences in a "crowdsourcing-type" experiment with a topic that has the potential to be controversial. The term crowdsourcing was coined by *Wired* contributing editor Jeff Howe in 2006 to name the new practice of engaging a specific group, community, or the general public to perform tasks as a group that previously were undertaken by staff or contractors. With the rise of social media sites such as Facebook, Twitter and YouTube, audiences are actively contributing to discussions, voicing their opinions and creating content in very public ways. Crowdsourcing is a natural extension of this participation. Increasingly, crowds are called upon to invent new products (for example Smiths Crisps' search for new flavours), innovate in the development of new services (for example,

DesignCrowd[6] an online graphic design outsourcing site) and interpret cultural content on their own terms (Collectish[7] an online collection tool developed by Museum Victoria). Proprietary systems for crowdsourcing are developing to enable community to not only voice their own opinions in a public forum but to co-create content and engage in a public assessment of new services prior to their being implemented or sent to market.

Web 2.0 as a value network

Collections, the mainstay of cultural institutions, are contextualised through their association and provenance with communities. Yet collections + communities is not enough. For audiences to make meaning of cultural content, museums use interpretative techniques such as exhibitions, public programs, educational and outreach programs. The rise of online activity has brought with it opportunities to create digital content which links collections and communities though compelling stories told by or for audience members. These raise important questions, particularly:

- How might experts be encouraged to engage in dialogue with audiences?
- In what ways can museums connect with audiences in public spaces?
- How could mobile technologies be used to enhance the visitor experience?
- Can social networking raise awareness of culturally diverse community issues?
- How can social media networks be harnessed to advocate with museums on issues that have global impact and that museums can legitimately have a voice?

Questions such as these are starting to shift emphasis from a community of practice to the development of "value networks". A value network brings together individuals, communities, institutions, organisations and technical resources via relationships which create social goods or economic value. This value may take the form of knowledge and other intangibles and / or is financial. Value networks can be internal and external, are focused on key activities, processes and relationships which cut across boundaries and are created through exchange and the relationship between roles. Cultural institutions have increasingly created significant internal value networks. Exhibitions, public, education and outreach programs are all examples of internal value networks where knowledge is created through a process of exchange between audience and institution. Cultural institutions have, for the most part, maintained ownership of the process and the value which has been created has been embedded within the organisation itself.

Value networks which are based on open innovation create new partnerships through exchange and the relationship between roles. They enable external partners, individuals and institutions to collaborate in the development and distribution of knowledge which has social and / or economic value through user innovation. But transformations in cultural communication are increasingly characterised by a shift towards open innovation and new partnerships outside of institutions to create and distribute new knowledge. Over the past 20 years, the communication of cultural materials has undergone the following transformations:

- early shifts from single institution, building-bound collections to first generation online cultural networks such as the Canadian Heritage Information Network (CHIN)[8] and the Collections Australia Network[9]
- recognition of the need to link content to communities through compelling stories and the development of second generation cultural networks which incorporate user innovation, such as Culture Victoria[10] and the National Museum Online Learning Project[11]
- a third generation shift from top-down cultural networks to bottom-up value networks which use open innovation models to embed audience experience in the interpretation process, with examples of this being Collectish and the *All About Evil* social media case study (described earlier).

User-innovation is primarily used in the early idea generating phases of new communication projects. Communities are asked to engage in a co-creative process to create new knowledge (such as through digital stories) which the organisation then disseminates through their own processes and internal innovation capabilities. Good examples of this include the Culture Victoria portal, which includes a number of commissioned digital stories and the National Museum Online Learning Project which incorporates commissioned audio and video to inspire audiences to create new content for their personal site.

Open innovation occurs when institutions engage in a co-creative process with communities and the new knowledge is then able to be used by both parties to create new business opportunities. For instance, Picture

Australia's Click and Flick[12] is both an example of user innovation (communities engage in a co-creative process which creates new knowledge for the Picture Australia archive) and an example of open innovation as Flickr contributors have access to their creative content, can continue to promote themselves and create new business opportunities outside of, and potentially strengthened by, the partnership with the National Library of Australia. Although this is a rich example, open innovation in cultural institutions is still in the formative stages.

First generation online cultural networks such as the Canadian Heritage Information Network and the Collections Australia Network demonstrated how institutions could partner to deliver their content online. These networks aggregate content from a number of organisations and make it available in one simple portal. Second generation cultural networks recognise the need to link content to communities through compelling stories which add audience experience to the process of interpretation. Third generation cultural networks take advantage of Web 2.0 to create new value networks based on open innovation models which incorporate crowdsourcing to enable audience experience and creativity to be integral to the understanding of cultural materials both within and outside of the institution.

Poole (2009) in musing on social media and social history, suggests that given the sheer volume of social and ephemeral material arising from contemporary digital culture, the only way museums could hope to curate it is by enabling users to become their own curators, suggesting that the time may be here of the "citizen curator".[13] Poole argues that as the first wave of Web 2.0 recedes "… it is leaving in its wake a new draft of the social contract with our users" (2009). He suggests that we may yet know whether this new draft is a game-changing rewrite, but for culture, he puts forward the following set of clauses for this new contract:

- You will talk, and we will listen
- They're your collections
- Many voices is better than one
- We will come to you
- You have a fundamental right to Culture
- We will provide the platform for Culture but it's not our job to construct it

More than ten years ago the sector tried valiantly to come to terms with the notion of the virtual curator (Kenderdine 1996) however the technology was not sophisticated enough to enable significant participation, the infrastructure was costly, difficult to build and, in time, the notion faded away. Today we have at our disposal aggregators, search engines and digital content which are forcing museums to revisit this notion and consider the citizen curator as a viable and important addition to their programs. Russo (2009) asserts that in this environment, Poole's draft contract might be reconsidered to address the plurality of voices and the types of engagement associated with networks of participants. She offers that the museum discourse might shift to reflect a changing paradigm where:

- They're our collections
- Many voices are critical to the interpretation of culture
- We will attempt to go where participation takes us
- We will provide the platform for audience engagement, the training and advocacy to support it and we would like to work together to construct the content.

This dialogue is challenging and one which takes into account the realities of participation as offered through Web 2.0. It is based on research demonstrating that until museums have significant impetus to do so (and economic difficulty may be that impetus) the first wave of social media may well become a fond memory and one which is increasingly seen as secondary to curatorial practice.

Web 2.0: museums harness communities of practice and create value networks

MacArthur (2007) identified that institutional bias is the most pressing problem in the uptake of Web 2.0 in museums. A community of practice, as it is generally understood, relates to the shared vision of a group of practitioners as they come together to solve problems and / or to resolve ideas related to their practice. Museums need to recognise that, not only visitors, but staff need to be active learners in a continually changing and evolving community of practice, that they are all members of a community of practice, novices and experts at the same time, and that we are all agents of change within it.

While communities of practice have served a pre-Web 2.0 museum world very well, future participatory models which draw audiences into discourse at times of their suiting and for the duration of their interest are yet to be tested. Research has demonstrated that the development of networks based around the value that contributors bring to the discussion, dropping in and out of their own accord, is increasingly a critical issue to address. The rise of crowdsourcing for the purpose of invention, innovation and interpretation will require frameworks which address the transitory nature of participation and the engagement patterns based on competition, content creation and kudos will increasingly pose new challenges to the museum environment. The next few years should prove to be challenging and exciting for museums as they seek to utilise their many value networks in an ever-changing set of technological and social spaces, while grappling with issues of concern to a global and connected citizenry.

References

Abu-Shumays, M. and G. Leinhardt. 2002. Two docents in three museums: Central and peripheral participation. In *Learning conversations in museums*. Ed. G. Leinhardt, K. Crowley and K. Knutson, 45–80. Mahwah, NJ: Lawrence Erlbaum Associates.

Bearman, D. and J. Trant, J. 2008. Technologies, like museums, are social. In *Museums and the Web 2008: Selected Papers from an International Conference*. Ed. D. Bearman and J. Trant, 3–9. Toronto: Archives and Museum Informatics.

Bennett, T. 1995. *The birth of the museum: history, theory, politics*. London: Routledge.

Bernstein, S. 2008. Where do we go from here? Continuing with Web 2.0 at the Brooklyn Museum. In *Museums and the Web 2008: Selected Papers from an International Conference*. Ed. J. Trant and D. Bearman, 37–47. Toronto: Archives and Museum Informatics.

Bricklin, D. 2000. The cornucopia of the commons: How to get volunteer labor. http://www.bricklin.com/cornucopia.htm (accessed 6 January 2009).

Cameron, F. 2006. Beyond surface representations: Museums, edgy topics, civic responsibilities and modes of engagement. *Open Museum Journal* 8.

Daniels, H. Ed. 1996. *An introduction to Vygotsky*. London: Routledge.

Ellenbogen, K. 2002. Museums in family life: An ethnographic case study. In *Learning conversations in museums*. Ed. G. Leinhardt, K. Crowley and K. Knutson, 81–101. Mahwah: Lawrence Erlbaum Associates.

Ellis, M. and B. Kelly. 2007. Web 2.0: How to stop thinking and start doing: Addressing organisational barriers.

http://www.archimuse.com/mw2007/papers/ellis/ellis.html (accessed 9 January 2009).

Falk, J. 2005. Free-choice environmental learning: Framing the discussion. *Environmental Education Research* 11(3): 265–280.

—. 2006. An identity-centered approach to understanding museum learning. *Curator* 49 (20): 151–166.

Falk, J., P. Brooks and R. Amin. 2001. Investigating the long-term impact of a science center on its community: The California Science Center L.A.S.E.R. Project. In *Free-choice science education: How we learn science outside of school*. Ed. J. Falk, 115–132. New York: Teachers' College Press, Columbia University.

Fasoli, L. 2001. *Young children in the art gallery: Excursions as induction to a community of practice*. Unpublished PhD, University of Canberra, Canberra.

Hansman, C. 2001. Context-based adult learning. In *The new update on adult learning theory*. Ed. S. Merriam, 43–52. San Francisco: Jossey-Bass.

Hein, G. 1998. *Learning in the museum*. London: Routledge.

Holden, J. and S. Jones. 2006. *Knowledge and inspiration: The democratic face of culture. Evidence in making the case for museums, libraries and archives*. London: Museums, Libraries and Archives Council.

Hooper-Greenhill, E. 2000. *Museums and the interpretation of visual culture*. London: Routledge.

Jensen, B. and L. Kelly. 2009. Exploring social media for front-end evaluation. *Exhibitionist* 28 (2): 19–25.

Kelly, L. 2006. Museums as sources of information and learning: The decision-making process. *Open Museum Journal* 8.

—. 2007. *Visitors and learners: Adult museum visitors' learning identities*. Unpublished PhD, University of Technology, Sydney.

—. 2009. The impact of social media on museum practice, http://www.australianmuseum.net.au/document/The-Impact-of-Social-Media-on-Museum-Practice/ (accessed 20 October 2009).

Kelly, L. and P. Gordon. 2002. Developing a community of practice: Museums and reconciliation in Australia. In *Museums, society, inequality*. Ed. R. Sandell, 153–174. London: Routledge.

Kelly, L. and S. Groundwater-Smith. 2009. Revisioning the physical and on-line museum: A partnership with the coalition of knowledge building schools. *Journal of Museum Education* 34 (4): 55–68.

Kelly, L. C. Cook and P. Gordon. 2006. Building relationships through communities of practice: Museums and indigenous people. *Curator* 49 (2): 217–234.

Kelly, L. and A. Russo. 2008. From ladders of participation to networks of participation: Social media and museum audiences. In *Museums and the Web 2008: Selected papers from an international conference*. Ed. J. Trant and D. Bearman, 83–92. Toronto: Archives and Museum Informatics.

Kenderdine, S. 1996. Diving into shipwrecks: Aquanauts in cyberspace. *Spectra* 24: 32–42.

Lake Snell Perry & Associates. 2001. *Americans identify a source of information they can really trust*. Washington: American Association of Museums.

Lave, J. and E. Wenger. 1991. *Situated learning: Legitimate peripheral participation*. Cambridge: Cambridge University Press.

Leinhardt, G. and M. Gregg. 2002. Burning buses, burning crosses: Student teachers see civil rights. In *Learning conversations in museums*. Ed. G. Leinhardt, K. Crowley and K. Knutson, 139–166. Mahwah: Lawrence Erlbaum Associates.

MacArthur, M. 2007. Can museums allow online users to become participants? In *The digital museum: A think guide*. Ed. H. Din and P. Hecht, 57–65. Washington: American Association of Museums.

Merriam, S. Ed.. 2001. *The new update on adult learning theory*. San Francisco: Jossey-Bass.

O'Reilly, T. 2005. What is Web 2.0: Design patterns and business models for the next generation of software. http://www.oreillynet.com/pub/a/oreilly/tim/news/2005/09/30/what-is-web-20.html (accessed 10 January 2009).

Paris, S. and M. Mercer. 2002. Finding self in objects: Identity exploration in museums. In *Learning conversations in museums*. Ed. G. Leinhardt, K. Crowley and K. Knutson, 401–423. Mahwah: Lawrence Erlbaum Associates.

Pearce, S. (Ed). 1994. *Interpreting objects and collections*. Routledge: London and New York.

Poole, N. 2009. Social media and social history. http://openculture.collectionstrustblogs.org.uk/2009/07/13/social-media-social-history/#more-105 (accessed 19 December 2009).

Russo, A. 2009. Blog response to Nick Poole: Social history or social memory. http://openculture.collectionstrustblogs.org.uk/2009/07/13/social-media-social-history/#comments (accessed 19 December 2009).

Russo, A., and J. Watkins. 2006. Establishing and maintaining cultural e-communities. *WSEAS Transactions on Advances in Engineering Education* 3 (1): 27–33.

Russo, A., J. Watkins, L. Kelly and S. Chan. 2008. Participatory communication with social media. *Curator* 51(1): 21–31.

Russo, A., and D. Peacock. 2009. Great expectations: Sustaining participation in social media spaces. http://www.archimuse.com/mw2009/papers/russo/russo.html (accessed 20 October 2009).

Schauble, L., G. Leinhardt and L. Martin. 1997. A framework for organising a cumulative research agenda in informal learning contexts. *Journal of Museum Education* 22: 3–8.

Seely Brown, J. and R. Adler. 2008. Minds on Fire: Open education, the long tail, and learning 2.0. *EDUCAUSE* January/February: 17–32.

Vygotsky, L. 1978. *Mind in society: The development of higher psychological processes*. Cambridge: Harvard University Press.

Watkins, C. and P. Mortimore. 1999. Pedagogy: What do we know? In *Understanding pedagogy and its impact on learning*. Ed. P. Mortimore, 1–20. London: Sage.

Wenger, E. 1998. *Communities of practice: Learning, meaning and identity*. Cambridge: Cambridge University Press.

Wenger, E., and W. Snyder. 2000. Learning in communities. http://www.linezine.com/1/features/ewwslc.htm (accessed 20 September 2009).

Notes

[1] http://socialmedia.wikispaces.com/ShortAZ (accessed October 20 2009)

[2] http://www.australianmuseum.net.au/research/Exhibitions-as-Contested-Sites/ (accessed December 19 2009)

[3] http://museum30.ning.com/ (accessed December 19 2009)

[4] http://allaboutevillk.blogspot.com/ (accessed December 19 2009)

[5] http://www.facebook.com/home.php?ref=home#/group.php?gid=63750884739 (accessed December 19 2009)

[6] http://www.designcrowd.com/ (accessed December 19 2009)

[7] http://collectish.com/ (accessed December 19 2009)

[8] http://www.chin.gc.ca/English/index.html (accessed December 19 2009)

[9] http://www.collectionsaustralia.net/ (accessed December 19 2009)

[10] http://www.cv.vic.gov.au/ (accessed December 19 2009)

[11] http://www.vam.ac.uk/about_va/online_learning/index.html (accessed December 19 2009)

[12] http://www.pictureaustralia.org/contribute/individual.html (accessed December 19 2009)

[13] http://openculture.collectionstrustblogs.org.uk/2009/07/13/social-media-social-history/#more-105 (accessed December 19 2009)

CHAPTER SIXTEEN

ARCHITECTURES OF COLLABORATION, WEBS OF CONTENTION

ELAINE LALLY

This chapter examines emerging social networks as conduits for interfacing audiences, museums and "hot" topics in public culture. New online social networks like Facebook and Twitter have been drawing a lot of attention as hot topics in their own right. While they are clearly becoming important recreational and social spaces, they are also increasingly being mobilised by interest groups, advocacy networks and organisers of topical events. Museums and galleries are exploring innovative ways of engaging with audiences through these new forms of organising. This chapter explores these shifting relationships around hot topics as new forms of collaboration between institutions and their active publics.

The rise of social software

In recent years, the world wide web has emerged from its origins as a medium for interacting with digitally published information to become a platform for interacting with people and online content in what has been referred to as the transition to "Web 2.0". Key to this transformation is that users are at the centre of both the publication and consumption of online content, which is aggregated and remixed to result in highly dynamic and interactive websites (Bruns 2008). Known also as "social networking" or "social media", these practices emphasise user-generation of online content, as well as the "folksonomies" or user-defined keyword "tags" that make digital content widely accessible. While many social media forms are geared to individualised recreational and entertainment uses, the fact that more and more people are integrating disparate areas of their everyday lives through these media means that they are increasingly amenable to uses that engage the individual, not just as consumer, but also as citizen, and help them to become part of building a diverse public culture (Couldry et al. 2007).

The current state of internet development is therefore opening up new possibilities for innovative forms of online engagement between cultural institutions and their constituencies. In recent years a large number of web-based environments have emerged which attract and support communities of people who share interests and activities and who are interested in exploring the interests and activities of others, most notably YouTube, Flickr, MySpace, Facebook, Bebo, delicious, Last.fm, Twitter and many others. While many of these services are specialised in the kinds of activity they support (such as video on YouTube, images on Flickr, 140-character message on Twitter), they are increasingly becoming inter-operable through their application programming interfaces (or APIs).

However, the domain of social networking is still very much in flux. New services appear on a regular basis, and while some quickly become very popular and move from the technology fringes to the mainstream, others die out quickly without leaving an impact (except perhaps on the bank balances of those who invested in them). It has been suggested that the functionality of Twitter, for example, is too limited for mainstream success, however it is currently experiencing a meteoric rise in popularity. It may be that its success will come from its niche as a short circuit, linking hot and breaking topics wherever they are on the web. It has yet to find a business model that will allow it to reach economic sustainability.

We interact with new technologies in social and cultural contexts of use, and how a technology is taken up by those who use it, and the kinds of utility it will have for them, "often emerges in complex ways because of the momentum of pre-existing social structures and cultural meanings" (Lally 2003, 162). Whether Twitter succeeds or fails will depend on how it is taken up and used throughout the user community.

What is distinctively social about the Web 2.0 online environment may be, as Charles Leadbeater has recently proposed, that "you are what you share" (2008). The popularity and value to users of these online social environments is that they allow people to share—information, expertise, opinions, videos, images, texts—indeed, anything that can be transmitted via the web. Amazon.com was arguably one of the first web services to recognise and leverage the sharing of opinion, expertise and information, through giving customers access to user reviews and information about the buying preferences of other users ("other people who bought this also bought ..."). The best applications of this principle exhibit a positive feedback effect, the more people use them, the more useful they become for all participants. Indeed, this "network effect" may be a defining characteristic of what we now know as social media or "social software": "the more they are used, the more value accrues to the system itself and thereby to all who participate in it" (Hammond et al. 2005, 3).

The emergence of social networking services as an important driver of online behaviour has occurred in tandem with broader changes in the technological context of online participation, which can be loosely captured in the notion of "convergence". Digital content now flows (more or less) seamlessly across multiple media platforms, and our "digital lives" can now follow us wherever we go—from home to work and back again on desktop computers and laptops, and on the move via smart phones and netbooks.

These changes in the online environment are occurring so rapidly that it is almost impossible for any institution to stay on top of the pace of change:

> Changes in communications technology are out-pacing our notions of what we thought was possible just five years ago … it is the very nature of convergence that it gets away from us and leads us to unexpected places in a veritable nanosecond. (Chapman 2008)

Jenkins has argued that "convergence represents a cultural shift as consumers are encouraged to seek out new information and make connections among dispersed media content" (2006, 3). Because these technologies are increasingly an integral part of who we are as well as what we do, people are becoming increasingly active in their online lives:

> If old consumers were assumed to be passive, the new consumers are active. If old consumers were predictable and stayed where you told them to stay, then new consumers are migratory, showing a declining loyalty to networks or media. If old consumers were isolated individuals, the new consumers are more socially connected. If the work of media consumers was once silent and invisible, the new consumers are now noisy and public. (Jenkins 2006, 18–19)

Audiences, then, are increasingly looking for active participation in online communities, but the proliferation of modes of online communication mean that the mode of address from institutions to their publics must increasingly take account of "individually preferred networks of personal and work contacts, and leisure and entertainment resources" (Nightingale 2007, 20). It is no longer enough then for cultural organisations to wait for online audiences to come to them; they must go out and find those audiences wherever they happen to be in their online lives. And, if participation online is focused increasingly around social networking sites, then not to participate in these arenas may be to miss out on important opportunities to share and collaborate with potential as well as actual audiences.

Cultural institutions engaging with active audiences

Cultural institutions, including art museums and galleries, are increasingly feeling the pressure to respond to the new opportunities that social networking sites offer for connecting with active publics. Sydney's Powerhouse Museum, for example, as a technology-oriented cultural institution, is understandably at the forefront of using social media to extend its outreach into the community. Active on Facebook (where it had over 750 fans at the time of writing), Flickr and YouTube, the Powerhouse is also actively involved in using the power of these sites to link content across platforms. Its Facebook page incorporates a number of Facebook applications (programs which use the Facebook Application Programming Interface, or API to share and aggregate content across different social media sites).

In June 2009, the Australian Museum relaunched its website incorporating extensive and embedded social media capabilities to engage users of the site. Users can register a profile that enables them to add comments and tags to content, or mark it as "favourite" throughout the site. The Museum invites users to help enrich its own offerings by adding user-generated content to the site in the form of uploaded images, video or audio. Accessing the content a user has aggregated is streamlined through the "My Museum" tab in the site's main navigation bar. As more and more users add comments and select favourites, the site is able to give visitors useful feedback on how other people are using the site, which content they found most interesting. At the same time, the Museum itself is able to gain insight into how its online community is interacting with its "virtual" identity.

Britain's Tate Galleries[1] are using Google Maps to match artworks in its collection to the locations they depict, and (once an initial process of linking artworks to locations is completed) is inviting visitors to its site to help identify and verify those locations through "crowdsourcing" their local knowledge. The Tate has also launched iTunes U, a segment of iTunes offering free education-oriented video and audio downloads. The Tate's iTunes U offerings consist of over 400 videos and audio files categorised to enable users to go directly to their area of interest and browse thematically under artist, exhibition, Tate Voices, Tate Live, Tate IQ, and includes guides for teachers.

The Public Library of Charlotte and Mecklenburg County, in Charlotte, North Carolina, has established a presence in Second Life. It aims to provide opportunities to develop skills for self-expression as well as access to special events, workshops and programs for teens, through activities associated with its Second Life island, the "Eye4You Alliance" island. Based on a philosophy of problem-solving through play, the Eye4You Alliance presence in Second Life links to other social networking sites, for example by allowing teens to create machinima (a style of animation based on screen captures in Second Life or video games) and add these to their MySpace pages, or allowing them to share images of the objects or environments they create.

Understandably, many cultural institutions are working with social media to try to connect with youth audiences. The State Library of Victoria, for example, has created the "Inside a dog" website for young people. (The site is named in reference to Groucho Marx's statement that "Outside of a dog, a book is a man's best friend. Inside a dog, it's too dark to read".) The site includes podcasts and fora, and allows readers to post their own reviews of books.

Middleton and Lee surveyed recent practices in Web 2.0 and cultural institutions, and conclude that what is underway is a "re-orientation away from one-way delivery of information towards an exchange between institutions and their users" (2007, 33). Or in other terms, it is about establishing a dialogue with participants who can become contributors to the interpretation of collections, and may indeed contribute to the collection itself.

As yet, however, there is little evidence available on how these initiatives are received by audiences, or how the relationship between audiences and institutions is being transformed in practice. There is, however, much analytical speculation on these trends. It has been suggested that the evolution in the relationship between public institutions and their constituencies heralds the emergence of a new type of user of online resources, which some commentators have referred to as "Generation C" (for "content"). Generation C is said to be a significant new social force, favouring "communal creation and communal use of knowledge" (Penman and Turnbull 2008, 14). Significantly, members of Generation C occupy "a hybrid, consumer-and-producer position. They both consume internet content and can be active producers of that content" (14). These "produsers" (Bruns 2008) mobilise new media literacies and capacities which include creativity, collaboration, and critical and communicative capabilities.

The circulation of public culture across competing media economies therefore now depends more than ever before on the active participation of a new kind of consumer / citizen who can be thought of as a collaborator with the public institutions they interact with (Cubitt 2005). Clark and Aufderheide (2009) coin the term "public media 2.0", to describe the new multiplatform, participatory digital shared platforms for dialogue between public institutions and their constituencies. Public media 2.0:

> will be an essential feature of truly democratic public life from here on in … The grassroots mobilization around the 2008 [US] electoral campaign is just one signal of how digital tools for making and sharing media open up new opportunities for civic engagement. (2009, 2)

Public media 2.0's core function, according to Clark and Aufderheide, is to generate publics around problems. Clark and Aufderheide survey a number of participatory media projects, and conclude that what they all have in common is that they "allow people from a variety of perspectives to work together to tackle a topic or problem—to share stories and facts, to ask hard questions, and then shape a judgment on which they can act" (2009: 11). These authors suggest that it is important to experiment and engage in debates about these technologies, in order to turn "isolated experimentation into pervasive public habit" (2009, 24).

A case study: Facebook

Nancy Baym (2007) argued that new forms of online community "may have more in common with geographically place-based communities than previous online communities of interest", and that these represent:

> a new form of online social organisation in which members move amongst a complex ecosystem of sites, building connections amongst themselves and their sites as they do. They avail themselves of multiple communicative platforms across the Internet: blogs, social networks, comments, discussion forums, private messages, shoutboxes, MP3 files, and videos.

If online community continues to have much in common with geographically-based communities, then it is clear that one of the largest neighbourhoods in the contemporary western world is Facebook.

It is clear that publics are already mobilising quite spontaneously around problems and hot topics in social media environments, including

Facebook, and this gives cultural institutions a way of connecting with individuals on topics of mutual interest in an environment where their public is already spending time online. Facebook provides simple and easy-to-use functionality that allows individuals and organisations to establish a "page" or a "group" which interested members of Facebook can subscribe to. (There are important differences between "pages" and "groups", which will be discussed further below).

In mid-December 2008, for example, the Australian Federal Government announced its policy on reduction in greenhouse gas emissions, with a cut of 5 per cent by 2020 based on 2000 levels. In response, two Facebook groups were established: one calling itself "5% by 2020 is so pathetic I don't even know where to begin!" and the other "Rudd's 5% Emissions cuts by 2020 are pissweak". The former gathered over 6,500 members, the latter around 1,500, a membership level that has remained stable over the months following the establishment of these groups. There is some overlap in the membership and content in these groups, and both continue to be used on an ongoing basis to announce events and news reports of interest to people interested in climate change. While it seems that such proliferation of different groups on Facebook might seem to disperse their impact, these groups and their members are embedded in a wider network of individuals and organisations using Facebook to communicate about climate change issues through links to related groups and organisations, which are accessible from the pages of these groups.

On a more formal level, the Australian Conservation Foundation's (ACF) "Who on Earth Cares" initiative also has a presence as a Facebook group, with over 5,500 members at the beginning of June 2009. The group is used to distribute information about events and announcements of interest, and to draw attention to the ACF's "Who on Earth Cares" campaign. This campaign is primarily an interactive website which allows people to "place" themselves on a map to make visible their commitment to action on climate change.

Many public cultural institutions have now established a presence on Facebook, and are creating Facebook pages to connect with actual and potential audiences who become "fans" of their page. Facebook allows for a high level of flexibility in customising the feature set that is available to users through the applications that organisations install. A reviews feature is common, for example. Fans may post announcements which may be of interest to others using the wall. Other standard features for pages include discussion boards, which allow fans to initiate and participate in discussions on topics of interest to them. Organisations and fans can share images and video.

Sydney's Powerhouse Museum, for example, publishes podcasts and video of lectures and events, and hosts a blog on new media and museums on its own website[2]. It also features prominent links to its Facebook and Flickr presences on the front page of its site.

The Sydney Observatory has a Facebook page, and is using the Blog RSS Reader application to provide people with a feed from the blog hosted on its own website[3]. This feature is supported by a Facebook application called Blog RSS Reader, which allows users to publish multiple RSS feeds to their profile or page. This provides for a flow of traffic from Facebook outwards towards an organisation or individual's blog or blogs. Feeds can be customised with images and text descriptions.

Organisations can send updates which appear as direct messages in the Facebook internal mailboxes of people who are fans. Items the organisation posts to its own page may appear on the home page of group members, and also when someone posts images or videos. These features of Facebook's architecture allow for a "push" model of interaction, where information that users have implicitly indicated they might be interested in by joining the group or becoming a fan is sent to appear on their home page. In contrast, some of the other Facebook features which might allow for a deeper and more dialogical engagement, such as the discussion boards, reviews and wall posts, must be actively sought out by users, through their visiting the organisation's page. In other terms, while Facebook allows organisations to "push" some kinds of information out to users, it requires the users to actively "pull" in other kinds of more direct interaction. This limits the extent to which organisations can use Facebook to take their messages out to their community, and requires them to wait for the community to come to them to be involved in dialogue.

Compounding these complexities, social networking services such as Facebook regularly change their user interface in minor or major ways, often, it seems, in response to the threat of the increasing popularity of other services. In March 2009, for example, it was reported (McCarthy 2009) that a Facebook home page redesign that emphasised a real-time streaming news feed was implemented to compete with the functionality offered by Twitter. In a mediascape where things are moving so rapidly, it is difficult to draw conclusions about where the field of interaction between institutions and their constituencies may be over timescales of months, much less years.

Architecture is politics

As the online world increasingly resembles and supports a full spectrum of ways that people interact and collaborate, and as it is able to capitalise on the convergence of our online and offline activities, it increasingly reflects what prominent internet publisher and commentator Tim O'Reilly has termed an "architecture of participation", whereby a grass-roots user base creates for itself a self-regulating collaborative network (O'Reilly 2005). Architectures of participation, in describing the nature of systems that are designed for user contribution,

> may actually be more central to the success of open source than the more frequently cited appeal to volunteerism. The architecture of Linux, the Internet, and the World Wide Web are such that users pursuing their own "selfish" interests build collective value as an automatic byproduct. In other words, these technologies demonstrate some of the same network effect as eBay and Napster, simply through the way they have been designed. (O'Reilly 2004)

However, as Mitch Kapor has pointed out, "architecture is politics" (O'Reilly 2004). This means that, as Lessig argues (1999), we must be aware of and give sustained attention to, the architecture of online systems of interaction, if we want to fully understand and take advantage of their social effects.

Facebook's participatory architecture is built around the site's philosophy, that its mission is to "give people the power to share and make the world more open and connected". The core functionality of Facebook privileges the individuals who are its members, and limits its capacity to allow organisations and less formal networks of individuals to mobilise interest around topics of interest. Moreover, the distinction Facebook makes between the pages of individuals ("profiles"), of formally constituted organisations ("pages") and loose networks ("groups"), and the changing functionality of these, appears to have resulted in some confusion about the best way to connect on Facebook.

Casula Powerhouse Arts Centre (in Liverpool, western Sydney), for example, has now established a page, having previously registered a profile. Perth Institute of Contemporary Arts (PICA), on the other hand, has its Facebook presence in the form of a group. The Museum of Contemporary Art in Sydney, which previously had an entry as a profile in Facebook, moved to a group entry in early 2009.

As these examples suggest, a number of early-mover organisations creating a Facebook presence did this as profiles. This is quite understandable, since the profile is the central mode of participation on Facebook. These organisations would, in all likelihood, have staff members using Facebook as individuals who would have drawn on their experience to assist the organisation to establish their social networking presence. To register a profile as an organisation, however, contravenes Facebook's Terms of Service, since profiles are limited to individuals. In June 2008 CarriageWorks Arts Centre in Eveleigh, Sydney posted a new page, along with the text: "If you were previously a friend of CarriageWorks Arts Centre, please BECOME A FAN, as our old page is now, sadly defunct". The background information on the page went on to describe how the page would bring fans opportunities to win tickets to shows and events, as well as updates and news. It went on to say: "Watch our space for all this and more. We lost over 3,000 friends when our first page was swallowed up by the powers that be .... so if you love CarriageWorks, please help us recreate our online community by inviting all of your friends to join both the fan page and the group." CarriageWorks Arts Centre had over 6,500 fans in June 2009.

Difficulties for institutions arise because Facebook's terms of service reserve personal accounts for individuals, who are expected to identify themselves using their real names:

> Each user is permitted to maintain a single account, which is represented by a profile. Profiles can only be used to represent an individual, and must be held under an individual name ... All personal site features, such as friending and messaging, are also for personal use only and may not be used for professional promotion ... Using personal site features for professional promotion, or creating unauthorized Pages, may result in your account being warned or disabled.[4]

As this example shows, however, organisations taking up the opportunity to connect with their communities through these external services are using technologies with associated policies (explicit and implicit) about how they are used that are largely outside their control, and which can indeed change at any time. Organisations are expected to establish their Facebook presence using the pages facility:

> Personal accounts are optimized for individuals, not artists, businesses, or brands. Facebook Pages allow artists, businesses, and brands to showcase their work and interact with fans. These pages come pre-installed with custom functionality designed for each category. For example, a band Page has a music player, video player, discography, reviews, tour dates, a discussion board that the artists can take advantage of.

> [A personal account can] be used to manage multiple Facebook Pages that represent businesses or other organizations. You may only create Facebook Pages to represent real organizations of which you are an authorized representative.[5]

Third party developed applications can be added to pages. Unlike personal accounts, which are subject to restrictions on the number of friends who may be invited, Facebook Pages can automatically accept fan requests and are not subject to a fan limit.

Groups are distinct from pages, and are able to be used for the purpose of assembling a community around a topic or issue of common interest:

> Pages can only be created to represent a real public figure, artist, brand or organization, and may only be created by an official representative of that entity. Groups can be created by any user and about any topic, as a space for users to share their opinions and interest in that subject.[6]

While pages can be customised with rich media and interactive applications to engage page visitors, applications cannot be added to groups, which clearly restricts the kinds of interactive capacity available to loose collectives of individuals mobilising around an issue:

> Pages are designed to allow Page admins to maintain a personal / professional distinction on Facebook, while groups are a part of your personal Facebook experience. If you're a group admin, your name will appear on that group, while Pages will never display their admins' names. Additionally, when you take actions on your group, such as posting on your group's wall, these actions will appear to come from you as an individual. However, if you post or take other actions on a Page you own, it will appear to come from the Page.[7]

These distinctions between profiles, pages and groups incorporate a set of policies about what Facebook considers appropriate uses of the service, that are made explicit within the site's terms of service. More importantly, they are made manifest within the technological architecture of the site, which recognises a limited range of potential entities to exist within the service and gives each of them differential access to functionality.

At the centre of these policies lies the Facebook philosophy that its core mission is to serve the individuals who are its registered members, and facilitate their own sharing of information while restricting the ability of organisations and institutions to direct information at them. This appears, in part at least, to be a response to an anxiety about not overloading the site with commercial content (or at least unpaid commercial content). The limit on direct messaging to individuals, for example, appears to be an attempt to pre-empt the possibilities for "spam": "The option to message all members will not appear on a group after it has passed 5,000 members. This measure is in place both for technical reasons and to prevent spam". [8]

Pages can send updates to fans, which appear in a separate "Updates" section of the fans' Facebook inboxes. While this distinguishes the pages' information from that sent by groups (which appears alongside the direct messages from friends), pages are not limited to a maximum number of fans to whom they may send an update. It is also possible to restrict access to a group, so that new members have to be approved, but access to a page can only be restricted by certain ages and locations.

Despite Facebook's policy of restricting profiles to real people using their real names, there are many Facebook participants who use a pseudonym on the site. There are also still organisations that use the profile mode for their Facebook presence. At the time of writing, This Is Not Art, an annual festival of emerging art and new media forms, held in Newcastle, NSW has its Facebook presence as a pseudo-person, named "ThisIs NotArt", rather than as an organisational page or group. As at June 2009 "ThisIs" had over 2,600 Facebook friends. Ironically, these policies have caused problems for real people with names which Facebook has (in a non-transparent process) deemed likely to be "fake" names. A prominent example is the common Japanese name Yoda.

Conclusion

Success in the social networking domain depends on an organisation's capacity to create a rich information space that will attract and engage potential participants in an ongoing dialogue and interaction. In order to do this, it must find or provide an online platform or digital infrastructure that is able to support shared processes of communication and meaning-making about the nature of the tasks and activities in which participants are engaged.

While services like Facebook and Twitter provide cultural organisations with unique opportunities to connect with their audiences, they are not without their dangers. In April 2009 the Facebook group of the Australia Council for the Arts was "hijacked" and renamed to "FACEBOOK Pirates has this group now". The group's profile picture was changed to a skull and cross-bones, as were the group information and administrators. Entries on the group's discussion board suggest that some group members were unsure whether this action was indeed the cyber-vandalism it appeared to be, or whether is was a creative intervention on the part of some disgruntled artists in response to rejection of their funding applications: "it's either real, or one of the best examples of guerilla installation digital art I've come across", suggested one commenter on the group's wall. "Yay! Innovation" commented another. Others responded in the spirit of the attack: "aarrghhh … looking for funding for a dance piece featuring a man with one wooden leg … yarrrrrr!!!!!!" While the group's former administrator, a member of the Australia Council's staff, posted a message indicating that Facebook had been contacted about the problem and was working to correct things, the problem was eventually only resolved after a delay of more than two months. A search of Facebook groups demonstrates that this is not an isolated incident. At the time of writing there were 25 groups with the name "FACEBOOK Pirates has this group now", all with the same skull and cross-bones profile image. Other groups affected include the group of a middle school in Ohio, although the Australia Council's group appears to be the largest one affected.

What are the implications for cultural institutions, we might ask, of taking seriously Kapor's challenge that online architectures must be considered as political? This includes not just technical aspects of interfaces but also such "social" aspects as terms of use, and indeed, the political economy of the global industry in providing online platforms for social interaction. The rhetorically reassuring articulation of Facebook's philosophy in terms of "giving people the power to share", and the user-friendliness of its support for users to upload their digital content should not obscure its nature as big business. Cultural institutions seeking to connect with their constituencies across these platforms do so on the basis that they do not make the rules of the game, and must accept that the technical infrastructures and service policies can be changed with little warning.

We might ask, then, what kind of public culture and engagement between institutions and their constituencies do social networking services like Facebook make possible? Lichterman (1992) coins the term "thin culture" as an insight gained from his research into readers of popular psychology or "self-help" books, to denote "the readers' shared understanding that the words and concepts put forth in these books can be read and adopted loosely, tentatively, sometimes interchangeably, without enduring conviction" (426). A thin culture does not support a deep commitment from readers.

> For these readers, the challenges of personal life in a time of cultural vertigo do not lend themselves easily to established ideologies. By

> participating in the thin culture, readers can name their personal situations, and discover new situations to name. (1992, 441)

Thin culture can be understood in terms of ambivalence, tentativeness and making do with the resources for personal development that are ready-to-hand in the social environment. Perhaps the kind of participation that is facilitated by Facebook's "architecture of participation"—becoming a "fan" of a cause, or joining a group focused around a particular purpose—can never be more than a "thin culture" in Lichterman's sense. Although it can make people feel like they are doing something, no matter how insignificant, and that they have made a positive step, it cannot be more than this without the functionality to support sustained dialogue.

References

Baym, N. 2007. The new shape of online community: The example of Swedish independent music fandom. *First Monday* 12 (8), http://firstmonday.org/htbin/cgiwrap/bin/ojs/index.php/fm/article/viewArticle/1978/1853 (accessed 3 June 2009).

Bruns, A. 2008. Reconfiguring television for a networked, produsage context. *Media International Australia* 126: 82–94.

Chapman, C. 2008. Top six trends in communications technology create regulatory pressure. Australian Communications and Media Authority, Media Release, 20 May, http://www.acma.gov.au/WEB/STANDARD/pc=PC_311166 (accessed 2 June 2009).

Clark, J. and P. Aufderheide. 2009. *Public media 2.0: Dynamic, engaged publics.* Washington: Center for Social Media, American University.

Couldry, N., S. Livingstone and T. Markham. 2007. *Media consumption and public engagement: Beyond the presumption of attention.* Basingstoke and New York: Palgrave Macmillan.

Cubitt, S. 2005. Consumer discipline and the work of audiencing. In *Consumption in an Age of Information.* Ed. S. Cohen and R.L. Rutsky, 79–95. Oxford: Berg.

Hammond, T., T. Hannay, B. Lund and J. Scott. 2005. Social bookmarking tools (I): A general review, *D-Lib Magazine* 11(4), http://www.dlib.org/dlib/april05/hammond/04hammond.html (accessed 2 June 2009).

Jenkins, H. 2006. *Convergence culture: Where old and new media collide.* New York: New York University Press.

Lally, E. 2003. Mods and overclockers: Technology, young people and cultural innovation. In *Ingenious: Emerging youth cultures in urban Australia.* Ed. M. Butcher and M. Thomas, 161–173. Sydney: Pluto Press.

Leadbeater, C. 2008. *We-think: Mass innovation, not mass production.* London: Profile Books.

Lessig, L. 1999. *Code and other laws of cyberspace.* New York: Basic Books.

Lichterman, P. 1992. Self-help reading as a thin culture. *Media, Culture and Society* 14 (3): 421–447.

McCarthy, C. 2009. Facebook vs. Twitter: How will you stream your world? *CNET News: The Social*, 5 March 2009, http://news.cnet.com/8301-13577_3-10189959-36.html (accessed 5 October 2009).

Middleton, M. and J. Lee 2007. *Cultural institutions and web 2.0.* Sydney: Smart Internet Technology CRC.

Nightingale, V. 2007. New media worlds? Challenges for convergence. In *New media worlds: Challenges for convergence.* Ed. V. Nightingale and T. Dwyer, 19–36. Oxford: Oxford University Press.

O'Reilly, T. 2004. The architecture of participation, http://www.oreillynet.com/pub/a/oreilly/tim/articles/architecture_of_participation.html (accessed 4 June 2009).

O'Reilly, Tim. 2005. What is web 2.0: Design patterns and business models for the next generation of software, http://www.oreillynet.com/pub/a/oreilly/tim/news/2005/09/30/what-is-web20.html (accessed 4 June 2009).

Penman, R. and S. Turnbull. 2008. *Media literacy—Concepts, research and regulatory issues.* Canberra: Australian Communications and Media Authority.

Notes

[1] www.tate.org.uk/artmap (accessed December 19 2009)

[2] http://www.powerhousemuseum.com /dmsblog/ (accessed December 19 2009)

[3] http://www.sydneyobservatory. com.au/blog/ (accessed December 19 2009)

[4] http://www.facebook.com/help.php. Facebook help topics unfortunately do not have persistent URLs, results are built from a range of potentially relevant topics on-the-fly in response to the search terms input. This quotation is extracted from the help response headed "How are Pages different than personal profiles?" (accessed June 4 2009).

[5] Facebook help response "Why is a Page a better solution than a personal account for artists, businesses, or brands" (accessed 4 June 2009).

[6] Facebook help topic "How are Pages different than Facebook Groups" (accessed June 4 2009).
[7] Facebook help topic "How are Pages different than Facebook Groups" (accessed June 4 2009).
[8] Facebook help topic "I no longer see the option to send a message to my group" (accessed June 4 2009).

CONTRIBUTORS

Dr Fiona Cameron is a Senior Research Fellow at the Centre for Cultural Research, University of Western Sydney, Australia. Fiona researches and writes about museums in contemporary societies; the agency of the museum sector in the engagement of controversial topics, most recently climate change, and digital media and heritage collections in global flows. Fiona publishes widely in leading international journals, has produced 10 book chapters, a co-edited collection, *Theorizing Digital Cultural Heritage: A Critical Discourse* (MIT Press 2007) and monograph, *Liquid governmentalities and the climate crisis* (forthcoming)

Dr Jenny Ellison has recently graduated with a PhD in history at York University in Toronto, Canada. Her research interests include consumption, self-esteem and femininities. Publications based on her research have appeared in the *Open Museum Journal* (2003), *Canadian Woman Studies: An Introductory Reader* (2006) and *The Journal of the Canadian Historical Association* (2007).

Linda Ferguson is the Evaluation and Visitor Research Manager at the Australian War Memorial. She has worked in the museum industry since 1986 and is a founding member and past president of the Evaluation and Visitor Research Special Interest Group of Museums Australia. Linda holds a Master of Assessment and Evaluation from the University of Melbourne and has a BA (Hons) in Communications from the University of Technology, Sydney.

Stuart Frost joined the British Museum as Head of Interpretation in September 2009. Prior to this he was a member of the Concept Team at the Victoria & Albert Museum, London, steering the development of the Museum's new *Medieval & Renaissance Europe 300-1600* galleries (opened in December 2009). Previously Stuart worked in the Education Departments of the British Museum and the National Maritime Museum, London. His research interests include the changing relationship between museums, sex and sexuality.

Elaine Heumann Gurian, a member of the Museum Group, is a consultant / advisor to museums and visitor centers that are beginning, building or reinventing themselves. Her volume, *Civilizing the Museum: the Collected Writings of Elaine Heumann Gurian* was published in 2006. She has received a Fulbright scholarship to Argentina, a Visiting scholar position to the University of Michigan, named to the 100 Centennial Honor Roll members by the American Association of Museums and awarded the Distinguished Service to Museums Award in 2004.

Dr Lynda Kelly is the Head of Audience Research at the Australian Museum, Sydney. She has published widely in museum evaluation and the impact of social media/Web 2.0 on contemporary museum practice. She administers Museum 3.0, a social networking group for museum professionals and in 2007 completed her PhD researching museum visitors' learning identities.

Dr Emlyn Koster advocates that the value of a science museum or science centre hinges on to how much the pressing science-based challenges and opportunities that surround society and the environment, regionally and globally, are illuminated. A geologist before leading the Royal Tyrrell Museum and Ontario Science Centre in Canada and now Liberty Science Center in the New York metro region, his relevancy-driven approach is infused with cultural and landscape experiences across the world.

Dr Elaine Lally is Associate Professor in Creative Practices, Faculty of Arts and Social Sciences at the University of Technology, Sydney. She researches in the areas of art and technology as material culture, and the role of arts and culture in urban and regional development. In 2006 she produced a Discussion Paper and co-authored the final report for the Australia Council's New Media Arts Scoping Study. She is the author of *At Home with Computers*, published by Berg in 2002.

Dr Margaret A. Lindauer is Associate Professor and Museum Studies Coordinator at VCUarts Department of Art History, Virginia Commonwealth University, in Richmond, Virginia, US. Her research—inspired in part from two decades of professional museum experience—focuses on the history, theory and practice of museums as educational institutions.

Dr Morgan Meyer is a postdoctoral researcher at the Center for the Sociology of Innovation, Ecole des Mines de Paris (ParisTech) and holds a PhD from the University of Sheffield. His research interests are: sociology and geography of science; boundaries and boundary-work; actor-network theory; museum studies; epistemic communities; culture and science in Luxembourg. He is currently co-editing a special issue of *Sociological Research Online* on the theme of 'epistemic communities'.

Dr Angelina Russo is Associate Professor in the Faculty of Design, Swinburne University, Melbourne, Australia. She researches the connections between museum communication processes, multimedia design and digital content creation. She is Chief Investigator on the research project *Engaging with Social Media in Museums* at Swinburne University. She holds an Australian Postdoctoral Fellowship and is a former Smithsonian Fellow.

Dr Juan Francisco Salazar is a Senior Lecturer in Communication and Media Studies at the School of Communication Arts, and a researcher at the Centre for Cultural Research, University of Western Sydney. He holds a PhD in Communication and a BA in Anthropology. His teaching, research and media practice are in the fields of community media, communication and social change, media anthropology, convergent media, documentary film studies.

Dr Richard Sandell is Head of the School of Museum Studies at the University of Leicester. He has been awarded research fellowships at the Smithsonian Institution (2004/5) and the Australian National University (2008) to pursue his research interests which focus on the social agency of museums. He has written and edited a number of books including, most recently, *Re-Presenting Disability: Activism and Agency in the Museum* (with Jocelyn Dodd and Rosemarie Garland-Thomson 2010).

Caleb Williams is Head Curator of the Justice & Police Museum, Sydney. His exhibitions and essays have examined subculture, protest, prisons, crime scene photography and popular culture. Caleb is interested in the idea of the museum as site of conscience and interpreter of buried and repressed histories. He is co-author of the recently published award winning book, *City of Shadows*.

Dr Paul Williams is a specialist in the area of museums and historical representation. His most recent publication is *Memorial Museums: The Global Rush to Commemorate Atrocities* (Oxford: Berg, 2007). Dr. Williams spent several years teaching in the MA Museum Studies program at New York University. Since 2008 he has worked for Ralph Appelbaum Associates, the New York-based museum planning and design firm.

Dr Andrea Witcomb is an Associate Professor in the Cultural Heritage Centre for Asia and the Pacific at Deakin University in Melbourne, Australia. Her research interests span relations between contemporary media and exhibition practices, the role of affect in museum contexts, the politics of interpretation and the history of museums and heritage bodies. She is the author of *Re-Imagining the Museum: Beyond the Mausoleum* (Routledge 2003) and, with Kate Gregory, *From the Barracks to the Burrup: The National Trust in Western Australia* (UNSW Press 2010). She is also the editor (with Chris Healy) of *South Pacific Museums: Experiments in Culture* (Monash e-press 2006).

INDEX